HOWARD THE DUCK

THE COMPLETE COLLECTION VOL. 1

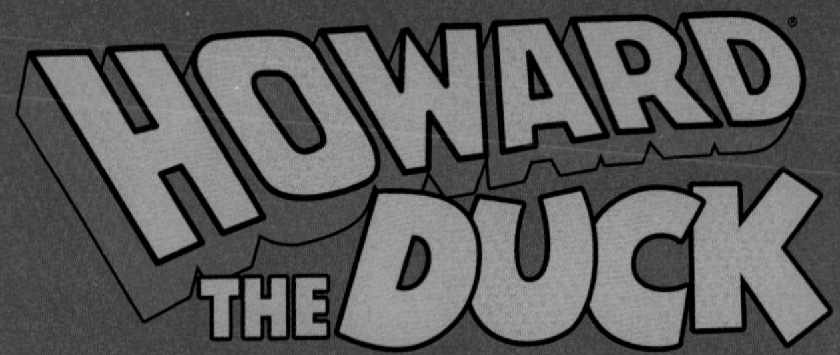

WRITERS:
Steve Gerber with Frank Brunner & Mary Skrenes

PENCILERS:
Val Mayerik, Frank Brunner, John Buscema, Gene Colan & Sal Buscema with Alan Weiss, Ed Hannigan, Dave Cockrum, Tom Palmer, Al Milgrom, Dick Giordano & Mike Nasser

INKERS:
Sal Trapani, Steve Leialoha, Klaus Janson & Val Mayerik with Frank Brunner, Tom Palmer, Alan Weiss, Ed Hannigan, Dave Cockrum, Al Milgrom, John Buscema, Dick Giordano & Terry Austin

COLORISTS:
Stan Goldberg, Dave Hunt, Frank Brunner, Glynis Wein, Michele Wolfman, Marie Severin, Jan Cohen, Irene Vartanoff, Klaus Janson & "Doc Martin"

LETTERERS:
Art Simek, John Costanza, Tom Orzechowski, Annette Kawecki, Irv Watanabe, Jim Novak & Joe Rosen

EDITORS:
Roy Thomas, Len Wein, Marv Wolfman, Archie Goodwin & Steve Gerber

FRONT COVER ARTISTS:
Frank Brunner & Matt Milla

BACK COVER ARTIST:
Gene Colan

Howard the Duck created by Steve Gerber & Val Mayerik

COLLECTION EDITOR: Mark D. Beazley
ASSISTANT MANAGING EDITOR: Joe Hochstein
ASSOCIATE MANAGING EDITOR: Alex Starbuck
EDITOR, SPECIAL PROJECTS: Jennifer Grünwald
SENIOR EDITOR, SPECIAL PROJECTS: Jeff Youngquist
RESEARCH: Mike Hansen
LAYOUT: Jeph York
BOOK DESIGNER: Adam Del Re
SVP PRINT, SALES & MARKETING: David Gabriel

EDITOR IN CHIEF: Axel Alonso
CHIEF CREATIVE OFFICER: Joe Quesada
PUBLISHER: Dan Buckley
EXECUTIVE PRODUCER: Alan Fine

Special Thanks to Gary Henderson, David Anthony Kraft, Don McGregor, Marty Pasko & Doug Shark of mycomicshop.com

HOWARD THE DUCK: THE COMPLETE COLLECTION VOL. 1. Contains material originally published in magazine form as FEAR #19, MAN-THING #1, HOWARD THE DUCK #1-16, HOWARD THE DUCK ANNUAL #1, MARVEL TREASURY EDITION #12 and GIANT-SIZE MAN-THING #4-5. First printing 2015. ISBN# 978-0-7851-9776-8. Published by MARVEL WORLDWIDE, INC., a subsidiary of MARVEL ENTERTAINMENT, LLC. OFFICE OF PUBLICATION: 135 West 50th Street, New York, NY 10020. **Printed in the U.S.A.** ALAN FINE, President, Marvel Entertainment; DAN BUCKLEY, President, TV, Publishing and Brand Management; JOE QUESADA, Chief Creative Officer; TOM BREVOORT, SVP of Publishing; DAVID BOGART, SVP of Operations & Procurement, Publishing; C.B. CEBULSKI, VP of International Development & Brand Management; DAVID GABRIEL, SVP Print, Sales & Marketing; JIM O'KEEFE, VP of Operations & Logistics; DAN CARR, Executive Director of Publishing Technology; SUSAN CRESPI, Editorial Operations Manager; ALEX MORALES, Publishing Operations Manager; STAN LEE, Chairman Emeritus. For information regarding advertising in Marvel Comics or on Marvel.com, please contact Jonathan Rheingold, VP of Custom Solutions & Ad Sales, at jrheingold@marvel.com. For Marvel subscription inquiries, please call 800-217-9158. **Manufactured between 5/1/2015 and 6/8/2015 by R.R. DONNELLEY, INC., SALEM, VA, USA.**

10 9 8 7 6 5 4 3 2 1

At Home with Howard the Duck

Mary Skrenes and Samantha Gerber remember Steve Gerber

As a tribute to her father, Samantha Gerber got a tattoo of Howard the Duck in 2012 with the years of Steve Gerber's birth and death. The tattoo is based on the corner box from Howard the Duck #8.

I first met Steve Gerber at Marvel in 1973. A bunch of us relative newcomers would meet up, after five, for food and drinks. We were mostly writers and a few artists. Witticisms, zingers and laughter abounded. I found Steve to be exceptionally smart and hilarious in a group of guys that were all knowledgeable and funny.

Steve Gerber was a kind, generous, very intelligent, funny, talented, humble and self-effacing man. He truly liked women and was very comfortable talking to them. Steve was a voracious reader. He was obsessed with world history and current world news. He was a great believer in Marshall McLuhan. He was the first man I ever knew that I felt was my verbal equal. That made him very interesting. His writing was good too.

Before collaborating with me on *Omega the Unknown* in 1976, Gerber wrote Marvel style while I worked DC style, "full script." When he saw some of my writing, he got jazzed. He wanted to work that way too! I had already done a couple of full scripts for Marvel and nobody questioned it. Of course, the writer still had to place the word balloons, which didn't happen at DC. Steve loved writing that way, and Gene Colan really liked the scripts.

We were at some kind of burger bar with Frank Brunner discussing *Howard the Duck #1*. Steve had a rough plot for the first issue and we were working out the details. Steve was describing Howard's climb up the credit card tower. As he got to the window, I said, "And inside is a scantily clad woman chained to the wall. Her name is Beverly Switzler. No, wait, I mean Swizzle!" Steve was adamant, shouting, "No, no, it's Switzler!" He loved the name for some reason. Thirty-three years later, after he died, I discovered that Switzler Hall was part of Gerber's college experience at the University of Missouri.

Although I contributed many ideas to the Howard books, and a lot of Beverly's dialogue, the book was all Steve's. It allowed him an unprecedented voice in a world of comics that seemed to be full of rehashed and regurgitated sameness. Everything in Howard's stories, protagonists, villains, even the background characters, stood for elements of the 1970s world that was rapidly moving toward the technobabble and security nightmare that we live in today.

Steve's daughter, Samantha, has her own special relationship with the Duck.

"I was three when Howard was born," Samantha said. "Six when he got his own book and ran for president. I didn't know the comic, at all, until I was much older. My dad bought me *ElfQuest* comics, which I loved. I do remember the cartoon shows he wrote, especially *Thundarr the Barbarian*. He gave me a copy of his Eclipse comic *Stewart the Rat*, but he told me I couldn't read it then. He said to just hold on to it for later. I really got into Howard in the past several years. He is so funny and outraged at everything. Even though I know he was my dad's alter ego, I began to think of him as my little brother."

And, George Lucas, director of the *Howard the Duck* film, played a part in her childhood:

"Some of my most special memories with my dad have to do with the *Star Wars* movies. He took me to the first one and I was instantly obsessed. As we were leaving he said, 'I think they will strike back.' Sure enough, we went to see *The Empire Strikes Back* when it came out. At the end I was a little worried and he said, 'I'm sure the Jedi will return.' Well, he was right, and I was stunned that he could see that far ahead. I was sure my dad was a genius! How did he know? I thought my dad was amazing!"

Steve, who could barely change a light bulb, dove instantly into computers in the early '80s. I was shocked and asked him, "How, why?" He looked at me, raising an imperious eyebrow, as if it should be obvious. "It's Star Trek, not auto mechanics!" he quacked.

In 1984, when, perhaps he could have been writing the Howard movie, Gerber was otherwise engaged. He was editing and writing some of fifty – count 'em, fifty – half-hour episodes of the *G.I. Joe* animated series. We sent in the scripts to a bulletin board that he set up on a computer in his apartment. (He was one of the first in the entertainment industry to require digital submissions.)

All that work meant Sami hardly saw her father in '86. He did take her and her grandmother, Bernice, to the premiere of the movie *Howard the Duck*.

"My grandma and I shopped for outfits on Rodeo Drive," Samantha said. "When we got to the theater, I was so excited. There were crowds of people and bright lights. Dad was stressed out for some reason. In the darkened movie theater, Grandma was telling Dad how proud she was of him that he had his own movie. He really didn't want to hear it.

"When it was over, the audiences applauded and made a lot of noise. I told him I liked it and he didn't say much about it. We went to the after-party at a nearby hotel and I got to meet Tim Robbins. They had food and drinks, and the centerpieces on the tables were the egg from the poster with Howard's beak cracking out of it. I took one home with me. I was clutching it so hard, afraid someone would take it away.

"After my dad passed, Howard and I both lost him. I could no longer have dad in my life and Howard didn't have life without him. I got Howard tattooed on my ankle, but only true Howard the Duck fans would recognize him.

"Recently, Marvel contacted me and I found out that Howard could continue on. Mary, my dad's best friend, said that my dad would want him to live on for me. I want my dad's legacy to prevail for him and the fans that still love Howard."

Is it funny or ironic that: Disney sued Marvel, Gerber sued Marvel, Lucas made the Duck movie, Disney bought Marvel, and Disney bought Lucas' seminal characters? Now, both Howard and Star Wars have a new lease on life.

Mary Skrenes and Samantha Gerber
Las Vegas, NV/Folsom, CA
4/10/2015

FEAR MARVEL COMICS GROUP™

APPROVED BY THE COMICS CODE AUTHORITY

20¢ 19 DEC 02448

ADVENTURE INTO FEAR™

WITH

THE MAN-THING™

Stan Lee PRESENTS: MAN-THING! TM
A VOYAGE BEYOND THE BEYOND BY... STEVE GERBER . Writer VAL MAYERIK . Artist SAL TRAPANI . Inker ART SIMEK, letterer . STAN G., Colorist ROY THOMAS Editor
The ENCHANTER'S APPRENTICE!
REALITY: SINCE THE DAWN OF TIME, MAN HAS SOUGHT TO UNRAVEL ITS FABRIC--EXAMINE THE WEAVE--DISCOVER ITS ESSENCE.
REALITY: PLATO FOUND IT IN THE SHADOWY CONFINES OF A CAVE-- DESCARTES, IN A SYLLOGISM... "COGITO ERGO SUM" ..."I THINK, THEREFORE I AM."
THEY BLEW IT--BOTH OF THEM.
REALITY: IT IS HERE--ON THIS BLOOD-RED PLAIN--'NEATH THIS VERDANT SKY--AMONG THESE STONES SURELY SCULPTED BY A SOMNAMBULANT LUNATIC.
REALITY: AYE, IT IS HERE--AND THE MACABRE MAN-THING IS ABOUT TO MEET IT--HEAD-ON!

FROM THE WEST THERE COMES A LOW ROAR--THE SOUND OF MEN AND MACHINES--MOVING--TRAMPLING THE EARTH BENEATH THEM--RAISING A MAMMOTH CRIMSON CLOUD.

THE CAUSE? THIS BATTALION OF COMBAT-TOUGHENED AMERICAN G.I.'S, BLAZING A TRAIL OF GUTS AND GLORY--AND DUST--ACROSS THIS WEIRD LANDSCAPE!

THE MAN-THING WHIRLS! ON THE EASTERN HORIZON, AN EQUALLY OMINOUS CLOUD APPEARS--ALSO ACCOMPANIED BY THE DIN OF MEN AND METAL.

AND WHEN ALL THESE FORCES COME TOGETHER--

--THE RESULTANT CLASH IS ALMOST MORE THAN MERE HUMAN CONSCIOUSNESS CAN FATHOM. NAKED, WANTON SLAUGHTER, WITHOUT RHYME, WITHOUT REASON...

...'TWIXT FOES WHO, IF LOGIC STILL HAS ANY MEANING...

...SHOULD NOT--COULD NOT!--EVER HAVE MET! NOT IN ANY KNOWN PLACE--NOT IN ANY KNOWN AGE!

FORWARD, MEN OF KATHARTA! SLAY THESE WIZARDS IN ZOKK'S NAME!

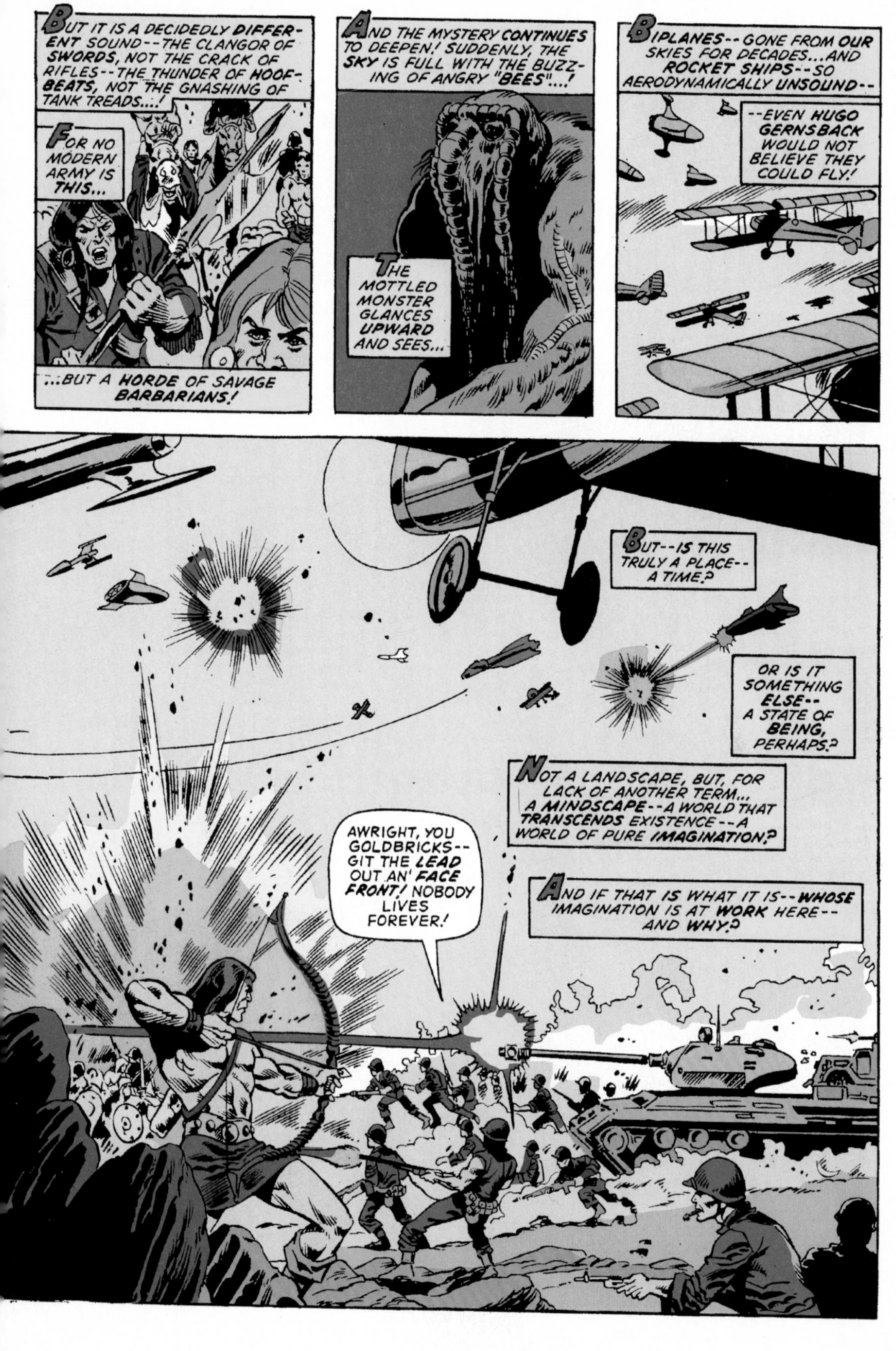

BUT IT IS A DECIDEDLY DIFFERENT SOUND--THE CLANGOR OF SWORDS, NOT THE CRACK OF RIFLES--THE THUNDER OF HOOF-BEATS, NOT THE GNASHING OF TANK TREADS...!
FOR NO MODERN ARMY IS THIS...
...BUT A HORDE OF SAVAGE BARBARIANS!

AND THE MYSTERY CONTINUES TO DEEPEN! SUDDENLY, THE SKY IS FULL WITH THE BUZZING OF ANGRY "BEES"...!
THE MOTTLED MONSTER GLANCES UPWARD AND SEES...

BIPLANES--GONE FROM OUR SKIES FOR DECADES...AND ROCKET SHIPS--SO AERODYNAMICALLY UNSOUND--
--EVEN HUGO GERNSBACK WOULD NOT BELIEVE THEY COULD FLY!

BUT--IS THIS TRULY A PLACE--A TIME?
OR IS IT SOMETHING ELSE--A STATE OF BEING, PERHAPS?
NOT A LANDSCAPE, BUT, FOR LACK OF ANOTHER TERM... A MINDSCAPE--A WORLD THAT TRANSCENDS EXISTENCE--A WORLD OF PURE IMAGINATION?
AWRIGHT, YOU GOLDBRICKS--GIT THE LEAD OUT AN' FACE FRONT! NOBODY LIVES FOREVER!
AND IF THAT IS WHAT IT IS--WHOSE IMAGINATION IS AT WORK HERE--AND WHY?

AND NOW... THE TRUTH:
IT IS BOTH-- IMAGINATION AND REALITY.
HERE, THEY ARE ONE AND THE SAME...
...JUST AS THEY ARE ON EARTH, THOUGH FEW REALIZE IT.
SARGE--LOOK! A LIGHT-BRIDGE FROM THE CASTLE!

THAT IS WHY THIS GIRL, JENNIFER KALE, CAN WALK ON A BEAM OF LIGHT--
--DOWN HUNDREDS OF FEET FROM THE CASTLE IN THE SKY...
...TO THE SPOT WHERE STANDS THE THING FROM THE SWAMP.

YOU SEE, SHE IS REAL... BUT SHE IS NOT TRULY HERE.
I--I KNOW YOU DON'T UNDERSTAND THIS--OR MY WORDS--BUT TRY TO FEEL WHAT I'M SAYING.
YOU MUST COME... HURRY TO SAFETY... AND TRY TO REMEMBER I'M YOUR FRIEND.
HERE... TAKE MY HAND AND WE'LL GO...!

ZOKK! IT'S THE WITCH-GIRL--AND SHE'S STOLEN THE SPOILS OF THIS BLOODY COMBAT!
AFTER HER--UP THE LIGHT-BRIDGE! FOLLOW ME--
--LEST ANY VICTORY WON THIS DAY GO FOR NAUGHT!
AYE, KORREK--LEAD ON!

DON'T BE AFRAID--THEY CAN'T CATCH US! JUST HURRY!
LOOK, KORREK--THE SWAMP DEMON CANNOT RUN! HE'S TOO SLOW--TOO AWKWARD!
AYE--WE'LL NET THE UNGODLY BEAST FOR SURE!

OR SO IT SEEMS, UNTIL SUDDENLY--!
YI-EEEE! THE LIGHT-BRIDGE FAILS!
ZOKK!
THEIR BODIES WILL BURST LIKE BLOOD-FILLED GRAPES ON THE ROCKS BELOW!

BUT THEIR DEATHS WON'T GO UNAVENGED --NOT WHILE I YET BREATHE!
NOT WHILE MY HAND STILL WIELDS A BLADE!

ORDER THIS HELLSPAWN ASIDE, WENCH! FACE ME WITH YOUR SPELLS ALONE-- IF YOU DARE!
OR MUST I BOWL THE SLIME-THING OVER TO REACH YOU?

VERY WELL, THEN--I SHALL! NOTHING MUST STAND IN MY-- URK
I AM...OOZING THROUGH THE MONSTER! IT MUST BE--

--AN ILLUSION! YES--YES! AN EVIL TRICK PLAYED ON MY MIND--TO MAKE ME FALTER-- AND SWAY FROM MY VENGEFUL PATH!
YOU ARE... FORMIDABLE, WOMAN.

...AND RAVISHING, AS WELL--THOUGH THAT, NO DOUBT, IS ALSO ILLUSORY--A LAST PLOY TO SAVE YOUR WRETCHED LIFE!
N-NO--PLEASE-- YOU MUST BELIEVE ME! I'M NOT THE CAUSE OF ANY OF THIS!
AND I'M NOT A SORCERESS! I--
YOU LIE! YOUR TONGUE IS AS CROOKED AS A HANGED MAN'S NECK!

AND IN A MOMENT, GOLDEN-HAIRED MALEFACTRESS, IT WILL ALSO BE AS BLOODLESS!
NO! NO! DON'T KILL ME! PLEASE-- DON'T--! STAY BACK!

DON'T KILL ME!!
DON'T-- OH!! HE'S GONE! IT'S ALL GONE!

BUT I CAN'T BE HERE--!
HOW CAN I BE AT HOME-- SAFE IN BED-- UNLESS--OH, LORD, NO!
I'M DEAD! I'M ALL ALONE... IN A DARK HEAVEN!!
I MUST BE DEAD! OR I'D STILL BE IN THE CASTLE--

--IN THE SKY-EEEEE!
GRANDPA! ANDY! I'M DEAD!! HE KILLED ME!
JENNIFER! GOOD LORD, GIRL--WHO? WHAT'S WRONG?
ANOTHER NUTTY NIGHTMARE, THAT'S WHAT!

ANDY! CAN'T YOU SEE HOW UPSET YOUR SISTER IS?
I'M UPSET, TOO! SINCE HER SCREWY DREAMS STARTED, I HAVEN'T HAD ONE GOOD NIGHT'S SLEEP!
ANDY-- I'M SORRY-- OH, GRAND-PA--!

THERE, NOW--JUST RELAX! YOU'RE FAR FROM DEAD--AND A DREAM CAN'T COME BACK TO HURT YOU.
-SOB- BUT, GRANDPA--
--IT WASN'T A DREAM! IT WAS REAL--AND UNREAL--ALL AT ONCE! I'M SCARED!

REST, JEN... WE'LL DISCUSS IT IN THE MORNING. YOU'LL BE MORE RATIONAL THEN.
THERE MAY BE SOMETHING TO WHAT YOU SAY, BUT....!
I--I KNOW. I'LL TRY TO SLEEP...
GOOD GIRL.

IT FRIGHTENS ME... BUT I THINK SHE'S RIGHT. THESE ARE MORE THAN DREAMS.
AND YET... DESPITE MY KNOWLEDGE OF OCCULT PHENOMENA--*
--I'M AT A LOSS TO EXPLAIN WHAT THEY ARE!
AT LEAST THIS TIME SHE SEEMS TO RECALL SOME DETAILS. THAT MAY HELP.
*WHICH IS CONSIDERABLE. SEE FEAR #'S 13-15. --R.T.

BUT WHATEVER THE ANSWER--I'VE GOT TO FIND IT SOON--BEFORE SHE'S DRIVEN INSANE.
THIS HAS PLAGUED HER FOR MONTHS NOW...EVER SINCE--EH?
ANDY? WHAT ARE YOU--?

PEANUT BUTTER! AT THIS TIME OF NIGHT, YOUNG MAN? YOU'LL NEVER GET BACK TO SLEEP.
CARLIN PEANUT BUTTER

IF I DON'T, IT'LL BE SCREAMING--NOT PEANUT BUTTER--THAT KEEPS ME AWAKE!
IS JEN GOING GA-GA, OR WHAT?
IF ONLY IT WERE THAT SIMPLE, ANDY!
UNFORTUNATELY... I DON'T BELIEVE IT IS. I'M WORRIED, SON.

JUST THINK BACK A MOMENT.
IT BEGAN WHEN THE PSYCHIC BOND BETWEEN JEN AND THE MAN-THING WAS BROKEN.*
I'M AFRAID THERE MAY BE SOME CONNECTION ...BUT WE CAN'T BE CERTAIN.
*FEAR #15. --ROY.

HOWEVER, I AM CERTAIN THAT IT'S LATE--AND WE'RE TIRED. SO...TO BED!
YEAH... OKAY. I'LL GO QUIETLY.
THUS, THEY LEAVE THE KITCHEN UNAWARE... THAT THIS KNIFE IS--GLOWING!

MORE...IT IS CHANGING! GROWING LARGER WITH EACH PULSATION OF ITS EERIE NEW AURA--

--UNTIL ITS VERY SHAPE IS ALTERED--
--UNTIL IT IS THE INNOCENT BUTTER-KNIFE NO MORE!

AND WHEN IT CEASES BECOMING--
A KATHARTAN WAR SWORD RESTS BESIDE THE JAR OF--

--PEANUT BUTTER?!

OR--

--IS IT A JAR OF... MAN??

HOWEVER YOU CHOOSE TO EXPLAIN IT--THE JAR'S CONTENTS HAVE BECOME--
KORREK--WARRIOR PRINCE OF KATHARTA!
A SOMEWHAT PUZZLED PRINCE JUST NOW...BUT NO LESS SAVAGE, NO LESS THE IRON-THEWED WESTLANDS GIANT FOR THAT--!

AND NO LESS HUNGRY FOR REVENGE, EITHER--!
I KNOW YOU ARE HERE, FOUL SORCERESS--THOUGH I KNOW NOT HOW I KNOW...
...NOR HOW I CAME TO BE HERE...
...NOR WHERE IT IS I HAVE COME TO BE....!

THERE IS NOTHING--
NORMAL ABOUT THIS PLACE! THE WALLS ARE CLOSE AND CRAMPED--THE ARCHITECTURE, GHASTLY AND GRIM!

INDEED...THE ONLY THING FAMILIAR IS ITS STENCH OF SORCERY! SO THIS MUST BE HER HAUNT! AYE--I'VE FOUND YOU--

--WITCH WOMAN!!
WHA--? NO! IT CAN'T BE! NOT YOU!!

YOU'RE--NOT EVEN REAL! YOU'RE JUST PART OF A DREAM! DO YOU HEAR ME--YOU CAN'T EXIST!!
BAH! YOUR PRETENSE AT MADNESS CANNOT SAVE YOU, SIREN!

SEE HOW REAL I AM!!
ANDY! GRANDPA! HELP!

JEN--WHAT ON EARTH--?
GOOD LORD! WHO ARE YOU? WHAT DO YOU WANT HERE?
OH, WOW.
WELCOME TO THE TWILIGHT ZONE, FOLKS!

BY AGOGIN'S BEARD! SHE HAS ALLIES HERE!

TWO MORE WEIRDLY GARBED WORKERS OF WIZARDRY!
ONE--EVEN TWO--I MIGHT OVERCOME! BUT NOT A WHOLE DEN OF THEM! SO--!

I MUST DEPART THIS HOUSE OF EVIL-- BY THE ONLY AVAILABLE EGRESS!
BUT, I'LL BE BACK FOR YOU, WIZARDESS!
THIS I SWEAR ON THE SKULL OF RABIS!
AND SO, AMID THE CRASH OF SHATTERING GLASS, THE CRACK OF SPLINTERING WOOD--

--KORREK HIES AWAY!
OKAY, FOLKS --IN TWENTY-FIVE WORDS OR LESS... WHAT IS THIS?

LIKE...WHO WAS THAT GUY? WHY'D HE TRY TO KILL MY SISTER? WHERE'D HE COME FROM?
I WISH I COULD ANSWER YOU, ANDY--BUT I CAN'T! I JUST DON'T KNOW!

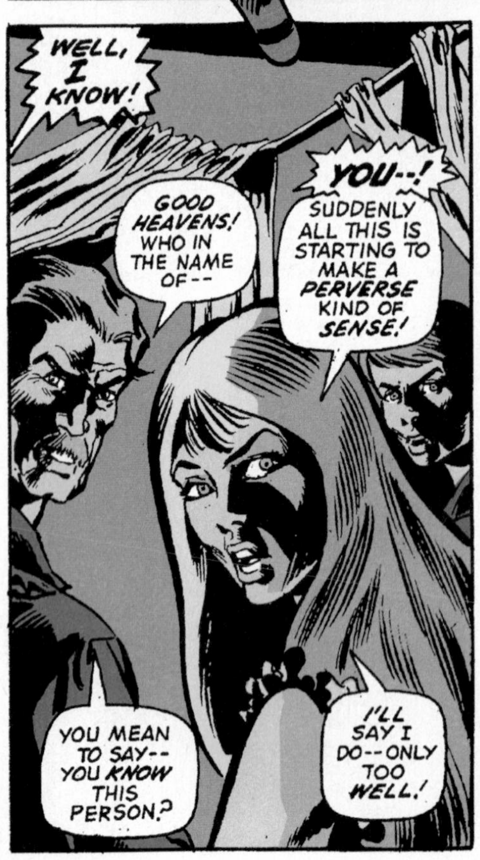
WELL, I KNOW!
GOOD HEAVENS! WHO IN THE NAME OF--
YOU--! SUDDENLY ALL THIS IS STARTING TO MAKE A PERVERSE KIND OF SENSE!
YOU MEAN TO SAY-- YOU KNOW THIS PERSON?
I'LL SAY I DO--ONLY TOO WELL!

OF COURSE, SHE DOES! 'TWAS I WHO LED HER--AND THE MAN-OBJECT--ACROSS THE DIMENSIONS TO THE DARK DOMAIN OF SOMINUS--
--TO RESCUE YOU, JOSHUA KALE, AND THE CULTISTS OF ZHERED-NA!* AH, YES--'TWAS I AND NONE OTHER--
--DAKIMH THE ENCHANTER!
*FEAR #15. --ROY.

HE'S THE MAGICIAN I TOLD YOU ABOUT, GRANDPA--THE ONE I CAN ALWAYS COUNT ON...
...TO DESERT ME WHEN I NEED HIM MOST!
IS ALL THIS CHAOS YOUR DOING?

SURELY YOU JEST, CHILD! THE TRUTH IS QUITE THE OPPOSITE! I'VE COME TO HELP YOU.
TOGETHER, WE CAN STOP IT--
--BEFORE IT'S TOO LATE.

WILL YOU KINDLY QUIT TALKING IN RIDDLES, MAN? STOP WHAT? BEFORE WHAT IS TOO LATE?
WE "SIMPLE FOLK" STILL DON'T UNDERSTAND ANY OF THIS!

ALLOW ME BUT A MOMENT, SIR, AND I'LL EXPLAIN EVERYTHING--LITERALLY, EVERYTHING. THE UNIVERSE!
NOW, SIMPLY STATED, THE COSMOS WORKS THUS: ON ANY GIVEN WORLD WHERE LIFE IS PRESENT--
--EVERY POSSIBLE PERMUTATION OF "REALITY" EXISTS.
THEY EXIST IN THE VERY SAME SPACE--BUT ON DIFFERENT DIMENSIONAL PLANES!

INDEED, WHAT IS REALITY ON ANY ONE SUCH PLANE--IS MERE FANTASY ON ALL THE OTHERS. ALL IS REAL, ALL IS ILLUSION.
AND, UNTIL RECENTLY, ALL THIS ALL WAS HELD IN A DELICATE COSMIC BALANCE--
--TO PREVENT ALTERNATE REALITIES FROM CONVERGING--AND POSSIBLY DESTROYING ONE ANOTHER.
AND NOW THAT BALANCE HAS BEEN DISTURBED--
--AT THE NEXUS POINT OF THE COSMIC FORCES--IN THE SWAMP WHERE THE MAN-OBJECT DWELLS!

"THE RECENT FLURRY OF ACTIVITY THERE--THE CONSTRUCTION CREW DRAINING THE SWAMP TO ERECT AN AIRPORT ON THE SITE*--COULD WELL RESULT IN CATASTROPHE!

"FOR IF THE BALANCE I SPOKE OF IS NOT SET ARIGHT, THE VERY STRUCTURE OF REALITY WILL COLLAPSE-- A MILLION MILLION ALTERNATE UNIVERSES WILL COLLIDE--!

IN THE END, A PLAGUE OF INSANITY WOULD SWEEP ACROSS THE COSMOS --AND NONE WOULD SURVIVE!

"YOUR WORLD WILL BE INUNDATED BY A TIDE OF BLADE-WIELDING BARBARIANS... OR BEASTS WHO WALK AND TALK LIKE MEN...!

"...OR BY DEMONS SPAWNED IN THE DARKEST PITS OF SOMINUS! OR BY ALL OF THESE-- AND MORE!"

*SEE FEAR #16-18. --R.

IT'S-- HORRIFYING! BUT WHY HAVE YOU COME TO ME? THERE'S NOTHING I CAN DO!
NO MATTER WHAT KORREK THINKS, I'M NO SORCERESS--!
NOT YET, IT'S TRUE. BUT YOU'VE SHOWN GREAT POTENTIAL!
SO GREAT, IN FACT--THAT I PROPOSE TO MAKE YOU MY APPRENTICE--
--IMPART TO YOU ALL THE KNOWLEDGE I'VE AMASSED IN 20,000 YEARS OF LIFE!
YOU HAVE THE TALENT--AND THE COURAGE. HAVE YOU THE DESIRE TO EMBARK ON ON SUCH A VENTURE?

OH, GRANDPA-- DO YOU THINK I COULD? I'VE WANTED TO STUDY CONJURY FOR SO LONG!
THINK OF THE ADVENTURE IT WOULD BE!
I AM THINKING OF THAT-- AND OF THE DANGER.
BUT IF IT IS WHAT YOU WANT...
I CAN'T STAND IN YOUR WAY.

EXCELLENT! YOU EXHIBIT GREAT WISDOM, JOSHUA KALE. YOU MUST SENSE, AS I DO--
--THAT YOUNG JENNIFER'S NAME MAY ONE DAY BE AS HALLOWED AS ZHERED-NA'S OWN.

SO HAVE NO FEAR, MY FRIENDS. SHE IS SAFE WITH ME--AND ONLY GREATNESS WAITS BEFORE HER...
...AS WE DEPART FOR WORLDS UNKNOWN! FAREWELL!
'BYE, GRANDPA-- 'BYE, ANDY...!
ZOT

THEY'RE GONE-- TO LORD KNOWS WHERE. I ONLY PRAY...THEY'LL RETURN ONE DAY.
YOUR SISTER IS A VERY BRAVE GIRL, ANDY. AND SHE'S TAKEN ON AN AWESOME RESPONSIBILITY --TO ALL WHO LIVE.
OKAY, OKAY--I'M IMPRESSED.
HOW COME I NEVER GET TO SAVE THE WORLD?

THAT QUESTION, NONE CAN ANSWER... JUST AS THERE IS NO ONE TO QUELL THE QUERIES OF THIS STRANGER IN A STRANGE SWAMP...!
NEVER HAVE I SEEN SUCH A QUAGMIRE! ALL THE FOLIAGE IS... GREEN!
WHERE ARE THE PURPLES AND GOLDS OF KATHARTA?

AND MORE... WHERE AM I?
HAVE I LOST MY ARMY... MY WORLD... EVEN MY MIND?

OF WHAT USE IS A BLADE TO A WARRIOR GONE MAD?

PERHAPS THIS WAS THE WITCH'S PLAN ALL ALONG-- TO TRAP ME HERE IN THIS NETHERWORLD--
--WHILE SHE HEAPS DOOM UPON MY FATHER'S KINGDOM.

SOMEWHERE... SOMEWHEN, THE SLIME-DWELLER HAS SEEN THIS MAN BEFORE--!
AND THOUGH HIS INSTINCT SEEMS TO SAY-- "UNFRIENDLY"-- STILL HE DRAWS CLOSER...!
BUT WHAT OF IT? I'VE NO LONGER THE SPIRIT IN ME TO CARE.
NO KATHARTAN PRINCE HAS EVER GIVEN UP BEFORE, BUT NOW--!

AND THEN...THE SOUND OF SLOSHING FEET CAUSES KORREK TO TURN--AND RECONSIDER!
ZOKK! THE DEMON-THING!

ONCE MORE, I AM FLOODED WITH HOPE--FOR IF THE SORCERESS SENT YOU TO DISPATCH ME-- THEN, PERHAPS...
...HER SPELLS ARE NOT SO POTENT AS I ASSUMED! PERHAPS I CAN ESCAPE!
BUT FIRST, MALODOROUS ONE, YOU DIE--

--SO!
ZOKK! THIS CANNOT BE! I'VE RUN YOU THROUGH!
WHY DO YOU YET STAND?

CAN YOU NOT ANSWER, BEAST? YOUR SILENCE DRIVES ME TO FURY AND FRENZY! BUT NOT FEAR!
NO KATHARTAN KNOWS FEAR!
WE ARE, AFTER ALL, NOT A BRIGHT RACE--BUT WE ARE STRONG!

STRONG ENOUGH TO SLICE YOU-- HACK YOU-- CLEAVE YOU-- STAB YOU--
WHY DON'T YOU FALL DOWN??

AGAIN AND AGAIN THE CRACKLING BLADE OOZES HARMLESSLY THROUGH THE MIRY MAN-THING...
...UNTIL, FINALLY, KORREK'S RAGE GIVES WAY TO DESPAIR. AND, SULLEN AND WEARY--

--HE CASTS HIS WEAPON AWAY...
WHAT ARE YOU MADE OF, MONSTER? CAN NOTHING HARM YOU?

...AND FINDS A CLUMP OF DRY GROUND WHERE HE MAY RESUME HIS BROODING.
I SUPPOSE YOU WILL SLAY ME NOW. SURELY THAT WAS YOUR MISSION. WELL-- PROCEED!
OR DO YOU WISH TO HUMBLE ME FIRST-- MAKE ME BEG FOR MY LIFE?

WELL, I'LL NOT GIVE YOU THAT SATISFACTION! AT THIS POINT, I WELCOME DEATH!
WHAT ELSE IS THERE--FOR ONE WHOSE LIFE HAS BECOME AN ABSURDITY?

AW, CLAM UP, BUD! YOU DON'T EVEN KNOW THE MEANING OF THE WORD!
FINDING YOURSELF IN A WORLD OF TALKING HAIRLESS APES-- NOW THAT'S ABSURDITY!

OH--NO! WHAT NEW HORROR IS THIS? IT VAGUELY RESEMBLES A DUCK, BUT--!

WHILE, A UNIVERSE AWAY, IN THE SKY-CASTLE...
YOU MEAN--MY EARLIER VISITS HERE WEREN'T DREAMS, DAKIMH?
I WAS ACTUALLY "BLINKING" BACK AND FORTH BETWEEN THIS WORLD AND EARTH DURING MY SLEEP--
--BECAUSE OF THIS PSYCHIC--OR EMPATHIC--OR WHATEVER--POWER I'VE GOT?
FAR OUT... I WAS SANE ALL ALONG. FOR ONCE, IT REALLY WAS THE REST OF THE WORLD THAT WENT BONKERS! I WAS SO AFRAID THAT--
PUT THOSE FEARS TO REST, JENNIFER. ALL I'VE TOLD YOU IS TRUE.
AND WE MUST TURN TO OTHER MATTERS.

LIKE STOPPING THIS CRAZINESS, I HOPE!
PRECISELY. FOR YOU WERE NOT ITS ONLY VICTIM, CHILD. BEINGS FROM ALL THE PLANES OF EXISTENCE HAVE BEEN AFFECTED.
LIKE THOSE SOLDIERS--AND KORREK, HUH?
AYE--AND MILLIONS MORE--BLINKING OUT OF THEIR OWN REALITIES AND INTO ALIEN ONES.*
*WHICH EXPLAINS BOTH THE PEANUT BUTTER AND THE DUCK. --R.T.

AND WE FACE ANOTHER--POTENTIALLY GREATER--THREAT, ALSO:
A CONGRESS OF TYRANTS WHO HOPE TO GAIN DOMINION OVER ALL REALITY--UNLESS WE HALT THEM.
WHAT IS IT YOU'RE LOOKING UP?

IS THAT A BOOK OF SPELLS, OR JUST AN ENCYCLOPE--
DAKIMH! LOOK OUT!!
THAT'S SOME KIND OF BOMB!!

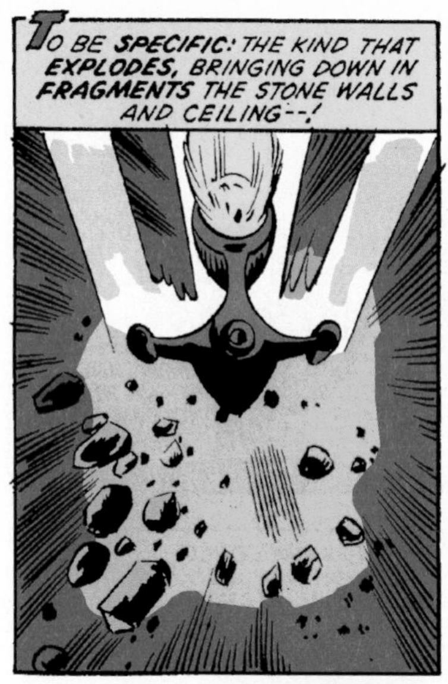
TO BE SPECIFIC: THE KIND THAT EXPLODES, BRINGING DOWN IN FRAGMENTS THE STONE WALLS AND CEILING--!

AND WHEN THE RESULTANT DUST CLEARS...
DAKIMH! HELP! I'M CAUGHT UNDER THE RUBBLE!
DAKIMH! ARE YOU OKAY? CAN YOU HEAR ME? OR--OH, NO!
HE'S DONE IT AGAIN! HE'S GONE!!

DON'T LET THAT TROUBLE YA, WENCH! WE'LL FIND 'IM--
--OR WE'LL GET OUR HEADS LOBBED OFF --WON'T WE, YA NO-GOOD SLOBBERIN' DOGS?
Y-YESSIR! SPREAD OUT, MEN!

PERSONNEL DEPLOYED FOR SEARCH-AND DESTROY OPERATIONS, SIR!
GOOD! NOW DIG THE GIRL OUTTA THAT HEAP! SHE'S COMIN' WITH US!
WE CAN'T RISK HER WRECKIN' OUR CONGRESS OF REALITIES, EITHER!

S-SIR... WE'VE TURNED THE CASTLE INSIDE OUT. THERE'S NO SIGN OF THE MAGICIAN, SIR.
HE--HE MUST'VE ESCAPED TO ANOTHER REALITY. I MEAN, HE IS A MAGICIAN, SIR.
SIR...?
SHUT UP! YOU CAN DISCUSS IT LATER--WITH THE OVERMASTER!

TO THE CASTLE BATTLEMENTS--ALL OF YOU! AND BRING THE GIRL! WE'RE FINISHED HERE.
IT'S TIME WE CLEARED OUT!
WE HEAR AND OBEY, WARLORD AKILLA! TO THE BALLOONS, MEN!

I DON'T BELIEVE I AM SEEING THIS....!

WAIT!!
AT LEAST TELL ME WHERE YOU'RE TAKING ME--AND WHY! I'M ENTITLED TO THAT!
VERY WELL, THEN--WE'RE TAKING YOU TO OUR CONGRESS--TO DIE!
NOW...DID THAT PUT YOU MORE AT EASE?

DAKIMH--HOW COULD YOU DESERT ME NOW? UNLESS...YOU INTENDED...!

AND THE BIZARRE SITUATION IN THE SWAMP IS ABOUT TO BECOME EQUALLY AS DESPERATE AS JENNIFER'S--!

WE AGREE, THEN, DUCK--TO SEARCH TOGETHER FOR A WAY OUT OF THIS SLOUGH--

--BACK TO OUR OWN WORLDS, WHERE'ER THEY MAY BE!

CUT THE SPEECH SHORT AND MARCH, KORREK!

NO! NOT AIMLESSLY! THIS BOG IS HUGE. WE MIGHT--

AIEEEE!

ZOKK! DID YOU HEAR THAT, DUCK? THE SOUND OF OTHER MEN! SALVATION!

WE MUST FIND ITS SOURCE!

YOU'RE GOING TO FOLLOW THAT? YOU'RE CRAZY! YOU WANT TO GET KILLED?

BUT KORREK FEARS NOTHING--AND DESIRES ESCAPE ABOVE ANYTHING--AND SO HE TRAMPS ON--CHASING THE SOUND--

--AND THE DUCK AND THE QUAG-DWELLER FOLLOW AT HIS HEELS.

AND SOON, TO THEIR UNQUALIFIED REGRET, THEY LOCATE THE ORIGIN POINT OF THE SCREAM:

THE F.A. SCHIST CONSTRUCTION CAMP--BESIEGED BY THINGS THAT SLITHER, THINGS THAT CRAWL, THINGS THAT SWARM THE SKY ON LEATHERN WINGS!

DEMONS--IN THE SERVICE OF THE MYSTERIOUS OVERMASTER!
BEHOLD, O MY BROTHERS--THE ONE WE HAVE COME TO DESTROY HAS ARRIVED! THE BEING SPAWNED BY THE SWAMP'S MYSTIC FORCES!
ZOKK AND MAFTRA! HE MEANS THE MONSTER--WHOM WE THOUGHT AN ENEMY!!
KILL HIM--AND WE OPEN THE GATES TO THE CONQUEST OF ALL!

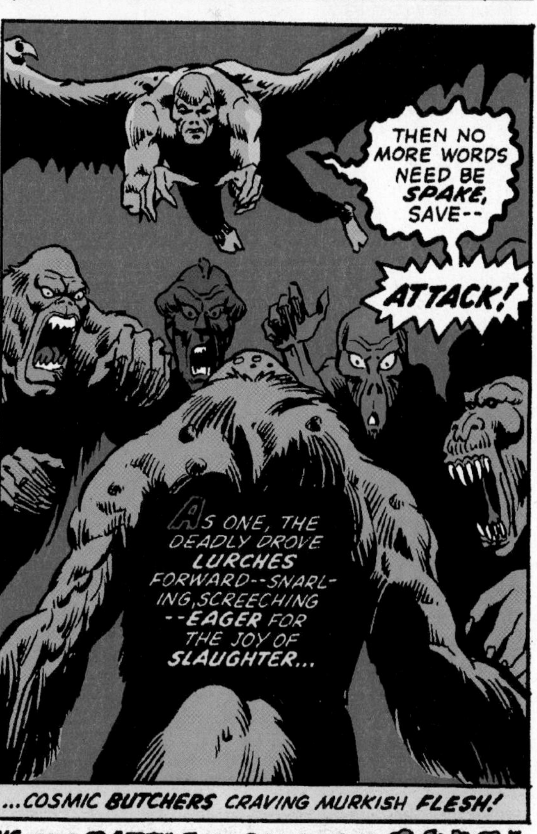

THEN NO MORE WORDS NEED BE SPAKE, SAVE--
ATTACK!
AS ONE, THE DEADLY DROVE LURCHES FORWARD--SNARLING, SCREECHING--EAGER FOR THE JOY OF SLAUGHTER...
...COSMIC BUTCHERS CRAVING MURKISH FLESH!

NEXT: THE SANITY-RENDING CONCLUSION FEATURING ALMOST EVERYTHING IN THE UNIVERSE, AND... THE BATTLE FOR THE PALACE OF THE GODS!

MAN·THING

MARVEL COMICS GROUP™

APPROVED BY THE COMICS CODE AUTHORITY

20¢

1 JAN 02912

THE MOST STARTLING *SWAMP·CREATURE* OF ALL!

THE MAN-THING

NOW IN HIS OWN MAGAZINE! FEAR·FRAUGHT FIRST ISSUE!

BRUNNER

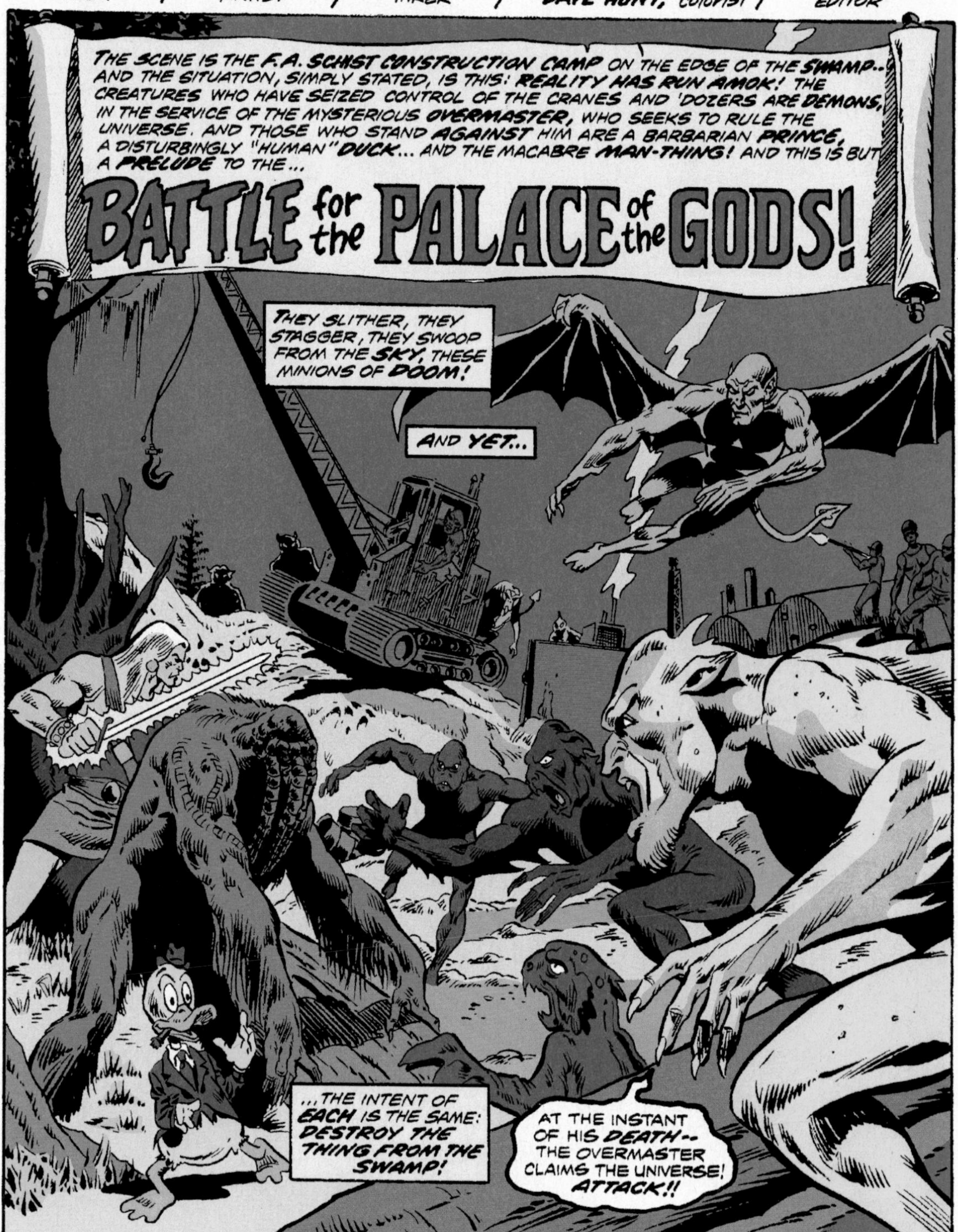
Stan Lee PRESENTS: MAN-THING!
STEVE GERBER WRITER / VAL MAYERIK ARTIST / SAL TRAPANI INKER / JOHN COSTANZA, letterer DAVE HUNT, colorist / ROY THOMAS EDITOR
THE SCENE IS THE F.A. SCHIST CONSTRUCTION CAMP ON THE EDGE OF THE SWAMP.. AND THE SITUATION, SIMPLY STATED, IS THIS: REALITY HAS RUN AMOK! THE CREATURES WHO HAVE SEIZED CONTROL OF THE CRANES AND 'DOZERS ARE DEMONS, IN THE SERVICE OF THE MYSTERIOUS OVERMASTER, WHO SEEKS TO RULE THE UNIVERSE. AND THOSE WHO STAND AGAINST HIM ARE A BARBARIAN PRINCE, A DISTURBINGLY "HUMAN" DUCK... AND THE MACABRE MAN-THING! AND THIS IS BUT A PRELUDE TO THE...
BATTLE for the PALACE of the GODS!
THEY SLITHER, THEY STAGGER, THEY SWOOP FROM THE SKY, THESE MINIONS OF DOOM!
AND YET...
...THE INTENT OF EACH IS THE SAME: DESTROY THE THING FROM THE SWAMP!
AT THE INSTANT OF HIS DEATH-- THE OVERMASTER CLAIMS THE UNIVERSE! ATTACK!!

WITH FANG AND BEAK, TALON AND TENTACLE--
--THEY POUNCE UPON THE SLIME-DWELLER--TEARING, GNAWING, CLAWING AT HIM--
--SLOWLY EATING AWAY AT THE MURKISH UN-FLESH OF WHICH MAN-THING IS MADE!

MORE OF THEM SPRING FORWARD TO ATTACK! FOLLOW ME, DUCK-- WE'LL WARD THEM OFF!
DON'T BE AN IDIOT, KORREK! WE CAN'T FIGHT THIS!

BUT THE WARRIOR PRINCE OF THE WESTLANDS PAYS NO HEED! HE BOUNDS BOLDLY INTO THE FRAY, HIS SWORD SPEWING ITS MYSTIC FIRE!
AND HE MAKES A MIND-STUNNING DISCOVERY--!

DIE, DEMON! DI--
WHA--? THIS THING... IS NOT ALIVE!

BEHOLD, DUCK! IT IS HOLLOW, LIKE A CHILD'S DOLL!
BEHIND THEIR FEAR-SOME VISAGE, THERE IS NO SUBSTANCE!

AND BEFORE THE CRACKLING SWORD OF KORREK-- THEY FALL!
LOOK, FEATHERED ONE! WE HAVE NOTHING TO FEAR FROM THESE MADMAN'S TOYS! WE WERE DUPED ONCE-- BUT NO LONGER, EH?

FOR FEAR WAS OUR TRUE FOE-- AND WE HAVE SLAIN IT!
PRAISE BE TO ZOKK! KORREK OF KATHARTA STANDS TRIUMPH-ANT!

AND WHEN HE RETURNS TO THAT FABLED LAND, THE MINSTRELS SHALL SING OF THIS D--
OH-- NO! NO!

THIS CANNOT BE! THE SEVERED PARTS YET LIVE!
BARBARIC FOOL!

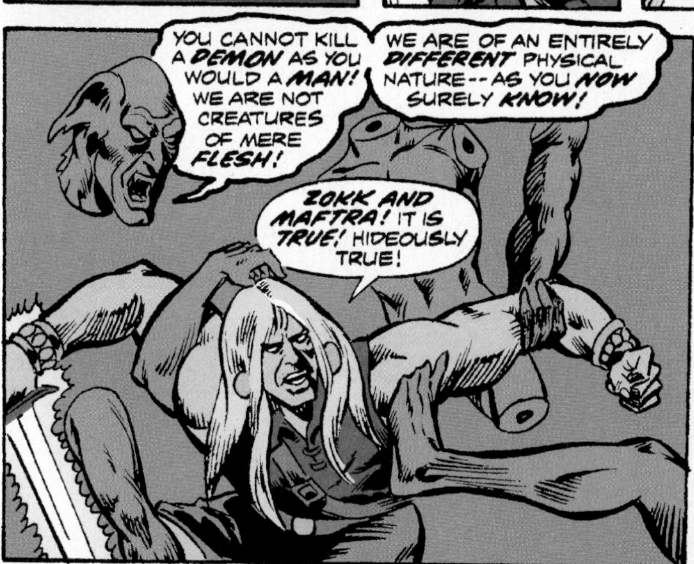
YOU CANNOT KILL A DEMON AS YOU WOULD A MAN! WE ARE NOT CREATURES OF MERE FLESH!
WE ARE OF AN ENTIRELY DIFFERENT PHYSICAL NATURE--AS YOU NOW SURELY KNOW!
ZOKK AND MAFTRA! IT IS TRUE! HIDEOUSLY TRUE!

SCANT YARDS AWAY, THE DUCK IS DRAWN INTO THE CONFLICT--!
UH-OH. THAT POOR GUY'S OUT FOR THE COUNT!
LIKE IT OR NOT-- HERE'S WHERE I GET INVOLVED.

THE DUCK--HOWARD, BY NAME--CASTS HIS BETTER JUDGEMENT TO THE WINDS, AND GRABS UP A GUN OF THE FALLEN WORK-MAN--!
OKAY, CREEPS-- HERE'S WHERE YOU GET YOURS, SEE?
I HAPPEN TO BE A CRACK SHOT --I NEVER MISS --AND--
BAM
OBOY!

I GOT YOU, BLAST IT! RIGHT IN THE HEART! WHY AREN'T YOU DEAD?
DEMONS DO NOT DIE, DUCK! THAT IS FOR YOU MORTALS TO DO-- AT OUR HANDS!

THEN, SUDDENLY, THE TIDE OF BATTLE TURNS-- AS THE MISSHAPEN ONCE-MAN STRIKES BACK!
AND HE BENDS THE FIEND'S WIRY FORM OVER UPON ITSELF...
HIS MOTTLED ARMS REACH BEHIND HIM-- RIP THE OUT-WORLDER FROM HIS BACK--!

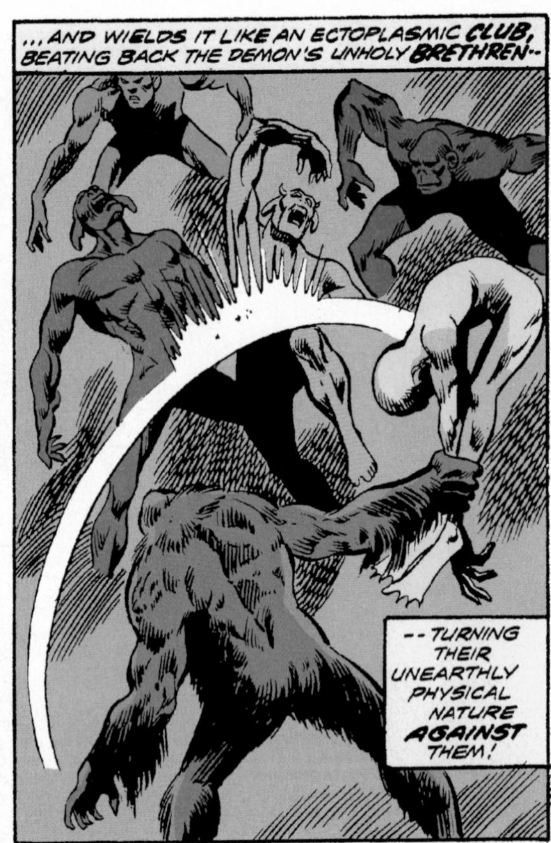
...AND WIELDS IT LIKE AN ECTOPLASMIC CLUB, BEATING BACK THE DEMON'S UNHOLY BRETHREN--
--TURNING THEIR UNEARTHLY PHYSICAL NATURE AGAINST THEM!

AND NOW, IN A BURST OF AMBER LIGHT COMES THE EQUALIZER IN THIS COMBAT OF MORTALS-VERSUS-MONSTERS--!
AW, NO! WILLYA LOOK AT THIS?! MORE LUNACY!
IT--IT'S HUMAN-- BUT WHOSE SIDE IS IT ON? WHO IS IT?

HE IS CALLED DAKIMH THE ENCHANTER-- THE MAGE WHO DWELLS IN THE CASTLE IN THE SKY IN THE LAND BETWEEN NIGHT AND DAY!
AND WITH A PASS OF HIS HAND THRU THE AIR...
...HE SUMMONS UP A WHITE WHIRLWIND THAT ROARS THRU THE CAMP, SWEEPING THE OVERMASTER'S SCREAMING HORDES INTO ITS VORTEX!

AND WHEN EACH AND EVERY DEVILKIN HAS BEEN THUS ENSNARED, THE CONJURER GESTURES AGAIN--
--CAUSING THE WHIRLWIND TO IMPLODE--AND ENDING THE DEMONS' BRIEF REIGN OF TERROR!
WHUK!
BEGONE, YE OGRES--TO YOUR FINAL REST IN THE FLAMING PITS OF SOMINUS! SO SPEAKS DAKIMH!

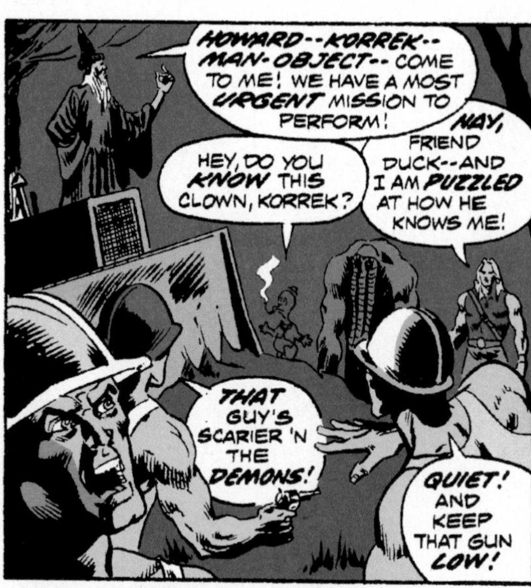
HOWARD--KORREK--MAN-OBJECT--COME TO ME! WE HAVE A MOST URGENT MISSION TO PERFORM!
HEY, DO YOU KNOW THIS CLOWN, KORREK?
NAY, FRIEND DUCK--AND I AM PUZZLED AT HOW HE KNOWS ME!
THAT GUY'S SCARIER 'N THE DEMONS!
QUIET! AND KEEP THAT GUN LOW!

THERE IS NO CAUSE FOR ALARM, GOOD PRINCE. I AM YOUR ALLY--AND YOU, I PRAY, SHALL SOON BE MINE...
...AS WE FIVE JOIN TO SAVE THE COSMOS!
BAH! I DON'T BELIEVE YOU! IT'S SOME SORCEROUS TRICK!
I BEG YOUR PARDON! THIS IS NO JEST, MY FRIEND! YOU AND THE DUCK HAVE BEEN CHOSEN BY FATE TO AID ME!
THAT IS WHY YOU ARE HERE--IN THE SWAMP--AT THE NEXUS OF ALL REALITIES!
ARE YOU SAYING THERE'S SOMETHING UNUSUAL ABOUT EACH OF US--THAT DREW US HERE FROM OUR OWN WORLDS, WHISKERS?
PRECISELY, HOWARD--AND I SHALL EXPLAIN IN FULL--

--WHEN WE ARE SAFELY ENSCONCED IN MY CASTLE--FAR FROM THE PRYING EYES OF MAN AND DEMON ALIKE! AND SO--
AWAY TO THAT REALM WE GO!
TH-THIS CAN'T BE REAL!

Y'KNOW, I THINK THE DUCK'S LAST WORDS SAY IT ALL--IT COULDN'T'VE BEEN REAL!
THEN WE'RE AGREED. IT--JUST DIDN'T HAPPEN, RIGHT?
WHAT--? WHAT DIDN'T HAPPEN?
RI-I-I-I-GHT!

WE, TOO, MIGHT TERM "IMPOSSIBLE" THE EVENTS THAT HAVE JUST TRANSPIRED... WERE WE NOT ABOUT TO WITNESS THIS SCENE!

THE CONGRESS OF REALITIES!! MEN FROM VIRTUALLY EVERY PLANE OF EXISTENCE-- BROUGHT TOGETHER BY THEIR COMMON ASPIRATION: GODHOOD.

I AM TOLD THE OVERMASTER HIMSELF WILL MAKE AN APPEARANCE TODAY--

--TO PRESIDE OVER THE WITCH-CHILD'S EXECUTION.

SO IT IS SAID, NORSEMAN.

Quid Est Reality?

GODHOOD: DEFINED AS DOMINATION OVER ALL THE PLANES OF REALITY FROM THE GREEN PASTURES OF THEREA TO THE DARK DOMAIN OF SOMINUS.

GODHOOD: IT BEGINS FOR THEM WITH THE KILLING OF THIS GIRL... JENNIFER KALE.

FOR SHE IS APPRENTICE TO DAKIMH-- AND HE IS THE FORCE THAT STANDS 'TWIXT THIS CONGRESS AND ITS DIVINE GOAL.

SUDDENLY-- THE CRY OF CLARION AND BUGLE--!
ALL HAIL! ALL HAIL! ALL HAIL THE LEADER!
THE GLORY WHO WALKS IS IN OUR MIDST!

THE OVERMASTER-- SOON-TO-BE LORD OF ALL REALITY!

A THUNDEROUS APPLAUSE GREETS HIS COMING, AS HE TAKES HIS PLACE AT THE ROSTRUM.
GLAD TIDINGS, MY FRIENDS! WE STAND UPON THE THRESHOLD OF VICTORY!
ONLY ONE OBSTACLE STANDS BETWEEN OUR FORCES AND THE DIMENSION CALLED THEREA-- HOME OF THE GODS!
THIS SORCERESS IS PART OF THAT OBSTACLE-- PART OF DAKIMH'S BAND!
SHE HAS BEEN BROUGHT HERE--TO DIE!

WITH THOSE WORDS, THE OVERMASTER'S FIRING SQUAD ASSEMBLES-- WEAPONS AND WARRIORS FROM ACROSS THE SPECTRUM OF SPACE AND TIME--!
YOU, JENNIFER KALE, HAVE BEEN FOUND IN CONTEMPT OF THIS CONGRESS-- GUILTY OF PROTECTING THE FREE BALANCE OF EXISTENCE!
PREPARE TO PAY THE PENALTY FOR THAT CRIME! SQUADRON -- READY--AIM--

BUT BEFORE THE FINAL COMMAND CAN BE GIVEN--
GOOD LORD! UNLESS MY RADAR SENSE HAS GONE CRAZY--
--HERE COMES DAREDEVIL, THE MAN WITHOUT FEAR!
--WE'RE PASSING THRU SOME KIND OF HOLE IN SPACE!
WE'RE SWINGING RIGHT BACK OUT AGAIN, IT APPEARS!
BUT IN BETWEEN-- WE'VE SAVED A LIFE! SEE THAT GIRL?
FAM
THOK
D.D AND THE WIDOW WILL WONDER ABOUT THAT EXPERIENCE UNTIL THE END OF THEIR DAYS. YET, IT PALES BESIDE-- THIS
OH-- NO! MY BODY!
IT'S MELTING! TURNING INTO WATER! HELP!!

WHILE, ONE DIMENSION BELOW THE MANIACAL CONGRESS --
AH! MY SPELL HAS BEEN SUCCESSFUL! OUR FIFTH MEMBER ARRIVES!
ARE YOU MAD, OLD MAN? 'TIS BUT A LEAK IN YOUR CASTLE'S ROOF!

"HARDLY, KORREK--OBSERVE! IT IS THE FEMALE YOU MISTAKENLY ASSUMED WAS YOUR ENEMY--MY APPRENTICE!"

AND PRAISE BE TO THEE, O' GODS OF THEREA, FOR PERMITTING HER SAFE RETURN!
SAVE THE ORAL ROBERTS ACT FOR LATER, DAKIMH. I WANT ANSWERS!

AND WHEN THE TWO HAVE EXCHANGED INCREDIBLE TALES--!
SO, WE'RE ALL FRIENDS NOW-- AND OUR JOB IS TO SET RIGHT THE COSMIC AXIS.
THAT'S PEACHY-- BUT IT STILL DOESN'T EXPLAIN ABOUT DAREDEVIL!
I KNOW NOT WHO THIS DARE-PERSON IS--BUT I THINK I CAN ACCOUNT FOR HIS APPEARANCE.

IMAGINE, CHILD, THAT THE NORMAL STRUCTURE OF REALITY APPEARS THUS:
ASCENDING LEVELS, HELD IN DELICATE BALANCE, A HAIR'S-BREATH APART.

THIS, HOWEVER, IS ITS CURRENT STATE--CHAOS! EVERY LEVEL COLLAPSED UPON ANOTHER.
WHERE ANY TWO OF THOSE LEVELS TOUCH, A JUNCTURE POINT IS CREATED--A DIMENSIONAL BRIDGE, OF SORTS.

I GET IT! D.D AND THE WIDOW PASSED THRU ONE OF THOSE JUNCTURE POINTS TOTALLY BY ACCIDENT, AND--!
EXACTLY! THEY CROSSED OVER INTO THE CONGRESS' WORLD. BUT... ENOUGH OF THIS.
WE HAVE A JOURNEY TO BEGIN-- NOW!

AND SO, HE LIFTS HIS HAND--
--AND THE WORLD VANISHES!
THERE IS NO NAME FOR WHERE THEY ARE NOW-- EXCEPT PERHAPS... "BETWEEN"!
FOR THIS IS A PLACE OUTSIDE REALITY--OUTSIDE BEING!

COME-- WE MUST CLIMB THE STAIR-CAGE TO ITS END.

BUT THE GOLDEN STAIRS ONLY WIND THEIR WAY TO --NOWHERE-- TO ANOTHER STATE OF UN-NESS...
...A RIBBON THAT LACES THRU THE BETWEEN, TYING IT TO YET ANOTHER KIND OF NULLITY--

--STEPPING STONES! AND ABOVE, BENEATH, AND BETWEEN THEM-- OBLIVION!
KORREK! DUCK! EXERCISE CAUTION! THE REST OF US ARE PROTECTED BY OUR SORCEROUS POWERS!
YOU TWO ARE NOT --YOU CAN DIE HERE!

DUCK! DID YOU HEAR HIM? GO SLOWER! TAKE TIME TO-- DUCK!
NO!!
I--I TRIPPED! I'M FALLING!!

DO NOT ATTEMPT TO FOLLOW, KORREK, LEST--
BUT--IS THERE NOTHING YOU CAN DO?

FOR POOR HOWARD-- NO. BUT I CAN DO SOMETHING I SHOULD HAVE DONE EARLIER--!

"I CAN PROTECT YOU -- WITH THIS MYSTIC HELMET."

NOW, YOU MAY FOLLOW WITHOUT FEAR, KORREK-- ON THIS NEXT LEG OF THE JOURNEY--
--THRU A SPACE DEVOID OF ALL BUT AIR AND LIGHT! COME!

'TWAS MY HASTE THAT COST THE DUCK HIS LIFE.
IF WE SUCCEED AT THIS QUEST-- I'LL HAVE TO LIVE WITH THAT TRUTH-- FOREVER.
AND SO, EACH IS ADRIFT WITH HIS OR HER OWN THOUGHTS--
--SAVE THE MAN-THING... WHO HAS NO THOUGHTS!
THEY TUMBLE ONWARD.

UNTIL...!
ZOKK! WHAT IS THIS PLACE?!
YOU ARE SEEING THE SWAMP--AS IT TRULY IS!

AND THERE IS THE CAUSE OF OUR INTERDIMENSIONAL TRAUMA-- THAT TOTTERING NEEDLE!
IT IS THE COSMIC AXIS-- AND WE MUST SET IT ARIGHT!

AND SO THEY SET THEM-SELVES TO THE AWESOME, YET DELICATE, TASK...!
BUT, NO SOONER HAVE THEY BEGUN-- THAN THE UTTERLY UNTHINKABLE OCCURS!

THE VERY FABRIC OF REALITY IS RENT ASUNDER-- AND FROM OUT OF THE RIP IN THE SKY-- THEY POUR IN A SEEMINGLY ENDLESS STREAM:
THE CONGRESS OF REALITIES!
DINOSAURS AND TANKS-- MUSKETS AND LASER PISTOLS-- CAVEMEN AND SUPERMEN-- FLYING, GALLOPING, ROLLING-- TOWARD INFINITY--!
SPECIAL NOTE FROM STEVE GERBER TO OUR DEMON PROOF-READERS: THIS PAGE IS SUPPOSED TO BE READ SIDE-WAYS, GANG! (OR, THE GERBER CURSE STRIKES AGAIN!)
BEINGS FROM THEN AND NOW AND WILL-BE...
...AND NEVER.

WE ARE--TOO LATE! THEY'VE FOUND THE WAY TO THEREA! ALL WILL BE LOST-- UNLESS WE FOLLOW AT ONCE!
BUT TO CATCH THEM-- WE WOULD NEED WINGS! SO--

--WINGS!
DAKIMH-- WHY WOULD THIS SPELL NOT HAVE SAVED THE DUCK?

ANSWER ME, DAKIMH-- WHY?
I...DID NOT THINK OF IT, KORREK. MY AGE HAS DULLED MY WITS, I FEAR.
MOMENTS LATER, THE WINGS DISSOLVE AS THE FOURSOME FLOATS LAZILY DOWNWARD TO THE VERDANT PARADISE CALLED THEREA--!

THANK HEAVENS-- WE STILL HAVE TIME! THE PALACE REMAINS INVIOLATE-- THE GODS, WELL AND SAFE.
SAFE? ARE YOU GOING BLIND, TOO, DAKIMH? THAT CLOUD OF DUST--
THAT'S THE ARMY-- ON THEIR WAY TO THE PALACE!
NO, CHILD-- YOU ARE WRONG.

FOR NOW, AT LEAST, THE PALACE IS IN NO DANGER. AND YOU WILL SEE WHY... ALL IN GOOD TIME. BUT...
...MEANWHILE, WE MUST STOP THE OVERMASTER BEFORE HE, TOO, LEARNS THE TRUTH.
SO--WHERE DOES THAT LEAVE US?

DAKIMH DOES NOT REPLY. RATHER... HE WINKS--!
DAKIMH!
SCREEE
AND THAT LEAVES THEM HERE: AT THE DRAW-BRIDGE ENTRANCE TO THE GODS' PALACE--AND DIRECTLY IN THE PATH OF THE OVERMASTER'S CAR!

DAKIMH, YOU OLD FOOL! YOU'RE LUCKY I DIDN'T RUN YOU OVER--AND I WOULD HAVE, IF I DIDN'T WISH TO SEE YOU HUMBLED BEFORE ME AFTER MY VICTORY!
NOW, STAND ASIDE! THE PALACE BELONGS TO ME! I AM RULER OF THE UNIVERSE!
ASIDE, I SAY! AT ONCE!

NO! YOUR CONQUEST IS A SHAM--UNTIL YOU DEFEAT YOUR ULTIMATE ENEMY! HIM! THE MAN-OBJECT!
THE RESULT OF ALL REALITIES GONE MAD--AT THEIR CROSSROADS, THE SWAMP!

DO YOU THINK I FEAR THAT WALKING MASS OF MURK, MAGE?
THEN, LET ME SHOW YOU SOME-THING...

THE OVERMASTER CLUTCH-ES AT HIS SCALP--AND PULLS--
--GATHERING SKIN INTO HIDEOUS FOLDS--STRETCHING IT--KNEEDING IT--!

AND THEN--
LOOK, DAKIMH!
LOOK UPON THE TRUE FACE OF YOUR FOE--UPON THE FIERY COUNTENANCE OF EVIL INCARNATE!
I AM THE "OVER-MASTER," DAKIMH! I--THE GODS' BANE!
I--WHO HAVE EVER BEEN BARRED FROM WALKING THE HALLOWED SOIL OF THEREA!

I--THE NETHER SPAWN!
ALL NEED FOR PRETENSE IS ENDED NOW--SO LET THE BATTLE COMMENCE!
TWICE BEFORE HAVE I CLASHED WITH THE SWAMP BEING--ONCE ON HIS HOME-GROUND, ONCE IN A LAND OF ILLUSION WHERE I COULD NOT HARM HIM--!

BUT HE HAS NO SUCH ADVANTAGE HERE! HERE, I SHALL EMERGE THE VICTOR!
FORWARD, MY LEGIONS! SEIZE THE PALACE, WHILE I DESTROY--
--OUR FINAL BARRIER TO GODHOOD!

THE WORDS SPOKEN IN THE ENSUING STRUGGLE--

--WORDS LIKE "POWER..." "MASTERY..." "MIGHT..." AND SO ON--ARE ALL SPOKEN BY THE NETHER-SPAWN...
...BECAUSE THE MONSTER FROM THE MIRE HAS NO MOUTH WITH WHICH TO SPEAK.
AND, IN TRUTH, THE SIGNIFICANCE OF THOSE WORDS IS MINIMAL.

SO LET US CONCENTRATE INSTEAD ON THE ACTIONS OF THE COMBATANTS-- AND WHAT THEY MEAN.
THE DEMON'S WEAPON IS THAT OF FLAME. IT DESTROYS--BUT IT CAN ALSO PART THE CURTAINS OF DARKNESS AND IGNORANCE.
WHICH IT CAN... DEPENDING UPON WHO WIELDS IT.

THE MAN-THING'S WEAPON IS BRUTE STRENGTH--APPLIED TO THE ERSTWHILE CONVEYANCE OF THIS WOULD-BE LORD OF THE COSMOS...
...THE VEHICLE WHICH HAS COME TO SYMBOLIZE MAN'S MATERIAL LUST.
IT IS NOT AN EASY TASK FOR HIM...

...TOPPLING THIS TWO-TON METAL MONSTROSITY. HE IS NOT EVEN CERTAIN WHY HE DOES IT--EXCEPT THAT THE DEMON REEKS OF EVIL, AND FOR SOME HAZY REASON, HE DOES NOT LIKE EVIL. IT... HURTS HIM.
LITERALLY... IT CAUSES PAIN TO HIS EMPATHIC NATURE.

IN SHORT, THE BRIEF SCENE WE HAVE JUST WITNESSED IS PREGNANT WITH PHILOSOPHICAL IMPLICATIONS. BUT THESE TWO OF THE NETHER-SPAWN'S--DON'T CARE!
HEY, ZADDAK! LOOK! OUR LEADER'S BEEN BEATEN!

DON'T YOU SEE? IF WE...!
AYE! IF WE CAN DEFEAT THE MONSTER--THEN WE'LL BE THE LEADERS! LET'S HAVE AT HIM, KONOG!

MORE EVIL... MORE PAIN... AND NOW, SOMETHING WORSE:
FEAR!

AND FEAR IS THE SINGLE EMOTION THE MAN-THING LOATHES! ON SENSING IT, HE LOSES ALL CONTROL--REACHES OUT--LAYS HIS HANDS HEAVY ON ITS SOURCE!

AND THE RESULTS ARE MOST HORRIFYING--!
FOR WHATEVER KNOWS FEAR, BURNS AT THE MAN-THING'S TOUCH!!
FOR NOW, THESE MEN STAND STARING IN SHOCK AT THE FIVE FINGERED SCARS UPON THEIR CHESTS. IN A MOMENT..

...THEY WILL COLLAPSE IN AGONY, EVEN AS THEIR MASTER RISES AGAIN!
OUR FIGHT IS NOT OVER, MONSTER! FAR FROM IT!
THE AIR SUDDENLY FILLS WITH THE STENCH OF SULFUR AS HE WELLS UP FROM THE MOLTEN SLAG THAT HAD BEEN THE CAR!

AND ALMOST AT ONCE, THE CONFLICT IS RENEWED-- FIERCER THAN EVER--!
MAKE NO ERROR, SLIME-DWELLER-- I INTEND TO KILL YOU!
THAT THE MONSTER DOES NOT DOUBT. IF ONLY HE KNEW-- WHY!!

DAKIMH--I DON'T GET IT! IF THIS IS THE PALACE OF GODS-- WHERE ARE THE GODS?
WHY AREN'T THEY HERE-- HELPING DEFEND THEIR OWN PALACE?

I CANNOT ANSWER YOU, CHILD... NOT YET.
EXCEPT TO SAY THAT IT IS... NOT THE NATURE OF GODS TO DO THAT. YOU WILL SEE.

A PUZZLE. AND WHETHER OR NOT WE LEARN ITS SOLUTION HINGES UPON THE OUTCOME OF THE MAN-MONSTER'S STRUGGLE--
--A STRUGGLE NEARING ITS MACABRE FINALE!

THE WATER OF THE CASTLE MOAT! SIMON-PURE THEREAN WATER! NO!!
THE MAN-THING CANNOT FATHOM HIS ADVERSARY'S WORDS--OR ANY WORDS--BUT AGAIN HE SENSES FEAR--TERRIBLE FEAR!
AND HE SENSES FURTHER THAT IT HAS TO DO WITH THE WATER--THIS PARTICULAR WATER, WHICH THE VEGETABLE PART OF HIS MAKE-UP TELLS HIM IT IS DIFFERENT FROM ANY OTHER--WHOLLY WITHOUT IMPURITY!

HE CANNOT, HOWEVER, MAKE THE MENTAL LEAP OF LOGIC--
--THAT WOULD TELL HIM WHY A CREATURE LIKE THE NETHER-SPAWN WOULD FIND TERROR IN SUCH A THING.
BUT HE ACCEPTS THE FACT-- AND LUNGES-- PUSHES--!

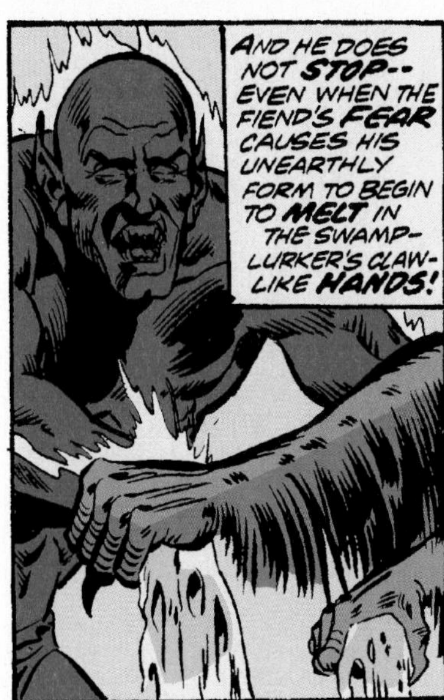
AND HE DOES NOT STOP-- EVEN WHEN THE FIEND'S FEAR CAUSES HIS UNEARTHLY FORM TO BEGIN TO MELT IN THE SWAMP-LURKER'S CLAW-LIKE HANDS!

YOU CAN'T HOLD ME! I CAN TEAR MYSELF LOOSE!
I WON'T LET YOU WIN!
I WON'T BE BEATEN BY A BEING THAT CAN'T EVEN THINK!!
IRONY: THE FLAME-DEMON'S OWN MOMENTUM--

--IS THAT FORCE THAT FINALLY SENDS HIM PLUNGING TO HIS DOOM.
STEAM RISES AS THE WATERS WASH OVER HIM--!

AND WHEN THE TORRID MIST CLEARS...
THE FLAME, THE PASSION OF THE EVIL IS DEAD. AND ALL THAT REMAINS IS...
...ITS GRAY, WITHERED CORE!

TO US, THE SIGHT OF THIS WIZENED, ATROPHIED MOUND OF METAPLASM IS MERELY APPALLING. BUT TO HIS FORMER FOLLOWERS--
IT'S THE END! CHARLIE-THING WON! C'MON, YOU SONS O' LEECHES-- RETREAT WITH HONOR!
AYE--LEST WE FALL VICTIM TO THE OLD MAN'S SORCERY!

IN MOMENTS, THE HORDES HAVE GONE-- BACK THRU THE BLACK HOLE INTO NON-BEING...!
AND DOVES SING THE SONG OF PEACE IN THE THEREAN SKY!
OKAY--SO WE WON! I'M STILL CURIOUS ABOUT THE GODS!
CAN YOU EXPLAIN NOW--WHY DIDN'T THEY HELP US?
AYE. I, TOO, AM TROUBLED BY THEIR SEEMING INDIFFERENCE. TROUBLED-- AND ANGRY.

BUT THERE IS NO CAUSE FOR ANGER, KORREK.
YOU SEE, THE PROBLEM IS NOT WITH THE GODS-- BUT RATHER WITH MAN'S CONCEPTION OF WHAT GODS SHOULD BE.
WE CONCEIVE THEM AS IMMENSE, COMPLEX BEINGS --WHO DWELL IN REALMS WITH TOWERS AND SPIRES OF GOLD.
BUT NOTHING COULD BE FURTHER FROM THE TRUTH!

YOU SEE--THIS IS THE REAL PALACE!
THIS HUMBLE COTTAGE, SURROUNDED BY THINGS-- OF NATURE, THINGS OF PEACE.
QUIET, SIMPLE, LOVING THINGS--LIKE THE GODS THEMSELVES-- UPON WHOM YOU NOW GAZE!

Y-YOU'RE KIDDING?! THAT ORDINARY PEASANT COUPLE-- THEY'RE THE GODS OF THEREA? THE MOVERS OF THE COSMOS!?
I--I CAN'T BELIEVE IT! IT'S TOO WEIRD. THEY CAN'T BE GODS!!

OF COURSE NOT, CHILD. THEY ARE MERE CARETAKERS.
THESE ARE THE GODS!
"THINK OF YOUR EARTHLY FOLKLORE ABOUT THEM: MAN'S BEST FRIEND-- EVER LOYAL-- WATCHERS OVER THE HOME.

"ZOKK AND MAFTRA!" EXCLAIMS KORREK, AND PERHAPS THOSE ARE THEIR NAMES...!
BUT NAMES MEAN NOTHING TO THE MAN-THING...

...AND NEITHER DOES COSMIC STATUS.

HE MERELY SENSES THAT THESE ARE FRIENDLY BEINGS, KIND AND GOOD.
THUS, HE REACHES OUT ALMOST SOFTLY-- TO TOUCH.

AND AS HIS MOTTLED FINGERS MAKE CONTACT--

IN A SINGLE DAZZLING INSTANT...

ALL EXISTENCE BURSTS OPEN!

THE FOURSOME SEES AND HEARS AND FEELS EVERY COLOR AND SOUND AND SENSATION THERE IS OR EVER WILL BE--!

AND THEY GO REELING ACROSS THE SPECTRUM OF REALITIES--

--BACK TO WHENCE THEY CAME!

KORREK, WARRIOR PRINCE OF KATHARTA--HIS SOUL NOW IMBUED WITH A SERENITY IT HAS NEVER KNOWN BEFORE--STANDS ATOP A SNOWSWEPT WESTLANDS PEAK--AND SMILES. HE IS HOME.

AND IN THE LAND BETWEEN NIGHT AND DAY, THE AGED ENCHANTER AND HIS YOUNG APPRENTICE RETURN TO THE CASTLE IN THE SKY... MORE THEN EVER AWARE OF THEIR AWESOME RESPONSIBILITY.

THE UNIVERSE IS SO--SO TOTAL, DAKIMH! NOW THAT I'VE SEEN IT--I MUST LEARN MORE!
IF ONLY HOWARD COULD HAVE SURVIVED TO--!
THAT IS WHY WE MUST RESUME YOUR LESSONS AT ONCE. MY TIME...IS SHORT.

THE MAN-THING, TOO, HAS RETURNED TO HIS RIGHTFUL PLACE--THOUGH THERE IS NO SENSE OF CALM OR WONDER IN HIM. THERE IS ONLY THE OMNIPRESENT HAZE, OBSCURING ALL THOUGHT, ALL MEMORY.

OH, HE RECALLS SOME OF THIS EXPERIENCE-- THE FRIENDLY D-O... OR WAS IT G-O-... OR...AND THEN, HE FORGETS EVEN THAT.

NEXT: DEATH-TRAP FOR A MAN-THING!

GIANT SIZE MAN-THING

4 MAY 02920

50¢

68 BIG PAGES

MARVEL COMICS GROUP

APPROVED BY THE COMICS CODE AUTHORITY

GIANT-SIZE MAN-THING

PANIC IN THE CITY... AS THE MOST STARTLING SLIME-CREATURE OF ALL STALKS THE HALLOWED HALLS OF A TERRIFIED HIGH SCHOOL!

EXTRA!

HOWARD THE DUCK FACES DEATH AT THE HANDS OF... GORKO, THE MAN-FROG

BRUNNER

THERE ARE WORLDS UPON WORLDS ... WORLDS WITHIN WORLDS ... WORLDS WITHOUT END.
EVERY MAN'S MIND IS A UNIVERSE.
AND BETWEEN THOSE UNIVERSES ARE PLACES LIKE THIS, WHERE REALITIES COLLIDE.
WORLDS WHERE ALL AND NOTHING ARE SYNONYMOUS...
...WORLDS NOT MEANT FOR LIVING BEINGS... UNFIT FOR CREATURES WHO MUST REASON...
FOR LOGIC, RATIONALE, EVEN SANITY HAVE NO MEANING HERE.
SO CONSIDER THE PLIGHT OF HOWARD THE DUCK!
FOR MONTHS, BY OUR RECKONING, HE HAS BEEN FALLING THROUGH THIS UN-WORLD, THIS VOID BETWEEN...
...ALONE WITH HIS THOUGHTS IN SOUNDLESS SPACE, LEFT TO WONDER WHETHER OR NOT HE EXISTS.
FROG DEATH!
INTRODUCING A NEW CONCEPT IN COMIC LITERATURE BY
STEVE GERBER Writer
FRANK BRUNNER Artist & Colorist
TOM ORZ lettering
CARL BARKS spiritual guide

AS HE DISCOVERS A MOMENT LATER-- HE DOES. FOR, BY DEFINITION, ONE CAN ONLY GO SO FAR IN A WORLD BETWEEN.

IT--IT'S GROUND! SOLID GROUND! I'M SITTING ON THE GROUND!! NOT FALLING--SITTING!
AND THERE'S GRASS--AND TREES--AND BUILDINGS. I'M HOME! I MADE IT!
MISTER, ARE YOU ALL RIGHT?

OH, SURE--JUST A LITTLE SHAKY, NATCH, BUT IT'S GREAT TO BE BACK, AN'--

WAAAAGH!
I'M BACK ON THE WORLD OF TALKING HAIRLESS APES!
HEY--YOU'RE A DUCK!

THERE AIN'T NO JUSTICE! YA SAVE THE UNIVERSE*, AN' WHAT DOES IT GET YA?
"YOU'RE A DUCK!" --THAT'S WHAT IT GETS YA!
M-MAYBE WE CAN HELP YOU?
*IN FEAR #19 AND MAN-THING #1. --LEN.

IF YA REALLY WANNA HELP--YOU'LL SHUT UP AN' POINT ME TOWARD THE NEAREST CIGAR STORE.
I-IT'S RIGHT AROUND THE BLOCK. C'MON. WE'LL TAKE YOU.

YEAH, I JUST BET YOU WILL! HOW DO I KNOW THIS AIN'T A WIZARD'S TRAP?
'CAUSE THERE AIN'T NO WIZARDS IN CLEVELAND, MAN! NOW, WALK ON!
TOBACCO
CLEVELAND! HOW COULD A PLACE POSSESS SO EERIE AND EVIL A NAME AND NOT BE RULED BY DEMONS, HOWARD WONDERS.

AND YET, SENSING THAT THESE TWO "APES" MEAN HIM NO HARM -- HE FOLLOWS.
WHAT'LL IT BE --?

THESE'LL BE FINE. HOW MUCH?
EVERYTHIN' ON THE COUNTER'S THREE FOR A BUCK.
EL ROPO

AT LEAST SOMETHING'S REASONABLE ON THIS WORLD! HERE, PAL.
A BUCK EVEN. THANKS, CHUM.
SPECIAL
WHEELING

HAVE A GOOD DAY--AN' COME BACK AGA-- URRK!
HEY! HOLD IT! WHAT'RE YA TRYIN' TA---
THE UNITED STATES OF
ONE DOLLAR

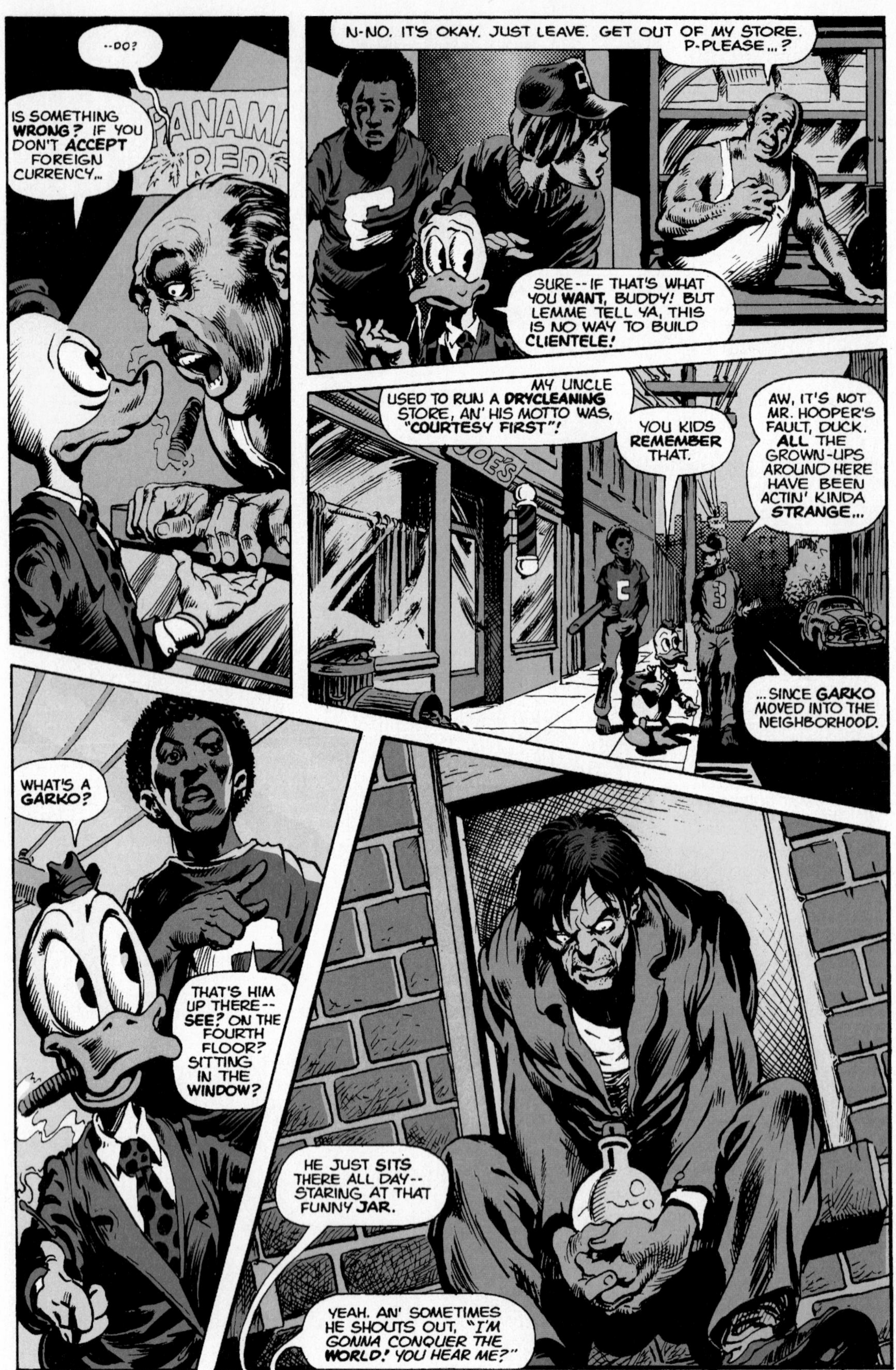
--DO?
IS SOMETHING WRONG? IF YOU DON'T ACCEPT FOREIGN CURRENCY...
PANAMA RED
N-NO. IT'S OKAY. JUST LEAVE. GET OUT OF MY STORE. P-PLEASE...?
SURE--IF THAT'S WHAT YOU WANT, BUDDY! BUT LEMME TELL YA, THIS IS NO WAY TO BUILD CLIENTELE!
MY UNCLE USED TO RUN A DRYCLEANING STORE, AN' HIS MOTTO WAS, "COURTESY FIRST"!
YOU KIDS REMEMBER THAT.
AW, IT'S NOT MR. HOOPER'S FAULT, DUCK. ALL THE GROWN-UPS AROUND HERE HAVE BEEN ACTIN' KINDA STRANGE...
...SINCE GARKO MOVED INTO THE NEIGHBORHOOD.
WHAT'S A GARKO?
THAT'S HIM UP THERE--SEE? ON THE FOURTH FLOOR? SITTING IN THE WINDOW?
HE JUST SITS THERE ALL DAY--STARING AT THAT FUNNY JAR.
YEAH. AN' SOMETIMES HE SHOUTS OUT, "I'M GONNA CONQUER THE WORLD! YOU HEAR ME?"

EVERYBODY HOPES HE WILL JUMP. BUT HE JUST SITS THERE...
YEAH, I CAN SEE WHY HE MAKES PEOPLE NERVOUS. IF HE EVER JUMPED--!
...BRINGIN' DOWN PROPERTY VALUES.
OH.
Y'KNOW, JUICE, I COULD DRINK YOU RIGHT NOW AND SHOW ALL THOSE FOOLS. I COULD BE MASTER OF THE WORLD!
BUT I KEEP ASKING MYSELF: WHY? WHY SHOULD I CONQUER THE WORLD?
I MEAN... ONCE I GOT THE WORLD, WHAT WOULD I DO WITH IT? THE ONLY THING POWER'S GOOD FOR... IS GETTING MORE POWER.
AND IF A MAN'S GOT ALL THE POWER-- ALL THAT'S LEFT FOR HIM IS TO USE IT.
TO GET RID OF HIS ENEMIES. TO KILL PEOPLE.
SO... KILLING PEOPLE, BEING FEARED IS REALLY WHAT WORLD DOMINATION IS ALL ABOUT, RIGHT?
SO WHY WASTE ALL THAT TIME CONQUERING THE WORLD -- WHEN I CAN JUST DRINK YOU-- AND KILL PEOPLE?
WHY, INDEED?
BOTTOMS UP!
YA-A-ARGH!
IT'S -- WORKING--!
I'M -- CHANGING--!
I'M A FR-- ARRRGH!

ARE THINGS REALLY SO DIFFERENT WHERE YOU COME FROM, MR. DUCK?
HOWARD-- CALL ME HOWARD.
NO. NOT SO DIFFERENT, I GUESS. MORE DUCKS -- APES DON'T TALK. THAT'S ALL.

CRASH!
THAT'S NOT ALL! YOUR WORLD ISN'T MENACED BY-- GARKO!

OKAY. SO I SEE IT. THAT DOESN'T MEAN I GOTTA BELIEVE IT!
I MEAN, I DON'T EVEN BELIEVE IN ME, ANYMORE!
YOU WILL BELIEVE IN ME-- OR YOU WILL DIE! FOR I KILL BECAUSE ALL ELSE IS FUTILE!
SUCH IS THE MISSION OF--
--GARKO, THE MAN-FROG!
SO CHOOSE! FEAR ME--FALL AT MY FEET -- OR PERISH!

HA HA HA
HA HA
HA HA
YEAH--WELL--HOW 'BOUT IF WE JUST RUN AWAY FROM YOU?
NEVER THOUGHT OF THAT, DIDJA?
Psst--YOU KIDS CALL THE COPS! I'LL KEEP HIM BUSY...
...IF I DON'T DIE FIRST.
HAHAHAHA! YOU ARE DOOMED, DUCK! THERE IS NO ESCAPE FROM A LEAPING MAN-FROG!
CRRAK
NUTS! I'M ACTING LIKE A LOON! I CAN'T RUN FROM HIM FOREVER!
I GOTTA FIND SOMETHING TO HIT HIM WITH! THERE--!
THIS IS MORE LIKE IT! I'M READY FOR THAT WARTY MANIAC NOW!
I KNOW YOU'RE HERE, DUCK! THERE'S NO USE HIDING. COME OUT--AND DIE!

ON MY WORLD, GARKO, WE NEVER SAY "DIE!" WE SAY--
--KILL!!
PERHAPS THE TIME HE HAS SPENT IN THE UN-WORLD HAS MADE HIM TOO RASH, TOO FOOLISHLY DARING--!
OR PERHAPS THE SUDDEN APPEARANCE OF THIS MONSTER HAS TAPPED A HITHERTO UNKNOWN RESERVOIR OF COURAGE WITHIN HIM--!
BUT HE FIGHTS WITH A SAVAGERY HE HAS NEVER KNOWN BEFORE!
WH-WHAT'S HAPPENING TO ME?
HE FINDS HIMSELF GROWLING WORDS OF DEFIANCE, WORDS OF ANGER!
OH MY GOD! I'M SHRINKING! BECOMING A REAL FROG!
HE IS FILLED WITH A DETERMINATION TO WIN, TO CARVE A PLACE FOR HIMSELF IN THIS STRANGE WORLD!
GETTING HARDER TO THINK! WANNA FIND A POND!

OW-W-W! HEY! WHAT DO YOU THINK YOU'RE--?
JOE! MIKE! IT'S HIM! THE MANIAC THE KIDS CALLED ABOUT!
HUH--?!
WHAT'RE YA DOIN'? YA GOT THE WRONG GUY, I TELL YA! IT'S A FROG YOU'RE AFTER!
A FROG. SURE, BUDDY. WE'LL TALK ABOUT IT AT THE STATION--
--AFTER WE GET YOU OUTTA THAT DUCK SUIT!
DUCK SUIT?? ARE YOU CRAZY? THIS IS MY BODY! I'M REAL, I TELL YA!
POL
SURE, SURE. WE KNOW. WE'RE JUST TAKING YOU IN FOR YOUR PROTECTION.

GIANT SIZE MAN-THING

68 BIG PAGES

MARVEL COMICS GROUP

APPROVED BY THE COMICS CODE AUTHORITY

5 AUG 02920

50¢

GIANT-SIZE MAN-THING™

ALL-NEW!

THREE FACES OF FEAR!

MACABRE DOUBLE-LENGTH MIND-BENDERS IN THE MYSTERIOUS MARVEL MANNER!

GK ADKINS

EXTRA!

HOWARD THE DUCK BATTLES FOR HIS LIFE AGAINST THE MOST INCREDIBLE VAMPIRE OF ALL!

From the time of his hatching, he was...different. A potentially brilliant scholar who dreaded the structured environment of school, he educated himself in the streets, taking whatever work was available, formulating his philosophy of self from what he learned of the world about him. And then the Cosmic Axis shifted...and that world *changed.* Suddenly, he was stranded in a universe he could not fathom. Without warning, he became a strange fowl in an even stranger land.

Stan Lee PRESENTS: HOWARD THE DUCK!™
HELLCOW!
IN A CLEVELAND, OHIO, JAIL CELL, A VICTIM OF BLIND JUSTICE LANGUISHES IN SOLITUDE. HE IS A HERO; HE HAS SAVED THE CITY FROM THE MONSTROUS MADNESS OF GARKO, THE MAN-FROG.
FREE the N.Y. 8 MILLION
BUT AS A DIRECT CONSEQUENCE, HE HAS BEEN ARRESTED...FOR CREATING A DISTURBANCE.
ANOTHER EXCURSION INTO BASIC WEIRDNESS BY
STEVE GERBER WRITER
FRANK BRUNNER ARTIST
TOM PALMER, INKER
ANNETTE KAWECKI, LETTERER
GLYNIS WEIN, COLORIST
LEN WEIN, EDITOR

SUDDENLY--
CLANG
WAUK!
AWRIGHT, "MR. DUCK"-- SNAP TO! YA GOT A VISITOR.
I DON'T BELIEVE IT. THIS IS THE PRISONER WHO'S STUMPED OUR BEST INVESTIGATORS-- THIS MIDGET IN A DUCK SUIT?!
YESSIR, COMMISSIONER GORDONSKI. WE FIGURED YOU'D WANT A LOOK AT 'IM.
OBOY.
YOU FIGURED I'D LIKE TO LOOK AT A DUCK SUIT, EH? I DON'T KNOW WHETHER TO LAUGH-- OR PUNCH YOU IN THE MOUTH!
I PRESUME YOU'VE AT LEAST GOTTEN HIS FINGER-PRINTS...?
W-WE TRIED, SIR...
TH-THEY WOULDN'T TAKE THROUGH THE FEATHERS...
...SIR?
SHUT UP! AND YOU-- WHOEVER YOU ARE-- TAKE OFF ALL YOUR CLOTHES--NOW!
OR WE'LL ADD OB-STRUCTION OF JUSTICE TO THE CHARGE AGAINST YOU.
OKAY... IF YOU SAY SO...
BUT I REALLY DON'T SEE HOW IT'S GONNA HELP... TO EMBARRASS ME...
SEE, IT ALL BEGAN WITH THIS FROG, AN'--
I SAID ALL YOUR CLOTHES!!
OKAY, OKAY... HERE... TAKE IT! BUT I'M TELLIN' YOU...
THAT DOES IT!

THIS HAS GONE FAR ENOUGH. COME HERE--THIS INSTANT!
I DON'T KNOW WHAT YOU HOPED TO GAIN BY THIS LUNATIC CHARADE, BUT IT'S OVER, DO YOU HEAR?
WH-WHAT'RE YA GONNA DO?

QUIET--AND KEEP THOSE WINGS--HANDS!--BEHIND YOUR BACK!
I'M GOING TO DO WHAT TOMPKINS HERE SHOULD'VE DONE!
I'M GOING TO FRISK YOU--

--UNTIL I FIND THE ZIPPER--
--ON THIS CRAZY OUTFIT OF--GOT TO BE--
--BUT THERE'S JUST--
--SKIN!

LORD HELP ME... IT'S REAL... THERE'S NO ZIPPER... NO MIDGET... IT'S A TALKING DUCK...!
IT'S A MUTANT... SOME SORT OF HORRIBLE FREAK...!
OH, BROTHER!

GET IT OUT OF HERE! I DON'T CARE WHAT YOU DO WITH IT--JUST GET IT OUT OF MY JAIL BEFORE THE PAPERS HEAR--
--WE'VE BOOKED A DUCK!
Y-YOU HEARD 'IM, DUCK--

YOU'RE FREE TA GO. GOOD-BYE!
I TRIED TO TELL YOU. NO HARD FEELINGS...?

POLICE
86th
PRECI
MAYBE I'M GETTIN' LUCKY, FINALLY. I THOUGHT SURE THEY WERE GONNA KEEP ME IN THERE 'TIL MOULTING SEASON.
ONLY--NOW WHAT? WHERE DO I GO? WHAT DOES A GUY DO TO MAKE A BUCK AN' SURVIVE...
...IN A WORLD WHERE HE DOESN'T BELONG?
SOBERING QUESTIONS INDEED--EVEN FOR THOSE OF US WITH-OUT HOWARD'S PECULIAR PROBLEM...
...EVEN FOR A MAN LIKE JUBAL BROWN, FARMER, WHO, THOUGH HE CANNOT SUSPECT IT...
...IS ABOUT TO CONFRONT HIS DESTINY.
WELL, I'LL BE!
WHERE'D YOU COME FROM? THAT CAPE AN' ALL, YA MUST BE SOME KINDA SHOW COW. A RUNAWAY, I BET.
SOMEBODY'LL BE LOOKIN' FOR YOU, SWEETHEART.
C'MON, YA KIN STAY IN HERE FER TH' NIGHT.
I'LL FIX UP THIS STALL FER YA, AN' COME MORNIN', WE'LL CALL TH'--
EEAAAGH
AND FARMER BROWN'S DESTINY IS DEATH!
RAZOR-SHARP FANGS SINK DEEP INTO THE FLESH OF HIS THROAT.
AND, A MOMENT LATER, HIS BODY IS UTTERLY DRAINED OF BLOOD!

AND THEN, HER THIRST SATED, THE COWLED COW UNDERGOES A WEIRD TRANS-FORMATION.
HER BILLOWING CAPE BECOMES LEATHERN WINGS...
...THE WINGS OF A VAMPIRE BAT!
DADDY? DADDY, WHAT'S--?
OH, NO--NO! STAY BACK--DON'T--
HAHAHAMOOO
THE STRANGE CREATURE SAILS OVER THE GIRL'S HEAD...INTO THE NIGHT...TOWARD CLEVELAND...
...WHERE, THE FOLLOWING EVENING...
ND PLAIN DEALE
5TH MYSTERY FARM DEATH
NUTS! IT AIN'T NO MYSTERY TO ME!
THE KILLER'S NOT ONE OF THE HAIRLESS APES--IT'S A FARM ANIMAL--A CHICKEN, MAYBE.
I NEVER DID TRUST CHICKENS.
BUT THE COPS HERE WOULD NEVER THINK OF THAT.
HEY! WHAT IF I CAUGHT THE KILLER!? MAYBE I COULD GET A JOB WITH THE COPS, AN'...
I'LL DO IT!

HOWARD SPENDS THAT NIGHT AND THE NEXT DAY IN THE PARK, CONCEIVING A DARING PLAN...A SCHEME THAT WILL COME TO FRUITION THIS NIGHT...FOR NOW THE BOVINE BLOOD-BEAST STALKS THE CITY!
MOOOOOOOOOO
AND SHE HAS COME SEEKING VENGEANCE!
VENGEANCE FOR A LIFE STOLEN AWAY FROM HER MORE THAN 300 YEARS AGO, A PEACEFUL EXISTENCE IN THE PLENTIFUL PASTURES OF SWITZERLAND...
...AS THE FAVORITE COW OF OLD HANS.

BUT LATE ONE NIGHT, WHILE HANS SLEPT, A DESPERATE STRANGER CAME TO THE LITTLE FARM.
ALL THE DOORS AND WINDOWS OF THE VILLAGE WERE LOCKED.
AND THE STRANGER WAS VERY THIRSTY.
...AND NOT FOR MILK.

HANS COULD NOT BEAR TO EAT HER BLOODLESS CORPSE. SHE HAD BEEN...TOO CLOSE TO HIS HEART FOR THAT.
BESSIE
TEARFULLY, HE COMMITTED HER BODY TO THE EARTH AND SAID A QUIET PRAYER...

...NEVER GUESSING...

...THAT THREE NIGHTS LATER...

...BESSIE WOULD RISE FROM HER GRAVE...UNDEAD!

--BY A COW?!

BUT SPYING BESSIE'S FANGS, THE DUCK QUICKLY REALIZES THIS COW IS ANYTHING BUT CONTENTED.

DAUNTLESSLY, HE LASHES OUT, SWINGING HIS WOODEN PROP AT THE HELLCOW'S HEAD. BUT...

WHAP

IT DISSOLVED--TURNED INTO MIST! IT'S GONE!

ONLY TEMPORARILY. SHE REMATERIALIZES A MOMENT LATER BEHIND THE WIDE-EYED WATERFOWL AND, MADDENED, CHARGES!

FOR A MOMENT, THE DUCK'S WORLD IS A MAD MELANGE OF SOUND:
RRRING
SPTANGL
KRAK
OWW
THUK
THE SHATTERING OF GLASS... THE CRACKING OF WOOD.. THE SHRILL RING OF THE SHOP'S BURGLAR ALARM...

AND THEN, THE HOT, WET SLURPING, THE LOW GROWL OF THE HORRIBLE HELLCOW!
CORNERED! I NEVER SAW A COW MOVE SO FAST! I'M DONE FOR--UNLESS--
WAIT! THAT LUG WRENCH!

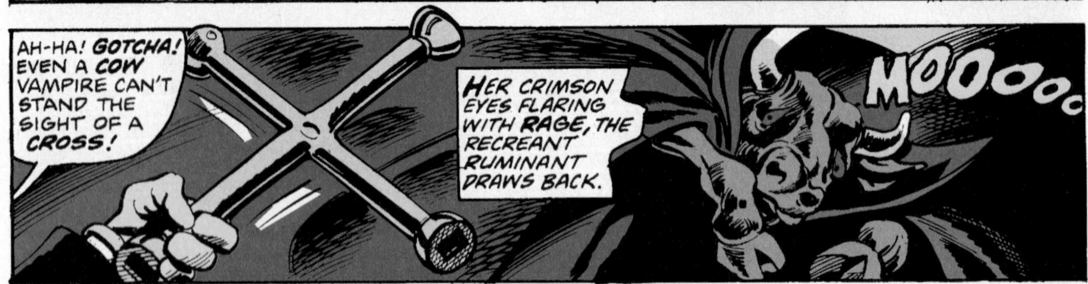
AH-HA! GOTCHA! EVEN A COW VAMPIRE CAN'T STAND THE SIGHT OF A CROSS!
HER CRIMSON EYES FLARING WITH RAGE, THE RECREANT RUMINANT DRAWS BACK.
MOOOooo

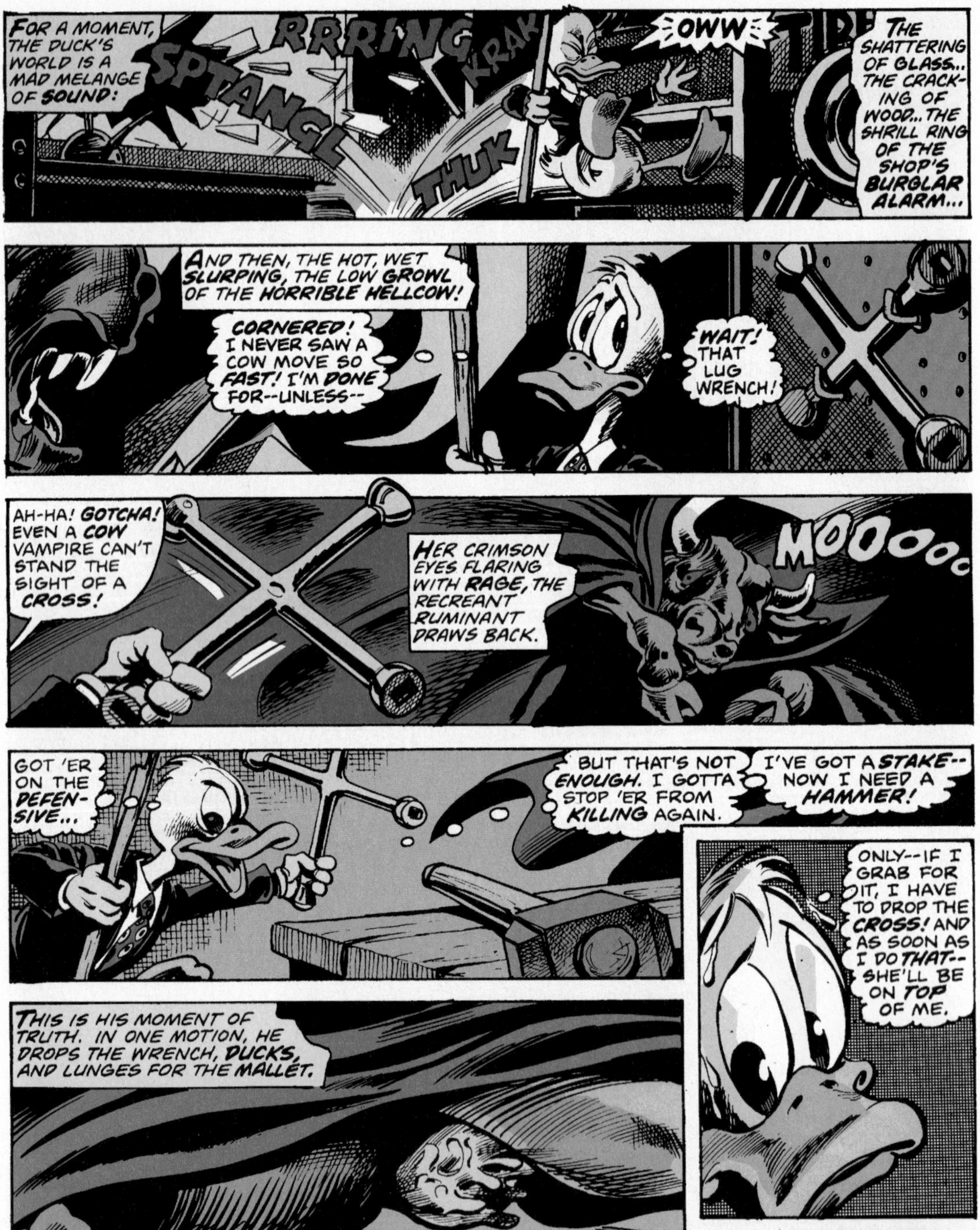

GOT 'ER ON THE DEFENSIVE...

BUT THAT'S NOT ENOUGH. I GOTTA STOP 'ER FROM KILLING AGAIN.

I'VE GOT A STAKE-- NOW I NEED A HAMMER!

ONLY--IF I GRAB FOR IT, I HAVE TO DROP THE CROSS! AND AS SOON AS I DO THAT-- SHE'LL BE ON TOP OF ME.

THIS IS HIS MOMENT OF TRUTH. IN ONE MOTION, HE DROPS THE WRENCH, DUCKS, AND LUNGES FOR THE MALLET.

THE HELLCOW, TOO, HURLS HERSELF AT HER TARGET--BUT MISSES, HER COLD, UNMILKABLE UDDER BARELY BRUSHING HOWARD'S FEATHERY CROWN.

AND, HOOVES FLAILING OUT OF CONTROL, SHE COMES TO A LOUD, UNGRACEFUL LANDING...
CRASH
...AMID A PILE OF STEEL-BELTED RADIAL RETREADS.
DAZED, THE BOVINE BLOOD-SUCKER STRUGGLES TO EXTRICATE HERSELF FROM THE RUBBERY RINGS--AND FAILS.
SHE SIGHS. A TEAR ROLLS DOWN HER HAIRY CHEEK. FOR HER FANGS ARE IMBEDDED IN A WHITEWALL.
AND SHE KNOWS HER NUMBER IS UP.
ONLY ONE THING LEFT TO DO NOW. IT'S PRETTY AWFUL, BUT...AW, NO--SHE'S CRYING!
I CAN'T DO IT. BUT I GOTTA DO IT. I'VE GOT NO CHOICE...!
FORGIVE ME, COW.
PRESSING SHUT HIS EYES, GRITTING HIS BEAK, HOWARD DASHES GRIMLY FORWARD.
AND WITH A SINGLE, SICKENING "THWUNT", HE SENDS THE HELLCOW TO HER FINAL REST.
MOOOOOOO
BUT NO SOONER HAS THE DEED BEEN DONE, THAN...
RAY'S AUTO SHOP
FREEZE, MISTER! PUT A LIGHT ON 'IM, TOMPKINS!
HUH...?

TOMPKINS! LOOK--IT'S ME--HOWARD! I DID IT! I GOT THE FARM KILLER!
SPARK PLUGS
TOMPKINS...?
AC
TOMPKINS--WAIT! WHERE ARE YA GOIN'? DON'T LEAVE!
STOP! COME BACK! THIS COW WAS THE--
TOMPKINS?
DON'T...

WAAAAAAAAUGH
OF ALL THE MISERABLE, UNGRATEFUL, CORRUPT, GRAFT-RIDDEN--!
DROP DEAD, TOMPKINS--SEE IF I CARE!!

BUT OUT ON THE STREET, HE WATCHES WITH A TWINGE OF SADNESS AS THE SQUAD CAR PULLS AWAY. IT WOULD'VE BEEN...NICE.

STEADY WORK... A ROOF OVER HIS HEAD... A RESPECTABLE POSITION IN SOCIETY...!
NOPE. THERE'S NO GETTING AWAY FROM IT.

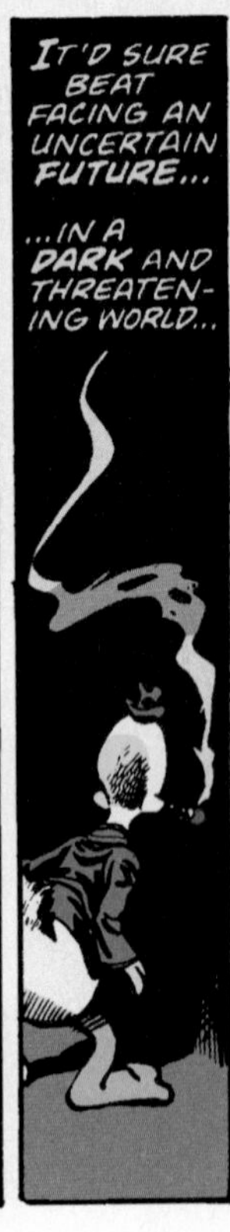
IT'D SURE BEAT FACING AN UNCERTAIN FUTURE...
...IN A DARK AND THREATENING WORLD...

...ALL ALONE.
END

HOWARD THE DUCK

MARVEL COMICS GROUP™

APPROVED BY THE COMICS CODE AUTHORITY

25¢ CC

1 JAN 02415

TRAPPED IN A WORLD HE NEVER MADE!

HOWARD THE DUCK™

BECAUSE YOU DEMANDED IT-- THE FABULOUS **FIRST ISSUE** OF MARVEL'S MOST SENSATIONAL NEW SUPER-STAR!

BRUNNER

AGAINST SWORD AND SORCERY, HOWARD STANDS SIDE-BY-SIDE WITH THE AMAZING

SPIDER-MAN!

Stan Lee PRESENTS: HOWARD THE DUCK! ™

CREATED & WRITTEN BY STEVE GERBER • ILLUSTRATED & COLORED BY FRANK BRUNNER
CO-PLOTTERS
INKED BY STEVE LEIALOHA
JOHN COSTANZA, letterer
MARV WOLFMAN, editor

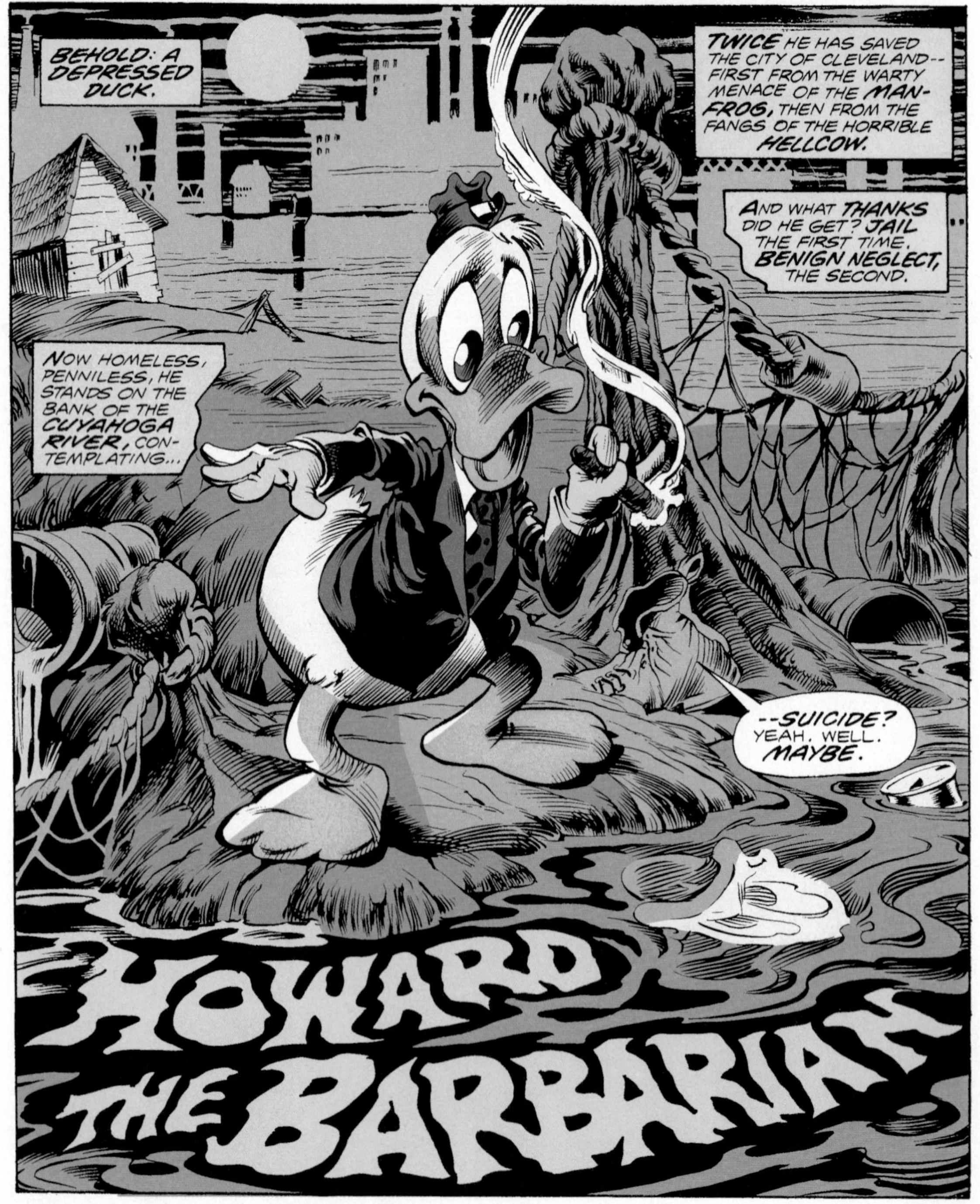

BEHOLD: A DEPRESSED DUCK.
TWICE HE HAS SAVED THE CITY OF CLEVELAND-- FIRST FROM THE WARTY MENACE OF THE MAN-FROG, THEN FROM THE FANGS OF THE HORRIBLE HELLCOW.
AND WHAT THANKS DID HE GET? JAIL THE FIRST TIME. BENIGN NEGLECT, THE SECOND.
NOW HOMELESS, PENNILESS, HE STANDS ON THE BANK OF THE CUYAHOGA RIVER, CONTEMPLATING...
--SUICIDE? YEAH. WELL. MAYBE.
HOWARD THE BARBARIAN

ON THE OTHER HAND, MAYBE SOMETHING LESS DRAS-TIC.
A LITTLE DIP TO CHEER ME UP, GIMME A CHANCE TO THINK.
THERE'S ALWAYS A WAY OUT, I SAY. THINGS ARE NEVER AS BLACK AS THEY--

--SLIME.

WAAUUGH
THAT DOES IT! I CAN'T STAND IT ANYMORE!! THIS WHOLE WORLD IS FOULED UP!!!

NAH... THAT'S WHAT'S WRONG WITH IT. IT'S RUN BY HAIRLESS APES INSTEAD OF FOWL.
WHAT AM I DOING HERE??

NOTHIN' PRODUCTIVE, THAT'S FOR SURE! SO WHY BOTHER STICK-ING AROUND? A MASOCHIST I AIN'T.
ONE LITTLE LEAP OFF THAT NUTTY TOWER AN' THIS LIFE OF GRIEF COULD BE OVER.

SURE. I'LL GO WITH A FLOURISH. THE BIG SPLASH. THE LAST HURRAH, WHY NOT?
I MEAN... IT'S NOT LIKE ANY-ONE'LL NOTICE.

SHORTLY, ACROSS THE WATERS...
FIGURES. THE JERK WHO DESIGNED THIS ARCHITEC-TURAL ABORTION FORGOT TO PUT IN A DOOR!
IT'S, AH, TALLER THAN I THOUGHT, TOO... BUT THERE'S NO TURNING BACK NOW.
LIKE THEY SAY, THE DIE IS CAST...

I'M ***ENTITLED*** TO A BREATHER BEFORE I DIE.

SHOULD'A KNOWN EVEN ***SUICIDE*** COULDN'T BE ***SIMPLE*** ON THIS WORL--

HELP!

HUH--?!

SPINNING ON HIS TAIL FEATHERS, HOWARD PEERS IN THE WINDOW TO SEE:

Y-YOU'RE A ***DUCK!***

YEAH. I KNOW. YOU HAIRLESS APES KEEP ***REMINDING*** ME.

WHAT'S WITH THE ***CHAINS***, SWEETHEART?

I'M THE ***PRISONER*** OF A ***MADMAN!*** YOU MUST ***SAVE*** ME... PLEASE... I BEG YOU...!

I REALIZE THIS IS ***STRANGE***, FOLKS ...BUT WHAT THE HECK?... IT BEATS DOING MYSELF IN. READY OR NOT, LADY, ***HERE I***--

--COME!
OH NO.
THE CEREMONIAL AXE! SEIZE IT! DEFEND YOURSELF!
"SEIZE IT," SHE SAYS! IT WEIGHS UHH: A TON!
AND IT'S STUCK IN THIS STUPID STUMP!
BESIDES... I CAN'T JUST SLICE OPEN A DUMB ANIMAL! WHAT'LL I DO IF I GET IT LOO--
OOOPS
THE FOWL IS FLUNG WILDLY ACROSS THE ROOM, AWAY FROM THE SPUMING BEAST, CARRIED BY THE WEIGHT OF THE BROBDINGNAGIAN BLADE...
THUD
...UNTIL HE STRIKES THE CHAMBER'S FAR WALL... AND A CERTAIN ROPE...
...BRINGING DOWN SALVATION FROM ABOVE...

...IN A VIOLENT, WHOLLY UNEXPECTED FASHION.
HOLY CROW! IT CRUSHED HIM! TALK ABOUT A DOG'S LUCK--!
POOR GUY. BUT AT LEAST HE DIDN'T SUFFER.
STILL, I'D'VE RATHER TAMED HIM WITH A DOG YUMMIE THAN--
UH-OH! HE'S STARTIN' TO GLOW!
AW, FER CRYIN' OUT LOUD, HE'S CHANGIN'!
"INTO-- ONE OF THEM!!"
TERRIFIC! JUST SWELL! NOW I'M A MURDERER! I COME HERE TO WIPE ME OUT, AND INSTEAD--
YOU'LL HAVE AMPLE OPPORTUNITY TO MEET YOUR DOOM. I SHALL SEE TO THAT.
HAVE NO FEAR, FEATHERED INTERLOPER.
WE-E-AUUGH

THUS, HOWARD LIES UNCONSCIOUS AS NIGHT PASSES INTO MORNING, AS, SOME 500 MILES AWAY...
PARKER! DON'T MOVE!

...IN THE OFFICES OF THE NEW YORK DAILY BUGLE, ACE SHUTTERBUG PETER PARKER IS ACCOSTED BY PUBLISHER J. JONAH JAMESON.
YOU'RE TOO LATE, J.J.J.-- I ALREADY CASHED MY CHECK.
VER-RY FUNNY, PARKER. YOU'RE A LOAD OF LAUGHS.
SO MAYBE YOU'D LIKE TO JUST LAUGH OFF THIS PLANE TICKET TO THE ASSIGNMENT OF THE CENTURY, TOO!

OBOY. J.J.J.'S SENT ME TO FLORIDA...CANADA ...EUROPE. THIS I DON'T WANNA BLOW!
I KNOW IT SOUNDS NUTTY, BUT THERE'RE WILD RUMORS FLYING AROUND WHERE YOU'RE HEADED...
...RUMORS ABOUT SOME STRANGE NEW MUTANT MENACE! I WANT PICTURES OF IT, PARKER!
GOOD ENOUGH.. WHERE AM I OFF TO?

CLEVE-LAND! AND WHAT YOU'RE AFTER IS... A DUCK THAT TALKS LIKE A MAN!
OKAY, NOW YOU CAN MOVE! AND DON'T COME BACK WITHOUT PHOTOS.
CLEVELAND. A DUCK. I'M GONNA BE SICK...!

NEVERTHELESS, THE YOUNG PHOTOG-RAPHER (WHO IS ALSO THE AMAZING SPIDER-MAN) WILL MAKE THE TRIP, ARRIVING AT HOPKINS INTERNA-TIONAL AIRPORT AROUND NOON...
...JUST AS THE FELLED FOWL RETURNS TO THE REAL WORLD.

MR. DUCK...?

MR. DUCK, ARE YOU AWAKE YET?

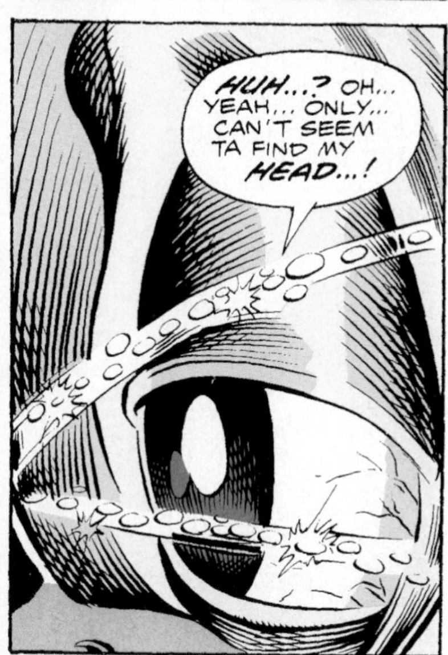
HUH...? OH... YEAH... ONLY... CAN'T SEEM TA FIND MY HEAD...!

WAAAGGH!
MY CLOTHES! WHERE ARE MY CLOTHES?!
WHERE AM I?!?

WE'RE IN THIS TOGETHER NOW, DUCKY.
WE'RE BOTH PRISONERS OF PRO-RATA, THE MAD FINANCIAL WIZARD.
YEAH -- BUT HOW'D I GET THIS SWORD? WHO DRESSED ME THIS WAY?
THE SWORD, YOU'LL NEED. AND I... WELL, I CHANGED YOUR CLOTHING... ON PRO-RATA'S ORDERS.

HOW TOUCHING. SHE'S EMBARRASSED.
FOLLOW ME, WOMAN AND WATER-FOWL...
ULP
...AND SEE WHY THAT SHOULD BE THE LEAST OF YOUR CONCERNS.
GAZE UPON THE OFFICE OF PRO-RATA, SOON TO BE CHIEF ACCOUNTANT OF THE UNIVERSE!
AND NOTE ESPECIALLY MY PRIZE OF PRIZES-- THE COSMIC CALCULATOR.
FOR YOUR FATES ARE INTIMATELY TIED TO ITS MISSING JEWELED KEY.
BY WHATEVER MEANS NECESSARY, I MUST PROCURE THAT KEY BY MIDNIGHT.
FOR AT THAT HOUR, THE STELLAR BALANCE SHEET COMES INTO ALIGNMENT,.. THE ASTRAL AUDIT MAY BE TAKEN... AND I--
I ALONE SHALL COLLECT THE COSMIC DIVIDEND!

YOU SHALL OBTAIN THE KEY FOR ME--THERE, THRU THE DIMENSIONAL PORTAL--AS MY HIRED BARBARIAN WOULD HAVE--
--HAD YOU NOT BROKEN EVERY BONE IN HIS BODY!
OH, SO THAT'S IT!
LOOK, THAT WAS AN ACCIDENT, AND I REALLY DON'T THINK IT'S FAIR TO BLAME ME--
IN, YOU FOOL!
WAAUK
THUS, WOMAN AND DUCK HURTLE BETWEEN UNIVERSES, PRO-RATA'S RASPING VOICE THEIR ONLY LINK WITH REALITY-- AND A TENUOUS LINK AT THAT: "MY ANCESTORS WERE EGYPTAIN SORCERERS, SLAVIC WITCHES, DRUIDS... AND THEY WERE FAILURES, MYSTICAL SLOBS, THE LOT OF THEM!
"ALL BECAUSE THEY FAILED TO SEE WORLD DOMINATION IN TERMS OF ACCOUNTANCY. THE UNIVERSE IS THE ULTIMATE FLOW CHART.
"AND HE WHO CAN JUGGLE THE BOOKS CAN RULE INFIN-ITY!"
WE LANDED IN SOME KINDA NEST-- REMINDS ME OF WHERE I WAS FIRST HATCHED.
HEY-- YOU OKAY?
UH-HUH... JUST SHOOK UP.

LOOK--THAT'S THE CITADEL OF SAI-FUUR, JUST AS PRO-RATA DESCRIBED IT TO ME. THE JEWEL-KEY'S IN THERE.
C'MON... LET'S GET IT AND SPLIT THIS SCENE.
WHY DON'T WE NOT GET IT AND SPLIT ANYWAY?
BY THE RED COLUMN!
'CAUSE PRO-RATA'S WATCHING US, DUCKY!
A DAMSEL--PURSUED BY A NEWLY-HATCHED BAHNDBIRD!
MUST SLAY IT--BEFORE IT MATURES!
WHY AM I SURE HE'S TALKING ABOUT ME?
EYES CLOSED AND A PRAYER ON HIS BEAK...
CRACK!
...HOWARD STRIKES!!
AND THE WARRIOR, HIS LANCE SHATTERED...
...PITCHES HEADLONG OFF HIS STRANGE STEED ONTO THE HARD GROUND...

...AND INTO UNCONSCIOUSNESS.
HIT HIS HEAD ON A ROCK, I GUESS. TOUGH BREAK... FOR HIM.
BUT IT GOT US FREE TRANSPORTATION.
Y'KNOW, BABE, I LIKE YOUR ATTITUDE. WE COULD GET TO BE FRIENDS.
YEAH. I COULD USE ONE OF THOSE.
QUESTION: WHY D'YA FIGURE HE SAID KILL ME BEFORE I "MATURE"? I AM MATURE.
I'VE SPENT MOST 'A MY LIFE TELLING EVERYBODY I'M MATURE.
NOW I'M EVEN GETTING THE "WHY-DON'T-YOU-GROW-UP" ROUTINE FROM BARBARIANS I'VE NEVER MET!
MMM. IT'S A HASSLE. I'VE HAD THE SAME PROBLEM...
AT THE CITADEL'S ZERO-SHAPED ENTRANCE, HOWARD AND FRIEND DISMOUNT... AND STARE WITH AWE AND TREPIDATION AT ITS TWO STONE-SILENT GUARDIANS.
THEY LOOK AS THOUGH THEY'RE ONLY SLEEPING, DON'T THEY?
YEAH... WELL... WALK ON TIPTOE. LET'S NOT WAKE 'EM UP, HUH?
FUNNY... NO REAL GUARDS FOR THIS PLACE.

YEAH. I EXPECTED AN OBSTACLE COURSE AT THE VERY LEAST.
BUT THERE'S THE JEWEL-KEY--RIGHT UP AHEAD. FAR OUT!
IF WE CAN'T GET THE KEY, PRO-RATA WILL ABANDON US HERE! WE'RE DOOMED!
I DIDN'T SAY THAT.
DON'T LET YOUR HEART LEAP WITH ANTICIPATION YET, KIDDO.
THERE'S A GOOD REASON WE COULD JUST WALTZ IN HERE.
CATCH WHAT HAPPENED TO THE LAST GUY WHO TRIED TO GET THAT KEY.
OOOH...!
I JUST GOTTA THINK, THAT'S ALL.
NUTS! WISH I HAD A CIGAR TA CHOMP ON. CAN'T CONCENTRATE...
OH, I CAN HELP YOU WITH THAT. LOOK IN YOUR SCABBARD, DUCKY.

MY LAST CIGAR!!

I FOUND IT IN YOUR BREAST POCKET... WITH YOUR MATCHES.

I THOUGHT YOU MIGHT WANT IT... FOR A MOMENT LIKE THIS. SO I RISKED PRO-RATA'S ANGER, AND...!

SAY NO MORE, KID. YOU'RE ONE OF THE GOOD PEOPLE IN MY BOOK.
NOW JUST LET ME COGITATE A SECOND OR TWO...

I GOT IT! HERE--TAKE MY HELMET, AND HOLD IT OUT UNDER THE GEM KEY...
AND KEEP A STEADY HAND-- WHILE I TAKE AIM!
SSST
WITH EAGLE-EYED PRECISION, HOWARD FLICKS THE STOGIE INTO FLIGHT...
CLUNK
...FREEING THE GEM-KEY!

THUS IS THE VICTORY WON... BUT AT A PRICE.
DON'T GET MISTY-EYED. THERE'LL BE OTHER CIGARS...
...WHEN WE'RE HOME SAFE. WE'VE GOTTA GET BACK TO THE NEST, SO PRO-RATA CAN OPEN THE RETURN PORTAL FOR US.
AND WE'VE GOTTA HURRY. SOMETHING'S GONNA HAPPEN. I CAN FEEL IT IN MY BONES.
KRE-E-ECK
PERCEPTIVE SKELETON YOU'VE GOT THERE, TOOTS!
WHEN WE PULLED OFF THIS LITTLE HEIST--
WE SET OFF THE BURGLAR ALARM!!
GET YOUR GIRDLE IN GEAR, KID. THEY'RE BIG--BUT SLOW.
MAYBE WE CAN OUT-RUN 'EM--!
OH, NO! NO!!

"YE GODZ," HOWARD CRIES. "THE NEST--THE SLUR ON MY MATURITY--IT ALL MAKES SENSE NOW--
"--MORE OR LESS."
"IT'S JUST ATTACKING ANYTHING THAT MOVES. MAYBE IT'LL TAKE OUT THE GRANITE TWINS FOR US," THE GIRL WHISPERS.
"SCORE ANOTHER POINT FOR YOUR BONES, SIS," THE DUCK RESPONDS.
QUICK--BEHIND THIS ROCK! IT HASN'T SEEN US YET!
'COURSE, IF IT'S HUNGRY... IT'S GONNA DOPE OUT PRETTY FAST THAT THOSE GUYS AIN'T EDIBLE.
YOU'RE RIGHT! IT'S TURNING--COMING AFTER US!
LISTEN... I KNOW IT SOUNDS SILLY... BUT IF WE'RE GOING TO DIE TOGETHER...
...I'D LIKE TO KNOW YOUR NAME.
HUH? OH--IT'S HOWARD.
MINE'S BEVERLY--BEVERLY SWITZLER. I--
WAIT! WHAT'S HAPPENING TO US?! WE'RE FADING AWAY--!!

AND AT THAT INSTANT, BACK IN CLEVELAND...
ADMIT IT, PARKER--YOU'VE BEEN HAD! JAMESON WINS THIS ONE.
YOU'D THINK, AFTER YEARS OF SUPERHEROING, I'D DEVELOP A HEALTHY SKEPTICISM.
BUT NO. J.J.J. SENDS ME TO THE ARMPIT OF THE NATION TO SNAP PIX OF A TALKING DUCK-- AND I FALL FOR IT!
BUT, BARELY A MILE AWAY...
UH... I THINK YA RANG UP MORE THAN YOU BAR-GAINED FOR, WIZ.
THE BAHND-BIRD! MUST'VE HIT THE WRONG DECIMAL!
"STAND ASIDE," PRO-RATA CRIES, "I MUST RECALCULATE-- SEND THE MONSTER BACK TO TO ITS NEST BEFORE--"
KRAAK!
--IT FLAPS ITS WINGS.
THE KEY! GIVE ME THE KEY!!
IT'S OUR ONLY HOPE OF CONTROLLING THE BIRD!

OKAY... SO I MAY NOT RECOGNIZE A JOKE WHEN IT HITS ME IN THE FACE.
BUT MY SPIDER-SENSE NEVER LIES ABOUT TROUBLE. THAT WAS AN EXPLOSION I HEARD.
AND THE DAY'S BEEN JUST DULL ENOUGH TO JUSTIFY HITCHING A RIDE TO CHECK IT OUT.
I'LL BROOK NO DAWDLING, DUCK! HAND OVER THE KEY-- AND YOU AND THE WOMAN ARE FREE TO GO!
WHILE YOU SET YOURSELF UP AS A GOD, RIGHT?
MASTER CHARGE
STOP! WHAT MADNESS IS--?
SORRY, MAC-- NO DICE! IF YOUR COSMIC CALCULATOR CAN REALLY DO THAT--
--IT'S TOO POWERFUL FOR ANY-BODY TO POSSESS!
YOU FOOL FOWL! YOU'VE THROWN AWAY OUR LIVES!
WHEN THIS MONSTROS-ITY ADAPTS TO ITS NEW REALITY--WE SHALL BE ITS PREY!
RIGHT, YOU'RE JUST LOOKING OUT FOR MY WELFARE. SURE.
'SCUSE THE INTRU-SION, BUT DID ANYBODY LOSE THIS?
BANK AMERICARD
I WAS JUST SWINGING BY AND--
HEY! WHAT'S GOING ON HERE?!

SPIDER-MAN!! I'VE NO NOTION WHAT YOU'RE DOING HERE--
--BUT I SHAN'T WASTE AMENITIES ON THE LIKES OF YOU! GIVE ME THAT KEY--
--OR DIE!!
HE MEANS IT! HE'S GONNA KILL THE GUY! UNLESS--!
THUK
AAARGH
HIS AIM SPOILED BY THE JARRING IMPACT OF THE SCABBARD--
--PRO-RATA'S MYSTICAL BOLT SAILS OVER THE WEB-SLINGER'S HEAD--
--INTO THE MURKISH CUYAHOGA, IGNITING THE VOLATILE POLLUTANTS THEREIN!
I'LL WORRY LATER OVER WHETHER I BELIEVE THIS.
FOR NOW, I'LL JUST MAKE SURE NONE OF US BECOMES DINNER FOR POLLY PARROT HERE!
THEN MAYBE I CAN HELP OUT THE LITTLE GUY WHO SAVED MY LIFE!

--BUT THERE WOULD BE NO BUDGETARY LOGIC IN THAT! NO WAY TO JUSTIFY THE EXPENDITURE OF MAGIC!
BUT SPIDER-MAN'S DEATH WILL NET ME THE GEM-KEY! I'LL PROFIT BY DESTROYING HIM!
BAH! I COULD REDUCE YOU TO DRUMSTICKS WITH A SINGLE SPELL, DUCK--
HE'S GONNA TRY AGAIN! AND THIS TIME I'VE GOT NOTHING TO THROW--
--EXCEPT MYSELF!!
SURE--WHY NOT? I WAS ABOUT TO OFF MYSELF ANYWAY.
MAY AS WELL USE MY LIFE TO STOP THIS WACKO!
YAAAAGG!
TTWIP
THUS, THE COURAGEOUS DUCK AND THE EVIL CONJURER PLUNGE DOWNWARD--DEATHWARD--TOGETHER! THE FLAMING WATERS SEEM TO RISE TO MEET THEM--HOWARD'S EYES PRESS SHUT IN HORROR--AND THEN--
--SALVATION!

HANDS GIFTED WITH THE PROPORTIONATE STRENGTH OF A SPIDER HAUL THE HARRIED HOWARD TO SAFETY.
AND SO COMES TO PASS PERHAPS THE WEIRDEST MOMENT IN THIS, THE MARVEL AGE OF COMICS, AS...
WEB-FOOT MEETS WEB-HEAD!!
YOU'RE FOR REAL! JAMESON DIDN'T CRACK HIS NUT! YOU'RE A TALKING DUCK!!
YOU'RE NOT EXACTLY MR. NORMAL, EITHER, Y' KNOW.
AND WHILE YOU WERE SPOUTIN' OFF, TELLIN' ME WHAT I ALREADY KNOW--
--PRO-RATA'S PARAKEET FLEW THE COOP!
LOOK--YOU KEEP THE JEWEL-KEY. I'LL SEE ABOUT TRACKING DOWN BIG BIRD.
GOTTA GO NOW. HERE COMES MY CONVENIENT HELICOPTER.
YEAH. SEE YA. BE SURE AN' WRITE.
WELL, HOWARD... THE DANGER'S PAST. AND WE'RE BOTH ALIVE AND WELL.
WHAT WILL YOU DO NOW? WHERE WILL YOU GO?
I DUNNO... BUT I SURE COULD USE A GOOD CIGAR.
NEXT: THE STAR-SPAWNED THREAT OF THE DEADLY SPACE TURNIP! BE HERE!

HOWARD THE DUCK
MARVEL COMICS GROUP
APPROVED BY THE COMICS CODE AUTHORITY
25¢
2 MAR 02415
TRAPPED IN A WORLD HE NEVER MADE!
HOWARD THE DUCK
NOTHING CAN SAVE YOU NOW, DUCK--YOU'RE AT THE MERCY OF--
--THE DEADLY SPACE TURNIP!
BRUNNER

Stan Lee PRESENTS: **HOWARD THE DUCK!**™

WRITTEN BY **STEVE GERBER** *ILLUSTRATIONS BY* **FRANK BRUNNER** *INKING BY* **STEVE LEIALOHA**
TOM ORZECHOWSKI, *LETTERING* MICHELE WOLFMAN, *COLORS* **MARV WOLFMAN**, *EDITOR*

CRY TURNIP!
IT HAD BEEN THIS WAY SINCE THE HOLOCAUST. TO SURVIVE, ONE HAD TO FIGHT EVERY DAY OF ONE'S LIFE. BLOOD HAD BECOME AS FAMILIAR A SIGHT TO ME AS THE UNDERSIDE OF BEVERLY'S KNEE.
BLOOD: THICK, HOT, RED, FLOWING IN RIVERS ACROSS THE ONCE-GREEN LANDSCAPE NOW QUICK-FRIED BROWN BY THE POSITRON CANNONS OF THE DREADED MUURKS.
THE MUURKS: NO ONE KNEW WHERE THEY'D COME FROM, NOR EVEN WHEN THEY'D ARRIVED, EXACTLY. BUT THEY'D QUICKLY WORN OUT THEIR WELCOME. IT'S HARD TO BE HOSPITABLE TO AN ALIEN RACE THAT WANTS YOUR PLANET FOR THEIR OWN.
IT'S NO USE, BEVERLY-- THEY'RE EVERYWHERE! WE'LL HAVE TO ATTEMPT AN ESCAPE!

ESCAPE: HOW IMPOSSIBLE IT SEEMED WITH THE MUURKS CLOSING IN NOW FROM EVERY SIDE.
BESIDES, I WASN'T SURE I WANTED TO ESCAPE.
McD

WHATEVER ELSE I MAY HAVE BEEN-- DISMAYED, PANIC-STRICKEN, TERRIFIED-- I WAS STILL KILLMALLARD THE WARRIOR.
AND I HAD A REP TO LIVE UP TO!
I WHIRLED-- FIRED IN A PATTERN-- SLICING SEVERAL OF THOSE SAVAGE, LEERING BEASTS NOT-SO-CLEANLY IN TWAIN!

I RECALLED THE HISTORY TEXTS, A PARAGRAPH ABOUT A SUB-GENRE OF LITERATURE KNOWN AS SPACE-OPERA THAT DEALT WITH TOPICS JUST SUCH AS THIS.

A GRIM SMILE. WHERE WAS THE "OPERA" IN MY STRUGGLE?
WHO WAS SINGING THE ARIAS? WHO WROTE THE LIBRETTO--THE AGONIZED DEATH-SQUEALS OF SEVERED MUURKS?

NO, THERE WERE NO SONGS THIS NIGHT. AND THE ONLY ORCHESTRATION WAS THE DIN OF DESTRUCTION. ALL ABOUT US...
... A RAUCOUS SYMPHONY OF SHATTERING ROCK AND CRACKLING, BURNING MUURKFLESH.

AND ONE OTHER SOUND:
BEVERLY AND I RECOGNIZED IT INSTANTLY.
CLUNCH CLUNCH
A MUURKIAN SEPTOPOD-- ONE OF THE SEVEN-LEGGED MECHANICAL MONSTROSITIES THE SCALY DEVILS HAD EMPLOYED IN THEIR SUCCESSFUL CAMPAIGN TO WALK ALL OVER US!
CONSTRUCTED OF THE ALIEN METAL MUURKONIUM, THEY WERE IMPERVIOUS TO OUR HIGHEST-INTENSITY PLASMA-BURSTS.
BEVERLY AND I WERE, IN A WORD, DOOMED TO THE MOST HORRIFYING AND BRUTAL DEMISE KNOWN ON THIS WORLD SINCE THE DAY WHEN CORPORATE MONSTERS ROSE ENCASED IN GLASS AND STEEL AND SWALLOWED OUR ANCESTORS WHOLE INTO THEIR BUREAUCRATIC DIGESTIVE TRACTS, REDUCING THEIR MINDS TO GELATIN AND THEIR BONES TO ROUGHAGE, MAKING WASTE-MATTER OF PEOPLE, THEN CALLOUSLY ELIMINATING THEM AT AGE SIXTY-FIVE, SIXTY-TWO FOR WOMEN.
NO HOPE. OUR RAY-FIRE SERVED ONLY TO HEAT THE ALLOY FOOT SO THAT WE WOULD NOT ONLY BE CRUSHED...
...BUT COOKED AS WELL.
WAAAUGH
HOWARD...?

WAAAUGH
WE'RE DEAD --DEAD! MURDERED BY THE MUURKS!
HOWARD, NO-- WE'RE FINE!

WE'RE HERE-- IN CLEVELAND-- IN MY HOUSE!
NO! NO! NO!!
YES, YES, YES! OPEN YOUR EYES! LOOK AROUND! SEE FOR YOURSELF!

HUH... oh... WHA' HAPPENED?
YOU HAD A NIGHTMARE, THAT'S ALL. YOU WERE READING ARTHUR'S STORY WHEN YOU FELL ASLEEP.
THERE AREN'T ANY MUURKS?
NO MUURKS.

BUT I'VE GOT COFFEE AND BALONEY SAND-WICHES READY, IF YOU'RE INTERESTED.
YEAH... YEAH, THAT SOUNDS GOOD. I'M STARVED.
YOU WOULDN'T BY ANY CHANCE... HAVE A CIGAR AROUND, TOO, WOULDJA?

SURPRISE. I KEEP 'EM AROUND FOR ARTHUR. I DON'T THINK HE'D MIND...!
WHEELING
GOAT
CUSTAR
NEW
TOOTS, I THINK YOU 'N' ME ARE GONNA GET ALONG...

...IF YOU PROMISE NOT TO GIMME ANY MORE OF THOSE STORIES TO READ... AT LEAST, NOT AT BEDTIME.
YOUR BOYFRIEND'S GOT A WEIRD IMAGINATION.
OH, ARTHUR'S NOT MY BOYFRIEND, EXACTLY. I'M SORT OF A SISTER TO HIM.

THAT'S... ENCOURAGING.
*PRO-RATA: THE MAD WIZARD WHO CAPTURED BOTH HOWARD AND BEV LAST ISSUE. --MARV.
HE HAD ME CHAINED UP THERE FOR A MONTH-- EVER SINCE I ANSWERED HIS AD FOR AN ARTIST'S MODEL AND FELL INTO HIS CLUTCHES.
BY NOW, HE PROBABLY THINKS I'VE SKIPPED TOWN.
I WASN'T ALLOWED TO MAKE PHONE CALLS FROM PRO-RATA'S TOWER.*
WE'D PROBABLY STILL BE THERE IF SPIDER-MAN HADN'T TOLD THAT 'COPTER PILOT TO COME BACK FOR US. haha
BLESS OUR PAD
WHAT'S SO FUNNY?
"THE LOOK ON THE PILOT'S FACE WHEN HE SAW YOU... AND YOU SPOKE TO HIM.
"THAT FLIGHT WAS MORE DANGEROUS THAN PRO-RATA AND ALL HIS MONSTERS PUT TOGETHER!"
LEMME SAY IT FOR YOU, HUH: "Y-YOU'RE A DUCK!"
B-BUT... AREN'T YOU?
HEY, YA JERK! KEEP YER EYES ON THE ROAD--
--AN' OFF MY FEATHERS, HUH?
B-BUT...!
ANYWAY, THAT'S ALL OVER WITH. AN' I'M BACK WHERE I STARTED-- NO JOB, NO HOME, NO BREAD--!
BUT YOU HAVE A FRIEND NOW-- ME. AND TOMORROW, YOU'LL HAVE ANOTHER.
WHO-- ARTHUR?
DON'T TELL ME YOU'RE JEALOUS-- JUST BECAUSE HE NAMES HIS HEROINES AFTER ME?
NAH!

WHAT IS IT, THEN -- THE HERO'S NAME? DON'T YOU LIKE "KILLMALLARD"?
Aaah... I GUESS IT'S JUST TOO EASY FOR ME TO IDENTIFY WITH.

WELL, I THINK IT HAS A NOBLE SOUND ABOUT IT. A RING OF STRENGTH AND SAVAGERY--!
YEAH. REAL COMMERCIAL POTENTIAL. HOT STUFF. HEAVY.

LO
VE
I'M NO CRITIC -- BUT PERSONALLY I THINK HE TRIES TOO HARD--HITS YA OVER THE HEAD WITH THE MESSAGE.
SO HE'S GOT A SOCIAL CONSCIENCE. YOU COULD USE A LITTLE OF THAT YOURSELF.

LISTEN, HONEY-- IF ANYBODY IN THIS WORLD KNOWS WHAT IT IS TO BE OPPRESSED--!
I'M A MINORITY OF ONE IN THIS SCREWY PLACE! EVERY INSTITUTIONAL STRUCTURE YOU GOT IS LOADED AGAINST ME!
THAT'S IT-- PROVE ME RIGHT!

YOU'RE ONLY CONCERNED ABOUT YOU! AND I'LL BET YOU WERE THAT WAY ON YOUR WORLD, TOO!
ARTHUR'S AN ARTIST! A SERIOUS ARTIST! HE'S WORKING AS A RENT-A-COP TO SUPPORT HIMSELF UNTIL HIS WRITING TAKES OFF.
Oh-- UNPUBLISHED, HUH? ONE O' THOSE?

WHAT'S THAT SUPPOSED TO MEAN?
NOTHIN'. NOTHIN' AT ALL...
G'NIGHT, TOOTS.

CLIK
GOOD NIGHT, ARTH-- HOWARD.

AS THE FOWL AND HIS LISSOME FRIEND DRIFT INTO **SLUMBER**...
UNIVERSAL IMPO

...THEIR TOPIC OF CONVERSATION, ONE **ARTHUR WINSLOW**, FIGHTS TO STAY **AWAKE.**
≡YAWN≡ OH, GAWD-- THREE HOURS TO **GO.**
HONK FOR UARD

THIS HAS GOT TO BE THE MOST **BORING** JOB I--
CRASH
HOLY CRUD! WHAT--?

FOR SEVEN MONTHS OF EVENTLESS NIGHTS HE'S **WAITED** FOR THIS MOMENT...
...PRAYED FOR THE SCENT OF **DANGER!**

AND NOW IT'S **COME**: A CHANCE TO STAND IN THE PRESENCE OF THE **UNKNOWN**...
...AND TO FACE IT **UNAFRAID**, AS DO HIS FICTIONAL ALTER EGOS!

BUT-- **NOTHING.** NO MOVEMENT WITHIN, SAVE FOR THAT OF THE **RATS.**
NO SIGN OF MENACE. NO CREEPING THREAT. ONLY... A **VEGETABLE.**

BUT IT'S A **BIG** VEGETABLE. AND IT **GLOWS.** AND IT'S THE CLOSEST THING TO **EXCITEMENT** THIS JOB HAS OFFERED **YET.**
SO HE DECIDES TO **INVESTIGATE.**

CHANCES ARE IT ISN'T REALLY DANGEROUS.
IT'S ONLY A TURNIP, AFTER ALL -- EVEN IF IT IS THE SIZE OF A BASKETBALL.
AND WHAT EARTHLY HARM COULD A TURNIP DO TO ANYONE?
ANSWER: NO EARTHLY HARM. BUT THEN, THIS ISN'T AN EARTHLY TURNIP.

THIS TURNIP CAME FROM OUTER SPACE-- AND IT WAS THE SIZE OF A HOUSE BEFORE AIR-FRICTION WHITTLED IT DOWN...
... BEFORE IT CAME HURTLING DOWN FROM THE SKY AND THROUGH THE WAREHOUSE WINDOW...

... BEFORE ITS POWERFUL, BUT DYING, INTELLIGENCE FORCE CAPTURED THE MIND AND SOUL OF ARTHUR WINSLOW.
YES... YES... NO!... WELL, MAYBE...!

ALMOST AT ONCE, A SINISTER SYMBIOSIS IS ESTABLISHED, AND ARTHUR'S MIND IS EXTENDED ACROSS A UNIVERSE...!
IN A SINGLE FLEETING-MOMENT, THE BELIEFS OF A LIFETIME ARE CONFIRMED.
THE COSMOS IS... AS HE ALWAYS THOUGHT IT WAS.
IT MUST BE. WOULD A STAR-SPAWNED TURNIP LIE??

"I am PHELCH," the turnip says telepathically, "and my race was old when the stars were young. We were a breed of aggressive, dynamic, success-oriented vegetables who overcame the limits of our roots and evolved into space-spanning GO-GETTERS, interstellar overachievers.
"Alas, we met our doom when we failed, in our vanity, to PICK ourselves at the first cosmic frost. I am the lone survivor, and I have wandered the trackless void for EONS in search of a more efficient BODY, suitable for framing my superior intellect and my incomparable power. Who are YOU? Speak, meat-being!"
Trepidatiously: "I am Arthur Winslow, author, and collector of old movie stills. I, too, am alone. For all my life I've been forced to endure a world in which no BACKGROUND MUSIC swells when boy meets girl, in which love has been dragged down from the spiritual HEIGHTS to the crass domain of PHYSICAL sensation.
"I stand APART, because I dare to believe in the power of what one man can do—the Lone Ranger, the Green Hornet, James Bond-the HEROES, the stuff of legends! I long to BE that kind of man, but all I can offer the world are FICTIONS that publishers refuse even to READ, because heroes have gone out of fashion!"
"Might I suggest a MERGER, then, Arthur-meat? You gain my insight into the universe, which has come to BORE me, whilst I avail myself of the mobility, the opposable thumb, and the pleasures of the flesh, which you DISDAIN, but which are denied to me by my form."
Winslow's eyes glow with anticipation. "If I agree to the joining, shall I get what it takes to become— a hero, a scourge of evil, a defender of the common man? Can you lend me power enough to fulfill my DREAM?"
"I can LEND you that. Yes," the turnip affirms. "But I demand an option on total control of your body if I DELIVER."
"What is the body but casing for what TRULY matters— the eternal soul! I agree to your bargain!" Winslow proclaims.
THERE FOLLOWS A BLINDING FLASH. FOR A MOMENT, ARTHUR WINSLOW LOSES TOUCH WITH HIS SURROUNDINGS, HIS BODY, EVEN HIS MIND. ALL IS BLACKNESS. ALL IS PURE CLEAR WHITE. AND THEN-- HE IS ONE WITH THE TURNIP!!

THE FOLLOWING AFTERNOON:
SMEGMA
CHEW
C'MON, TOOTS-- LET'S GET OFF AN' HOOF IT THE REST O' THE WAY TO ARTHUR'S HOUSE.
IT'S TOO FAR TO WALK. YOU'LL JUST HAVE TO LIVE WITH THE STARES A WHILE LONGER.
I'M STARTIN' TO FEEL... SLIMY.

BESIDES, I'M ENJOYING THIS. FOR ONCE, ALL EYES ARE GLUED TO MY NAVEL.
YEAH. SWELL. I'M TICKLED PINK FOR YA.
ME, I DON'T EVEN HAVE A NAVEL. I ATTRACT LOOKS ON SHEER CHARISMA ALONE.
GUESS THAT'S THE PRICE OF--
YOU--YOU ANIMAL!
WAUUK

NO SMOKING! NO SMOKING ON THIS BUS! I WON'T LOSE MY KIDNEYS TO THE LIKES OF YOU!
KIDNEYS! K-I-D-N-I-E-S! I KNOW YOU'RE OUT TO GET 'EM!
NIXON DEFENSE FUND
DRINK
CBS
wha...?

I RIDE THIS BUS ALL DAY-- BACK AND FORTH, BACK AND FORTH-- TO PROTECT MY KIDNEYS FROM YOU BEASTS!
YOU AND YOUR TOBACCO-- YOUR DEEP-FRIED FOODS-- YOUR WANTON WOMEN AND LOW MORALS--
--YOUR INTERNATIONAL KIDNEY-POISONING CONSPIRACY!

NO OFFENSE, GRANDMA, BUT YOU NEED HELP.
LOTS OF IT.
AND FAST.

OH, THAT'S SO TYPICAL OF YOUR KIND! MOCKING ME, BECAUSE I CAN'T FIND ALLIES!
YOU'RE SO SECURE IN YOUR ZEALOUSLY-GUARDED SECRECY--SO SURE JOHN Q. PUBLIC WON'T BELIEVE IN THE THREAT TO HIS KIDNEYS.
WELL, I'LL SHOW YOU!
SQUATCH!

I'M WISE TO YOU, BOY! THE WORLD MAY SNICKER NOW, BUT YOU'LL SEE--YOU CAN'T HIDE THE TRUTH FOREVER. YOU'LL NEVER GET MY--
Aaah, SHUDDUP, YA BUG-BRAINED OLD BAG! WHO CARES ABOUT YOUR KIDNEYS?

I'M GOIN' FOR THE THROAT!!
YOU SQUASHED MY LAST CIGAR!
aaahk MURDER! MURDER!!

CITY OF TRANSIT
HEY--HEY! WHAT'S GOIN' ON BACK THERE?! KNOCK IT--

--OFF.
OWTCH
WHAT'RE YA--? MOVE! LEMME STEER! GET OFF THAT WHEEL--

--OR YOU'LL KILL US ALL!
AT LAST! A CRISIS OF LIFE OR DEATH, MANAGEABLE ONLY BY--
EeEeEk
OoOh
WAAAUGH
PINK FLAMINGOS
OUR FATHER...
--TURNIP-MAN, GARDEN-FRESH GUARDIAN OF THE GOOD!
2915 D
SMOKE DEATH
TURNING INWARD WHAT LITTLE MENTAL ENERGY HE STILL POSSESSES, ARTHUR WINSLOW CALLS UPON THE SPACE-TURNIP'S ABILITY TO EXERT CONTROL OVER ITS OWN CHLOROPLASTS, ITS PHOTOSYNTHETIC CELLS. AND--
MARY
JANE st.
--HIS GRADE-A FANCY BEAM HALTS THE HURTLING VEHICLE IN MID-FLIGHT AND LOWERS IT SAFELY TO A ROADSIDE LANDING!
STAN 'N' SOL'S MARKET
HOLY SPIT! WE'VE BEEN RESCUED-- BY A FLYING VEGETABLE!
HOWARD-- uh, I THINK THAT'S ARTHUR!
THE GUY IN THE SALAD SUIT?!
HE'S ON MY SIDE! SALADS ARE GOOD FOR THE KIDNEYS!
SMO

I'M NOT JUST PLAIN ARTHUR WINSLOW ANY LONGER, BEV. I'M LEADING A DOUBLE LIFE NOW.

SO I'D APPRECIATE IT IF YOU'D CALL ME TURNIP-MAN WHEN I'M IN UNIFORM.

BUT, ARTHUR, HOW DID YOU GET THIS WAY? THESE STRANGE NEW POWERS--!

THAT MUST REMAIN MY LITTLE SECRET, BEV--ER, MISS SWITZLER. FOR NOW, FAREW--

HEY, WHAT IS THIS? WHY CAN'T I FLY?

BECAUSE I AM NOT YET READY TO DEPART, ARTHUR-MEAT!

SHORTLY, YOU'LL BE UNABLE TO DO ANYTHING WITHOUT MY PERMISSION.

I TOLD YOU-- I WANTED ALL OF YOU--AND MY ADVANCED INTELLECT IS TAKING IT, BIT BY BIT!

HEY, WAITAMINIT, BUB! TAKE YER SLEAZY LEAVES OFF HER!

I WISH TO EXPERIENCE WHAT YOU MEAT-BEINGS TERM... THE MAKING OF WHOOPIE.

waark NO FAIR! COME BACK AN' FIGHT, YA FRESH-PICKED FREAK!

SCRIPT FOR DUCK #2

LISTEN, ARTHUR-MEAT-- THERE'S THE BACKGROUND MUSIC YOU CRAVED. DO YOU LIKE IT?
ARTHUR, WHO ARE YOU TALKING TO? WHAT'S THAT MUSIC?
NO! YOU BETRAYED ME! AND NOW YOU'RE TAUNTING ME! I DESPISE YOU!
OH, COME NOW. YOU MERELY DISLIKE ME. I'VE HURT YOUR FEELINGS, THAT'S ALL.

DON'T YOU SEE -- IT'S YOUR PREDILECTION FOR MELODRAMATIC ABSOLUTES THAT'S MADE YOUR SILLY LIFE SUCH TORTURE ALL THESE YEARS?
HERE, ARTHUR-MEAT-- LET'S COME IN FOR A LANDING.
ARTHUR, THAT'S THE JAMES BOND THEME--!

THERE ARE NO HEROES, ARTHUR-MEAT-- NOR VILLAINS, EITHER. MERELY VARIOUS ENTITIES WITH VARIOUS DESIRES.
WHEN SOCIETY APPROVES OF THESE DESIRES, THE ENTITY IS DEEMED GOOD-- OR AT LEAST RESPECTABLE.
NO! IT'S A LIE!

WH-WHAT ABOUT STORIES WHERE THE HERO IS THE RENEGADE-- THE ANTI-ESTABLISHMENT FIGURE?
ESCAPIST CLAPTRAP, ARTHUR-MEAT-- A SAFETY VALVE FOR THE FRUSTRATIONS OF THE MASSES, ALLOWING THEM TO VENT THEIR HOSTILITIES VICARIOUSLY.

THAT'S WHAT YOU'VE BEEN DOING-ARTHUR-- LIVING YOUR LIFE THROUGH OTHERS' FANTASIES AND YOUR OWN.

AND IT IS A PITY: NOW THAT YOU'RE IN A POSITION TO EXPERIENCE A REAL SENSATION...
... IT'S I WHO'LL REAP THE BENEFITS.

IF I HAD ANY BRAINS AT ALL, I'D PRETEND THIS NEVER HAPPENED.
RIGHT. I'D TELL MY-SELF: "SELF, FORGET THE CHICK AND THINK ABOUT NUMERO UNO."
BUT YOU KIDNEY-ROBBERS STICK TOGETHER! YOU CAN'T FOOL ME!
WELL, I DO!
I MEAN... THAT LEAFY LUNATIC COULD MAKE DUCK SOUP OUTTA ME...
AND I DON'T EVEN KNOW WHERE HE'D TAKE HER...
HE'D TAKE HER TO A GREEN PLACE-- AWAY FROM THE FILTH OF THE CITY-- WHERE HER KIDNEYS COULD RECOVER AND SHE'D REGAIN HER SANITY!
HE'D TAKE HER TO SUNSPOT SLOPE--SO NAMED BE-CAUSE IT'S THE ONLY SPOT IN CLEVELAND THAT GETS ANY SUN!
HUH--? WHERE? THERE?
GRANNY, IF I WEREN'T POSITIVE YOUR LIPS ARE AS CALCIFIED AS YOUR BRAIN-- I'D KISS YA!
YOU WOULDN'T DARE! ORAL INTIMACY DISGUSTS ME! AND IT PLAYS HAVOC WITH THE KIDNEYS!
BETTER YOU SHOULD FLEE! THESE OLD LEGS CAN'T FOLLOW-- BUT I KNOW TWO NEW LEGS THAT CAN!
AND I WARN YOU-- I'LL BE IN TOUCH WITH THOSE LEGS SOON!
AND WHEN THE PERSON WHO OWNS THEM FINDS OUT WHAT YOU TRIED TO DO TO MY KIDNEYS--!
BUT THE FOWL IS ALREADY OUT OF EARSHOT AND DOES NOT HEAR THE WOMAN'S PECULIAR THREAT.
HE MAY LIVE TO REGRET THAT LAPSE--AND THEN AGAIN, HE MAY NOT. FOR HE HAS CHOSEN TO SNEAK A RIDE INTO THE MAW OF DEATH...!
EGESTION EXPRESS
WELL, HECK, HE DOES OWE THE GIRL A FAVOR.

EXACTLY 54 MINUTES LATER:
Y-YOU SURE CAN SUSTAIN A LEVEL OF AROUSAL, ARTHUR...!
DRESSING UP AS A TURNIP SEEMS TO HAVE CHANGED YOU SOMEHOW.
WOULD YOU LIKE TO TURN OVER SOME OF MY NEW LEAVES, BEVERLY?

OOH! THE SAME OLD NAIVE DOUBLE-ENTENDRES!
WHY DOES SHE REACT THUS? I FOLLOWED YOUR THOUGHT-PATTERNS IN CONSTRUCTING IT.
BEV, PLEASE-- I DIDN'T SAY THAT!

BUT YOU DID. OR YOU WOULD HAVE IF YOU WERE CONTROLLING YOUR TONGUE AT THE TIME.
IT DID PUZZLE ME... YOUR NEED TO MASK YOUR TRUE FEELINGS IN MULTIPLE MEANINGS...!
SHUT UP! STOP MAKING FUN OF ME!

ARTHUR, I WASN'T-- I MEAN-- IT'S JUST-- WELL, SOMEONE SO CLEVER SHOULDN'T HAVE TO BE SO CHILDISH!
OH, LORD-- BEV, IT'S THE TURNIP! IT'S TAKEN CONTROL OF MY BODY! IT'S TRYING TO DESTROY MY MIND NOW, TOO!
SHE WON'T BELIEVE YOU, ARTHUR-MEAT. I WON'T ALLOW HER TO.

I'LL MOVE YOUR TONGUE AGAIN -- MAKE YOUR LIPS SAY IT WAS ALL A JOKE.
GIVE UP, ARTHUR-MEAT. I'VE FULFILLED MY PART OF THE BARGAIN AND MADE YOU A "HERO".
NOW, AS A MATTER OF HONOR-- HAND OVER YOUR HEAD!!
NO!

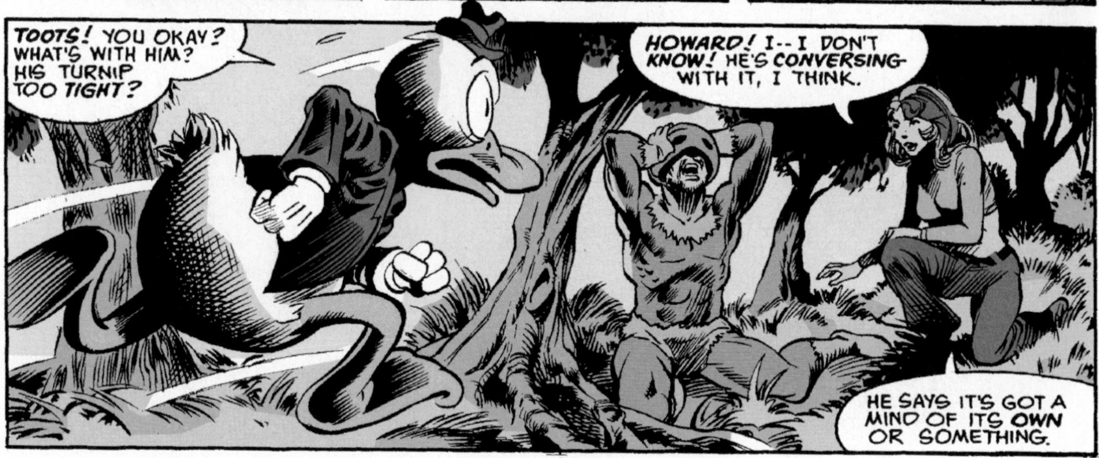
TOOTS! YOU OKAY? WHAT'S WITH HIM? HIS TURNIP TOO TIGHT?
HOWARD! I-- I DON'T KNOW! HE'S CONVERSING WITH IT, I THINK.
HE SAYS IT'S GOT A MIND OF ITS OWN OR SOMETHING.

owtch
MAYBE... WHAT'S NEEDED HERE IS ANOTHER APPROACH.

LET'S GO AT IT LOGICALLY. NO SENTIENT TURNIP WITH A SURVIVAL INSTINCT IS GONNA LET ITSELF BE HOLLOWED OUT AND USED AS SOME WACKO'S CHAPEAU, UNLESS--

AW, FOR CRYIN' OUT LOUD--OF COURSE! THE BULB IS JUST DECORATION!

THE BRAINS ARE IN THE GREENS!

FOOL! THIS WON'T STOP ME! YOU, TOO, ARE MERE MEAT!

MEAT-- TO BE BRUISED! AND BONES-- TO BE CRUSHED!

Uh-oh.

NEXT: THE KIDNEY LADY'S BIZARRE REVENGE -- AS HOWARD, HIS LIFE PLACED ONCE MORE IN PERIL, IS **FORCED** TO SEEK INNER PEACE AND A MEANS BY WHICH TO SMASH FACES IN...

MASTER OF QUAK-FU

SPECIAL THANKS TO JUDO JIM STARLIN FOR HIS ASSISTANCE IN LAYING OUT THIS MOST **CHALLENGING** SCRIPT!

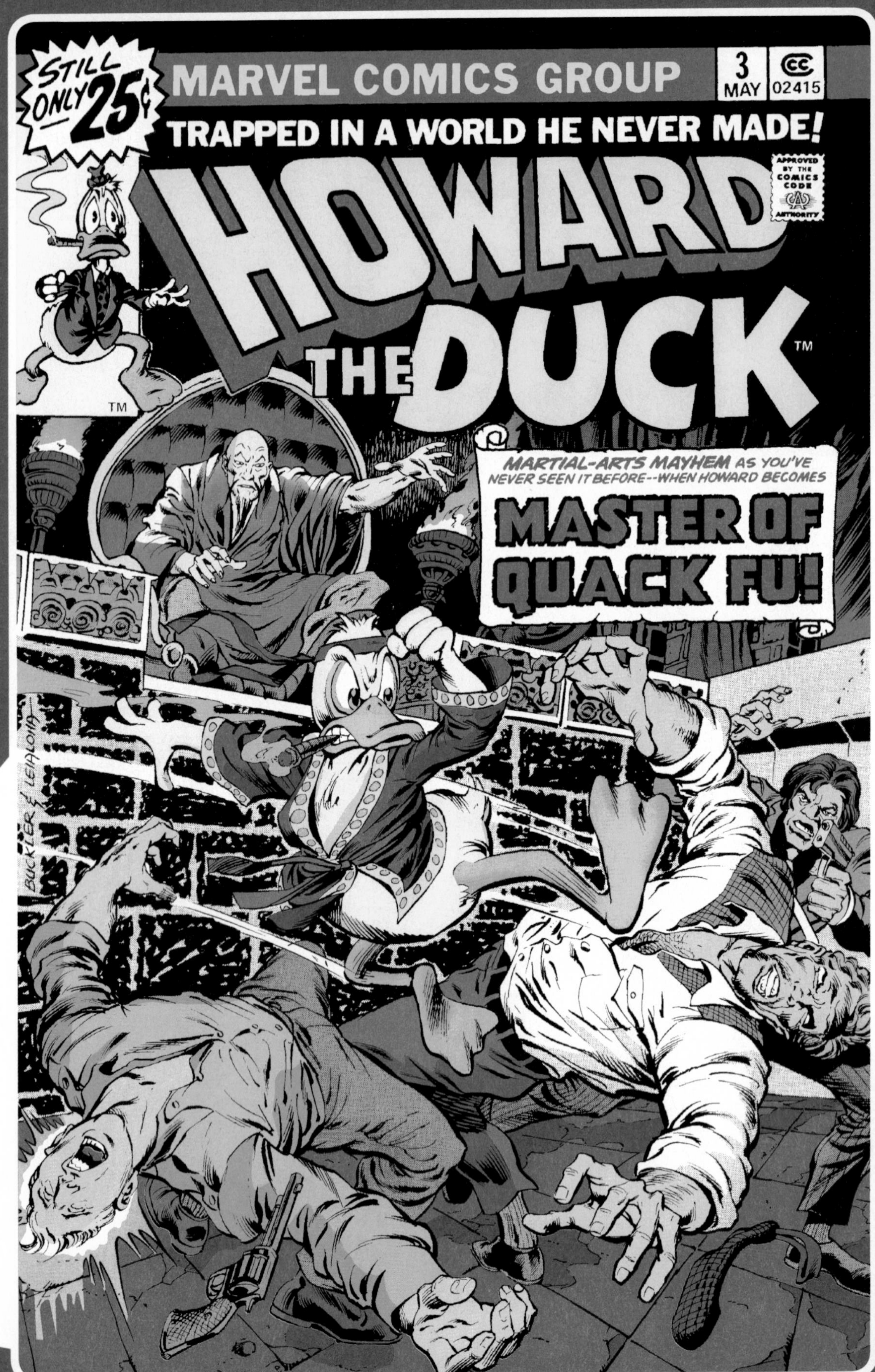
STILL ONLY 25¢
MARVEL COMICS GROUP
3 MAY
CC 02415
TRAPPED IN A WORLD HE NEVER MADE!
APPROVED BY THE COMICS CODE AUTHORITY
HOWARD THE DUCK™
TM
MARTIAL-ARTS MAYHEM AS YOU'VE NEVER SEEN IT BEFORE--WHEN HOWARD BECOMES
MASTER OF QUACK FU!
BUCKLER & LEIALOHA

From the time of his hatching, he was...different. A potentially brilliant scholar who dreaded the structured environment of school, he educated himself in the streets, taking whatever work was available, formulating his philosophy of self from what he learned of the world about him. And then the Cosmic Axis shifted...and that world *changed.* Suddenly, he was stranded in a universe he could not fathom. Without warning, he became a strange fowl in an even stranger land.

Stan Lee PRESENTS: HOWARD THE DUCK!™

WRITTEN BY STEVE GERBER * ILLUSTRATED BY JOHN BUSCEMA * INKED BY STEVE LEIALOHA * EDITED BY MARV WOLFMAN

ANNETTE KAWECKI, LETTERER MICHELE WOLFMAN, COLORIST

FOUR FEATHERS OF DEATH!
or: ENTER: THE DUCK!
SATURDAY NIGHT IN CLEVELAND: THE MID-NIGHT SHOWING OF THE YEAR'S HIGHEST-GROSSING (AND, COINCIDENTALLY, GORIEST) KUNG FU THRILLER HAS JUST CONCLUDED, AND AN APPRECIATIVE AUDIENCE TAKES TO THE STREETS.
BEVERLY SWITZLER AND HOWARD THE DUCK ALSO DEPART THE THEATRE.
HOW CAN YOU CALL RIPPING OUT SOMEBODY'S TONGUE "ENTERTAINMENT"?
HOW CAN YOU CALL IT A MARTIAL ART?
JEEZ, IT'S ONLY A MOVIE, HOWARD.
AND PHWAUGGH HOW CAN YOU EAT AFTER WATCHING THAT?!

YEAH? LOOKS MORE LIKE BASIC TRAINING FOR THE NEIGHBORHOOD TROOPS! I--
HAI-EEE-TSA!!
WAAAUGH
MAKE ROOM-- FOR A TRUE BROTHER OF THE PANTHER!

IS THAT YOUR WHOLE ACT, KID? CAN WE APPLAUD AN' MOVE ON, OR--?
Y-YOU'RE A DUCK!! A TALKING DUCK!!
AN' YOU'RE THE POOR MAN'S SONNY CHIBA. SO WHAT ELSE IS NEW?

N-NOTHIN', I GUESS. I MEAN, I DIDN'T MEAN--UH, SEE YA!
CHEESH--LIKE YOU HAIRLESS APES HAVEN'T SCREWED UP YOUR WORLD ENOUGH!
YOU MISREPRESENT AN ANCIENT PHILOSOPHY, PACKAGE IT AS A VIOLENT ENTERTAINMENT-- AND SELL IT TO YOUR YOUNG TO EMULATE!
WECCH
WOW...!
ONE WAY

SOMEHOW I NEVER PEGGED YOU AS AN INTELLECTUAL, DUCKY.
DON'T CALL ME NAMES, TOOTS.
YOU DON'T GOTTA TAKE OUT A MORTGAGE ON AN IVORY TOWER TO RECOGNIZE STUPIDITY WHEN YOU SEE IT!

C'MON, LET'S GRAB A BITE, AN--
WAULP
YA FREAKIN' FORTUNE COOKIES! WATCH WHERE YER--
SHH! HOWARD-- ENOUGH. DON'T PROVOKE THEM! SHOO--INSIDE-- GO.
HAIEE HEEYAH CHOYEE

INSIDE...
HOLY CROW-- THEY'RE EVERY-WHERE! IT'S A DISEASE!
--HOWARD--KNOCK IT OFF, WILLYA? OR AT LEAST DROP YOUR QUACK A FEW THOUSAND DECIBELS? DON'T BROADCAST YOUR OPINION TO--

LOOK, SISTER--YOU'RE RAISING A WHOLE GENERATION HERE WHO'RE GONNA THINK THE STREET FIGHT IS THE HIGHEST FORM OF ARTISTIC EXPRESSION.
EVER BEEN IN A STREET BRAWL, BEV? EVER SEE A KID'S FACE AFTER A CLUB OR BRASS KNUCKLES OR A BROKEN BOTTLE HAS DONE ITS WORK?
NO...

YEAH, WELL... SOME PUNKS FEED ON THE SIGHT, 'SPECIALLY IF THEY DID THE DAMAGE.
THEY NEED IT, Y'KNOW? 'CAUSE THEY AIN'T GOT THE MENTAL EQUIPMENT TO BE SURE THEY EXIST, UNLESS THEY FEEL THAT SENSE OF POWER.
SO YOU GLORIFY VIOLENCE LIKE THIS, MAKE IT SOCIALLY ACCEPTABLE, AN' BELIEVE ME--

OOOH
--SOMEBODY'S GONNA GET HURT.
SPLSHANGL!
HIT THE DECK!
CRIPES, WE'RE BEIN' FIRED ON-- BY A HUMAN CANNONBALL!

HOWARD, IT'S THE KID WHO--!
I KNEW IT, I KNEW IT...!
STAND AWAY! TOUCH HIM, TRY TO HELP HIM--AND YOU, TOO, WILL BE MAIMED, CRIPPLED, OR DISFIGURED BY--
--COUNT MACHO!

UH, LOOK, CHAMP--YOU'RE COMIN' ON PRETTY HEAVY.
I THINK THE KID GOT THE MESSAGE. WHY DON'TCHA--?

HE ATTACKED ME! BLOCKED MY PATH! RAISED HIS HAND TO STRIKE ME!
NO MAN THREATENS COUNT MACHO --AND LIVES!
TWAP!
WAAAUK!

B-BUT HE'S NOT A MAN! HE'S BARELY INTO PUBERTY!
WHY DON'T YOU PICK ON SOMEONE YOUR OWN SIZE?
MAN OR BOY--HE MUST PAY THE PRICE--FOR AFFRONTING A MASTER OF THE DEADLY ARTS!

Y-YOU'RE CRAZY, MAN--IT WAS A JOKE, THAT'S ALL! I DIDN'T MEAN--
I AM NOT ONE TO BE TOYED WITH. I CONSIDER EVERY ATTACK TO BE REAL...

...AND DEAL WITH IT ACCORDINGLY.
HAI-EEEE!!
RUNK
UHHHNH!

HIEE-YAW!
SOME MASTER! COMES EQUIPPED WITH FOUR GOONS TO BACK HIM UP IF A KID HALF HIS SIZE PROVES TOO MUCH--
NUNUNGH
JEFFREY!!
THE YOUNG MAN FALLS-- AND SUDDENLY THE FRACAS IS NO LONGER MERELY AN INCIDENT, BUT A CREATURE, SUCKING, VORACIOUS, WITH A LIFE OF ITS OWN.

ONE BY ONE, OTHERS ARE DRAWN INTO THE FRAY, SPURRED BY A SENSE OF FAIR PLAY, BY FEAR OF DANGER TO THEIR COMPANIONS...
...OR BY THE SHEER JOY THAT SOME PERVERTED SOULS DERIVE FROM PUNCHING ANOTHER HUMAN BEING IN THE FACE.

IN MOMENTS, BEFORE EVEN THE COMBATANTS REALIZE WHAT HAS OCCURRED, ONE MAN'S NEED TO PROVE HIS POTENCY...

...HAS ESCALATED INTO A MELÉE.

SPEECHLESS, THE DUCK GAPES AT WHAT SEEMS A WALL OF BALD-APE BODIES, A MONOLITHIC MASS OF FLESH THAT EXPANDS, CONTRACTS, EXPANDS...

...AS IF ATTEMPTING TO SQUEEZE ITSELF TO DEATH.

AND THEN HOWARD'S EYES RIVET ON A SINGLE DETAIL.

THE INEVITABLE WEAPON, WIELDED ANONYMOUSLY.

A SHRILL TREBLE SLICES THROUGH THE DULL BASS DIN OF THE ROW.
A PIERCING CRY OF PAIN. A CRY OF PIERCING PAIN. WHICHEVER.

THE BOY'S BRIGHT FACE GOES PALLID. THE STRENGTH DRAINS FROM HIS LEGS.
HE FALLS TO THE COUNTER CLUTCHING AT--BUT IT CAN'T BE!--A HOLE IN HIS BODY?
MY GOD--HE'S BEEN STABBED!!

AS SWIFTLY AS IT APPEARED, THE BLADE HAS VANISHED. THE FIGHT-CREATURE DISSOLVES IN PANIC. ITS LIMBS DETACH AND GO THEIR SEPARATE WAYS.
AND CERTAIN OF THOSE LIMBS SEEM INORDINATELY CONTENTED, EVEN JOCUND, ABOUT THE CIRCUMSTANCES OF THE CREATURE'S DEMISE.
UH... HOLD IT, YOU TURKEYS!

MAYBE YOU BOZOS DIDN'T NOTICE--BEIN' MASTERS AN' ALL--I MEAN, I FIGURE YOU'RE SO USED TO IT--
--BUT THAT KID BACK THERE WAS BLEEDIN'!
HUNNGGH

AND, SEE, MUCH AS I HATE TA POKE MY BEAK INTA THINGS LIKE THIS, I--
WEE-AAUGH
HAI-EE!
OFF ME! INSINUATE WHAT YOU PLEASE--BUT KNOW YOU DO SO IN PERIL OF YOUR LIFE!

WHILE THE WATERFOWL LIES SPRAWLED ON THE PAVEMENT, MACHO ESCAPES. AND INSIDE THE DINER...
...STOP THE BLEEDING!
PUT HIS LEGS UP!
TALK TO 'IM! KEEP 'IM AWAKE!
OH, GOD-- I'M GONNA BE SICK!
AGITATION OF A DIFFERENT SORT PERMEATES THE CROWD. THEY ARE CHARGED PARTICLES, WHIRLING ABOUT THE NUCLEUS OF THEIR CONCERN--THE WOUNDED BOY.

BUT THE VALENCES ARE ALL WRONG--NO COHESION-- THE ELECTRONS COLLIDE, HAMPER ONE ANOTHER'S MOVEMENT.
AND THE NUCLEUS IS SPLITTING, DYING.

IN ALL THE FLURRY OF ACTIVITY, TWO WORDS HAVE GONE UNSPOKEN:
POLICE... AMBULANCE...
SHE PRAYS THEY ARRIVE IN TIME TO SAVE THE BOY FROM THE CROWD'S ATTEMPTS TO HELP HIM.

AND WHILE SHE WAITS, A COLD, CLAMMY SWEAT BEADS ON HER PALMS.
HER EYES CANNOT FIND THE DUCK.

HE FOLLOWED COUNT MACHO OUT THE WIN-DOW, SHE REMEMBERS.
HE WAS ALONE, UN-ARMED. WHAT IF--?

BUT--NO.
HOWARD!! ARE YOU ALL RIGHT?!
I'M SWELL. CAN'TCHA TELL BY LOOKIN'?
HOW'S THE KID? WHAT'S GOIN' ON IN HERE?
PANIC-- BLIND AND DEAF.

I CAN'T GET CLOSE ENOUGH TO FIND OUT--
IF YOU COULD-- COULDJA HELP?
WELL...I TOOK FIRST AID THE SUMMER I WORKED AS A LIFEGUARD...
SAY NO MORE.

JUST LEAVE IT TO ME. THE WORST WE CAN DO IS KEEP 'EM FROM SUFFOCATIN' THE POOR GUY!
B-BE CAREFUL, DUCKY...!
DON'T WORRY, TOOTS--DANGER IS MY BUSINESS.

SHARP, SPINDLY ELBOWS PUSHING, PRODDING, POKING PAST KNEES AND THIGHS, HOWARD REACHES THE CENTER OF THE MOB...!
I'M ONLY GONNA SAY THIS ONCE: BACK OFF! YOU ARE ALL BEHAVING ABOMINABLY!

Y-YOU'RE A DUCK!!
GIVE THE LADY A CIGAR --LONG AS IT AIN'T ONE O' MINE--AN' KEEP 'ER MOVIN.
NURSE! YOUR PATIENT'S WAITIN' IMPATIENTLY!
HUH? OH...!

C'MON-- BE GOOD SHEEP. BA-A-ACK! BA-A-A-ACK!
WHO MADE YOU THE GENERAL?
YEAH-- WE DON'T WANNA MISS NOTHIN'-- AN' WE AIN'T TAKIN' ORDERS FROM A MIDGET IN A DUCK SUIT!

TOUGH, MAC--THE SHOW'S OVER. MOVE YOUR BUTT!
TOMPKINS!*
YOU!!

* WHOM THE DUCK FIRST MET IN GIANT-SIZE MAN-THING #4. --MARV.

I SHOULD'A KNOWN! THAT BROAD A FRIEND O' YOURS? WHAT'S SHE--?
STOW IT, FLAT-FOOT! SHE'S A NURSE! AN' THE KID'S BLEEDIN' TO DEATH!
SAVE THE HARD-BOILED COP ROUTINE FOR LATER!

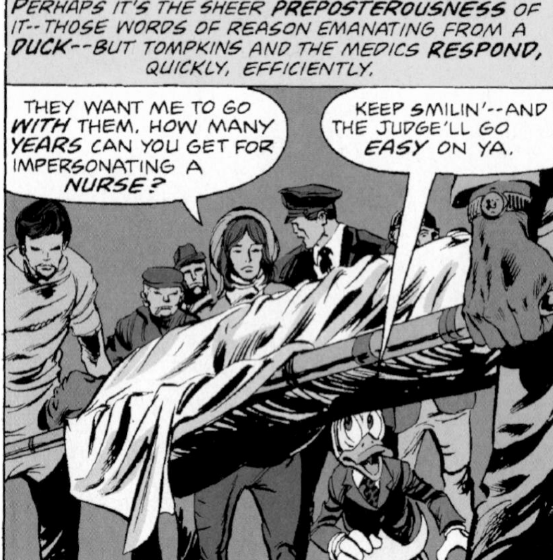

PERHAPS IT'S THE SHEER PREPOSTEROUSNESS OF IT--THOSE WORDS OF REASON EMANATING FROM A DUCK--BUT TOMPKINS AND THE MEDICS RESPOND, QUICKLY, EFFICIENTLY.
THEY WANT ME TO GO WITH THEM. HOW MANY YEARS CAN YOU GET FOR IMPERSONATING A NURSE?
KEEP SMILIN'--AND THE JUDGE'LL GO EASY ON YA.

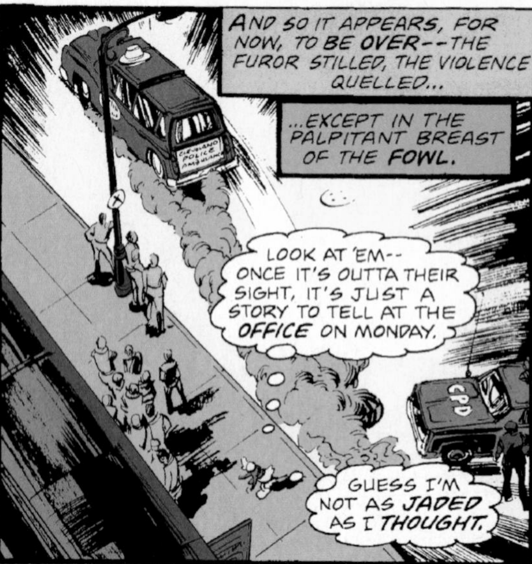

AND SO IT APPEARS, FOR NOW, TO BE OVER--THE FUROR STILLED, THE VIOLENCE QUELLED...
...EXCEPT IN THE PALPITANT BREAST OF THE FOWL.
LOOK AT 'EM-- ONCE IT'S OUTTA THEIR SIGHT, IT'S JUST A STORY TO TELL AT THE OFFICE ON MONDAY.
CPD
GUESS I'M NOT AS JADED AS I THOUGHT.

FOR THE DISCRIMINATING ADULT BIBLIOPHILE
BEV HAS THE KEYS...CAN'T GO HOME...TOO WIRED, ANYWAY, TO RELAX...
LAVENDER FLAMINGO BOOK
HMMM... MAYBE SOME READING MATTER... TAKE MY WEARY MIND OFF...

...MARTIAL ARTS.
UH, I THINK I'M GONNA BE ILL.
ADULTS ONL
MARTIAL ARTS
NO BROWSING!
YOU TOO CAN GROW!

THE DUCK'S NAUSEA TURNS TO GRIM, ALMOST MACABRE FASCINATION. SMALL WONDER THIS WORLD SEEMS SO GRIM, SO HUMORLESS...
...IF, AS EVIDENCED BY THESE PERIODICALS, IT IS FUELED ON CHEAP SEX AND VICARIOUS VIOLENCE.
DEADLY FEET OF KUNG FU!
BLACK BELT KIL
KARATE DEAT
FEBRUARY '76

"POISON FINGERS OF KUNG FU"..."THE NINJA: MASTER OF SILENT DEATH"..."HOW TO BE PREPARED WHEN A SAMURAI ATTACKS YOU"...
PHWAAUGH I DON'T BELIEVE-- HUH--WAITAMINIT-- WHAT'S THIS...?
FREE! HOW TO MAKE MILLIONS IN YOUR SPARE TIME!
DEADLY FE OF KUN

SECRETS OF KUNG FU REVEALED!
NO TRICKS! NO SKILL OR PREVIOUS TRAINING REQUIRED! MIND AND BODY TUNED IN MINUTES! LEARN KUNG FU, KARATE, T'AI CHI, AIKIDO, AND EASTERN PROVERBS FOR ALL OCCASIONS.
MASTER C'HAAJ MARTIAL ARTS EXTRAVAGANZA
7014 OAK STREET (AT CORNER ELM)
LEVELAND, OHIO
HOURS
IF THIS IS ON THE LEVEL, I COULD TRACK DOWN MACHO MYSELF--GIVE 'IM A TASTE OF HIS OWN MEDICINE.
THE SCHOOL'S HERE IN CLEVELAND--JUST A COUPLE BLOCKS AWAY--WHAT THE HECK?--WHY NOT?!
NAME
ADDRESS
AGE
PHONE

SHORTLY...
MASTER CHAAJ MARTIAL EXTRAVAGANZA (COME IN AND BROWSE
FUNNY... I'VE GOT THE SPOOKIEST FEELING I'VE WALKED IN A CIRCLE...!
IN FACT, EXCEPT FOR THE SIGN...

...AAH, BUT EVERYTHING IN CLEVELAND LOOKS ALIKE!
IF I WASN'T PUT OFF BY A SLEAZOID BOOK-STORE, WHY SHOULD A SEAMY GYM RUFFLE MY FEATHERS?

HECK, A LITTLE DOWN-HOME DEGENERACY NEVER ST--
WAAAUGH
WELCOME, INITIATE--ENTER AND BE AT PEACE. YOU HAVE BEEN SHOWN YOUR FIRST LESSON, FREE OF CHARGE.
THE FACE WHICH A MAN PRESENTS TO THE WORLD NEED IN NO WAY BE INDICATIVE OF THE SOUL IT MASKS.
BE SEATED.

EVEN AS HOWARD ATTEMPTS TO COPE WITH THIS MASSIVE INCONGRUITY, BEVERLY FACES A LOGICAL--AND TRAGIC--CONCLUSION.
...JUST A MINUTE AGO. THE DOCTORS DID WHAT THEY COULD, BUT...
I'LL BE GOING NOW, OFFICER TOMPKINS. YOU HAVE MY ADDRESS IF YOU NEED ME.
SURE. I UNDERSTAND IT'S ROUGH...!

WILL ANYTHING BE DONE, BEV WONDERS. WILL DOING ANYTHING MATTER? DEATH IS DEATH, ISN'T IT? UNCHANGEABLE? IRREVERSIBLE?
LOST IN THOUGHT, SHE WALKS ON MECHANICALLY, MIND DETACHED FROM BODY, FROM SENSORIUM...!

SHE NEVER HEARS MACHO'S CRONIES PADDING CATLIKE AT HER HEELS. INDEED, EVEN WHEN THEY ARE UPON HER...
...A MOMENT PASSES BEFORE HER BRAIN INTERPRETS AND INFORMS HER OF THE TACTILE SENSATION, THE STEELY-COLD CLAMP OF THEIR FINGERS.

SHE IS SPIRITED AWAY, INTO THE NIGHT... WHILE HOWARD'S SPIRIT RETURNS AND IS NOURISHED.
...AND THAT, IN A NUTSHELL, IS WHAT BROUGHT ME HERE. I CAN'T HACK SITTIN' ON MY TAIL FEATHERS WHILE THAT MANIAC IS ON THE LOOSE.
MOST ADMIRABLE. BUT PRUDENCE GUIDES EVERY ACTION OF THE SUPERIOR MAN. WHAT DO YOU KNOW OF YOUR ADVERSARY BESIDES HIS SELF-AGGRANDIZING NAME?

ZILCH--EXCEPT THAT HE WAS WEARIN' THIS. IT CAME UNHOOKED WHEN I TACKLED 'IM.
I FEAR... HE WAS ONE OF MY OWN STUDENTS, THEN. WE OFFER THAT CHARM-- FOR ONLY $5.98--TO ALL OUR GRADUATES.
BUT THIS PERSON, OBVIOUSLY, IS OF UNSCRUPULOUS CHARACTER AND MISUSES MY TEACHINGS.

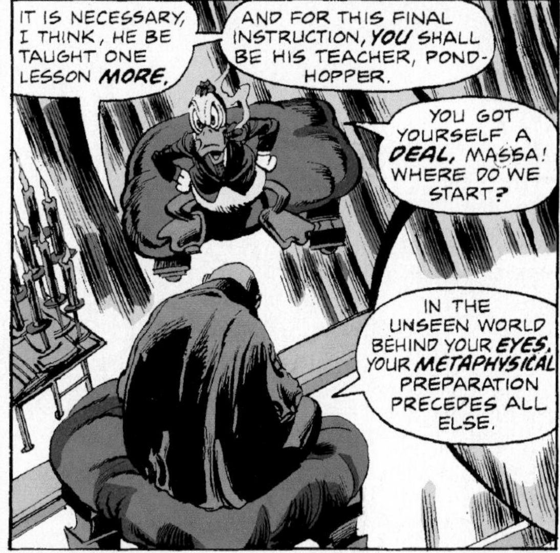
IT IS NECESSARY, I THINK, HE BE TAUGHT ONE LESSON MORE.
AND FOR THIS FINAL INSTRUCTION, YOU SHALL BE HIS TEACHER, POND-HOPPER.
YOU GOT YOURSELF A DEAL, MASSA! WHERE DO WE START?
IN THE UNSEEN WORLD BEHIND YOUR EYES. YOUR METAPHYSICAL PREPARATION PRECEDES ALL ELSE.

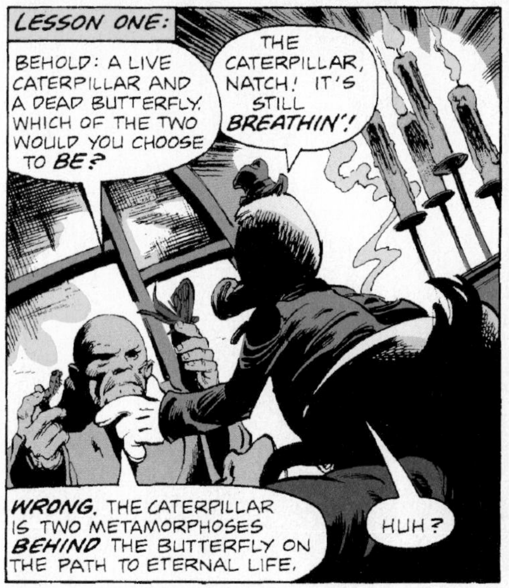
LESSON ONE:
BEHOLD: A LIVE CATERPILLAR AND A DEAD BUTTERFLY. WHICH OF THE TWO WOULD YOU CHOOSE TO BE?
THE CATERPILLAR, NATCH! IT'S STILL BREATHIN'!
WRONG. THE CATERPILLAR IS TWO METAMORPHOSES BEHIND THE BUTTERFLY ON THE PATH TO ETERNAL LIFE.
HUH?

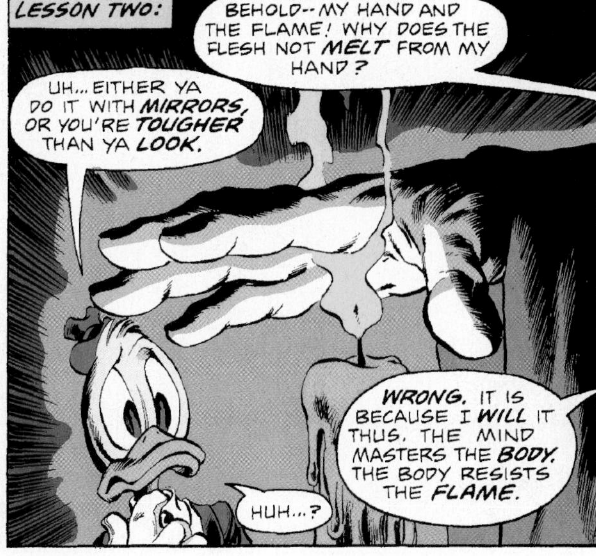
LESSON TWO:
BEHOLD-- MY HAND AND THE FLAME! WHY DOES THE FLESH NOT MELT FROM MY HAND?
UH... EITHER YA DO IT WITH MIRRORS, OR YOU'RE TOUGHER THAN YA LOOK.
WRONG. IT IS BECAUSE I WILL IT THUS. THE MIND MASTERS THE BODY. THE BODY RESISTS THE FLAME.
HUH...?

THE **PHYSICAL** ASPECT OF THE DUCK IS DEVELOPED NEXT. HE LEARNS THE BALANCE AND POISE NECESSARY TO MASTER THE **STAFF.** HIS REFLEXES ARE HONED TO PRECISION. HE LEARNS TO **MOVE** FASTER THAN THE EYE CAN FOLLOW, TO REACT FASTER THAN EVEN A STEEL BLADE CAN TRAVEL.

HE LEARNS THE POSTURES OF ATTACK AND DEFENSE.

HE LEARNS TO APPLY THE STRENGTH OF HIS **WILL** TO THE BREAKING OF **MATERIAL** BARRIERS.

YOUR FINAL LESSON, PONDHOPPER: THE IRRELEVANCE OF CHRONOLOGICAL TIME TO THE ENLIGHTENMENT OF MAN OR FOWL.
YOUR WILL TO ACHIEVE HAS ENABLED YOU TO COMPLETE A LIFETIME OF STUDY IN A MERE THREE HOURS AND SEVENTEEN MINUTES!
YOUR MEDALLION...!
CHOKE I AM HONORED, MASTER.

AND THIS MOST SPECIAL OF GIFTS IS ALSO FOR YOU...
NEW THREADS?
SILKEN ONES, HOWARD THE DUCK. GO BEHIND THE CURTAIN. CHANGE.

DON THIS NEW GARB, THIS UNSULLIED CLOTH IN WHICH TO DRAPE YOUR BODY...
...THIS OUTWARD REFLECTION OF YOUR NEWLY-RAISED CONSCIOUSNESS.

I RECHRISTEN YOU SHANG-OP--WHICH MEANS THE "RISING AND ADVANCING OF A DUCK."
SHANG-OP--WHOSE FLASHING FEATHERED FINGERS AND INDOMITABLE COURAGE MAKE HIM--MASTER OF QUAK FU!

I DUNNO IF I'D GO THAT FAR--BUT I GOTTA ADMIT, IT'S BEEN A VALUABLE THREE HOURS.
WHICH, UH, REMINDS ME--

HOW MUCH DO I OWE Y--
WAAUGH!

I'M STILL IN THE LAVENDER FLAMINGO!!
I MUST'A FANTASIZED THE WHOLE THING! I MUST'A BEEN STANDIN' HERE ALL THE TI--
THIS WAY TO EXIT
ONLY... IF THAT'S WHAT HAPPENED, WHERE'D I GET THESE YIN-YANG P.J.'S?

NO... IT WASN'T A DREAM. IT COULDN'T'VE BEEN. AND ANYWAY, WHAT IF IT WAS?
DREAMS'RE JUST ANOTHER LEVEL OF REALITY, RIGHT? I TOOK THAT MARTIAL ARTS COURSE --I CAN FEEL IT-- I CAN REMEMBER ALL THE MOVES!
I JUST CAN'T BELIEVE HE LET ME GO WITHOUT PAYING-- THAT'S WHAT'S WEIRD!

HIS WADDLE ACCELERATES TO A RUN. HE IS ANXIOUS TO LEAVE THIS SEEDY NEIGHBORHOOD WITH ALL ITS SHADOW-CLOAKED MYSTERIES BEHIND HIM.
HE LONGS TO RECOUNT HIS STRANGE EXPERIENCE TO BEVERLY, TO SHARE WITH HER THE AWE, THE WONDER, THE SPACEY STOMACH OF HAVING PASSED THROUGH THE REALM OF THE UNEXPLAINABLE.

WHEN HE ARRIVES AT THE APARTMENT, HOWEVER, THOSE CONCERNS ARE SUPERCEDED BY ANOTHER--FAR MORE URGENT... AND SINISTER.
NUTS, YOU'D THINK HE COULD JUST USE TAPE, BUT NO, HE--

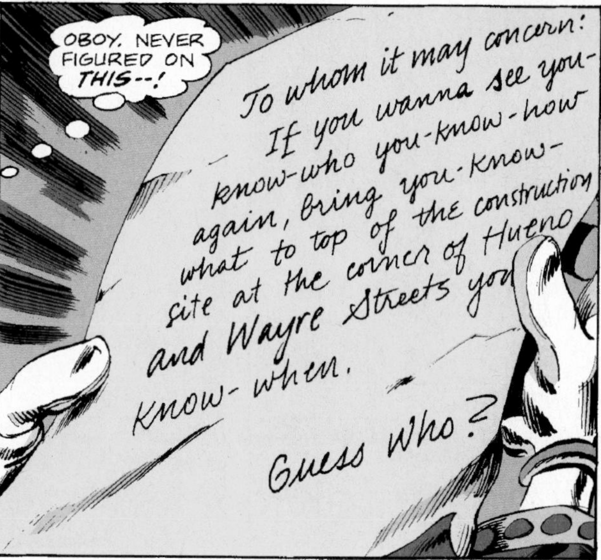
OBOY. NEVER FIGURED ON THIS--!
To whom it may concern:
If you wanna see you-know-who you-know-how again, bring you-know-what to top of the construction site at the corner of Hueno and Wayre Streets you know-when.
Guess Who?

"MACHO WANTS HIS DRAGON MEDALLION BACK," HOWARD MUTTERS, "AND HE'S WILLING TO KILL TO GET IT."
ANSWERS, PRETTY LADY-- OR MY NUNCHAKU WILL CRUSH YOUR LOVELY HIGH CHEEK-BONES INTO POWDER.
WHO WAS YOUR FRIEND-- THE MIDGET IN THE DUCK-SUIT-- AND WHERE HAS HE TAKEN MY MEDALLION?
THE TRUTH, PRETTY LADY!
I TOLD YOU THE TRUTH!

THERE IS NO "MIDGET"--HOWARD'S REALLY A DUCK. AND I DON'T KNOW ABOUT ANY MED--
YOU POOR LITTLE FOOL. TO PERSIST IN THOSE LIES--HAS COST YOU YOUR LIFE.

SWING HER OUT-- OVER THE EDGE OF THE ROOF!
HEAR ME WELL, PRETTY LADY. YOU'VE SEEN FOR YOURSELF THAT I WILL GO TO ANY LENGTH TO PRESERVE MY HONOR.
I AM CAPABLE OF FAR MORE VIOLENCE WHEN MY FREEDOM IS AT STAKE.

SPEAK! TELL THE TRUTH! NOW! OR--
AW, BUTTON YER LIP, YA PUNY, PUSILLANIMOUS, PEA-BRAINED PUGILIST!
WHAT?! WHO DARES--?!

AH, C'MON-- KNOCK OFF THE COMIC-BOOK DIALOGUE, WILLYA?
WHAT'S SO DARING ABOUT CALLING YOU NAMES? YOU'RE A BIG, HAIRY, BARREL-CHESTED MOUTH WITH NOTHIN' TO BACK IT UP!
WHY YOU--!

GET HIM! BREAK THOSE PIPECLEANERS HE CALLS ARMS-- AND WASTE HIM!
NOW THAT'S MORE LIKE IT. BACK TO YOUR ROOTS--THE GUTTER.

HAI-
FONK
DONP
EEE-
CHUNT
BRUK
CHI!
YA-

YOU'RE FRESH OUTTA GOONS, COUNT. LOOKS LIKE YER GONNA HAVE TA TAKE ME ON YOURSELF--
--ASSUMING YOU'RE MAN ENOUGH, YA SISSY!
THE ULTIMATE INSULT--SIGNED, SEALED, DELIVERED.

LIVID WITH RAGE, MACHO CEASES HIS BOASTFUL DECLAMATIONS. HIS VOICE BECOMES AN ANIMALISTIC GRUNT AND SNARL AS, SUCKING IN AIR, TENSING EVERY MUSCLE, HE WORKS UP HIS CHI--HIS FIGHTING SPIRIT.

WHEN HIS BODY AND MIND ARE NAUGHT BUT PURE DESTRUCTIVE ENERGY--
HE ATTACKS!!

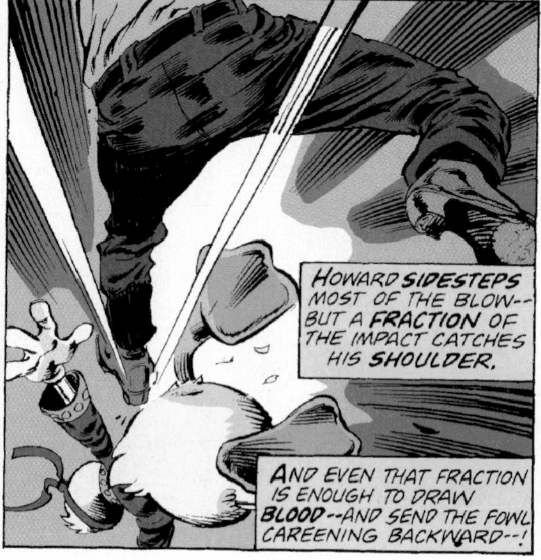
HOWARD SIDESTEPS MOST OF THE BLOW--BUT A FRACTION OF THE IMPACT CATCHES HIS SHOULDER.
AND EVEN THAT FRACTION IS ENOUGH TO DRAW BLOOD--AND SEND THE FOWL CAREENING BACKWARD--!

HE PLUNGES TOWARD WHAT SHOULD BE CERTAIN DOOM.
BUT HE DOES NOT DIE.

"PAIN IS A CONDITION OF THE MIND," ACCORDING TO MASTER C'HAAJ, "IT CAN BE OVERCOME BY CONCENTRATION, IF NEED BE.

"FIX YOUR EYE ON YOUR OPPONENT, YOUR MIND ON YOUR STRATEGY, YOUR HEARING ON YOUR OWN HEARTBEAT.
"STRIVE FOR THE MOMENT OF TOTAL AWARENESS...

"...AND YOU SHALL ACCOMPLISH WHAT LESSER MEN WOULD TERM MIRACLES."
NO!

A FLUKE--THAT'S WHAT IT IS! MY FOUR LIEUTENANTS--THE NUNCHAKU--
--BEGINNER'S LUCK, NOTHING MORE!

WELL, YOUR GOOD FORTUNE HAS JUST COME TO AN END, SHORTY!
DIE!!

NO.

TEETH CLENCHED, EYES BULGING, FACE RUBICUND WITH FURY, MACHO MAKES A FINAL, HATE-BLINDED CHARGE.
YES! YES! DIE WHEN I TELL YOU TO DIE!

I'LL MAKE YOU DIE! I'LL SHRED YOUR SKIN WITH MY NAILS! I'LL CHEW YOU INTO LITTLE PIECES!
I'LL TEAR YOU APA--A-AAAAGH!

FROM THE INSTANT HE LEAVES THE ROOF, HE IS CLUTCHING FURIOUSLY.
FORTUNATELY, HE HAS PLACED SOMETHING THERE IN THE EMPTY AIR TO GRAB.

UNFORTUNATELY, HIS SLICK, SWEATY PALMS AND FINGERS CANNOT MAINTAIN THEIR HOLD.

AND HE FALLS, STILL SCREAMING CURSES AT THE WOMAN AND THE DUCK, STILL PROTESTING FATE'S UNFAIRNESS--
--THAT HE, A MAN'S MAN, A FIGHTER, A STREET WARRIOR WHO NEVER LET ANYONE PUSH HIM AROUND, SHOULD BE SQUASHED LIKE AN INSECT ON THE PAVEMENT 42 STORIES BELOW--
--BY A DWARF WITH NO STRENGTH, NO RAW MUSCLE--ONLY A LITTLE TECHNIQUE.

DON'T SUFFER ANY SELF-RECRIMINATION. MACHO GOT WHAT HE DESERVED. THE KID... DIDN'T MAKE IT.
FUNNY... IT DOESN'T MAKE ME FEEL ANY BETTER. DEATH IS DEATH. MACHO DESERVED WORSE, REALLY...
AN' HE GOT IT. SEE, BEV--HE DIED A CATERPILLAR. THE KID DIED A BUTTER-FLY...!

NEXT:
HOWARD FACES THE SOMNAMBULENT MENACE OF:
THE SIXTH SLEEPER!

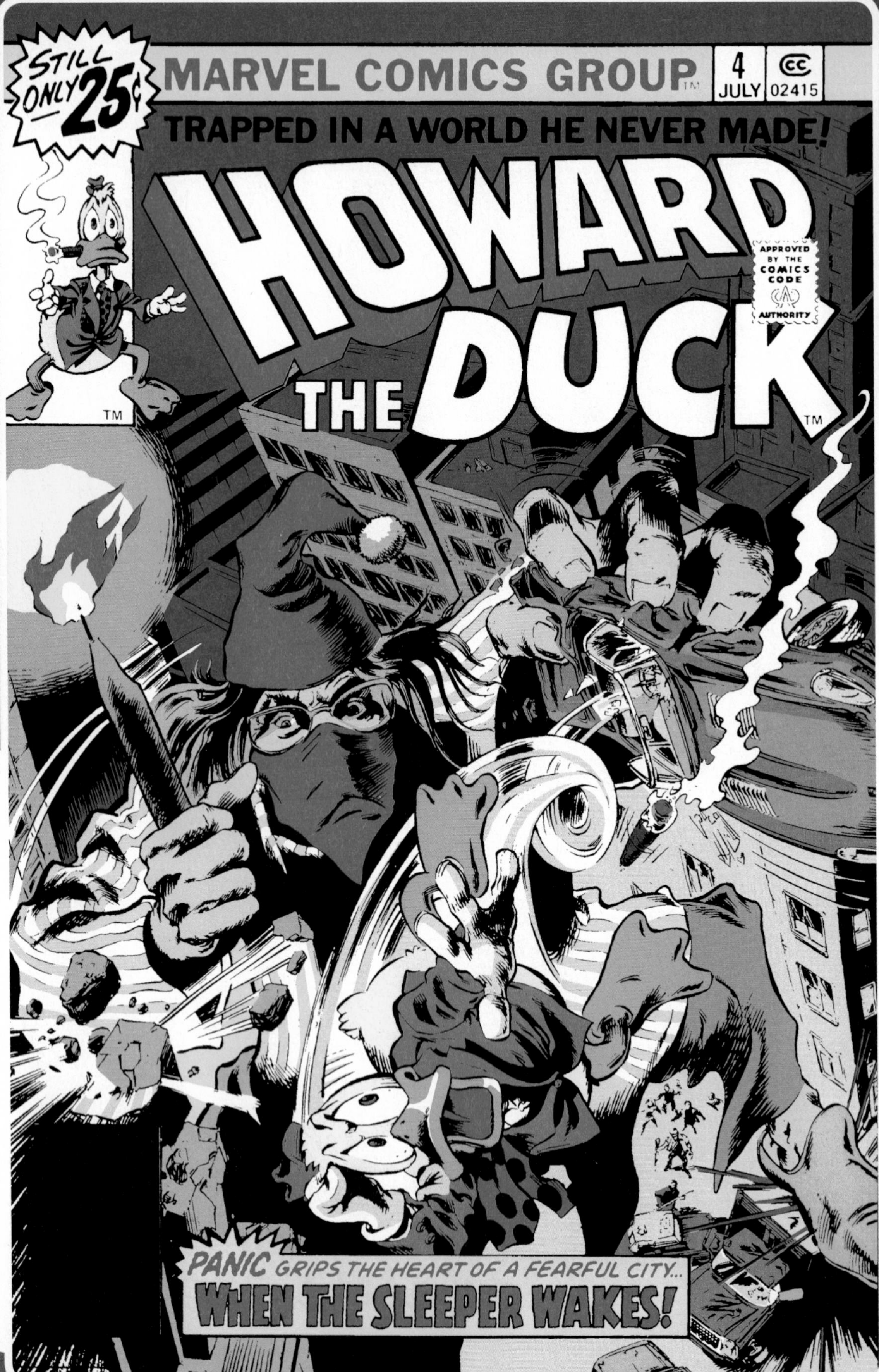
STILL ONLY 25¢
MARVEL COMICS GROUP
4 JULY
CC 02415
TRAPPED IN A WORLD HE NEVER MADE!
HOWARD THE DUCK
APPROVED BY THE COMICS CODE AUTHORITY
PANIC GRIPS THE HEART OF A FEARFUL CITY...
WHEN THE SLEEPER WAKES!

From the time of his hatching, he was...different. A potentially brilliant scholar who dreaded the structured environment of school, he educated himself in the streets, taking whatever work was available, formulating his philosophy of self from what he learned of the world about him. And then the Cosmic Axis shifted...and that world *changed.* Suddenly, he was stranded in a universe he could not fathom. Without warning, he became a strange fowl in an even stranger land.

Stan Lee PRESENTS: HOWARD THE DUCK!™

WRITTEN BY STEVE GERBER * ILLUSTRATED BY GENE COLAN * S. LEIALOHA INKER * A. KAWECKI, LETTERER MICHELE W., COLORIST * MARV WOLFMAN EDITOR

MHM...WHAT DO YOU SUPPOSE CAUSED--?
WHO'S GOTTA SUP-POSE? DON'T TELL ME YOU SLEPT THRU THAT RACKET FROM UPSTAIRS?!
OUR FRIENDLY NEIGHBOR'S BEEN POUNDIN' ON THAT SAME SPOT FOR HALF AN HOUR!

AN' OFFHAND, I'D SAY HE'S NOT ABOUT TA LET UP.
THUMP
DUCKY... YOU'RE GETTING EXCITED.

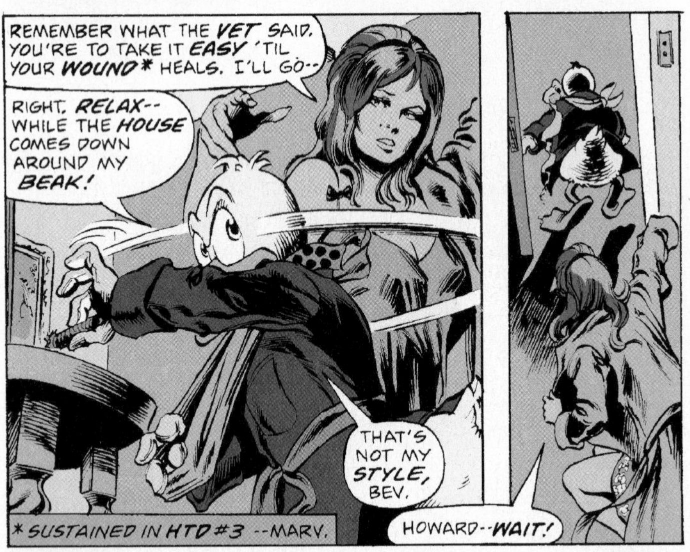
REMEMBER WHAT THE VET SAID. YOU'RE TO TAKE IT EASY 'TIL YOUR WOUND* HEALS. I'LL GO--
RIGHT. RELAX-- WHILE THE HOUSE COMES DOWN AROUND MY BEAK!
THAT'S NOT MY STYLE, BEV.
*SUSTAINED IN HTD #3 --MARV.
HOWARD--WAIT!

NO DICE, TOOTS--I'VE WAITED LONG ENOUGH! ANOTHER CALM, COOL, SELF-CONTROLLED SECOND--AN' I'LL FLAKE OUT!
NEVER REALIZED ...HOW WIRED I GET IF I DON'T KEEP MOVIN'.

UPSTAIRS...
AWRIGHT, AWRIGHT-- PULL YER EYEBALLS BACK IN YER HEADS AN' YER HEADS BACK IN YER DOORS.
I'LL HANDLE OUR HUMAN JACKHAMMER.

BUT--YOU'RE-- A DUCK!!

YEP--AN' UNLESS YOU FIGGER A PRUNE IS BETTER SUITED TO THE JOB--STAY OUTTA MY WAY!

AWRIGHT, YA BLASTED BATTERING RAM-- OPEN UP! FOOT-STOMPIN' TIME IS OVER! IT'S AFTER MIDNIGHT!
THUMP THUMP
HOWARD--?
TRY THE DOOR.
I'VE MET THE GUY WHO LIVES HERE. I'D BET HE LEAVES IT--
--UNLOCKED! RIGHT AS RAIN, TOOTS!
STAY BEHIND ME, NOW--THIS NUT COULD BE DANGEROUS!

GEE, I DON'T THINK SO, DUCKY. CHECK OUT HIS EYES. THEY'RE SHUT.
SO WHAT? IF MY PLACE WERE THIS CRUMMY-LOOKING, I'D--
WAIT--CRIPES, YOU MEAN--HE'S ASLEEP?!
PRECISELY--AND STRIKING OUT IN VAIN AGAINST SOME NAMELESS, INVISIBLE NIGHT TERROR.
MOMENTARILY, THE MACABRE SIGHT HOLDS HOWARD AND BEV TRANSFIXED.

BUT ONLY MOMENTARILY.
C'MON, SLEEPING BEAUTY--WAKE UP! THIS MAY BE A PEACEFUL SNOOZE FOR YOU, BUT--!
TWAP

THE STINGING SLAP OF HOWARD'S WEBBED FOOT DOES WRENCH THE YOUNG MAN'S EYE-LIDS OPEN...

...BUT HIS OUTLOOK REMAINS SOMEWHAT DISTORTED BY SLEEP.
THE DUCK APPEARS A CRIMSON-EYED, CARNIVOR-OUS MONSTROSITY... BEVERLY SWITZLER, A SARDONIC, SADISTIC SORCERESS WHOM THE DUCK-DEMON SERVES.
THEY INTEND TO HARM HIM... EVEN SLASH HIM TO RIBBONS IF NECESSARY... AND WHY?
JUST TO GET HIM TO--
WAKE UP!!
AAAGH
HADDA POP YA ONE, PAL-- YOU WERE FLAKIN' OUT. DIDN'T MEAN TO HURT YOU THAT BAD...!
YOU DIDN'T... I'M SORRY... I THOUGHT... BUT I GUESS... I'M NOT BLEEDING, AM I?
NOPE. IT WAS ALL A DREAM.
NIGHTMARE, YOU MEAN.
REALLY WEIRD, HUH? YOU HAVE THIS PROBLEM A LOT?
ONLY WHEN I SLEEP-- THAT IS, MOST OF MY LIFE.
LORD, I SOUND DEPRESSING.
YEAH, WELL-- THAT'S OKAY.
WHAT'S AN ARTIST WITHOUT A TEMPERAMENT?
UH-UH. THE QUESTION IS: "WHAT'S A TEMPERAMENT WITHOUT AN ARTIST?"
ANSWER: ME--PAUL SAME-- SPECIALIST IN UNFINISHED WORKS.
WANNA TALK ABOUT IT-- OR SHOULD WE JUST BUZZ OFF?

OBOY. HERE IT COMES, FOLKS-- THE TALE OF WOE YOU'VE ALL BEEN WAITING FOR!

OH, HOWARD-- SHUSH!
DON'T LET MY FEATHERED FRIEND INHIBIT YOU, PAUL. JUST POUR OUT YOUR HEART. I'LL PUT ON SOME COFFEE.
YOU'RE SURE YOU WANT TO LISTEN TO THIS?

I MEAN-- IT GOES BACK TO WHEN I WAS JUST A KID.

"SEE, I WAS SORT OF A MINOR-LEAGUE PRODIGY. I COULD READ AT AGE THREE. I WAS MY PARENTS' PRIDE AND JOY--THE STAR ATTRACTION AT ALL THEIR PARTIES.

"THEY EXPECTED GREAT THINGS FROM ME IN SCHOOL. THEY MIGHT'VE GOTTEN 'EM, TOO--
NO, PAUL-- IT'S HAMMERING TIME, NOT PAINTING TIME. YOU HAVE TO JOIN THE OTHER CHILDREN--
--OR THEY WON'T LIKE YOU.

"--IF I HADN'T BEEN SO BORED WITH WHAT THEY WERE TEACHING AND THE DULL, DRONING WAY THEY TAUGHT IT. AS IT WAS, I DAYDREAMED A LOT.

"SO IT WENT ON MY RECORD THAT I WAS AN UNDERACHIEVER, A PROBLEM LEARNER WITH NO ATTENTION SPAN.
THWACK

"AND THE KIDS NICK-NAMED ME 'SLEEPY.'
"REAL CREATIVE TYPES, THOSE LITTLE RASCALS.

"ANYWAY, EVERY REPORT CARD BECAME AN OCCASION TO READ ME THE RIOT ACT.
"THE TWO WORDS THAT MOST REMIND ME OF MY CHILD-HOOD ARE 'OR' AND 'ELSE.'

MMM... FOR ME, IT'S "WHEN YOU'RE OLD ENOUGH."
THAT'S WHEN I WAS SUPPOSED TO LEARN ABOUT ANYTHING THAT STRUCK ME AS INTERESTING.
EVERY TIME I GOT A REPORT CARD, I LOST A PRIVILEGE.
BY FOURTH GRADE, I HAD TO RAISE MY HAND TO GO TO THE JOHN--AT HOME!
YEAH... I HAD PROBLEMS WITH SCHOOL, TOO.

I DON'T WONDER... IF YOU'VE ALWAYS DRESSED LIKE THAT!
WAUUGH!
LISTEN, BUSTER--I DIDN'T STICK AROUND HERE TO BE INSULTED!

BESIDES--THESE THREADS HAPPEN TO BE THE HEIGHT OF ELEGANCE! BEV PICKED 'EM OUT HERSELF--
--AN' SHE KNOWS CLASS, SEE?

SURE. NOTHING PERSONAL. I CAN SEE HOW SOME WOMEN COULD GET OFF ON A TOUGH LITTLE GUY--
--EVEN IN A DUCK SUIT! DIFFERENT STROKES AND ALL THAT.
UH, PAUL... THAT'S NOT A COSTUME. HE'S FOR REAL. HIS DUCKNESS IS INBORN.

OKAY, OKAY--IF THAT'S HOW YOU WANT TO PLAY IT, I DON'T CARE.
I'LL SWALLOW YOUR STORY IF YOU'LL BELIEVE MINE.
DEAL! JUST GET ON WITH IT, HUH?

"IF YOU INSIST:
"PHASE TWO HIT WHEN I WAS TEN OR SO, BORED, ANGRY, FRUSTRATED, BUT BASICALLY PASSIVE BY NATURE--
BEEP
BEEP
"I BEGAN DOZING OFF WHENEVER THE PRESSURES STARTED TO BUILD--WHENEVER AND WHEREVER.

"IT WAS THE ONLY SAFETY VALVE I HAD--BUT IT LED TO SOME PRETTY STRANGE SCENES.
"NOTHING COULD ROUSE ME FROM THAT STATE, NOT THE SCREAMING DIPS AND DIVES OF A ROLLER COASTER--

"--NOT EVEN THE THRILL OF YOUNG LOVE.
"I SLEPT THROUGH MY FIRST KISS.

"MEANWHILE, OF COURSE, THERE WAS ALL THIS HOSTILITY SWELLING LIKE A TUMOR INSIDE ME, AND AS I SPENT MORE AND MORE OF MY LIFE ASLEEP--
"--IT BEGAN TO SURFACE IN VIOLENT DREAMS. I SAW MYSELF AS A RAMPAGING COLOSSUS.
"I'D TRAMPLE WHOLE CITIES--CRUSH ANYTHING, ANYONE THAT STOOD IN MY WAY OR TRIED TO JACK ME AROUND."

IT GETS SO BAD I CAN'T TELL ANYMORE WHEN I'M AWAKE OR ASLEEP. AND MY FURY AT THE WORLD KEEPS GROWING!
WALKING DOWN THE STREET... I GET THE URGE TO PUNCH OUT TOTAL STRANGERS!

I HOPE YOU DON'T EXPECT US TO SYMPATHIZE! DIDN'T YOU EVER FIGHT BACK AT--?

OH, NO! I'VE NEVER BEEN ABLE TO HURT ANYONE!
IF SOMEONE STANDS ON MY TOE, I'D RATHER WAIT FOR THEM TO MOVE THAN RISK OFFENDING THEM BY ASKING...!

'COURSE--THAT DOESN'T STOP YA FROM BANGIN' IN CEILINGS AT THREE A.M.!
HECK, YOU GOT THE PERFECT EXCUSE FOR ANY ACTION... YOU DID IT IN YOUR SLEEP!

SLAM

OKAY. WHAT IS THIS? I'VE HEARD SLIMIER STORIES THAN THAT!
WHY'D I FLAKE OUT? WHAT GETS TO ME ABOUT THAT GUY?

PAUL, I'M SORRY ABOUT HOWARD'S TEMPER. HE--
LISTEN, GET SOME REST NOW, HUH? WE CAN TALK SOME MORE IN THE MORNING IF YOU WANT.
THE PERFECT... YES... IN THE MORNING... SURE, IN THE MORNING...
...BUT UNDER THE COVER OF DARKNESS... YES ... THE PERFECT... GOODNIGHT, BEV.

DOWNSTAIRS...
CAME DOWN A LITTLE HARD ON THE GUY, DON'TCHA THINK?
NAH! HE PROBABLY NEVER EVEN FELT IT. HIS HEAD'S OUT TO LUNCH, TOOTS-- COULDN'T YOU TELL?
HE'S JUST A WAD OF SELF-PITY.

CLICK
SO LET HIM SLEEPWALK THROUGH LIFE! WHO CARES?!
I JUST WANNA GET SOME SHUT-EYE FOR MYSELF!

I MEAN... IT'S NOT LIKE IT'S MY PROBLEM. THESE HAIRLESS APES MANUFACTURE NEUROSES FOR THEMSELVES US DUCKS NEVER DREAMED OF!
NEVER "DREAMED" OF. HEH. FUNNY. HEH-HEH.

I DON'T BLAME SAME FOR NODDIN' OUT. IF I HADDA PLAY BY THIS WORLD'S NUTTY RULES... WHERE THEY PENALIZE YA FOR BEING CLEVER AN' REWARD MEDIOCRITY...
...AND THEN GLAMORIZE THE OUTLAW, 'CAUSE HE MAKES IT ON HIS OWN TERMS, EVEN IF THEY'RE STUPID AND DESTRUCTIVE...

I CAN'T SLEEP.
CLICK

I GOTTA GET OUT AN' DO SOME THINKING. I SHOULD'A KNOWN!
EVERY TIME I LET MY MIND SLIP LIKE THAT...!
I START OFF TRYIN' TO MINIMIZE ONE PUNK'S PROBLEM AND WIND UP DISSECTING A WHOLE SOCIAL STRUCTURE!
WAUGGH

ELSEWHERE...
BUT, I SWEAR... I'VE ONLY ENOUGH FOR CAR-FARE AND A HAMBURGER!
SO YOU'RE POOR! YOU'LL BE POOR AN' DEAD IF YA DON'T LEMME CHECK THAT PURSE FOR MYSELF, GRAND-MA!
YA GOT TEN SECONDS!

10--9--8--7--
--SICK! SICK, SICK, SICK!
HUH--?

OVER THE WALL, OUT OF THE NIGHT, TO ANSWER THE CALL OF THIS WOMAN IN FRIGHT--
--COMES WINKY-MAN, BOLD AND DARING AND FREE, TO PUT THE KIBOSH ON THIS DUMB ROBBERY!
I DON'T BELIEVE I'M SEEIN' THIS...!

ARE YOU FOR REAL?! I HEARD O' HEROES IN LONG UNDERWEAR --BUT A NIGHT-GOWN?!
AN WHAT'S THAT FOR? YA GONNA DRIP WAX ON ME?

HAW! LOOK, MAN--IF YOU'RE SMART, YOU'LL GO BACK TO BED AN' FORGET YA EVER--

DERIDE ME AND MOCK ME AND SCOFF IF YOU WILL! YOU'LL JUST HAVE TO SWALLOW YOUR OWN BITTER PILL!
FOR WHILE YOUR BIG MOUTH HAS BEEN TAUNTIN' AND FOAMIN', YOU'VE NEGLECTED TO NOTICE MY CANDLE IS ROMAN!

FAREWELL--SUCKER!

MEANWHILE, JUST AROUND THE CORNER, THE FOWL SEEKS DISTRACTION IN THE HAZY, VIBRATING ATMOSPHERE OF JOE'S BAR.
ME, I FIGGER LIVIN'S SORTA LIKE FOOTBALL... OR SQUASH, KNOW WHAT I MEAN?
SHTRATEGY... FAS' MOVES... BEER COMMERCIALS...
AAAH... GO EAT A BEEF JERKY!
BETTER YET... LET'S CHANGE THE SUBJECT.

YEAH... LIVIN'S A DRAG... LIKE FOOTBALL. LET'SH TALK ABOUT YOU.
YOU RILLY A DUCK? LEMME HEAR YA QUACK!

HE-E-EY! HE'S MY BUDDY! YOU LET 'IM ALONE!

DON' TELL ME WHADDA DO! I WANT 'IM TA QUACK--OR I'LL BASH YER HEAD IN!
HEY!!

HEY, WHAD?
HEY, YOU!
GUYS... YOU'RE GASSIN' ME...!

SOCK
DON' WORRY, PAL--I WON' LET IM' GET AWAY WI' DAT!
WAAUUK

ALCOHOL, OF COURSE, IS HIGHLY FLAMMABLE. SO WHEN TEMPERS IGNITE IN A JOINT LIKE JOE'S...
IT TAKES ONLY MOMENTS FOR THE FLAME TO LEAP FROM PATRON TO PATRON UNTIL THE SPARK HAS BECOME A FOREST FIRE.
BUT THE RAGING FIRE FREEZES AT THE SUDDEN CRY OF:
KNOCK IT OFF, YOU DRUNKEN BUMS!

SOMETHING WINKY THIS WAY COMES!
YOU, TOO, MADAM--IT'D MAKE ME EDGY FOR THAT MAN'S FACE TO FEEL YOUR WEDGIE!

HEAR ME NOW, AND HEAR ME WELL!
MY ANGER'S ONLY BEGUN TO SWELL!
OH, NO...!
YOU'VE HELPED MAKE MY WORLD THE MESS IT IS--YOU AND YOUR DRINKS THAT SPARKLE AND FIZZ!

I'LL SEE EVERY ONE OF YOU PUT IN TRACTION!
AND I WON'T BE RESPONSIBLE FOR MY ACTION!
PAUL... THEY'RE GETTIN' UGLY.

S'POZE WE SPLIT--TO A NICE, SAFE, DARK ALLEY!
YOU'RE ASLEEP, AREN'T YOU, PAUL?

C'MON, YA DOPE--SNAP OUT OF IT! YOU COULD'A BEEN KILLED!
WHA?--WHERE AM I--?

OH, SWELL! HE WAKES UP, AN' HIS MEMORY FIZZLES! HE DOESN'T KNOW HE COULD'A GOT SNUFFED!
WHY IS IT I FORESEE... COMPLICATIONS?

SEVERAL DAYS LATER...
YOU SAY YA SCULPTED IT FROM MEMORY?
WELL... AND IMAGINATION.
IT'S AMAZING! YOU'VE BEEN SO PRODUCTIVE LATELY! I JUST WISH I COULD FANTASIZE MY BODY INTO SUCH GOOD SHAPE!

WEEKS PASS.
PAUL'S PRODUCTIVITY INCREASES STEADILY... AS WINKY-MAN'S NIGHT-TIME EXPLOITS GROW EVER MORE OUTRAGEOUS.

SHATTERING SYMBOLS OF RIGIDITY AND CONFORMITY, PUNCTURING POMPOSITY AND PRETENSE, HE IS ELEVATED TO LEGEND STATUS.
ELAND PLAIN DEAL
FINAL
NIGHTSHIRT GUERRI
TERRORIZES CITY
APRIL 1, 1976
20 CENTS
MYSTERIOUS NIGHT STALKER
EYEWITNESS REPORTS
FAMOUS ARTIST DISAPPEARS

HIS PLACE IS SPOTLESS, HIS WORK UNDER CONTROL...
AN' HE STILL DOESN'T KNOW IT'S 'CAUSE WINKY'S WORKING OUT ALL HIS HOSTILITIES IN HIS SLEEP!
HOW LONG BEFORE HE WANTS A PIECE OF PAUL'S WAKING ACTION, TOO--?
NEATO!
I DID IT SPECIALLY--FOR MY ONE-MAN SHOW NEXT WEEK!

NEXT WEEK:
THE GUY WITH THE BEARD IS XAVIER COUTURE--THE ART CRITIC.
VERY INFLUENTIAL. IF HE'S IMPRESSED, I'VE LAUNCHED MYSELF A CAREER.
IF NOT... WELL, I CAN STILL BE A PAINTER... AT EARL SCHEIB'S.

JUNK. PURE JUNK.
JUNGLE ROT ON CANVAS.

NOTE THE ABSENCE OF AUTHORITY IN THE BRUSH STROKE. OUR YOUNG GENIUS HAS SPREAD HIMSELF TOO THIN, I'D SAY. HEH HEH
ARE YOU GONNA LET THAT CREEP GET AWAY WITH THAT?!
I... DON'T KNOW...!

YEESH--YOU'RE GOING PALE! C'MON OVER TO THE COUCH!
FEEL... DROWSY... EYES BLURRING...
UH-OH.

SEE IF THERE'S A DOCTOR IN THE HOUSE, TOOTS--AND HURRY!
BETTER ASK AROUND FOR A STRAITJACKET, TOO.
"JUNK," HE SAID...!

IT'S--NOT--JUNK!!
THUNK
OUTTA MY WAY! I'LL SHOW HIM! HE'LL EAT THOSE WORDS! I'LL STUFF 'EM DOWN HIS THROAT A SYLLABLE AT A TIME!!

MOMENTS LATER, AFTER A QUICK TRIP TO THE PARKING LOT...
...EXCEEDED ONLY BY THE BANALITY OF THE SUBJECT. THE FEMALE BODY IS PASSÉ.
ONLY THROUGH REINTERPRETATION IN LESS CONCRETE TERMS--
I'VE HEARD QUITE ENOUGH OF YOUR CRITIC'S LAMENT! IT'S YOUR HEAD, NOT HER BODY, THAT'S MADE OF CEMENT!
WHERE'D HE GO-- WHA' HOPPEN?--
YOU MAY THINK YOUR COMMENTS ARE WITTY AND WRY--
--BUT THEY'RE VAIN AND THEY'RE SILLY AND YOU'RE GONNA DIE!
OH, NO YA DON'T! YOU'RE AN ARTIST--NOT A HIT MAN!
YA GOTTA PLAY THE PART-- ACT SENSITIVE! CAN'T RUN AROUND SKAGGIN' PEOPLE! GIMME THAT ROD--
BLAMM
--BEFORE IT GOES OFF.

MY GOD! THE MAN WHO SAVED COUTURE'S LIFE--IS A DUCK!
SHWOOSHH
LISTEN... I SEEM TO HAVE HIT THE WRONG SWITCH ON THIS THING.
ASK THE TURKEY IN NIGHTSHIRT HOW TO TURN IT--
WHACK
WAAUGH!
THE FLAILING FOWL'S PLEA GOES UNHEARD AMID THE CONFUSION, BUT FORTUITOUS FATE--IN THE FORM OF A HEAT-SENSITIVE SPRINKLER SYSTEM--SAVES THE DAY.
THE FIERY CANDLE ELICITS A DOWNPOUR--AND THE COLD WATER NOT ONLY DOWNS THE DUCK, BUT DRENCHES PAUL AWAKE!
OKAY, CHUM--THIS IS THE MOMENT OF TRUTH! BE YOURSELF! TELL THAT BUM OFF!
HUH--?
OH--YEAH!
COOL YOUR HEELS, FUZZY! DON'T RUN OFF YET! I--
QUICK--WHAT DO I SAY?
HE'S A PHONY!
YOU'RE A PHONY! YOU WOULDN'T KNOW ART IF IT CAME UP AND BIT THE PSORIASIS OFF YOUR ELBOW!
I'LL HAVE YOU KNOW, MR. SAME, THAT I AM AN AUTHORITY!

PHOOEY! YOU'RE NO AUTHORITY-- YOU'RE JUST A BALD GUY!

HA! THE ART WORLD'S BEEN WAITING FOR YEARS FOR SOMEONE TO POP THAT POMPOUS BAG OF WIND!
GIVE THAT MAN A HAND! GIVE HIM A MEDAL!

HIP HIP HOORAY
HM.
HIP HIP

THE FOLKS ENJOYED OUR LITTLE EXHIBITION OF LIFE-AS-ART, WOULDN'T YOU SAY, PAUL?
A PROFOUND STATEMENT ON MAN'S INCLINATION TO ARTIFICIALITY...!

NUTS! CO-OPTED AGAIN! NEXT, HE'LL TAKE CREDIT FOR PAINTING THE PICTURES!
IT'S NOT IMPORTANT. THE PEOPLE SAW WHAT HAPPENED. THEY KNOW.
THEY DON'T KNOW!
THEY KNOW!
THEY DON'T!
WELL... PAUL KNOWS.

LATER...
LOOK AT HIM-- SLEEPING LIKE A BABY. I THINK YOU CHANGED HIS DESTINY TODAY.

AAH--HE'S GOT A LONG WAY TA GO. COUTURE WAS A CINCH.
WHAT IF IT'D BEEN A WOMAN CRITIC? THE CROWD WON'T CHEER IF YA YANK OFF A BALD LADY'S WIG!
NEXT TIRED, BROKE, AND WEB-FOOTED!

HOWARD THE DUCK

MARVEL COMICS GROUP™

APPROVED BY THE COMICS CODE AUTHORITY

30¢ 5 SEPT 02415

CC

TRAPPED IN A WORLD HE NEVER MADE!

HOWARD THE DUCK™

TM

WAAAUGH!

IT'S THE FEATHERED FURY VERSUS THE MAN-MOUNTAIN-- KLOUT!

ARENA OF NO RETURN

EVERLAST

From the time of his hatching, he was...different. A potentially brilliant scholar who dreaded the structured environment of school, he educated himself in the streets, taking whatever work was available, formulating his philosophy of self from what he learned of the world about him. And then the Cosmic Axis shifted...and that world *changed.* Suddenly, he was stranded in a universe he could not fathom. Without warning, he became a strange fowl in an even stranger land.

Stan Lee PRESENTS: HOWARD THE DUCK!™

STEVE GERBER *AVARICIOUS WRITER* / **GENE COLAN** *PENURIOUS PENCILLER* / **STEVE LEIALOHA** *INSATIABLE INKER* / **ARCHIE GOODWIN** *TIGHTFISTED EDITOR*

WELL, THE BEST THINGS IN LIFE ARE FREE--BUT YOU CAN GIVE 'EM TO THE BIRDS AN' BEES--
I WANT MO-O-ONEY!
EUREKA!! I FOUND MY STASH!!
LOVE
LOOK, HOWARD! HERE IT IS--A WHOLE QUARTER--A SHINY NEW BICENTENNIAL QUARTER--OURS, ALL OURS!!
AND I ONLY HAD TO RANSACK HALF THE APARTMENT TO TURN IT UP!
IRV WATANABE LETTERER
MICHELE WOLFMAN COLORIST
JV354

LET'S SEE...
WITH THE CHANGE WE FOUND IN DRAWERS...YEP! JUST ENOUGH FOR A CANDY BAR APIECE FOR DINNER!
WAAUGH! $108 IN UNPAID BILLS-- THE RENT DUE--AND WE'VE GOT FIFTY CENTS--FIFTY MEASLY CENTS!
HOW COULD YOU GET YOURSELF INTO A FISCAL FIASCO LIKE THIS?!

GEE, IT'S EASY TO LET ALL THOSE BILLS LANGUISH ON THE SHELF--WHEN YOU DON'T HAVE THE BREAD TO PAY 'EM.
WHAT DID YOU THINK--I WAS INDEPENDENTLY WEALTHY?

MORE OR LESS... YEAH.
I MEAN--YA HAVEN'T WORKED A DAY SINCE I'VE KNOWN YA.

I TOLD YOU--WHEN I NEED MONEY, I POSE FOR A LIFE-DRAWING CLASS.
IT'S A STANDING OFFER-- THERE'S ALWAYS WORK. I'LL CALL THE SCHOOL TOMORROW.

YEAH. SWELL--MEANTIME, WE FEAST BY CANDLELIGHT ON TWO SNICKERS!
I'LL BE BACK, BEV.

I'M HEADIN' FOR THE DRUGSTORE TA--
HOWARD--WAIT! LET'S GET RICH!

COME AGAIN?
LET'S MAKE A MILLION DOLLARS AND GO OFF WHERE NOBODY CAN FIND US AND RULE THE WORLD!

ON THE $2.10 AN HOUR YOU EARN AS A MODEL?
SURE, BEV.

JEEZ, HOWARD, YOU'RE ALWAYS SO REALISTIC!
HAVEN'T YOU EVER HAD A FANTASY?
UH-HUH. I GET 'EM A LOT--
--'SPECIALLY WHEN I'M HUNGRY!

I GET A LITTLE SHORT-TEMPERED ON AN EMPTY STOMACH, TOO.
MAYBE I'LL TAKE MY TIME--NOSE AROUND THE AISLES FOR SOME EXCITEMENT.

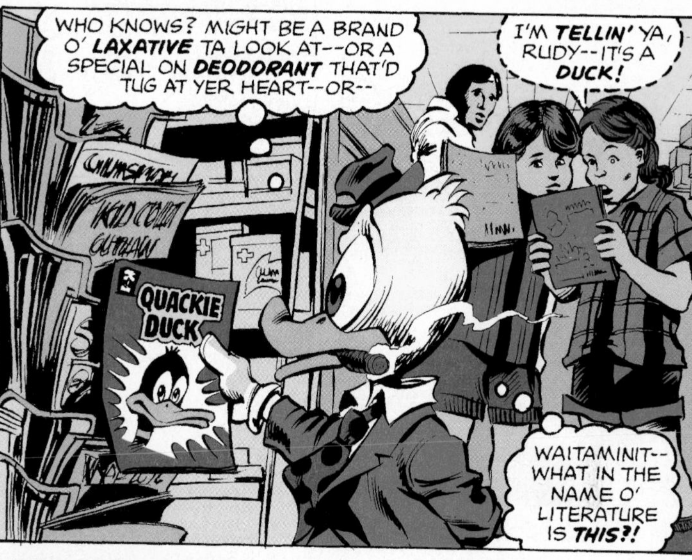
WHO KNOWS? MIGHT BE A BRAND O' LAXATIVE TA LOOK AT--OR A SPECIAL ON DEODORANT THAT'D TUG AT YER HEART--OR--
I'M TELLIN' YA, RUDY--IT'S A DUCK!
QUACKIE DUCK
WAITAMINIT--WHAT IN THE NAME O' LITERATURE IS THIS?!

HIS CURIOSITY PIQUED, HOWARD LEAFS THROUGH THE STRANGE MAGAZINE, PAUSING HERE AND THERE TO READ...!
QUACKIE DUCK
in...THE BEAR FACTS
BETCHA CAN'T CATCH ME! BETCHA! BETCHA!
OH, YEAH? I'LL SHOW YOU!
WRONG AGAIN --DUMMY! DIE, BEAR!
OOPS.

WAAAUGH
OF ALL THE BIASED, STEREOTYPIC TRASH!
WHAM
THIS IS AN UNFAIR REPRESENTATION OF DUCKS! IT MAKES US OUT AS SADISTS--PICKING ON THE POOR, STUPID BEARS!

UH-HUH...WELL, NOW THAT YOU'VE MANGLED THAT FUNNY-BOOK, YOU'VE BOUGHT IT, PAL.
THIRTY CENTS!
THIRTY--?!

THAT'S HIGHWAY ROBBERY! I REMEMBER WHEN A DIME--
AAAH-- SKIP IT! JUST GIMME A SNICKERS, TOO, HUH?

CERTAINLY, SIR.
DO COME SEE US AGAIN.

OVER MY DEAD BODY! PATRONIZE A PLACE THAT SELLS REACTIONARY PROPAGANDA TO KIDS?!
SALE
BUY ONE GET ONE FREE
NO, THANKS! I'LL TAKE MY BUSINESS ELSEWHERE!

SHORTLY...
WHAT TOOK SO LONG? AND WHERE'S OUR CANDY?
WE'RE DOWN TA ONE BAR. I SQUANDERED THIRTY CENTS ON MY PRINCIPLES!

A COMIC BOOK? I DON'T GET IT!
DON'T JUST LOOK AT THE PICTURES! READ! IT'S A WHOLE PAMPHLET FULL O' FOWL ASPERSIONS!
IF THERE'S ONE GOOD WORD ABOUT DUCKS IN THERE, SHOW ME!

AND NOW IT'S LISTENER'S LINE ON WDUM--THE NUMBER TO CALL, 754-034--
ON THE OTHER HAND...

HOWARD, WHAT--?
QUACKIE DUCK
IF YOU HAIRLESS APES GET SUCH A CHARGE OUTTA TALKIN' FOWL--
--ALL I GOTTA DO TO MAKE US A FORTUNE IS SELL OUT--EXPLOIT MYSELF!

HUH? WHAT DO YOU MEAN?
BEEP
BOO
BOP
JUST LEND AN EAR, TOOTS --YOU'LL FIND OUT.

GOT A LIVE ONE, BOSS!
SOME NUT WHO SAYS COMIC BOOKS ARE QUOTE "PROMULGATING RACIST MYTHS AND PERPETUATING PREJUDICE".
GREAT!
ABOUT TIME WE GOT SOMETHING CONTROVERSIAL!

THAT'S RIGHT, BUDDY--DUCKS! SLANTED, ONE-SIDED, DEFAMATORY PORTRAYALS OF DUCKS!
AND I KNOW, 'CAUSE I AM ONE!
WHADDAYA MEAN, "ONE WHAT"? ONE TALKING DUCK, YA--

YEEOWAAGH
CLACK
I DON'T THINK HE BELIEVED ME.

SORRY ABOUT THAT ONE, FOLKS. FOR SOME MIS-GUIDED SOULS, FREEDOM OF SPEECH IS A LICENSE TO...
YA FIGGER I CAME ON TOO SHRILL, OR WHAT?
NAH.

"BUT MAYBE YOU SHOULD TRY A MORE VISUAL MEDIUM."
WHAP-TV
NEXT DAY...
CHANNEL 81
AHEM HI, THERE! I--
AHEM
AHEM
SO THIS IS SHOW-BIZ.

HEADS UP, TOOTS! A STAR'S JUST EN-TERED THE PREMISES, SEE?!
WHAM

OH. THE NEW DUCK.
STUDIO "B"--THAT WAY. AND YOU BETTER GET A MOVE ON.
HUH? OH! SURE, DOLL.

SOME VISUAL MEDIUM! THEY DON'T EVEN LOOK ATCHA WHEN THEY TALK TO YA!
BUT WHAT THEY HECK--IF THEY WERE EXPECTIN' ME--!

MAY AS W--
WEEAUGHPHF
CRIPES, IT'S ABOUT TIME! OVER HERE!

HERE--GET ON THE CHALKMARK!
AND JUST STAND STOCK STILL 'TIL WE TELL YOU TO MOVE! GOT THAT?!
OH, AND GIMME THAT STOGIE!

WHAT'RE YOU--TRYIN' TO CORRUPT THESE KIDS? GONZO'S GOT AN IMAGE TO PROTECT!
GONZO...?

"AND NOW, KIDS, GET READY FOR--**GONZO!**"

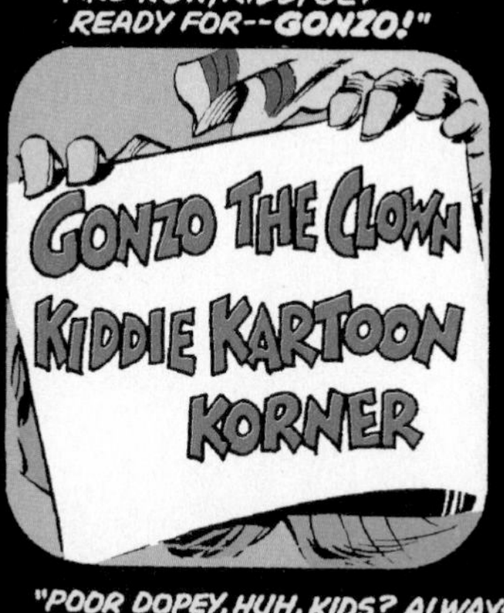

"FEATURING YOUR FAVORITE FEATHER-BRAIN--**DOPEY DUCK!**"

"POOR DOPEY, HUH, KIDS? ALWAYS GETTING HIT WITH THOSE **PIES!** ISN'T HE **FUNNY?**"

"NOT **HALF** AS FUNNY AS **YOU'RE** GONNA BE WITHOUT **TEETH,** YA TURKEY!!"

"**HEY**--**WHA'**--**AAAGH!**--

PLEASE STAND BY KIDS

"**HALP!** THIS DWARF'S TRYING TO **KILL ME!**"

YAY! ATTA WAY, DOPEY! BEAT THE LIVING **SPIT** OUTTA THAT MEALY-MOUTHED CLOWN!

HEY, NO **FAIR!** WATCH OUT, DOPEY! THE GUY WITH THE **BEARD'S** SNEAKIN' UP ON YA!

HEE-HEE. HEE-HEE. HEE-HEE.

LOOKIT! GONZO'S GOT A **NOSEBLEED!**

-HEH HEH- OKAY, DOPEY--FUN'S FUN--BUT YOU DON'T WANT TO HURT GONZO, DO YOU?
RRRIP
TAKE YER PAWS OFF ME, YA BIG GOON--!
THWIP
YEAH, YA BIG GOON--LET 'IM GO!
YEAH! WE WANNA SEE GONZA GET IT!
SPLAT
HEH HEH AW, KIDS--Y-YOU DON'T MEAN THAT--?

IF THIS'S THE STANDARD INTELLECTUAL CALIBER OF THE ENTERTAINMENT YOU FEED 'EM, FUZZY--I BET THEY DO.
ANYWAY, I GOTTA SPLIT.
BUT IF I WERE YOU, I'D SEIZE THIS OPPORTUNITY TO MEET YOUR CRITICS. YA MIGHT LEARN SOMETHING.

OUTSIDE...
SWELL! SO I ESCAPED WITH MY DIGNITY AND DID MY BIT IN THE CRUSADE TO IMPROVE CHILDREN'S TV...!
BIG DEAL!

E-Z CREDIT-APPLIA
I'M STILL FLAT BROKE...
...AND NOT EXACTLY BESIEGED WITH OFFERS OF EMPLOYMENT.

I DUNNO...I GUESS SOMETIMES YA JUST GOTTA SETTLE FOR THE PERSONAL SATISFACTION OF A JOB WELL DONE!
RIGHT, KIDS?

SUDDENLY, A GRUFF WHISKEY VOICE INTRUDES ON THE DUCK'S REVERIE...
HEY--AIN'T YOU THE GUY--?
YEAH. SO WHAT?

SO CONGRATULATIONS, SHORTY! LEMME SHAKE YOUR HAND! YOU'RE MY KINDA MAN!
I AM...?
I BEEN WAITIN' TEN YEARS TO SEE THAT SHNOOK GET WHAT'S COMIN' TO 'IM! I HATE THAT CLOWN! HE AIN'T FUNNY!

YOU'RE PROB'LY OUT OF A JOB NOW, HUH?
WELL, LISSEN--ANYBODY MAKES A FOOL OUTTA GONZO CAN'T BE ALL BAD!
YOU GOT WORK WITH ME IF YOU WANT IT, PAL! COME ON IN!

REAL CUSHY POSITION I GOT IN MIND FOR YOU. YOU JUST DIAL THE PHONE--
--AND ASK PEOPLE NICELY TO KEEP UP WITH THEIR PAYMENTS.
OH, AND IN A RARE INSTANCE, IT MIGHT BE NECESSARY TO CALL ON A CUSTOMER AT HOME.
YOU KNOW HOW IT IS--SOME PEOPLE JUST HAVETA BE REMINDED TO BE HONEST. SIGH

OKAY, NOW THIS IS OUR "SLOW-PAY" FILE.
YOU START AT THE FRONT AND KEEP CALLIN' 'TIL YOU GET TO THE BACK. SIMPLE, RIGHT?

YOU CAN START RIGHT NOW, GUY.
I'M GONNA WAIT ON THE SWEET YOUNG THING JUST STROLLED IN.
PROB'LY "JUST LOOKING"--THAT TYPE ALWAYS IS. SO I FIGGER I'LL "JUST LOOK" AT HER! WHY NOT, HUH?

OKAY, SO THE BOSS LEANS A LITTLE TO THE SLIMEY SIDE--YOUR BASIC SELF-MADE RETAILER.
BOO BOO BEE
SO WHAT? IT'S A JOB... AND IT LOOKS TO BE A CINCH.

HEL-LO, I'M CALLING FOR THE E-Z CREDIT APPLIANCE COMPANY, MRS. ADLER.
ACCORDING TO OUR RECORDS, YOU'RE TWO MONTHS IN ARREARS ON--

MRS. ADLER--WHAT?--NO--HEY, I DIDN'T--
ULP DON'T CRY--!
SOMETHIN' SMELLS FISHY AROUND HERE.

AND I'M GONNA FIND OUT WHAT IT IS!

SHORTLY...
NOT EXACTLY ANYBODY'S IDEA OF XANADU, IS IT? HOPE I GOT THE RIGHT ADDRESS.
SOMEHOW, I CAN'T PICTURE THE FOLKS WHO LIVE IN THIS DUMP AS SLAVES TO CONSPICUOUS CONSUMPTION.

YOU'D FIGURE THEY'D HANG ONTA THEIR DOUGH FOR FOOD...OR HOME IMPROVEMENTS...
KNOCK
KNOCK
...INSTEAD O' BLOWIN' IT ON A DELUXE MAHOGANY CABINET 27-INCH CONSOLE COLOR TV!

YES? OH--!!
HI. I'M FROM THE E-Z CREDIT--
Y--YOU'RE --A DUCK!!
RIGHT. A DUCK FROM THE E-Z CREDIT APPLIANCE STORE.

I...SUPPOSE YOU'VE COME TO REPOSSESS THE TV?
NAH! I JUST GOTTA COLLECT THE $59.50 IN BACK PAYMENTS YOU OWE.
GUESS YOU'LL **HAVETA** TAKE THE SET, THEN. I AIN'T GOT THE MONEY.
HOPE YOU CAN EXPLAIN IT TO **THEM.**
WAAUGH UH, LOOK... I **REALIZE** IT'S NONE O' MY BUSINESS, BUT... WHY'D YA **BUY** THE THING, IF--
I MEAN... WITH YOUR CIRCUMSTANCES SO **TIGHT,** AN' ALL?
I **DIDN'T** BUY IT--**BOBBY** DID. HE'S MY **HUSBAND**--WHO I AIN'T **SEEN** FOR A YEAR AND A HALF.
HE BELIEVED THE **ADS,** Y'KNOW? "COLOR TV FOR 50¢ A DAY"?

THEY DON'T **TELL** YOU IT'S FOR **FIVE YEARS**...OR THAT A $400 SET WINDS UP COSTIN' **$900...**
...OR THAT THE SET WON'T **LAST** THE FIVE YEARS YOU'RE PAYIN' ON IT...
...OR THAT IT'S SOME CHEAPIE **OFF-BRAND...**

...AND THE **REPAIRS** RUN TO SIXTY, SEVENTY DOLLARS A YEAR, AN' IT ONLY GUARANTEED FOR **NINETY DAYS!**
I BEEN KEEPIN' UP THE PAY-MENTS ALL THIS TIME...'CAUSE THE **KIDS** LOVE IT SO MUCH.
STOP IT, LADY--YOU'RE TEARIN' MY **HEART** OUT!

JUST KEEP THE TV. FORGET WHAT I SAID.
FORGET YOU EVER SAW ME.
BUT--

NO "BUTS" ABOUT IT, LADY. IT'S ON THE HOUSE.
I PAID FOR IT WITH MY JOB.

LATER...
NO KIDDIN', BEV-- ANOTHER SECOND AN' I'D'VE BEEN BAWLIN'!
I TRIED-- HONEST! BUT BOTH JOBS WERE SO DEMEANING--!
AT LEAST I MADE US DINNER MONEY MODELING TODAY.

YEAH, BUT WE CAN'T GO ON LIVIN' HAND-TO-BEAK LIKE THIS!
I GOTTA FIND SOMETHING STEADY --AN' LEGIT!
TWAP

I BET IT'S YOUR MALE EGO THAT'S BRUISED, NOT YOUR SENSE OF DECENCY. YOU MEN ARE ALL ALIKE.
CAN'T STAND HAVING A WOMAN SUPPORT YA, CAN YA?
OKAY, SO FLIP THROUGH THE WANT ADS! SEE WHAT YOU CAN SCROUNGE UP.

THANKS. I WILL...
CLEV
...AFTER I SKIM THE NEWS, IF THAT'S PERMISSIBLE. I'M JUST A LITTLE FED UP WITH--
WELL...!

WELL, WELL, WELL!
FORGET THE WANT ADS, TOOTS!

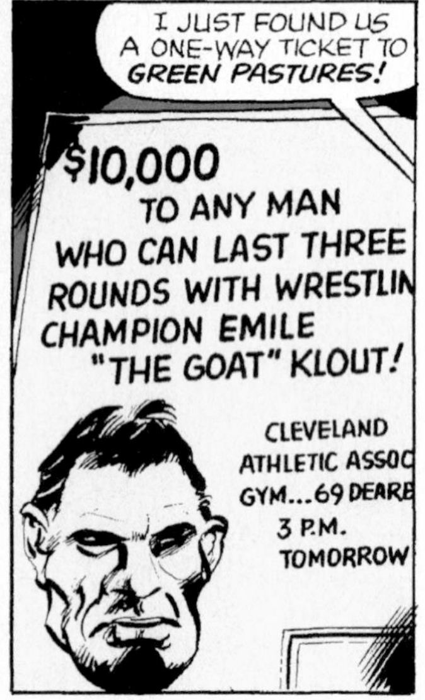
I JUST FOUND US A ONE-WAY TICKET TO GREEN PASTURES!
$10,000
TO ANY MAN
WHO CAN LAST THREE
ROUNDS WITH WRESTLIN
CHAMPION EMILE
"THE GOAT" KLOUT!
CLEVELAND
ATHLETIC ASSOC
GYM...69 DEARB
3 P.M.
TOMORROW

BEVERLY SWITZLER GASPS: "A CEMETERY PLOT, YOU MEAN! I'VE SEEN THAT BRUTE WRESTLE ON TV. THEY CALL HIM 'THE GOAT' BECAUSE HE CHEWS UP HIS OPPONENTS! EVEN HOWARD COSELL IS SCARED OF HIM!"
"YEAH? WELL, HOWARD THE DUCK ISN'T! SO THERE!
"TOMORROW, TOOTS, WE'RE GONNA BE SITTIN' PRETTY ON TEN GRAND!"
AND FURTHERMORE, WHEN THIS MATCH IS OVER--

YOU 'N' ME ARE GONNA BLOW THIS TOWN, SISTER!
CLEVELAND IS TOO SMALL-TIME FOR US--THE STICKS, THE BOONIES!

I THINK IT'S TIME WE GOT A TASTE OF THE BIG CITY-- AND ON $10,000 WE CAN DO IT WITH PANACHE! I--
YOU!!
I KNEW WE SHOULD'A TOOK A TAXI.
IT'S HER, ISN'T IT-- THE KIDNEY LADY!*
I SAW WHAT YOU DID TO GONZO YESTERDAY-- YOU BEAST!
I SAW YOU HUMILIATE THAT WHOLESOME SYMBOL OF FUN AND NICENESS BEFORE ALL THE KIDDIES WHO ADORE HIM!
*WHOM WE FIRST MET IN HTD #2.--A.G.

THAT'S YOUR WAY, ISN'T IT--YOUR SUBTLE SCHEME TO SYSTEMATICALLY SUBVERT OUR SYSTEM OF VALUES!
CALL'ER OFF, BEV. I WANNA SAVE MYSELF FOR THE RING.
WELL-- ISN'T IT-- KIDNEY THIEF??

REALLY, MA'AM, HE'S NOT IN THE MOOD TO...
HIS KIND IS NEVER IN THE MOOD TO TALK TRUTH AND RIGHTEOUSNESS!
YOU FOOLISH LITTLE GIRL! DON'T YOU KNOW HE'S ONLY AFTER YOUR KIDNEYS!?

C'MON, DUCKY-- THIS'S OUR STOP.
YOU WON'T ESCAPE BY GETTING OFF THIS BUS! I'M ONTO YOU!
YOU'RE THE OVER-ALL HEAD OF THE MASSIVE INTERNA-TIONAL KIDNEY-POISONING CONSPIRACY!
YOU WAIT AND SEE--SOON I'LL HAVE PROOF!

WHAT IS IT WITH ME, BEV? WHY AM I A MAG-NET FOR EVERY WEIRDO--?
AH-AH! NO INTROSPECTION 'TIL AFTER THE MATCH!
GYM

INSIDE THE GYM...
WELL, LOOK WHAT JUST WIGGLED IN!
YOU LIKE RASSLIN', DO YA, SWEETIE?
UH-HUH. AND I'M GOOD AT IT, SEE?
SO BUG OFF BEFORE I BREAK YOUR ARM!
EH...PARK YOUR BOD, BEV. I'M GONNA SLIP INTA MY FIGHTIN' TOGS.

BEV NODS AND DANCES LIGHTLY OVER A ROW OF WING-TIPPED FEET TO AN UNOCCUPIED SEAT.
ONLY THEN, SAFELY EN-SCONCED AS JUST ANOTHER SPECTATOR...
...DOES SHE GLANCE TOWARD THE RING.

ON BEV'S TELEVISION SCREEN, EMILE KLOUT APPEARED FORMIDABLE INDEED. IN THE FLESH, HIS MOUNTAINOUS MUS-CULATURE GLISTENING WITH SWEAT, HIS FELL FACE FAIRLY RADIATING CRUELTY, HE IS NOTHING SHORT OF MONSTROUS.
OH, MY GOD...!

ONE BY ONE, CONTENDERS ENTER THE RING.
ONE BY ONE, THEY ARE CARRIED OUT.
IN A MATCH LASTING 37 SECONDS--THE WINNER--EMILE "THE GOAT" KLOUT!
THROUGH IT ALL, "THE GOAT" SPEAKS NOT A WORD.
MUNNGH
HE GRUNTS, SNORTS, ROARS, BLEATS...!
HIS ENTIRE VOCABULARY SEEMS TO CONSIST OF INARTICULATE CREATURE SOUNDS.
SNNNF
BAA-HAHA
BUT HE WINS. OVER AND OVER AGAIN, HE WINS.
AND WHEN HE ISSUES HIS FINAL CHALLENGE...
THUMP
THUMP
...THERE'S NOT A TAKER IN THE HOUSE.

EXCEPT ONE.
DON'T TAKE YER BOWS YET, GRUESOME.
YOU BET YOUR SWEET CHEST-HAIRS YOU GOT AN OPPONENT!
HECCH
...BY THE RULES OF THE OHIO STATE PINOCHLE COMMISSION, NO HITTING BELOW THE KNEES!
BONG
NOW, GET TO YOUR CORNERS AND WHEN THE BELL RINGS-- KILL!!
I'LL TRY AN' MAKE THIS PAINLESS AS POSSIBLE, EMILE.
SEE, I KNOW, QUAK-FU!
THE GOAT CHORTLES.
THE DUCK QUICKLY LEARNS WHY.
FANCY DANCING IS OF LITTLE USE AGAINST A FOE WHOSE PROFESSION IS WITHSTANDING PAIN.
INFURIATED BY THE FOWL'S ELUSIVENESS, BUT UNIMPAIRED BY HIS BLOW, THE GOAT CHARGES!
THE DUCK SIDESTEPS.
CRASH
CRIPES, HE'S ALREADY GETTING UP!
HE CAN STAND AROUND AN' TAKE THIS FOREVER--'TIL I'M ALL TUCKERED OUT!

NEXT: THE SECRET HOUSE OF FORBIDDEN COOKIES!

HOWARD THE DUCK

MARVEL COMICS GROUP™

APPROVED BY THE COMICS CODE AUTHORITY

30¢ 6 NOV 02415

TRAPPED IN A WORLD HE NEVER MADE!

HOWARD THE DUCK™

THE SECRET OF THE CELLAR SINISTER!

THERE ARE SOME THINGS THAT MAN--AND DUCK--WERE NOT **MEANT** TO KNOW!

From the time of his hatching, he was...different. A potentially brilliant scholar who dreaded the structured environment of school, he educated himself in the streets, taking whatever work was available, formulating his philosophy of self from what he learned of the world about him. And then the Cosmic Axis shifted...and that world *changed.* Suddenly, he was stranded in a universe he could not fathom. Without warning, he became a strange fowl in an even stranger land.

STEVE GERBER. WRITER
GENE COLAN. ARTIST
STEVE LEIALOHA. INKER
JOHN COSTANZA, letterer
GLYNIS WEIN colorist
ARCHIE GOODWIN EDITOR

A LONELY HIGHWAY IN PENNSYLVANIA MOUNTAIN COUNTRY, LATE ONE STORMY NIGHT. CRAZES OF CRACKLING ELECTRICITY GERRYMANDER THE SKY. THUNDER ECHOES DULLY OFF THE SIDES OF ANCIENT HILLS.
AND TWO CIRCLES OF LIGHT CREEP WARILY THROUGH THE ALL-ENSHROUDING FOG.

STEERING THOSE TWIN MOONS ON THEIR COURSE IS JOE MOUNTBATTEN, REGIONAL SALES MANAGER OF RUBBERCORP INTERNATIONAL...
...HEADED HOME FROM THE AMERICAN BALL MANUFACTURERS ASSOCIATION CONVENTION IN DAYTON, WHERE EARLIER TONIGHT HE CLOSED A MILLION-DOLLAR DEAL.

SADLY, HIS MIND IS ON HIS TRIUMPH, NOT ON THE BALL. AND THUS, HE IS TOTALLY UNPREPARED...
oh my god...

...FOR THE MIND-NUMBING SIGHT THAT SPRINGS INTO VIEW AS HE ROUNDS THE NEXT BEND!

HIS HEART GOES OUT TO THE LADY IN DISTRESS...

...TO HER BARE, FRAGILE SHOULDERS, BEATEN AND BATTERED BY THE UNCARING ELEMENTS... TO HER PLEADING EYES AND WIND-RAVAGED HAIR... BUT HIS SYMPATHY HITS A SNAG AT THE WEIRD CREATURE BY HER SIDE.

IT--IT'S HIDEOUS--INHUMAN--NOT A MAN AT ALL--IT'S SOME MONSTROUS KIND OF--

THE SECRET HOUSE OF FORBIDDEN COOKIES!

DUCK!! HE'S COMIN' RIGHT AT US!!
HE :GLUP: LOST CONTROL OF THE WHEEL! HE--
SCR
EEEEEF
SQUISHHH

"LOST CONTROL" MY FOOT! HE WAS TRYIN' TA KILL US!!
C'MON BACK AN' FIGHT, YA--
OH, SAVE YOUR BREATH-- OR AT LEAST SQUAWK SOME-THING ORIGINAL, WILLYA?
HE CAN'T HEAR YOU-- SO THE LEAST YOU COULD DO IS ENTER-TAIN ME--

--'CAUSE, MAN, THIS IS ALL YOUR FAULT!!
WE'VE HITCHHIKED ALL THIS WAY FROM MY WARM APART-MENT IN CLEVE-LAND--
AW, BEV--
--ONLY TO WIND UP HUNDREDS OF MILES FROM NOWHERE--

--ALL BECAUSE YOU WOULDN'T PUT OUT YOUR BLASTED CIGAR TO APPEASE OUR LAST DRIVER!

A LOTTA GOOD IT DIDJA, HUH?
HERE!!
THWIP
HOPE YOU'RE HAPPY!

'CAUSE :SOB: THAT MAKES ONE OF US.
:SOB: 'CAUSE I'M NOT HAPPY AT ALL! :WAAAAA:
AW, NUTS!

DON'T CRY, TOOTS. SOMEBODY'S BOUND TO COME ALONG.
EVERYTHING'LL BE ALL RIGHT. YOU'LL SEE.
NO, I WON'T. NO I WON'T!
NOBODY'LL EVER COME ALONG!

NOBODY'LL EVER USE THIS ROAD AGAIN!
OWWAAUGH
WUMP
WE'LL BE FORGOTTEN! WE'LL HAVE TO EAT EACH OTHER TO SURVIVE!

I MEAN--THAT'D BE UNDERSTANDABLE IN THE ANDES, HOWARD--BUT NOT IN THE POCONOS!
NO WAY IN THE POCONOS!

SO I'M--I'M LEAVING YOU, DUCKY. OUR PARTNERSHIP JUST SORTA DISSOLVED. GET IT?
NAH--YOU PROB'LY DON'T. DUCKS LIKE THIS KIND OF WEATHER, DON'T THEY?
WELL, ANYWAY... THIS IS GOOD-BYE.

IT'S BEEN FUN-- BUT I CAN'T TOLERATE YOUR STUBBORNNESS OR YOUR PETTY FITS OF RAGE ANYMORE!

S-SURE. SHUCKS, IF THIS'S WHAT YA REALLY WANT. I CAN'T DENY I'M HELL TO LIVE WITH...
...SO I WON'T TRY TO STOP YA. I'LL JUST WAVE "ADIEU"... AFTER ALL, WE'RE BOTH MATURE ADULTS...
BEV!!
YEAH? NOW WHADDAYA WANT?

NOTHIN'.
FERGIT IT.

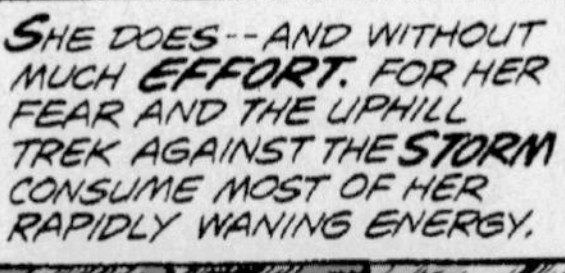
SHE DOES--AND WITHOUT MUCH EFFORT. FOR HER FEAR AND THE UPHILL TREK AGAINST THE STORM CONSUME MOST OF HER RAPIDLY WANING ENERGY.

SHE TRUDGES ON FOR HOURS, THOUGH, ON SHEER DETERMINATION, DEEPER INTO THE ENVELOPING BLACKNESS...
IDLE HANDS
2 MILES
...WITH NO HAVEN IN SIGHT...

...UNTIL THE SKY DETONATES WITH A BRISANCE OF THUNDER AND A BRILLIANT FLASH OF LIGHT...
CRRRAACKKKK
...WHICH MOMENTARILY LIMNS THE OUTLINE...
...OF A LOWERING, BROODING VICTORIAN MANSION. BUT OF COURSE IT MUST BE DESERTED, SHE ASSUMES. PERHAPS SHE EVEN HOPES IT IS SO.

BUT--NO.
A LIGHT BURNS IN THE TOP-MOST TOWER WINDOW.

AND SO BEVERLY SWITZLER SIMPLY SETS ASIDE HER INSTINCTIVE CAUTION...
...AND HEEDS INSTEAD HER INSTINCT FOR SELF-PRESERVATION.

KNOCK
KNOCK
HELLO, IN THERE! ANYBODY HOME?
HOLDING HER BREATH INVOLUNTARILY, SHE WAITS. THE SECONDS DRAG.

UNTIL, AT LAST, THE DOOR CREAKS OPEN TO REVEAL...
WHO'S THERE?
H-HELLO--I'M BEVERLY SW--

OH, YES. YOU MUST BE THE NEW GOVERNESS.

NEW GOV--?
OH, HECK-- WHY NOT? ANYTHING THAT'LL GET ME IN THE DOOR!

HOURS LATER, THE DAWN BREAKS... AND WITH IT, THE STORM.
BORNE ON THE GENTLE WIND OUT OF THE WEST, THE DARK CLOUDS SCUD ACROSS THE SKY...
...ALLOWING SHAFTS OF GOLDEN SUNLIGHT ACCESS TO THE EARTH.

THAT SAME SOFT BREEZE ALSO PARTS THE LEAVES OF THE TREES, PERMITTING THE TOASTY WARMTH TO PENETRATE TO THE GROUND...
...WHERE HOWARD, NESTLED ON A BED OF GRASS IN THE WOODS NEAR THE ROADSIDE...

...STIRS AWAKE AT THE SOUND OF APPROACHING FOOTSTEPS AND EXCITED VOICES.
GOLLY! LOOK AT THAT!
WHAT IS IT?
IT'S A BIRD-- LOOK AT THE FEATHERS!
GOSH! IS IT DEAD?
I DUNNO!

WOW-- MUST BE AN EAGLE, FROM THE SIZE OF IT!
AN EAGLE? WITH WEBBED FEET?
UH-OH!

JEEPERS! IT'S MOVING!
IT IS-- IT'S ALIVE! AND IT'S GOT CLOTHES ON--AND IT'S A DUCK!

THE YOUNGSTERS STEP BACKWARD, CONFER IN WHISPERS...
...THE LAST DAYS...
...SATAN...
...REVELATIONS...
...KILL IT?

UH, LISTEN, GANG... I FARE MUCH BETTER AS A PARTICIPANT THAN AS A TOPIC IN CONVERSATION.
AAAGH IT TALKS!!

RUN AND DON'T LOOK BACK! WE'VE GOTTA TELL THE HOLY FATHER WHAT WE'VE SEEN-- AND HEARD!
HUH?

NOW WHAT BROUGHT THAT ON?
SURE, I'VE EVOKED SOME PRETTY VIOLENT REACTIONS FROM HAIRLESS APES ON OCCASION, BUT--!
THOSE PUNKS WEREN'T JUST SURPRISED.

THEY WERE SCARED HALF OUTTA THEIR BALD SKINS!
AN' I CAN'T AFFORD TO OFFEND ANYBODY WHO'S GOT WHEELS!
HEAVEN

THERE, MASTER! LURKING IN THE BRUSH! THERE IT IS! IT'S COMING!
SO I SEE. THANK YOU, WALLACE.
NOW REMAIN CALM. TRUST IN ME. WE HAVE NOTHING TO FEAR FROM SATAN.

GREETINGS, BEAST. I AM REV. JOON MOON YUC, SERVANT OF THE LORD.
AND THESE ARE MY DISCIPLES-- MY YUCCHIES.
YEAH, WELL-- I'M HOWARD THE DUCK--

--AN' THOSE'RE THE WOODS I SLEPT IN ALL LAST NIGHT.
FIGGER YOU COULD SPARE A LIFT?

I THINK... THE LORD WILLS OTHERWISE, FOWL--DON'T YOU?
ACTUALLY, WE HAVEN'T SPOKEN RECENTLY.
I DO NOT HAVE TO ASK! MY WORD IS AS THE LORD'S!
GATHER 'ROUND ME, MY YUCCHIES!
WHY DON'TCHA BUZZ 'IM AN' ASK?
THIS DEVIL-DUCK HAS BEEN SENT TO TEST YOUR FAITH! SHIELD YOUR EYES WITH YOUR GOOD BOOKS--AND JOIN ME IN PRAYER!
TOGETHER, WE SHALL PREVAIL UPON THE LORD--
GULP
--TO STRIKE THIS CREATURE DEAD WITH A BOLT FROM HEAVEN!
LET US PRAY. HEAVENLY FATHER WHO DELIVERED THESE INNOCENT HEARTS AND MINDS INTO MY HANDS, WE BESEECH THEE TO--EH?
WHEEEHEEHEEH
BAM
THAT RUMBLE--LIKE GATHERING THUNDER! BUT I HAVEN'T EVEN FINISHED--
WAAUGH I DO NOT BELIEVE THIS--THE CAVALRY TO THE RESCUE!
AND NONE TOO SOON.
AND YET, THE DUCK'S UNEASE REFUSES TO SUBSIDE.
PERHAPS IT'S BECAUSE THE HORSEMAN'S GARB MORE RESEMBLES THAT OF A HIGHWAYMAN THAN A SOLDIER. OR PERHAPS IT'S THE SLIGHTLY MANIACAL GLINT IN THE STRANGER'S RIGHT EYE. OR MAYBE IT'S JUST DUE TO A LONGSTANDING AESTHETIC PREJUDICE AGAINST OVERLY MELODRAMATIC ENTRANCES.

WHICHEVER, HOWARD MAINTAINS HIS GUARD...!
HOPE I'M NOT INTERRUPTING ANYTHING, FOLKS.

IT'S NOT MY HABIT TO BARGE IN THIS WAY...
...BUT MY PRESENT MISSION IS OF UTMOST URGENCY.
MY CARD, SIR.

WAAAUGH! YOU'RE A REAL ESTATE BROKER??
SEVEN GABLES REALT
CORP. &
ALL NITE KEY GRINDING SERVICE
SPECIALIZING IN
DECAYING VICTORIAN
MANSIONS OF
PERNICIOUS REPUTE
Heathcliff Rochester
agent
I FAVOR THE TERM "LIFESTYLE CONSULTANT."

BUT WE'VE NO TIME TO WASTE OVER SEMANTICS, MY FRIEND... NOT IF YOU'RE STILL INTENT UPON SECURING THE DRAGONWORTH PROPERTY.
THE TOWNSPEOPLE ARE UP IN ARMS ABOUT HAVING YOUR... UNCONVENTIONAL RELIGIOUS CULT AT SUCH CLOSE PROXIMITY.
MY--?

I'M UNDER STRICT ORDERS FROM MY CHIEF AT SEVEN GABLES TO UNLOAD THIS ONE FAST.
DESPITE OUR UNUSUAL AREA OF SPECIALIZATION, WE ARE NOT ENAMORED OF, SHALL WE SAY... CONTROVERSY?
IT'S PREMIUM PROPERTY... BUT YOU CAN SNATCH IT UP FOR A SONG... IF YOU HUSTLE.

WHAT SAY YOU--
--REVEREND DUCK?
REV--? OH!! WELL!

I KNEW WE'D SEE EYE-TO-EYE, SIR!
WEEEE HEH
LET US HIE TO THE PROPERTY AT ONCE, THEN, EH?
YOU'RE CALLIN' THE SHOTS, PAL.
NO! WAIT!!

YOU'RE MAKING A TERRIBLE MIS-TAKE! IT'S "REVEREND YUC!"
YUC, DO YOU HEAR? YUC! YUC!!
I'M THE SECOND COMING! HE'S JUST A STUPID DUCK!!

MEANWHILE, IN THE BREAKFAST NOOK AT DRAGONWORTH...
THANK YOU FOR WAKING UP TO MAKE ME BREAKFAST, BEV.
BEV?
IS SOMETHING WRONG? DON'T YOU LIKE IT HERE, BEV?
BEV?!?

OH, NO. IT'S REALLY... COZY.
I WAS JUST LOOKING AT THE FAMILY PORTRAITS...
...LOOKING AT ME.

THAT'S GRANDMA. SHE'S DEAD.
THE TOWNS-PEOPLE STONED HER. IT HAP-PENED LAST WEEK.

YOU'LL HAVE TO SPEAK UP, PATSY! I CAN BARELY HEAR YOU DOWN HERE!
HOW ARE YOUR CORN FLAKES, DEAR?

SOGGY. I DON'T THINK YOU'RE GONNA CUT IT AS A GOVERNESS, BEV.
YOU EVER TACKLE THIS KIND OF WORK BEFORE?

NAH. I WAS AN ARTISTS' MODEL.
HEY--YOU LIVE ALONE IN THIS PLACE? I HAVEN'T SEEN ANY-BODY ELSE SINCE--

C'MON-- I'M ONLY A KID! YOU THINK THEY'D JUST LET ME TAKE CARE OF MYSELF?
MY INSANE MOTHER LIVES HERE WITH ME.
I TAKE CARE OF HER TOO.
OH, YES-- SHE DOES-- CRUELLY!

SHE NEVER LEARNS-- ONLY TEACHES.
ANYWAY, I FELT YOU SHOULD KNOW, PATSY--
THEY'RE COMING AGAIN.

THE TOWNSPEOPLE ARE COMING TO EAT YOU, MY DARLING DAUGHTER!
WHAAT? LET ME SEE!

GOSH, PATSY-- THE WHOLE TOWN'S COMING UP THE HILL!
IT'S LIKE A SCENE OUT OF "FRANKENSTEIN"-- WITH A FEW CONTEMPORARY TOUCHES.
KILL!
WRECK!
RAZE!
DESTROY!
EAT!

WHAT'RE WE GONNA DO?
OH, DON'T WORRY. THIS HAPPENS ONCE A WEEK LIKE CLOCKWORK.

HEATHCLIFF WILL DRIVE THEM AWAY.
HEATHCLIFF?!?
UH-HUH. WITH THE HOUNDS.
AROOW
RUFF
ARF

AW, FUDGE! IT'S THEM DRATTED, DAD-BLAMED DAWGS AGIN!
SOMEBODY TELL ARNIE T'GIT HIS BUTT UP HERE WITH THAT FLAME-THROWER!
HE WON'T BURN DOGS--ONLY PEOPLE!
HE LIKES DOGS.

BAM
TURN BACK, YE PROVINCIAL SWINE!
THIS ACREAGE IS ZONED RESIDENTIAL! I'LL NOT LET YOU TURN IT INTO A WHOLESALE SLAUGHTER-HOUSE!

WAAAUGH BETWEEN THE MIXED METAPHORS AND THE WORN-OUT SHOCKS ON THIS NAG-- I'M RATTLING TO PIECES!
C-COULDJA TAKE IT A LITTLE EASIER, CLIFFY? HUH? Y'THINK?

AN' WHILE YOU'RE AT IT, YOU MIGHT EXPLAIN--
BEV!!
INCONGRUITY UPON INCONGRUITY! THE FAMILIAR FACE AMID THE CHAOS IS THE FINAL STRAW!

HOWARD COMES UNGLUED.

WAAUGH
THUMP
OH WOW, HERE COMES THE NEAT PART, BEV! THE DOGS ARE CIRCLING BACK FOR THE KILL!
AND SO IT IS THAT BEFORE THE DUCK'S DIGNITY--LET ALONE HIS TAIL--CAN RECOVER...

HE IS TRAMPLED, DRAGGED THROUGH THE DIRT ONCE MORE...
IT'S TIMES LIKE THIS... I WISHED I'D BEEN RAISED A STOIC.
AT LEAST THEN, I WOULDN'T HAVE THE URGE TO SCREAM WHEN I'M UNABLE.

LOGICALLY, THOUGH, I SHOULD BE MORE CONCERNED THAT SUCH AN INANE THOUGHT WOULD EVEN CROSS MY MIND.
COULD IT BE? I MEAN, I REALIZE "SANITY" IS DEFINED RELATIVISTIC-ALLY--
HOWARD, ARE YOU OKAY? THE COAST IS CLEAR. THE TOWNSPEOPLE HAVE BEEN ROUTED!
--BUT TAKE MY RELATIONSHIP WITH BEVERLY AS A PRIME EXAMPLE.
TALK ABOUT EVIDENCE OF MENTAL IMBALANCE!

WAITAMINIT... WE'RE NOT SUPPOSED TO BE SPEAKING, ARE WE?
WHY?

WHY SHOULD I CARE IF I NEVER SEE HER AGAIN? WHAT POSSIBLE MUTUAL ATTRACTION COULD RATIONALLY EXIST BETWEEN A DUCK AND--THAT?
IT DEFIES EVERY LAW OF NATURE.
OF COURSE, I'M NOT INFLEXIBLE. I MIGHT BE PERSUADED... OR CHARMED...

ON THE OTHER HAND, I'VE NEVER FELT CONSTRAINED TO FOLLOW CONVENTION!
WHAT THE HECK. I GUESS IT'S DESTINY, TOOTS!

HOW COULD THIS BE WRONG--OR INSANE--WHEN IT FEELS SO GOOD?
Y'KNOW, DUCKY... I'M ASHAMED TO ADMIT THIS...

...BUT I MISSED YOU. I ALWAYS CONSIDERED MYSELF SO SELF-SUFFICIENT, BUT...
YEAH. I KNOW HOW IT GOES. LOVE IS STRANGE, AN ALL THAT!
BLOOP

WE BETTER SAVE THIS PERSONAL STUFF FOR LATER, THOUGH... IN PRIVATE.
RIGHT NOW, I'D APPRECIATE THE COWDOWN ON WHAT'S HAPPENING HERE...
AS NEAR AS I CAN FIGURE, WE'VE HITCH-HIKED INTO A CROSS BETWEEN "FRANKENSTEIN" AND "JANE EYRE"
NOT TO MENTION "BETTER HOMES & GARDENS"...
...AND "KING OF KINGS"! OR HAVEN'T YOU MET CLIFFY AND JOON YET?
WANNA BUY THIS DUMP?

HELLO, I'M PATSY'S MOTHER, THE MAD-WOMAN.
IT'S OKAY, HOWARD. SHE'S HARM-LESS.

OH, YES! I JUST LIKE TO PLAY!
AND YOU LOOK LIKE YOU'D BE LOTSA FUN TO PLAY WITH--ALSO UPON!
YEAH?

RIPE ON! COME IN! CHEW THE FAT! CHOMP THE CORN FLAKES!
WATCH ME MAKE A FUNNY NECK!
:WAAAUGH:

KEEP YOUR DISTANCE, LADY--OKAY? YOU BOTHER ME.
AW! BUT I LIKE TO PLAY UP CLOSE!

WELL! LOOK WHO'S HERE!
IT'S BEAN-SPILLING TIME, CLIFFY! MY SURVIVAL MAY DEPEND ON KNOWING WHAT RILED UP THOSE TURKEYS!
BUT OF COURSE, REVEREND.
SO TALK!
THE TOWNS-PEOPLE SUSPECT LITTLE PATSY HERE OF BEING SOME SORT OF... WITCH.

THAT'S WHY HER MOTHER HAS WISELY DECIDED TO MOVE OUT OF THIS CRUMBLING VICTORIAN MANSION...
...AND LEASE ANOTHER CRUMBLING VICTORIAN MANSE...FAR AWAY IN WISCONSIN.

GEE WHIZ, VILLAGERS ARE SUCH A DRAG!
THEY THINK I'M TRYING TO CREATE A MONSTER OR SOMETHING --JUST CAUSE MOM'S BRAIN'S BEEN WHITED OUT!
HECK, I'M NOT MAKIN' MONSTERS-- I'M JUST BAKIN' COOKIES!

AH, BUT THEY'RE GODLESS COOKIES, AREN'T THEY, LITTLE GIRL?
THAT'S WHY THE LORD SENT ME TO PURCHASE THIS HOUSE AND CONSECRATE IT AS MY SEMINARY--

--SO MY YUCCHIES AND I COULD EXORCISE THE EVIL FORCES YOU'VE QUARTERED HERE!
HMMM... SPEAKING FOR SEVEN GABLES--
--WE REALLY DON'T CARE WHO THE BUYER IS...
...SO LONG AS THE DOWN-PAYMENT IS SUFFICIENT AND WE GET FHA APPROVAL FOR FINANCING.
JEEPERS! ALL YOU GUYS EVER THINK ABOUT IS BUSINESS! WHAT ABOUT MY GOOD NAME?

I THINK PATSY IS A VERY GOOD NAME!
I PICKED IT, BUT MY MOTHER WOULDN'T LET ME KEEP IT, THE OLD CHESTNUT!
WELL, I THINK IT'S A GOOD NAME, TOO, SEE?!
SO FOLLOW ME-- ALL OF YOU--TO THE TOWER!

I'M SICK OF SEEING "PATSY" BESMIRCHED!
SO I'M GONNA PROVE TO YOU-- ONCE AND FOR ALL--THAT I'M REALLY JUST BAKING COOKIES!
UH, SWEET-HEART... THIS ISN'T EXACTLY A HOME EC LAB.
AND MUCH AS I DESPERATELY WANNA BELIEVE YOU--NO CHEF I EVER KNEW HADDA STRAP DOWN HIS PASTRIES.

TSK-TSK! I'M TELLING YOU--THIS WHOLE SET-UP IS NOTHING MORE THAN A GLORIFIED SUZY HOMEMAKER OVEN!
ALL THESE DIALS AND GAUGES ARE JUST ORNAMENTATION.
THE STUPID THING WOULDN'T EVEN WORK--

--WITHOUT THESE TWO "D" BATTERIES!
EVEREADY
ALL PURPOSE
EVEREADY
AND GRANDMA DIDN'T EVEN INCLUDE 'EM IN HER WILL!

I HADDA BUY 'EM MYSELF-- OUTTA MY PITTANCE OF AN ALLOWANCE!

OTHER KIDS GET PATTED ON THE HEAD FOR LEARNING THRIFT-- BUT NOT ME! I GET HASSLED BY DUMB VILLAGERS!!
PATSY, WAIT! WE BELIEVE YOU--HONEST!
BE A GOOD GIRL! DON'T--

NO!! YOU'RE LYING!!
YOU'RE SCARED OF ME-- JUST LIKE ALL THE OTHER IGNORANT, UNSCIENTIFIC RABBLE!
WELL, I'LL SHOW YOU!!
BANZAI!

FOR THREE LONG, AGONIZING MOMENTS, THE CHAMBER PULSATES WITH AN EERIE BLUISH GLOW. THE WALLS TREMBLE AND THE BASSO PROFUNDO RUMBLE OF MACHINERY.
AND THE COOKIE SHEET SHUDDERS.
HOWARD--I THINK IT'S OVER NOW...!
PATSY'S HEADED FOR THE TABLE!
RIGHT! FOR THE UNVEILING! SEE?
HERE'S WHAT YOU WERE AFRAID OF!
SON OF A CONTRACTOR...!
WH-WHAT IS IT?
A--A GIANT GINGERBREAD MAN!
HEAVING A FIVE-THROATED SIGH OF RELIEF, THE FOUR ADULTS AND ONE DUCK STAGGER TO THE DOOR...
...AND FIND IT LOCKED...
...WHILE FIVE YEASTY FINGERS...
...RISE UP ANGRY!
AGH
ARRR
WAAAUGH!
NEXT
"THE WAY THE COOKIE CRUMBLES!"
PLUS 2nd BIG LAFF RIOT!
"THE MANCHURIAN DUCK-- PART ONE!"

HOWARD THE DUCK

MARVEL COMICS GROUP™

APPROVED BY THE COMICS CODE AUTHORITY

30¢ 7 DEC 02415

TRAPPED IN A WORLD HE NEVER MADE!

HOWARD THE DUCK

TM

FROM THE OVEN... IT RISES!

ONLY ONE FIGHTING FOWL STANDS BETWEEN AN UNSUSPECTING WORLD AND... THE INCREDIBLE COOKIE CREATURE!

From the time of his hatching, he was...different. A potentially brilliant scholar who dreaded the structured environment of school, he educated himself in the streets, taking whatever work was available, formulating his philosophy of self from what he learned of the world about him. And then the Cosmic Axis shifted...and that world *changed.* Suddenly, he was stranded in a universe he could not fathom. Without warning, he became a strange fowl in an even stranger land.

Stan Lee PRESENTS: HOWARD THE DUCK!™

STEVE GERBER WRITER / **GENE COLAN** ILLUSTRATOR / **STEVE LEIALOHA** EMBELLISHER / **JIM NOVAK,** LETTERER **M. SEVERIN,** COLORIST / **ARCHIE GOODWIN** EDITOR

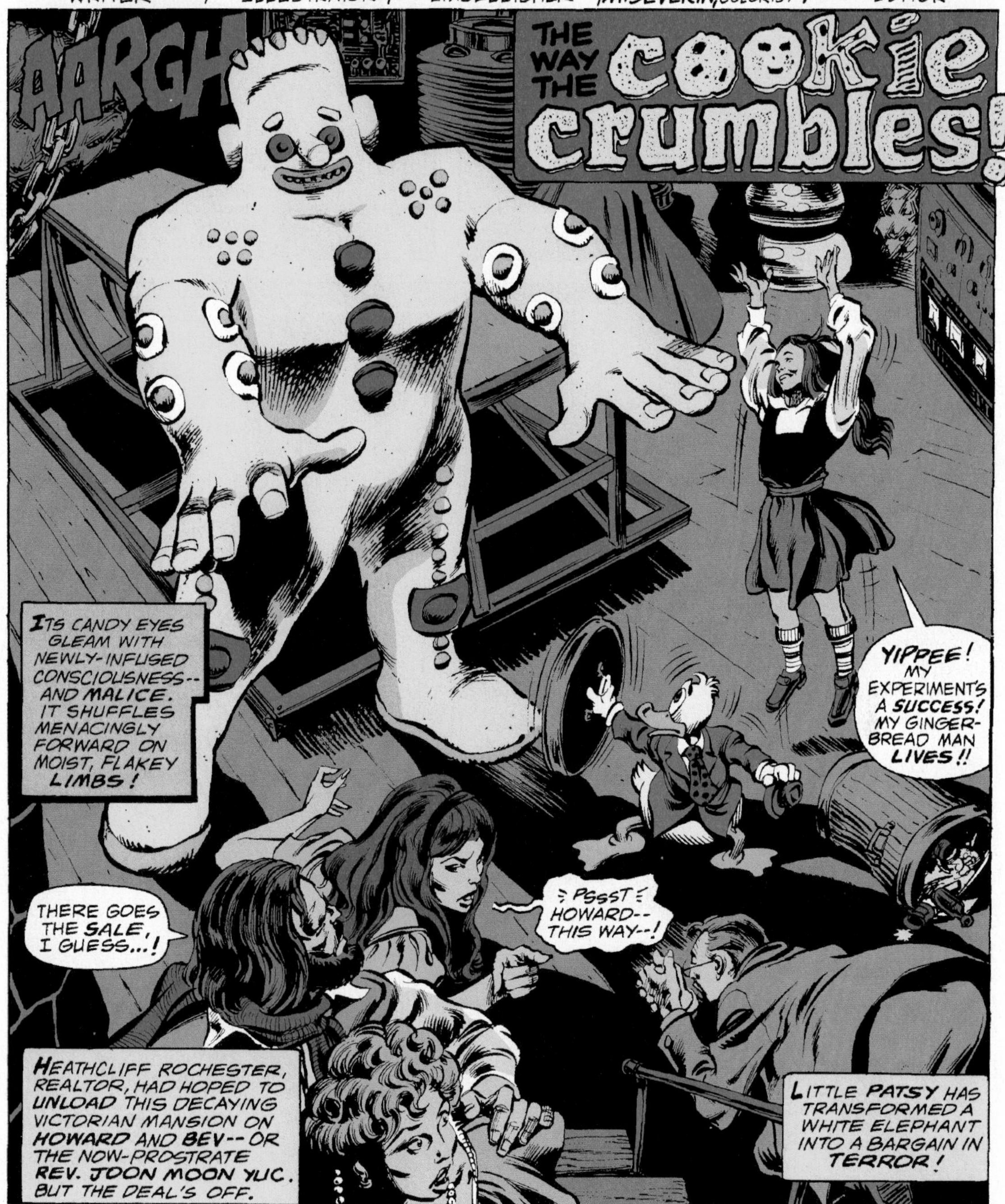

AARGH
THE WAY THE COOKIE CRUMBLES!
ITS CANDY EYES GLEAM WITH NEWLY-INFUSED CONSCIOUSNESS-- AND MALICE. IT SHUFFLES MENACINGLY FORWARD ON MOIST, FLAKEY LIMBS!
YIPPEE! MY EXPERIMENT'S A SUCCESS! MY GINGER-BREAD MAN LIVES!!
THERE GOES THE SALE, I GUESS...!
PSSST HOWARD-- THIS WAY--!
HEATHCLIFF ROCHESTER, REALTOR, HAD HOPED TO UNLOAD THIS DECAYING VICTORIAN MANSION ON HOWARD AND BEV--OR THE NOW-PROSTRATE REV. JOON MOON YUC. BUT THE DEAL'S OFF.
LITTLE PATSY HAS TRANSFORMED A WHITE ELEPHANT INTO A BARGAIN IN TERROR!

DON'T TRY TO FIGHT IT, DUCKY!
IT'S BIGGER THAN BOTH OF US! LET'S JUST SLIP QUIETLY OUT OF THE ROOM-- OUT OF THE HOUSE--
--OUT OF THE STATE OF PENNSYLVANIA!
I'M HOT ON YER HEELS, TOOTS. MARCH!

ULP! IT'S LOCKED! WE'RE TRAPPED!
OH, GOD! DO YOU KNOW WHAT THIS MEANS? DID YOU SEE THE LOOK IN THAT MONSTER'S EYES?
IT CRAVES REVENGE! IT WANTS TO DEVOUR US-- WITH MILK!!

WHAT A STUPID WAY TA DIE!
I MEAN-- WHO EVER GOT EATEN BY A COOKIE BEFORE?
I DUNNO ABOUT YOU, BUT I'M NOT ABOUT TO BECOME AN AFTERNOON SNACK FOR THIS CRUMB!

THE WAY I FIGURE IT--THE SOLUTION IS GROSS... BUT OBVIOUS.
IT CAN'T EAT US--

--IF WE EAT IT FIRST!!
CHOMP
CHOMP

GLUTTONOUS MOMENTS LATER, THE "SURGERY" IS COMPLETED.
ITS RIGHT LEG SEVERED BY THE FOWL'S RUTHLESSLY CHOMPING BEAK, THE MONSTER COOKIE TOTTERS... TIPS... TOPPLES INTO LITTLE PATSY'S JURY-RIGGED ELECTRICAL SYSTEM.
VROOOOM
=URP= OKAY, BEV! FOLLOW ME!
B-BUT, HOWARD, THIS EXIT LEADS TO THE TOWER!
=URP= RIGHT!
WE'RE GONNA MAKE OUR WAY CALMLY, UNHURRIEDLY. AN' WHEN WE GET THERE--
CRASH!
WE'RE GONNA JUMP FOR OUR LIVES!!

GOSH, HOWARD! YOU THINK PATSY AND THE OTHERS GOT OUT?
MAYBE. MAYBE NOT. BUT WE'RE NOT GOIN' BACK TO CHECK!
B-BUT, HOWARD-- SHE'S JUST A LITTLE GIRL!
UH-HUH... AN' ONLY SLIGHTLY HOMICIDAL!
NONE OF WHICH, UNFORTUNATELY, ALTERS THE FACT--
--THAT THIS JOINT IS GONNA BLOW ANY MINUTE!!!
SO HUSTLE YOUR TOESIES, SWEETS! AN' WHEN I TELL YA--
HIT THE DIRT!
BLAMMM

FOR A TIME THE GHASTLY RUMBLE OF THE EXPLOSION REVERBERATES OFF THE POCONO MOUNTAINSIDES-- A SONOROUS DEATH-BURP ECHOING INTO ETERNITY--
THEN, THE DIN SUBSIDES, THE SMOKE CLEARS TO REVEAL:
JUST DEBRIS. ≷SIGH≶ GUESS THE OTHERS GOT WASTED, HUH?
YUP. JET-PROPELLED ON THEIR WAY TO THAT BIG ASHTRAY IN THE SKY.

IT'S KIND OF A SHAME ABOUT POOR PATSY.
I DON'T THINK SHE MEANT TO HURT ANYBODY WITH HER EXPERIMENTS.

YEAH--WELL-- THAT'S EASY FOR YOU TO SAY.
YOU DIDN'T TASTE THE COOKIE!
PHWAAAUGH

PERSONALLY, I'M CONVINCED SHE WAS A 37-YEAR-OLD MIDGET-- AN ESCAPEE FROM SOME PENITENTIARY'S DEATH ROW--
--A HATE-DRIVEN, BLOODTHIRSTY, ANTI-SOCIAL DEVIANT-- A WARPED, CALLOUS, CALCULATING--
NAH, SHE WAS JUST A PRODUCT OF HER ENVIRONMENT. C'MON, LET'S HIKE TO THE NEXT GAS STATION.
WE'LL NEVER THUMB A RIDE LOOKING THIS GRIMY.
YOU FIGURE WE'LL HIT NEW YORK BY NOON? I WANTED TO TAKE A STROLL DOWN FIFTH AVENUE BEFORE--

CHAPTER II GET DOWN AMERICA!

NEW YORK, HALF PAST ONE:
--AND THEN HOWARD ATE OFF ITS LEG, AND WE ESCAPED.
ARE YOU REALLY DREYFUSS GULTCH?

IF MUH TRANSPORTATION AIN'T CONVINCED YUH, MA'AM, AH SHORE DON'T KNOW WHAT WILL.
IT'S JUST SO HARD TO BELIEVE!
D G
'76 TEXAS
D*G

NO TOUGHER 'N THAT YARN YOU JUST SPUN, HON.
NO, I MEAN-- WHAT'S A COUNTRY-WESTERN STAR DOING IN, UH, THESE PARTS?
I WAS JUST ASKIN' MYSELF THE SAME--

AH'M HERE BY INVITATION, SWEETHEART!
GONNA SING THE NATIONAL ANTHEM AT THE OPENIN' O' THE ALL-NIGHT NATIONAL CONVENTION.

THE WHAT?
WEST SIDE DRIVE
KEEP RIGHT
'76 TEXAS
D*G
THE ALL-NIGHT PARTY. Y'KNOW, LIKE THE DEMOCRATIC PARTY AN' THE REPUBLICAN PARTY?
THEY'RE HAVIN' THEIR GIT-TOGETHER IN NEW YORK TO PICK THEIR PRESIDENTIAL NOMINEE.
AN' SHUCKS IF THEY DIDN'T ASK ME TA STAR-SPANGLE THE LIVIN' BANNER OUTTA 'EM!

GEE, I DON'T THINK I'VE EVER HEARD OF THAT PARTY. HAVE YOU, HOWARD?
DON'T MENTION POLITICS TO ME, BEV.
I NEVER TOUCH THE STUFF.

IT'S A LAW OF NATURE: YOU CAN'T CHANGE ANYBODY'S MIND ABOUT POLITICS OR RELIGION.
REV. YUC'S BICENTENNIAL PRAYER MEETING AND KOREAN KARATE EXHIBITION NEXT WEEK
SPEAKING OF WHICH... GUESS THEY'LL HAVE TO CALL OFF THAT DOUBLE-BONANZA. TOO BAD.

MR. GULTCH, THERE WOULDN'T BE ANY JOBS OPEN AT THE CONVENTION, WOULD THERE?
WE'RE FLAT BROKE. WE NEED TO RUSTLE UP SOME QUICK BREAD TO GET AN APARTMENT.
WA-A-ALL--

ORDINARILY, AH DON'T LAHK T' USE MAH POWERFUL INFL'ENCE THAT WAY--BUT AH S'POSE AH COULD MAKE AN EXCEPTION...
...FOR SUCH AN EXCEPTIONAL PAIR AS YOU.

HEY, HOWIE--MAYBE WE CAN GITCHA A JOB AS THE MAIN COURSE AT THE BANQUET. WHATCHA THINK?
KILL.

HEAH'S THE HOTEL. NOW Y'ALL JES' STICK CLOSE BY ME, HEAR?
'CAUSE SOON'S AH STEP OUTTA THE DOOR, WE'LL BE MOBBED, SEE?
REPORTERS, AUTOGRAPH HOUNDS--Y'ALL WATCH.
WELCOME ALL-NIGHT PARTY

AND, SHORE 'NUFF:
GIVE US A SMILE, MR. GULTCH!
NOT TILL AH SEE MUH HOST IN THIS FAIR CITY, SON. WHERE IS HE? WHERE'S THE PARTY CHAIRMAN?
HERE!!

WALL, ASSERT YOURSELF, BOY-- SHOVE ON THROUGH!
GOT SOME FRIENDS AH WANTCHA TA MEET. THET THERE'S HOWIE--
HEL-LO, GLAD TO-- GULP! Y-YOU'RE A DUCK!!

AN' THIS'S BEVERLY
Y'ALL FIGGER WE COULD DIG UP A ROOM AN' A COUPL'A JOBS FOR 'EM DURIN' THIS HERE SHINDIG?
WELL, I-- YOU'VE CERTAINLY PUT ME ON THE SPOT, DREY, BUT-- FOLLOW ME. WE'LL TRY OUR BEST.

AND SHORTLY...
YAH-HOO!! A SUITE AT THE PLAZA! WE MADE IT!! WE MADE IT!!
KNOCK KNOCK
ALL THE WAY FROM CLEVELAND TO LUXURY!!

GET THE DOOR, WILLYA, BEV? I'M BUSY--
--EXULTING!

MS. SWITZLER AND MISTER... DUCK?
OH, WOW-- PRESENTS!
AND A MESSAGE, YES MA'AM.

I'LL TAKE THEM. YOU DON'T--
IS THERE SOMETHING ELSE? I--
OH.

YES--HOW RUDE OF ME--I'M SORRY-- THANK YOU--THANK YOU-- ≡MMMNMPH≡--OH, GOD, YES -- THANK YOU-- ≡MMMMNNMPHF≡

TH-THAT'S OKAY, LADY--REALLY-- I'D'VE SETTLED FOR TWO BITS!
SEE YA.

HEY, WHAT'S GOIN' ON OUT THERE? WHO WAS IT?
STAY PUT! I'LL SHOW YA IN A SEC!

TA-DAH!!
HI, I'M BEV, YOUR HOSPITALITY GIRL!
HOW'S THAT SOUND?

LIKE A COME-ON. WHAT'S THE NOTE SAY?
I DUNNO. I MEAN, I KNOW THE WORDS...
is in
Just

BUT I CAN'T MAKE SENSE OF IT.
HERE-- LOOK.

≡HMPH≡ SOUNDS LIKE GULTCH ACCEPTING YOUR OFFER OF HOSPITALITY.
The mix is in the pan. Just thought you'd like to know. A friend.
LET'S SEE WHAT KINDA GET-UP THEY SENT ME.

SOON...
GEE... HOWARD THE PIG. YOU SWING THAT STICK LIKE A NATURAL.
THAT'S WHAT THEY ALL SAY-- TILL THEY PUT ON THE UNIFORM!
CAN IT, BEV. YOU KNOW I'M UNCOMFORTABLE AS AN AUTHORITY FIGURE.

YOU REVEL IN THAT SENSE OF POWER-- AND YOU KNOW IT.
LISTEN, TOOTS-- ANY CHUMP THAT'S DEPENDENT ON DUDS FOR HIS POWER DOESN'T REVEL TOO LONG.

MMM...LOOKS LIKE THIS IS WHERE WE PART COMPANY, PAL.
WANNA MEET BACK HERE AFTER WORK?
SECURITY
HOSPITALITY
OKAY BY ME. CATCH YA LATER.

"SENSE OF POWER"-- NUTS! SURE, EVEN ON MY WORLD FOLKS COSTUMED THEMSELVES TO ACHIEVE OR REINFORCE A SOUGHT-AFTER SELF-IMAGE...!

...BUT YA DON'T IMMEDIATELY INTERNALIZE-- --AHH, SKIP IT!
THEY'RE NOT PAYIN' ME TA THINK.
SECURITY OFFICE

SHIELD 1242 REPORTING FOR DU--
AW, NO.

WHAT CAN I DO FOR YA, DEPUTY? TALK FAST. I'M A BUSY, BUSY MAN.
AIN'T THAT RIGHT, LINDA?
BUSY MAKING ME FEEL SECURE, CHIEF.
YEAH. RIGHT. I WAS JUST WONDERIN' WHAT MY DETAIL'S GONNA BE.

I DUNNO. I DON'T CARE.
SHOP AROUND--FIND SOMETHING YA LIKE.

OKAY, LOVER-BOY... YOU'RE THE BOSS. I'LL JUST PLAY TROUBLE-SHOOTER!
AMBLE AROUND TILL SOMETHIN' CATCHES MY EAR OR EYE AN'--
AAAGH!

WELL. THAT DIDN'T TAKE FOREVER, DID IT?
AH-HAH! JUST AS I SUSPECTED-- A COMMITTEE MEETING!
IF THIS WERE ANYTHING BUT POLITICS, THAT SCREAM WOULD'A BEEN GOOD FOR MURDER ONE!
I REPEAT, MR. SANGOR HAS THE FLOOR!

THANK YOU, MR. CHAIRMAN! AS I WAS SAYING, THIS IS THE REAL WORLD--WHERE THE RUSSKIES WILL KILL THEIR OWN PEOPLE IN THE INTEREST OF NATIONAL SECURITY!

OUR INTELLIGENCE AGENCIES MUST HAVE THE SAME FREEDOM TO OPERATE IF--
NO!!

THE CIA MUST LEARN MODERATION! OF COURSE, OUR MEN IN MUFTI DESERVE OUR SUPPORT...
...BUT WE CANNOT STOOP TO CONDONE ASSASSINATION--EXCEPT IN SELF-DEFENSE!

I'M AFRAID MR. SANGOR'S PREDICTABLY ANIMALISTIC CONSERVATISM AND MR. LANGOR'S JELLYFISH LIBERALISM BOTH FAIL TO ADDRESS THE REAL ISSUE, MR. CHAIRMAN.
WE'VE GOT TO GET THE DUMB PEOPLE OUT OF INTELLIGENCE!

WAAUGH
THAT'S IT. I'M SPLITTIN'.

WAIT!!

YOU! WHAT'S YOUR OPINION? SPEAK UP! DON'T BE SHY! WE NEED A PLATFORM PLANK AND WE'RE DEAD-LOCKED!
WE'LL TAKE ANYTHING!

THE FIRST THING YOU'LL TAKE IS YOUR HANDS OFF ME!!
THEN, ANSWER ONE SIMPLE QUESTION:

"ANY O' YOU TURKEYS KNOW ANY-THING ABOUT INTELLIGENCE??"
WELL...
EH...
NOT FIRST-HAND, BUT...

TELL THE TRUTH, THEN! SAY YA DON'T KNOW-- BUT THAT YOU'LL FIND OUT ALL YA CAN-- AN' WHEN YA DO--
PLOP
--THE BAD GUYS BETTER WATCH OUT!

BRAVO! A MAGNIFICENT STATEMENT! REVOLU-TIONARY! DID ANYONE WRITE IT DOWN?
EVERY WORD! WHY DO YOU SUPPOSE HE WEARS THAT DUCK SUIT?

EARLY EVENING, AT THE APPOINTED PLACE...
--AND THEN HE SAID, "WHADDAYA MEAN, NOT ON THE CONVENTION FLOOR?" SO I HADDA--
I DON'T THINK I CAN SIT, DUCKY-- MY POOR BOTTOM HAS BEEN PINCHED WITH-IN AN INCH OF ITS LIFE!
HEY, YOU LOOK BUSHED. WHY DON'T I FINISH THE STORY OVER A CUP O' COFFEE?
LET'S GO BACK TO THE HOTEL WHERE I CAN LIE DOWN, HUH? PLEASE?

AND SO...
OBOY. THE PRAIRIE TROUBADOUR MUST'A STOPPED BY AGAIN.

YEP.
The ice cream's on the cake. Just thought you'd like to know. A friend.
LET ME SEE...

HOWARD...Y'KNOW, I DON'T THINK GULTCH WROTE THIS NOTE.
THE SPELLING IS BETTER THAN YOU'D EXPECT, BUT--AAH, WHAT DO WE CARE?!

NEXT DAY...
OHIO
I DON'T LIKE IT. IT'S TOO PLACID. IT CAN'T LAST!
...DEBATE ON MINORITY OPINION...
...IN A DIGNIFIED FASHION...
...WITHOUT COMPROMISING THE PRINCIPLES UPON...
VOTE FOR

BEEF JERKIES?? WHY, YOU--!
I KNEW IT.
WACK

OKAY, OKAY--BREAK IT UP, YA BOZOS!
LET'S HAVE A LITTLE DECORUM, SEE--OR I'LL BASH YER TEETH IN!!

THIS--TURNCOAT BACKED OUT ON OUR SECOND-BALLOT BARGAIN!
WE HAD A DEAL!

WE'D THROW OUR SUPPORT TO WAULDRAP ON THE THIRD BALLOT--
WAULDROP
WAULDRAP
--IF WE PROMISED HALF OUR VOTES TO WAULDROP ON--
ENOUGH!!

GIMME THOSE PLACARDS! I'LL SHOW YA HOW TA SWAP VOTING BLOCS!
NOW WATCH CAREFULLY...

YA JUST SORTA FLIP 'EM, SEE? OKAY, WAULDROP JUST GOT ONE VOTE!
NOW, GATHER UP ALL YER PLACARDS... AN' JUST KEEP FLIPPIN'--
WAULDROP

--TILL ONE OR THE OTHER OF YA HAS ALL THE CARDS.
YA GOT IT? NOT TOO COMPLEX?
GOOD!

HAW NICE SHOT, LI'L BUDDY. AH LAHK YORE STYLE.
HOW'S THING'S GOIN' FOR YOU AN' THET LUSCIOUS LADY?
SWELL, GULTCH. REAL PEACHY.

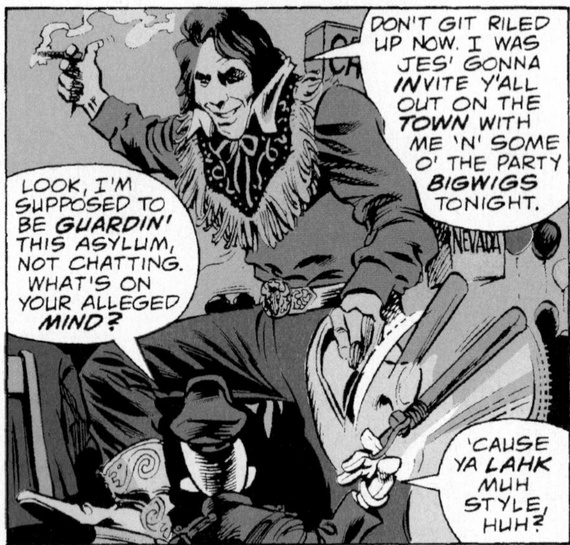
DON'T GIT RILED UP NOW. I WAS JES' GONNA INVITE Y'ALL OUT ON THE TOWN WITH ME 'N' SOME O' THE PARTY BIGWIGS TONIGHT.
LOOK, I'M SUPPOSED TO BE GUARDIN' THIS ASYLUM, NOT CHATTING. WHAT'S ON YOUR ALLEGED MIND?
'CAUSE YA LAHK MUH STYLE, HUH?
NEVADA

WEL-L-L, AW--WHY NOT? I NEED A LITTLE DISTRACTION, IF I'M GONNA AVOID GETTIN' DRIVEN THERE!

ALAS, THAT NIGHT...
SOME DISTRACTION! THIS HAS GOTTA BE THE ONLY SPOT IN NEW YORK--
--LOUDER AN' SLEAZIER THAN THE CONVENTION!

YOUR CHECK, SIR.
HUH...?

HOPE THOSE BUMS CAN PAY UP FOR WHAT THEY KNOCKED BACK, PAL.
YEAH. I--
HEY! WAIT! COME BACK!

BLUE GARTER
GUEST CHECK
It's all in the oven. Just thought you'd like to know.
Beverages— $74.32
--A friend
IT'S OUR PLE
TO SERVE

NEXT DAY:
I DON'T GET IT. SOUNDS MORE LIKE SOMEBODY'S MAKING BAKED ALASKA THAN PLOTTING ANYTHING SINISTER.
MADISON SQUARE GARDEN
RIGHT. WE GOT A COMPULSIVELY SHY RECIPE AUTHOR ON OUR--

WAAAAUGH
LATER, BEV! I GOTTA REPORT TO THE CHIEF-- FAST!

MUSTER THE TROOPS, BOSS! THERE'S A BOMB ON THE CONVENTION FLOOR!
I'LL SAY! THEY'RE GOING WITH WAULDROP AS THE NOMINEE.

NEVER ONE TO PERSIST IN THE FACE OF FUTILITY, THE DUCK RACES ALONE TO THE ROSTRUM.
ALASKA
YEP. JUST LIKE I FIGURED. THE DELEGATIONS ARE SEATED ALPHABETICALLY. ALASKA'S RIGHT UP FRONT.

SO NOW I GOTTA ASK MYSELF-- DO I REALLY WANNA GET INVOLVED IN THIS? OR WOULD THE SUPERIOR DUCK JUST SCRAM AND SAVE HIS OWN TAIL FEATHERS?

IT'S NOT LIKE ANY-BODY'D MISS WAULDROP.
FSSSST
ALASKA

AAH-- WHO'M I KIDDING? I CAN'T KNOWINGLY LET EVEN A POLITICIAN DIE!
AND SO I SAY TO THIS CONVENTION-- PUSH! THROTTLE! WHINE!
HE DOESN'T EVEN SEE WHAT'S HAPPENIN'!
WAULDRO

TOO MESMERIZED BY THE SOUND OF HIS OWN BANALITIES!
ALASKA
LOOK! THE ALASKA STANDARD'S ON FIRE!!

FIRE, NOTHIN'! IT'S A BOMB! EVERYBODY--
--SCATTER!!
ALASKA
EEEEEEE

GREAT! NOW I'VE GOT THE THING, WHAT DO I DO WITH--
AH-HAH! SEVEN LAYERS OF SALVATION!

THE PARTY'S BICENTENNIAL BIRTHDAY CAKE! THIS MUST BE MY WEEK FOR BAKED GOODS!

NEXT **OPEN SEASON** OR: "THE ROAD TO THE WHITE HOUSE IS PAVED WITH SHELL-CASINGS"

Howard the Duck 1976 lithograph by Bernie Wrightson

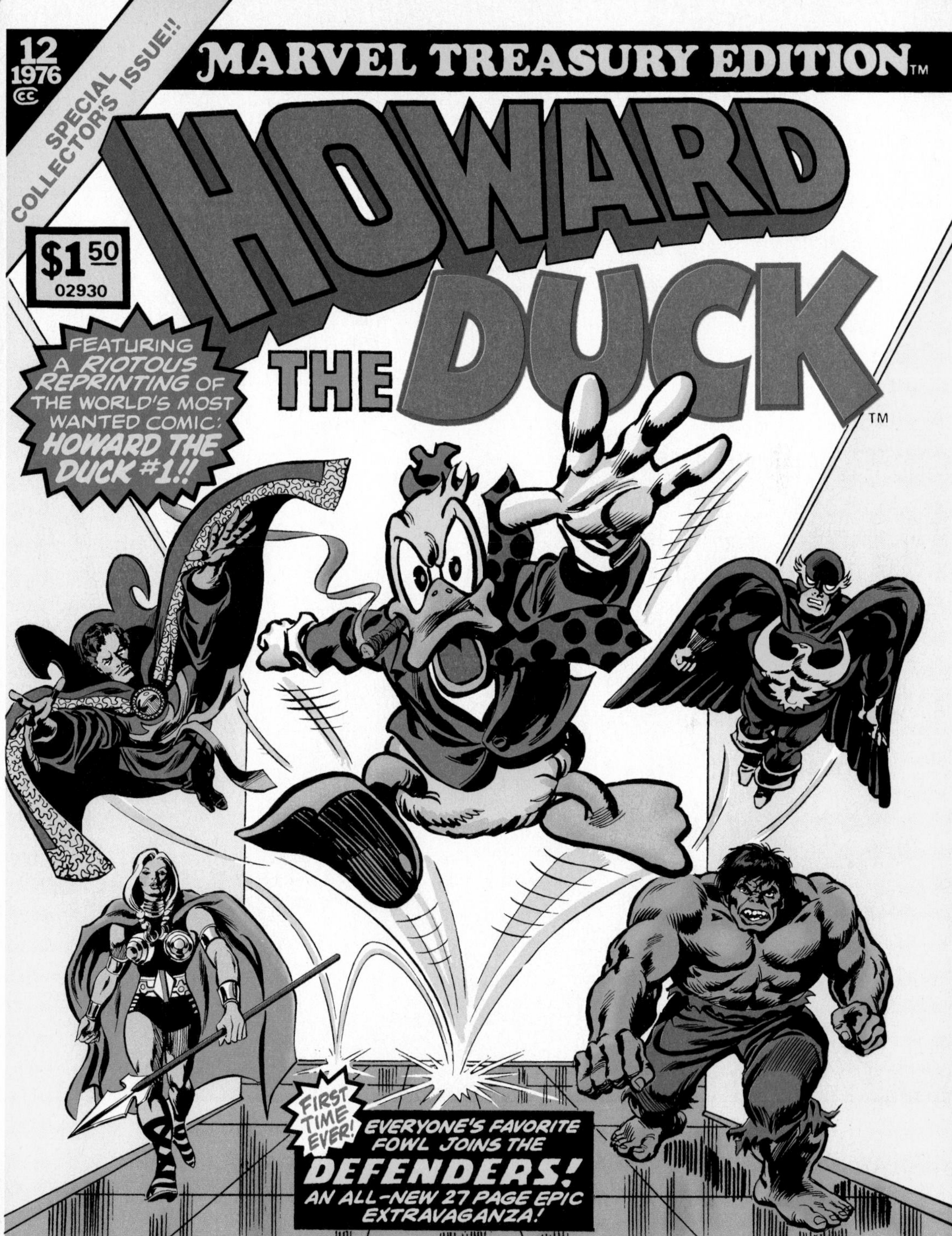

12
1976
CC
SPECIAL COLLECTOR'S ISSUE!!
MARVEL TREASURY EDITION™
HOWARD THE DUCK™
$1.50
02930
FEATURING A RIOTOUS REPRINTING OF THE WORLD'S MOST WANTED COMIC: HOWARD THE DUCK #1!!
FIRST TIME EVER!
EVERYONE'S FAVORITE FOWL JOINS THE
DEFENDERS!
AN ALL-NEW 27 PAGE EPIC EXTRAVAGANZA!

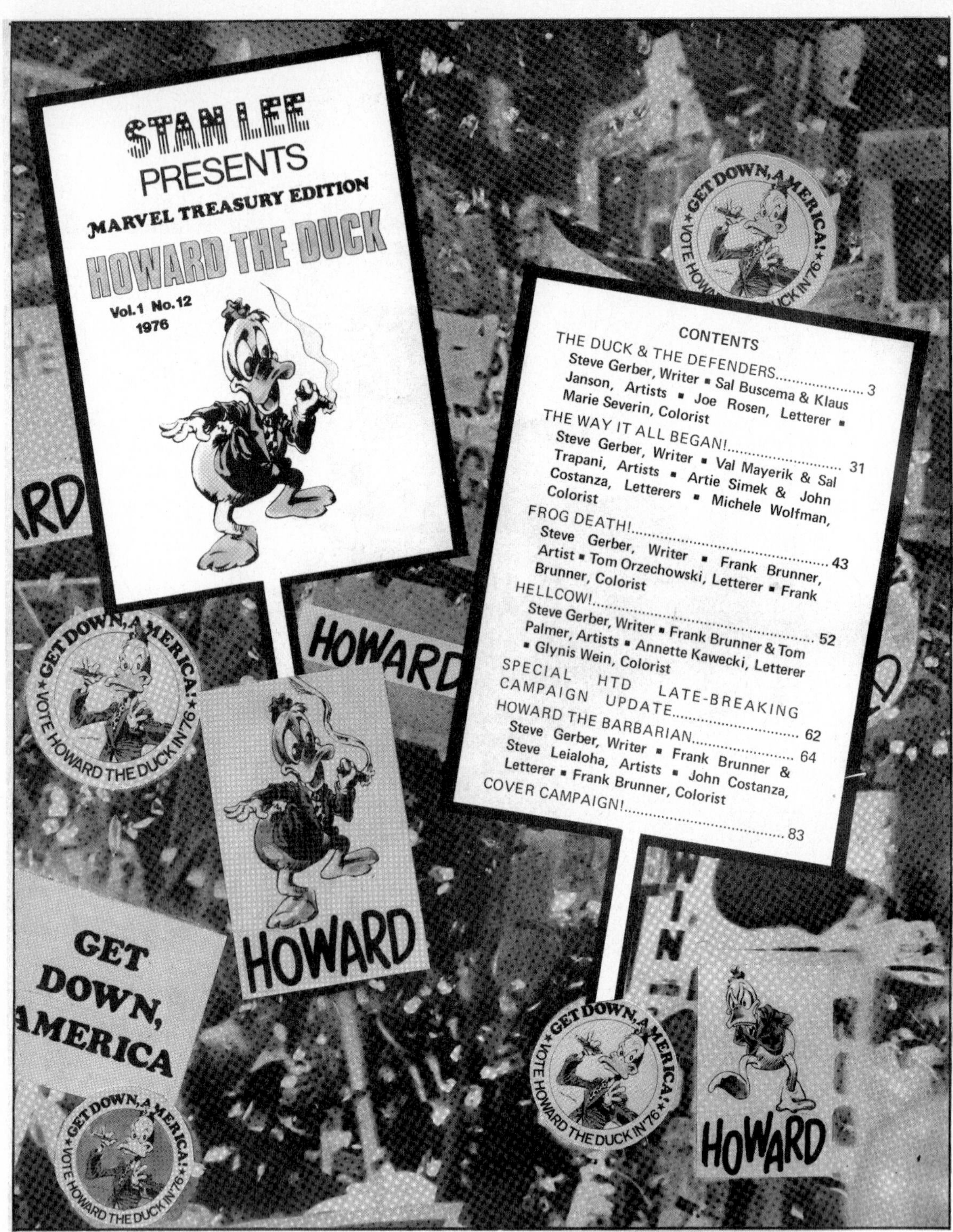
STAN LEE
PRESENTS
MARVEL TREASURY EDITION
HOWARD THE DUCK
Vol.1 No.12
1976
CONTENTS
THE DUCK & THE DEFENDERS..................... 3
Steve Gerber, Writer ▪ Sal Buscema & Klaus Janson, Artists ▪ Joe Rosen, Letterer ▪ Marie Severin, Colorist
THE WAY IT ALL BEGAN!.......................... 31
Steve Gerber, Writer ▪ Val Mayerik & Sal Trapani, Artists ▪ Artie Simek & John Costanza, Letterers ▪ Michele Wolfman, Colorist
FROG DEATH!.. 43
Steve Gerber, Writer ▪ Frank Brunner, Artist ▪ Tom Orzechowski, Letterer ▪ Frank Brunner, Colorist
HELLCOW!.. 52
Steve Gerber, Writer ▪ Frank Brunner & Tom Palmer, Artists ▪ Annette Kawecki, Letterer ▪ Glynis Wein, Colorist
SPECIAL HTD LATE-BREAKING CAMPAIGN UPDATE........................... 62
HOWARD THE BARBARIAN........................ 64
Steve Gerber, Writer ▪ Frank Brunner & Steve Leialoha, Artists ▪ John Costanza, Letterer ▪ Frank Brunner, Colorist
COVER CAMPAIGN!.................................. 83
GET DOWN, AMERICA!
VOTE HOWARD THE DUCK IN '76
HOWARD
GET DOWN, AMERICA

PROLOGUE
FIVE VILLAINS IN SEARCH OF A PLOT!
THEY'RE HERE-- JUST AS HE SAID THEY'D BE.
YEP. RIGHT HERE IN CENTRAL PARK-- AT MIDNIGHT!
Oh, Suzanna
JAHWOHL! SO LET'S GET THIS MARSH-MALLOW ROAST COOKIN'--
--YOU SWINE!
INTRODUCE YOURSELVES-- ALL OF YOU-- OR I'LL GIVE YOU SUCH A LICKIN'--!

I'M SITTING BULLSEYE, EX-CIA OPERATIVE--'TIL I INFILTRATED THE AMERICAN INDIAN MOVEMENT LOOKIN' FOR PROOF THEY WAS MAKIN' BOOTLEG FIRE WATER!
THEM REDSKINS CRACKED MY COVER--
--TATTOOED A TARGET ON MY CHEST, AND CHASED ME OFF THE RESERVATION. I LOST MY JOB, NATCH.

I MEAN, HOW COULD I WORK UNDERCOVER WITH AN IDENTIFYING MARK LIKE THIS?!
EMBITTERED, I--
AAH-- SHUDDUP!
I'M TILLIE THE HUN!

AND I AM-- THE SPANKER, FORMER HEAD-MASTER OF AN EXCLUSIVE PRIVATE PREP SCHOOL--
--WRENCHED FROM MY POSITION FOR ADMINISTERING EXCESSIVE CORPORAL PUNISHMENT.

=urk= YOU CAN CALL ME "BLACK HOLE." I WAS PLAYIN' HAND-BALL IN BROOKLYN ONE DAY WHEN A GRAIN OF DWARF STAR MATTER FELL FROM SPACE--
--AND IMBEDDED ITSELF IN MY BREASTBONE.
THIS ENDOWED ME WITH AN EXTREMELY GROSS POWER. I--

SUDDENLY--
AWRIGHT, YOU CLOWNS!
THE JIG'S UP! OPEN FIRES ARE AGAINST THE LAW IN THIS BURG!
BESIDES, THIS PARK CLOSES AT TEN P.M.!

CHANK
OH, YEAH??
SEZ YOU, FLATFOOT!!

FREEZE, TONTO! I GOT A BEAD DEAD CENTER ON--
I KNOW. THEY ALWAYS DO.
BUT FORTUNATELY FOR ME--

TWAK
I LEARNED A LOT FROM THEM INJUNS BEFORE THEY GOT WISE TO ME!

I LEARNED, ALSO--
-- FROM THE LILY-LIVERED LIBERAL PARENTS OF MY STUDENTS!
I LEARNED THAT IF JUSTICE IS TO TRIUMPH--

-- A MAN MUST SOMETIMES TAKE THE LAW INTO HIS OWN HANDS AND OVER HIS KNEE!
WHAP

STAND ASIDE, YOU TURKEYS! I'M GONNA SHOW YOU WHY I LOST THAT HANDBALL GAME AND EARNED THE CONTEMPT OF ALL THE POPULAR KIDS!
HIS EYES SQUEEZE SHUT, HIS BROW FURROWS--!
--HE CONCENTRATES MIGHTILY...
...AND AN EBONY CAVITY YAWNS OPEN IN HIS CHEST!
AND LIKE THE COSMIC PHENOMENON WHICH IS HIS NAMESAKE...
THE BLACK HOLE SUCKS!!
AAAARGH

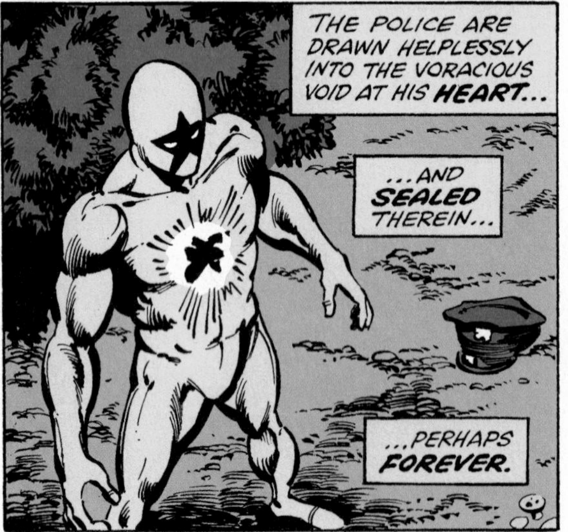

YES! YES! IT'S UGLY-- LOATHESOME-- UNSPEAKABLY GROTESQUE--
--KNOWING IT WAS I WHO SUMMONED YOU FOUR TO THIS PLACE-- I WHO PRE-CIPITATED THE DEATHS OF THOSE INNOCENT MEN--!
--IT'S PSYCHOLOGI-CAL TORTURE!!

AND I'M LOVING EVERY HORRIFIC MINUTE OF IT!

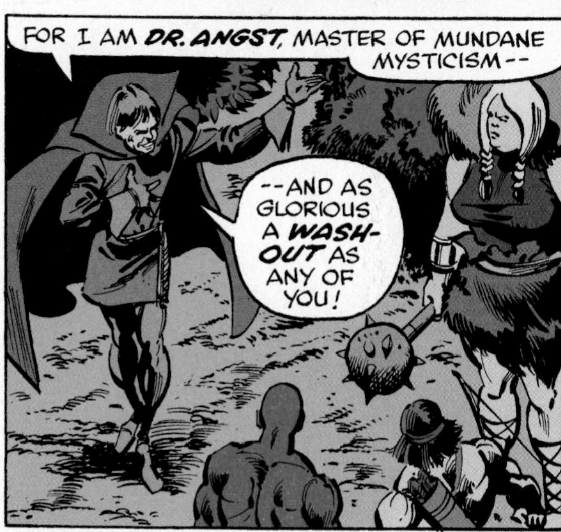
FOR I AM DR. ANGST, MASTER OF MUNDANE MYSTICISM--
--AND AS GLORIOUS A WASH-OUT AS ANY OF YOU!

DON'T ATTEMPT TO DENY IT! WE ALL SHARE A COMMON FAULT! NONE OF US HAS EVER HAD AN ORIGINAL THOUGHT IN HIS OR HER LIFE!
THAT'S WHY-- DESPITE OUR PRODIGIOUS TALENTS--NO ONE'S EVER HEARD OF ANY OF US!

WE'RE TOO DERIVATIVE--TOO STEREOTYPICAL--
--EVEN TO MAKE NAMES FOR OURSELVES AS 'SUPER-VILLAINS!'
BUT NO MORE!!

I'VE FOUND OUR WAY OUT OF ANONYMITY--AND INTO THE BIG BUCKS!
JOIN ME-- AND YOU'LL ALL BE ON THE COVER OF NEXT MONTH'S ISSUE OF "CELEBRITY!"
HUH...?

JOIN ME--IN MY PLOT TO ASSASSINATE THE ALL-NIGHT PARTY'S CANDI-DATE FOR PRESIDENT!
WAAAUGH.

THE DUCK AND DEFENDERS
QUIET DIGNITY AND UNDERSTATED ELEGANCE ARE THE HALLMARKS OF NEW YORK'S PARKSIDE PLAZA HOTEL.
EVEN WHEN THE MANAGEMENT BOOTS A GUEST OUT ONTO THE SIDEWALK FOR NON-PAYMENT OF HIS BILL, THE MATTER IS HANDLED WITH TASTE.
WAAAUGH
TCH.

GO! AND NEVER DARKEN OUR DOOR AGAIN!
AAH, CUT THE ARISTOCRATIC ROUTINE, CURLY! IF YOU REALLY HAD ANY CLASS--
--YOU'D'VE HAD THAT UNDERBITE FIXED YEARS AGO!

WELL...IT WAS FUN WHILE IT LASTED, HUH?
AW, C'MON, DUCKY.
YEAH. A BALL. I SPOTTED THOSE ALL-NIGHT CREEPS FOR WELCHERS FROM THE START!
IT WAS PROBABLY JUST AN OVERSIGHT.

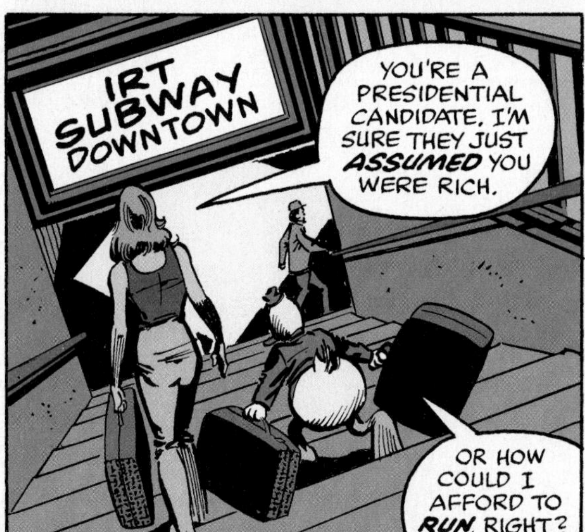
IRT SUBWAY DOWNTOWN
YOU'RE A PRESIDENTIAL CANDIDATE, I'M SURE THEY JUST ASSUMED YOU WERE RICH.
OR HOW COULD I AFFORD TO RUN, RIGHT?

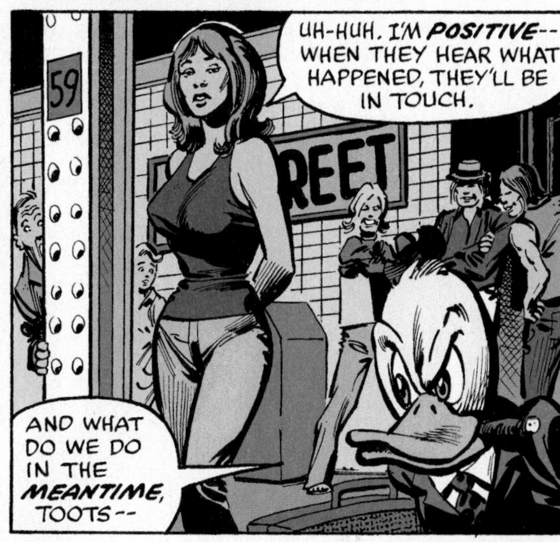
UH-HUH. I'M POSITIVE-- WHEN THEY HEAR WHAT HAPPENED, THEY'LL BE IN TOUCH.
59
REET
AND WHAT DO WE DO IN THE MEANTIME, TOOTS--

--RIDE BACK'N'FORTH BETWEEN HERE AND CONEY ISLAND 'TIL WE DROP?
NAH.

I KNOW SOME STEWARDESSES--OLD HIGH SCHOOL CHUMS FROM CLEVELAND--WHO'VE GOT A HOUSE IN GREENWICH VILLAGE.
SWELL, SO ALL WE GOTTA DO IS GET THERE ALIVE, RIGHT?

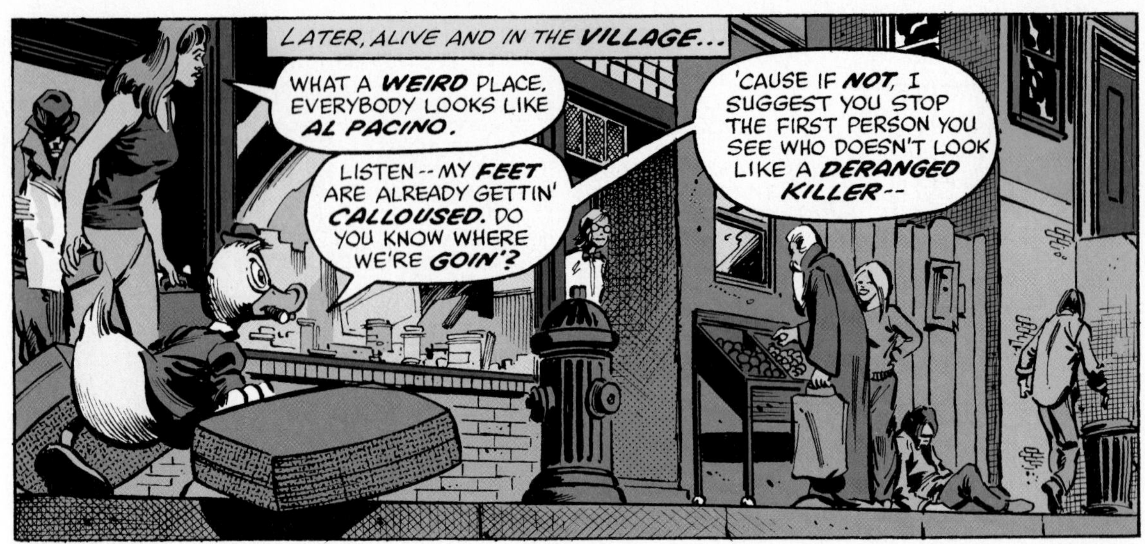
LATER, ALIVE AND IN THE VILLAGE...
WHAT A WEIRD PLACE. EVERYBODY LOOKS LIKE AL PACINO.
LISTEN--MY FEET ARE ALREADY GETTIN' CALLOUSED. DO YOU KNOW WHERE WE'RE GOIN'?
'CAUSE IF NOT, I SUGGEST YOU STOP THE FIRST PERSON YOU SEE WHO DOESN'T LOOK LIKE A DERANGED KILLER--

--AND ASK DIRECTIONS. RIGHT!

EXCUSE ME, YOU LOOK PRETTY HARMLESS. COULD YOU--?
I BEG YOUR PARDON?

HEY--HI! HOW'VE YOU BEEN? I HAVEN'T SEEN YOU SINCE--
SINCE BEFORE WE GOT IT ON, I HOPE--PAL.
OH, NO. HE'S NEVER SEEN ME AT ALL.

I'M NEW IN TOWN--FRESH FROM CLEVELAND.
UH-HUH. AN' SPEAKING OF FRESH--!
GULP! NOW I RECOGNIZE HER--AND BARELY IN TIME TO PROTECT MY SPIDER-MAN IDENTITY!

SHE'S BEVERLY SWITZLER. I'D KNOW HER DUCK ANYWHERE!
I, UH--I'M SORRY. SHE LOOKS JUST LIKE--
CHARLES STREET? SURE!

"SIX BLOCKS EAST AND HANG A LEFT," SHE SAID.
WHATEVER--AS LONG AS WE'RE TRUDGIN' AWAY FROM THAT BABY-FACED MASHER!

SIX BLOCKS EAST, ETC., ETC....
ARE YOU SURE THIS'S THE ADDRESS?!

IT IS KINDA SPACIOUS FOR TWO STEWARDESSES AND A CAT, HUH?
RRRING
FOR THE RENT ON THIS PLACE THEY COULD BUY THEIR OWN AIRLINE.
BUT--NOTHIN' TO LOSE BY ASKIN', I GUESS.

RELAX, WONG! I'M RIGHT HERE, I'LL ANSWER IT.
YES, WHAT CAN I DO FOR Y--

Y-YOU'RE--A DUCK!
chortle
NO OFFENSE, PAL--BUT YOU'RE HARDLY IN A POSITION TO CRITICIZE!
OH, WOW--!

I KNOW YOU! I'VE SEEN YOUR PICTURE IN THE PAPERS!
YOU'RE-- WAITAMINIT-- IT'S ON THE TIP OF MY--
YOU'RE THE FALCON, AREN'T YOU?!
SOMETHING LIKE THAT.

HEY, DOC--VISITORS! AND FROM THE LOOK OF 'EM, THEY COULD ONLY BE FOR YOU!
NO, NO-- THIS IS ALL A MISTAKE.
WE DON'T NEED A DOCTOR.

IN RESPONSE TO NIGHTHAWK'S SUMMONS, THREE IMPOSING FIGURES EMERGE FROM THE DOUBLE-DOORS OF THE PARLOR.
VALKYRIE: LIVING EMBODIMENT OF AN ANCIENT NORSE LEGEND!
DR. STRANGE: MASTER OF THE MYSTIC ARTS, AND, INCIDENTALLY, OWNER OF THIS SANCTUM SANCTORUM!
THE INCREDIBLE HULK: BRUTAL, BESTIAL BEHEMOTH BORN OF GAMMA RAYS!
TOGETHER WITH NIGHTHAWK, THEY FORM THE NEXUS OF A LOOSE CONFEDERATION OF SUPERHUMANS KNOWN AS THE DEFENDERS!
NATURALLY. A WHOLE NEST OF ZANIES. MY DAY IS COMPLETE.

HELA'S GHOSTS! STEPHEN, WHO--?!
VISITORS, VAL-- JUST AS KYLE PRESUMED.
THOUGH I SUSPECT ONE OF THEM HAS TRAVELLED AN INORDINATE DISTANCE TO PAY US THIS CALL.
JEEZ--!
DON'T FLATTER YOURSELF, MAC. WE JUST TOOK A WRONG TURN.

LET'S SPLIT, BEV.
I DON'T LIKE THE LOOK O' THIS--

WAAAWPGH
TWAP
PLEASE FORGIVE THE MYSTIC BARRIER I'VE ERECTED, MY FRIEND.

MYSTIC--?! I KNEW IT! A SORCERER! I CAN SMELL 'EM A MILE AWAY!!
WELL, DON'T THINK I'M SCARED, BUSTER-- BY YOU OR THE GREEN GUY OR THE SWORD-LADY OR THAT WACKO WITH THE CASE OF FEATHER-ENVY!
SUCH WAS NEVER MY INTENTION. I MERELY BELIEVE-- WE MAY HAVE MUCH-- TO DISCUSS.

MEANWHILE...
Feelgood's FUNHOUSE
GUILT! GUILT FOR THE PLIGHT OF THE MASSES--!

THAT'S WHAT DROVE ME TO ESTABLISH MY CITADEL OF MUNDANE MAGIC IN THIS DINGY APARTMENT--
--OVER A SEEDY MASSAGE PARLOR IN THE MOST SQUALID SECTION OF THIS DEGENERATE CITY!
IT KEEPS ME IN TOUCH WITH REALITY...

...AS DO THE TERRESTRIAL TALISMANS UPON MY ALTAR!
MY EUCHA-RITZ CRACKERS, MY ALL-SEEING ICE--

--AND MY BARBECUE TRIDENT AND BOWL OF CHERRIES!
BEHOLD-- FOR HEREIN LIES OUR SALVATION!

WE MAY YET ESCHEW OUR SLAVISH ADHERENCE TO OUTMODED TRADITION--

--WITH THESE!
METTLE SPHERES-- CAST FROM THE OTHER-WORLDLY ALLOY PROMETHIUM!

THAT'S RIGHT-- COME AND GET IT--
--THE COURAGE TO CREATE, TO QUESTION, TO EXPLORE.

H-HEY-- THESE THINGS'RE RED HOT!! WHADDA WE DO WITH 'EM?!

SWALLOW THEM, MY FRIENDS. MANUAL MANIPULATION OF YOUR SPHERES AMOUNTS TO MERE POSTURING.
THEY MUST BE INTERNALIZED.

FOUR GULPS LATER:
IT'S TRUE! I'M STRONGER! I CAN FEEL IT!
ME, TOO! WHAT MUSCLES!
I FEEL LIKE I COULD SUCK IN A HORSE!

OF COURSE, THE EFFECT IS PURELY TRANSITORY. TO PROLONG THE INVIGORATION INDEFINITELY--
--ONE REQUIRES A LIFETIME SUPPLY OF SPHERES.

ALAS, MY WORLDLY WIZARDRY CANNOT CREATE THEM. I STUMBLED UPON THESE IN A RUMMAGE SALE.
BUT DESPAIR NOT! GAZE WITH ME INTO MY PEDESTRIAN PROGNOSTICATOR.

"THAT MAN HAS THE MYSTIC TOOLS WE NEED. WE MUST SEIZE THEM--AND MAKE SOME CASH ON THE SIDE--
"--BY KILLING THE DUCK! WHAT SAY YOU?"

IF THIS IS WHAT IT'S LIKE TO POSSESS SPHERES--
--LET'S GO GET 'EM!!
SO SAY WE ALL!!

EXCELLENT--
--YOU FOOLS. HEH HEH

--AND THESE ARE PREDILUVEAN SCULPTURES CULLED FROM--
UH--NOT TO INTERRUPT, DOC, BUT FOR A SORCERER YOU'RE SORTA LOOSE-TONGUED, AREN'T CHA?
MOST GUYS IN YOUR PROFESSION ARE PRETTY SECRETIVE--UNLESS THEY WANT SOMETHING. TRUE?

QUITE CORRECT, BUT ALL I DESIRE IS YOUR OPINION--AS A BEING WHO ALSO HAS SEEN BEYOND THIS REALITY.
I'VE NOTED AN UNUSUAL DEGREE OF MYSTICAL ACTIVITY IN THE WIND RECENTY. I WONDERED--
NAH.

CLOSEST I EVER CAME TO STIRRING UP MAGIC WAS AN ACT I USEDTA DO AT BIRTHDAY PARTIES.
EVERYTHING ELSE, I JUST KINDA GOT STIRRED INTO.

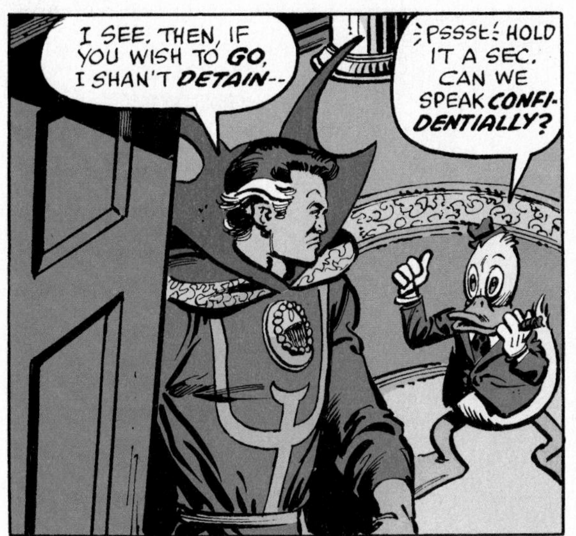
I SEE. THEN, IF YOU WISH TO GO, I SHAN'T DETAIN--
PSSST! HOLD IT A SEC. CAN WE SPEAK CONFI-DENTIALLY?

OF COURSE. WHAT--?
LISTEN... IF YOU'VE REALLY GOT ALL THIS ABRACADABRA STUFF DOWN PAT--
--COULDJA SPARE JUST A DAB OF IT TA SEND ME HOME?

IT'S...POSSIBLE. BUT WHAT OF YOUR POLITICAL CAREER--AND THE WOMAN BEVERLY?

SAME ANSWER FOR BOTH: I HADDA OCCUPY MY TIME ON THIS WORLD OR I'D GO CRAZY.

I MEAN--BEV'S A SWEET KID, BUT--
BUT NOT YOUR SPECIES. I UNDER-STAND.

BEHOLD, DUCK--THE ORB OF AGAMOTTO!
IN ITS INFINITE LUCID DEPTHS, WE SHALL LOCATE YOUR DIMENSIONAL WORLD...
...AND THEN, BY THE POWER OF THE ETERNAL VISHANTI...
ULP! SKIP THE SPOOKY DETAILS? PLEASE?

AS YOU WISH. DRAW CLOSE BESIDE ME.
WE SHALL COMMENCE AT ONCE.

PEER WITH ME AS-- EH? THE ORB GROWS MURKISH!
SOME-THING IS AMISS! BUT WHAT--?

EYES OF OSHTUR!!
"EYES" MY FOOT! THOSE'RE TENNIS BALLS!!

CRIPES! EITHER HIS MAGIC WAS OFF THE MARK--
--OR WE'RE UNDER ATTACK BY A SORCERER WITH A HELL OF A MEAN SERVE!

THOKATHOKATHOKA
DEMONS OF THE NORN-- THAT CLATTER!
SOUNDS LIKE TWO STIGAS IN A GRUDGE MATCH! WAIT HERE!

I'M GONNA DASH UPSTAIRS AND--
OOOMPH
AAAGH-- I'VE BEEN STABBED! WHAT THE--?

A WHITE PICKET FENCE?!
I'VE MET SOME STRANGE OBSTRUCTIONS IN MY TIME, BUT THIS IS THE MOST MUNDANE--

SUDDENLY--
SMILE, YOU SAPS! COMPANY'S COMING!
KLAAASH

YOO-HOO! DOC--?
OH, SWELL! HE'S OUT COLD!

AN' JUDGIN' FROM THE HUBBUB DOWNSTAIRS--
--THE WINDOW'S MY BEST BET FOR A QUICK EXIT!

HATE T' LEAVE BEV IN A SPOT LIKE THIS, BUT--
WAAAUGH

NABISCO
SHREDDED WHEAT
IT-- IT'S **CARDBOARD!** WE'RE ALL **BOXED-IN!**
PERHAPS... BUT NOT WITHOUT **RECOURSE.**

HUH? WHO **SAID** THAT?! WHERE-- WHAT--
WH-- **AAAUGH**

YOU.
LISTEN CAREFULLY, FOR I CANNOT LONG MAINTAIN THIS FORM WITH NO ACCESS TO THE ENERGY OF MY CONSCIOUS MIND.
YOU MUST RESCUE MY DEFENDERS AND MS. SWITZLER!

I SHALL GUIDE YOUR HAND AND MIND **TELE-PATHICALLY**--

--BUT **YOURS** MUST BE THE INDOMITABLE WILL WHICH **DIRECTS** THE MYSTIC ENERGIES!
AW, NO...!

GO! BE BRAVE! AND MAY THE OMNIPOTENT **OSHTUR** LIGHT YOUR WAY!
UH-HUH. AN' IT BETTER BE WITH A **250-WATT BULB!**

AND SO, ONE MORE TIME, I GO RACING **HEAD-ON** INTO THE SLOBBERING **ORIFICE** OF DEATH--
--LIKE THE **FOOL** I AM.
HUH?! WHO **THOUGHT** THAT?
I--DOCTOR STRANGE. THIS IS **TELEPATHY**, HOWARD.
YOU'VE NO TIME FOR **SELF-REPROACH**, DUCK.

NO **KIDDIN'**? IT'S-- UH-OH.
EMULATE THE **PICTURE** I'M PROJECTING BEFORE YOUR **MIND'S EYE**...

...AND **REPEAT** AFTER ME:
COME YE, **VAPORS OF VALTORR**, YE BILLOWS OF ENCHANTMENT--
--AND WAFT AWAY THESE COMBATANTS 'PON YOUR WIND OF SORROW AND **SILENCE!**

AND WHEN THE VAPORS DISSIPATE...
THEY'RE GONE! BUT WHERE, DOC?
DOC?
DOC??

HE CANNOT ANSWER YOU, FOWL. I'VE SEEN TO THAT...
...JUST AS I SHALL NOW TEND TO YOUR DOOM.

DOC-- BE A PAL-- HELP!!
THINK ALL YOU WISH. IT WILL AVAIL YOU NAUGHT.

"I'VE PLACED A MASK OF CONTAINMENT ABOUT STRANGE'S THOUGHTS.
"HE TRANSFERRED SOME OF HIS ARCANE KNOWLEDGE TO YOU BEFORE THE STRAPS TIGHTENED--"

--BUT NOWHERE NEAR ENOUGH! YOU'RE GONNA DIE, YOU FEATHERED FOOL!
AND I'M GOING TO BE RICH!!

MEANWHILE, IN SHEA STADIUM, THE CROWD ROARS ITS DISAPPROVAL AS THE HOME TEAM EVACUATES THE FIELD TO MAKE ROOM FOR-- THE HEROES AND VILLAINS.
WHAK WHAK WHAK
OW! OW! OW!!
THUK
SPOING
DOC MUST'VE ARRANGED THIS-- TO GIVE US SOME ELBOW, KNEE, AND FIST ROOM.
AND SINCE I'D HATE TO SEE HIS SPELL GO TO WASTE--
--LET'S SEE IF I CAN SPARE THE ROD AND SPOIL BEV!
HEY! STOP WRIGGLING! YOU'LL--
--FALL, NIGHT-HAWK?
BUT THAT'S PRECISELY WHAT I WANT!
I'M FREE NOW-- TO EMPLOY MY WEAPONRY!

TH-THAT THING?! BUT IT'S PLASTIC! IT'S JUST A TOY!
TRUE! BUT I AM... THE SPANKER! I DON'T NEED A REAL GUN--

--TO PISTOL-WHIP YOU!!

FIGHT, YOU MALE CHAUVINIST GARGOYLE! I'M TILLIE THE HUN! I CAN BEAT ANY MAN--
--AND IF I LOSE, I'LL BE YOUR BRIDE!
BUT-- HULK CAN'T SMASH-- GIRL!

TOO BAD I'M NOT AS CHIVALROUS AS GREENSKIN, HUH? NOW THAT I'VE VIBRATED THAT SWORD OUTTA YER HAND--

--YOU'VE LEFT YOUR GUARD AS OPEN AS YOUR MOUTH, ARCHER!
WHAM

LEARNED YOUR LESSON YET, BIRD-MAN? OR--?
KLOP
ACTUALLY, I'M SELF-TAUGHT--THROUGH BITTER EXPERIENCE. CAPISH?

I WARN YOU, BEAST--FALL OR BE MY MATE!
NO!!

WEARY OF TILLIE'S BLOWS AND REPELLED AT THE NOTION OF HER AFFECTION, THE GREEN BEHEMOTH SEIZES THE STADIUM'S CARPET OF ASTROTURF, AND...!

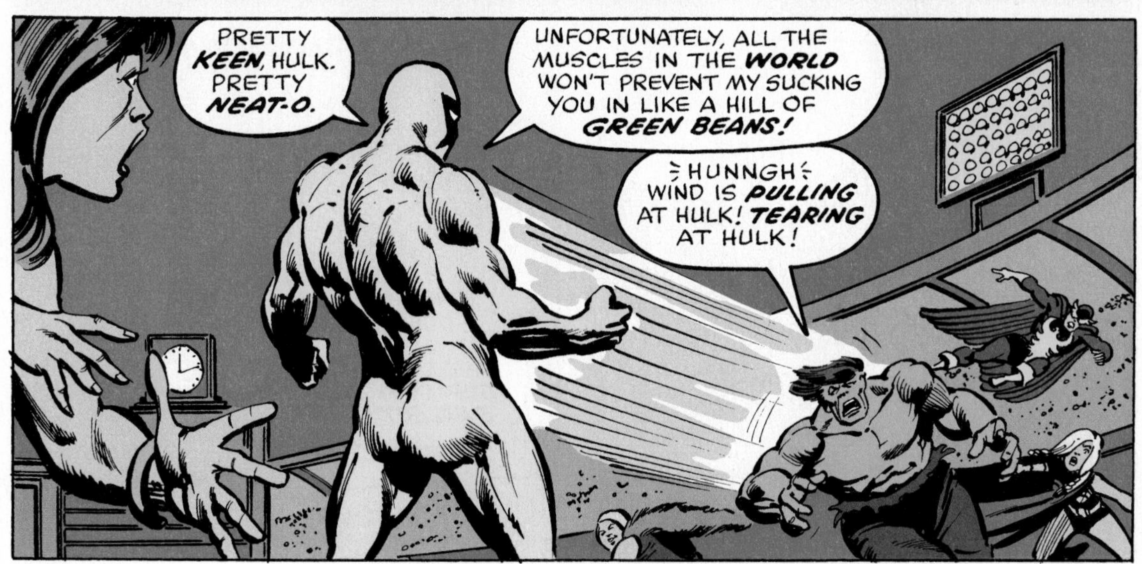
PRETTY KEEN, HULK. PRETTY NEAT-O.
UNFORTUNATELY, ALL THE MUSCLES IN THE WORLD WON'T PREVENT MY SUCKING YOU IN LIKE A HILL OF GREEN BEANS!
HUNNGH WIND IS PULLING AT HULK! TEARING AT HULK!

DON'T TAKE IT PERSONALLY, CHUMP. THIS WHOLE STADIUM-- EH?
'SCUSE ME...

...BUT I REALLY JUST CAN'T LET YOU DO THIS, Y'KNOW?

IN A SINGLE, TERRIBLE "FWOOMP," THE ALL-CONSUMING VILLAIN IS HIDEOUSLY SELF-SWALLOWED.
AAAAAA

BEV--DON'T!!
WE SPECIALIZE IN WEIRD VILLAINS--BOZOS, BABY DEER, HEADMEN--!
WE KNOW--IT COULD BE DANGEROUS.

WHILE, BACK AT THE SANCTUM...
YOU MEAN--SOME-ONE'S PAYING YOU TO WASTE ME?
BY THE WAY--I'M FREE!

SO I NOTICED. AND OF COURSE, I'M IN IT FOR THE MONEY!
WHAT ELSE COULD MOTIVATE A MATERIAL-ISTIC MYSTIC TO SEND A SIX-PLY RADIAL DEATH ROLLING YOUR WAY?

I DUNNO. BUT BY THE SHIELD OF THE SERAPHIM--I'LL DEFLECT IT!

AND IF THE INFO DOC IMPLANTED IN MY BRAIN WAS RIGHT--
--I CAN TRANSFORM THAT SHIELD INTO STRANDS OF ENERGY, AND--!
FOOL!

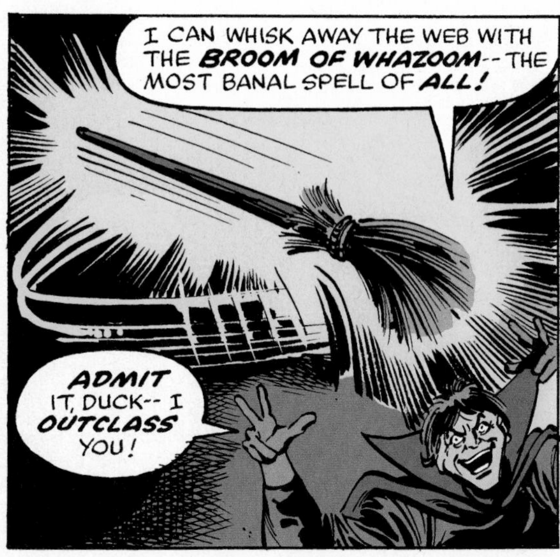
I CAN WHISK AWAY THE WEB WITH THE BROOM OF WHAZOOM-- THE MOST BANAL SPELL OF ALL!
ADMIT IT, DUCK-- I OUTCLASS YOU!

EXPERTISE, I'LL CONCEDE TO HIM-- BUT CLASS? NEVER!

DOC SHOWED ME ONE LAST BASIC MOVE. IF THIS DOESN'T WRAP IT UP--!
THROWING IN THE TOWEL, EH?

SO IT SEEMS... UNTIL THE SCARLET FABRIC SNAPS TO LIFE!
WHAT THE--?!

IT'S A CLOAK OF LEVITATION, PAL--SOMETHING YOU'D NEVER THOUGHT OF, 'CAUSE YOUR EYES NEVER LEAVE THE GROUND!
BUT ENOUGH REPARTEE.

JUST YOU KEEP FLOATIN' RIGHT THERE...
WHOMP
...WHILE I DELIVER THE PUNCH-LINE!

EXCELLENT, HOWARD-- YOU'VE FREED ME! I'M ON MY WAY DOWN!
YEAH. ME, TOO. TO THE PITS OF EXHAUSTION.

I'M QUITE IMPRESSED, MY FRIEND. YOU SHOW A NATURAL APTITUDE FOR THE MYSTIC ARTS.
IF YOU DESIRE, I COULD TUTOR YOU--

WAAAUGH! NOPE. SORRY. NO DICE. UH-UH.
JUST GET ME OUTTA THIS SMOCK AN' SEND ME HOME!

IN A MOMENT-- AFTER I RECALL OUR COMRADES...
...WHOM, I SENSE, HAVE ALSO MET WITH SUCCESS THIS DAY.

HOME AGAIN, HOME AGAIN, JIGGEDY-JIG.
DOC, I AM NEVER GONNA GET USED TO THIS KIND OF TRAVEL.
NUTS! FORGOT BEV WOULD BE WITH 'EM!
WHAT'M I GONNA TELL 'ER WHEN IT'S TIME FOR ME TA SHOVE OFF?

I KNEW IT! I KNEW SHE'D GO LACHRYMOSE ON ME!
OH, DUCKY, I WAS SO FRIGHTENED FOR YOU! THESE GOONS SAY THEY WERE PAID TO KILL YOU!

AAAH, WE DIDN'T CARE ABOUT THE DUMB DUCK! WE JUST WANTED THE METTLE SPHERES ANGST PROMISED US!
HE SAID STRANGE HAD THE TOOLS TO MAKE THEM!

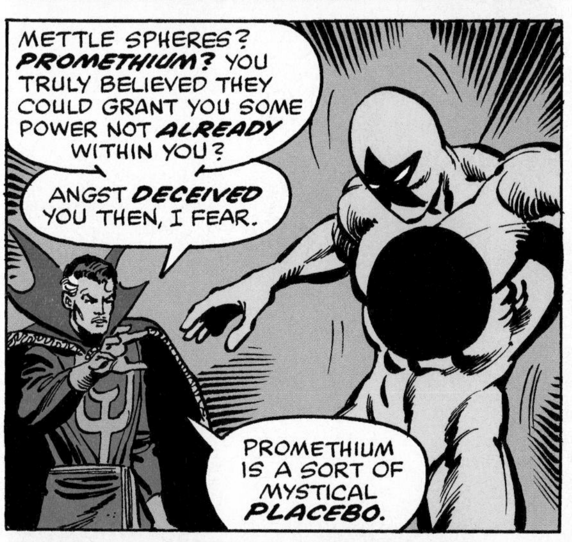
METTLE SPHERES? PROMETHIUM? YOU TRULY BELIEVED THEY COULD GRANT YOU SOME POWER NOT ALREADY WITHIN YOU?
ANGST DECEIVED YOU THEN, I FEAR.
PROMETHIUM IS A SORT OF MYSTICAL PLACEBO.

AND SPHERES, AS THEY SAY, ARE LIKE SOUL-- IF ONE LACKS IT, NO EXTERIOR FORCE MAY IMPART IT.

WHICH BRINGS US BACK TO YOU, FRIEND DUCK, AND YOUR MYSTIC JOURNEY--
SKIP IT, DOC. JUST LEMME NAP AWHILE, OKAY?
THEN YOU CAN LOAN ME A BUCK FOR THE JOURNEY BACK UPTOWN ON A BUS, HUH?
FIN

GET DOWN, AMERICA!
CAMPAIGN HEADQUARTERS
GET DOWN, AMERICA!
HOWARD THE DUCK CAMPAIGN HEADQUARTERS

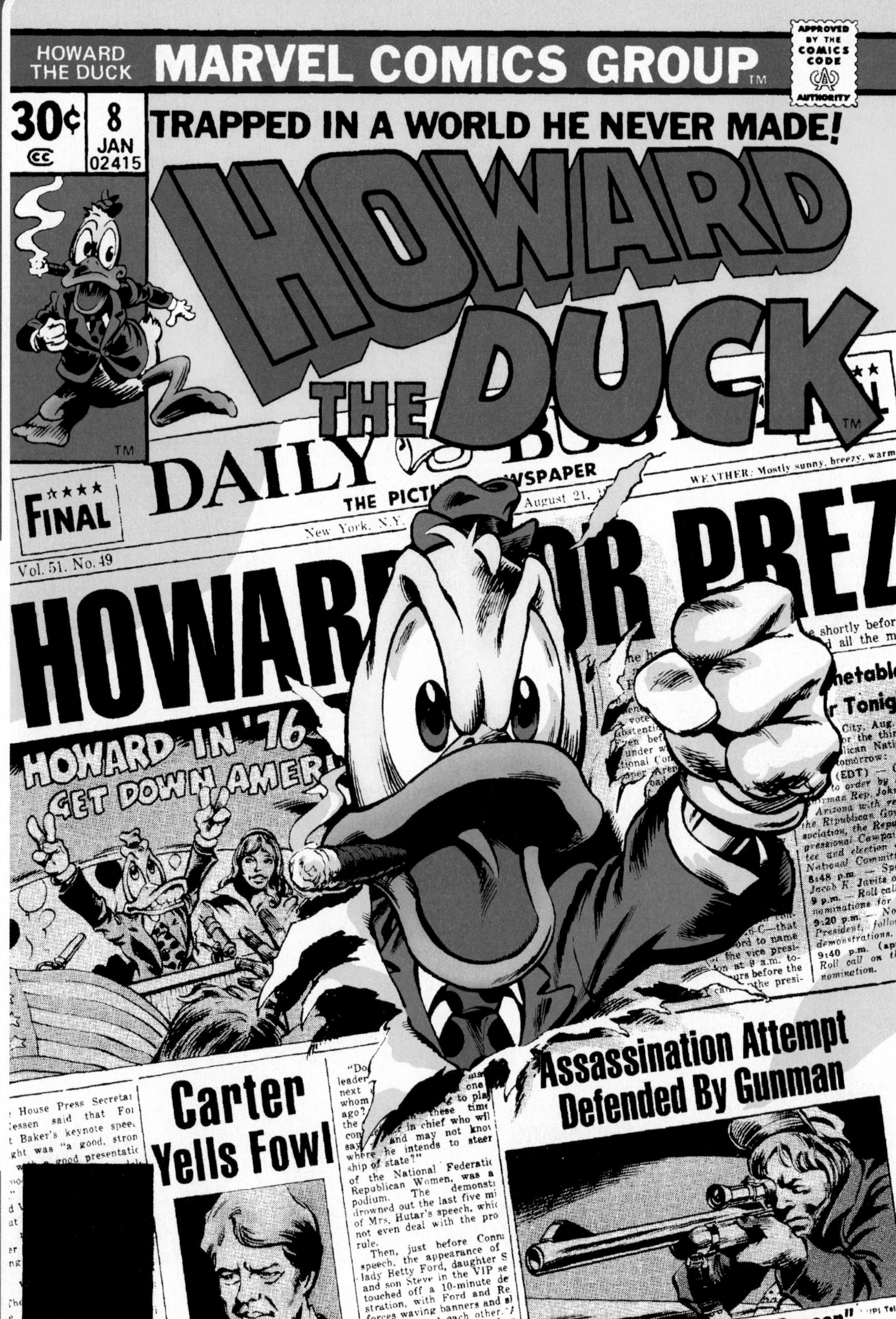

HOWARD THE DUCK
MARVEL COMICS GROUP
APPROVED BY THE COMICS CODE AUTHORITY
30¢
8
JAN
02415
TRAPPED IN A WORLD HE NEVER MADE!
HOWARD THE DUCK
FINAL
Vol. 51. No. 49
WEATHER: Mostly sunny, breezy, warm.
Carter Yells Fowl
UPI photo
Assassination Attempt Defended By Gunman
"Thought He Was In Season," Explains Prisoner

From the time of his hatching, he was...different. A potentially brilliant scholar who dreaded the structured environment of school, he educated himself in the streets, taking whatever work was available, formulating his philosophy of self from what he learned of the world about him. And then the Cosmic Axis shifted...and that world *changed.* Suddenly, he was stranded in a universe he could not fathom. Without warning, he became a strange fowl in an even stranger land.

Stan Lee PRESENTS: HOWARD THE DUCK!™

STEVE GERBER WRITER * GENE COLAN ARTIST * STEVE LEIALOHA INKER * I. WATANABE LETTERER * JAN COHEN COLORIST * ARCHIE GOODWIN EDITOR

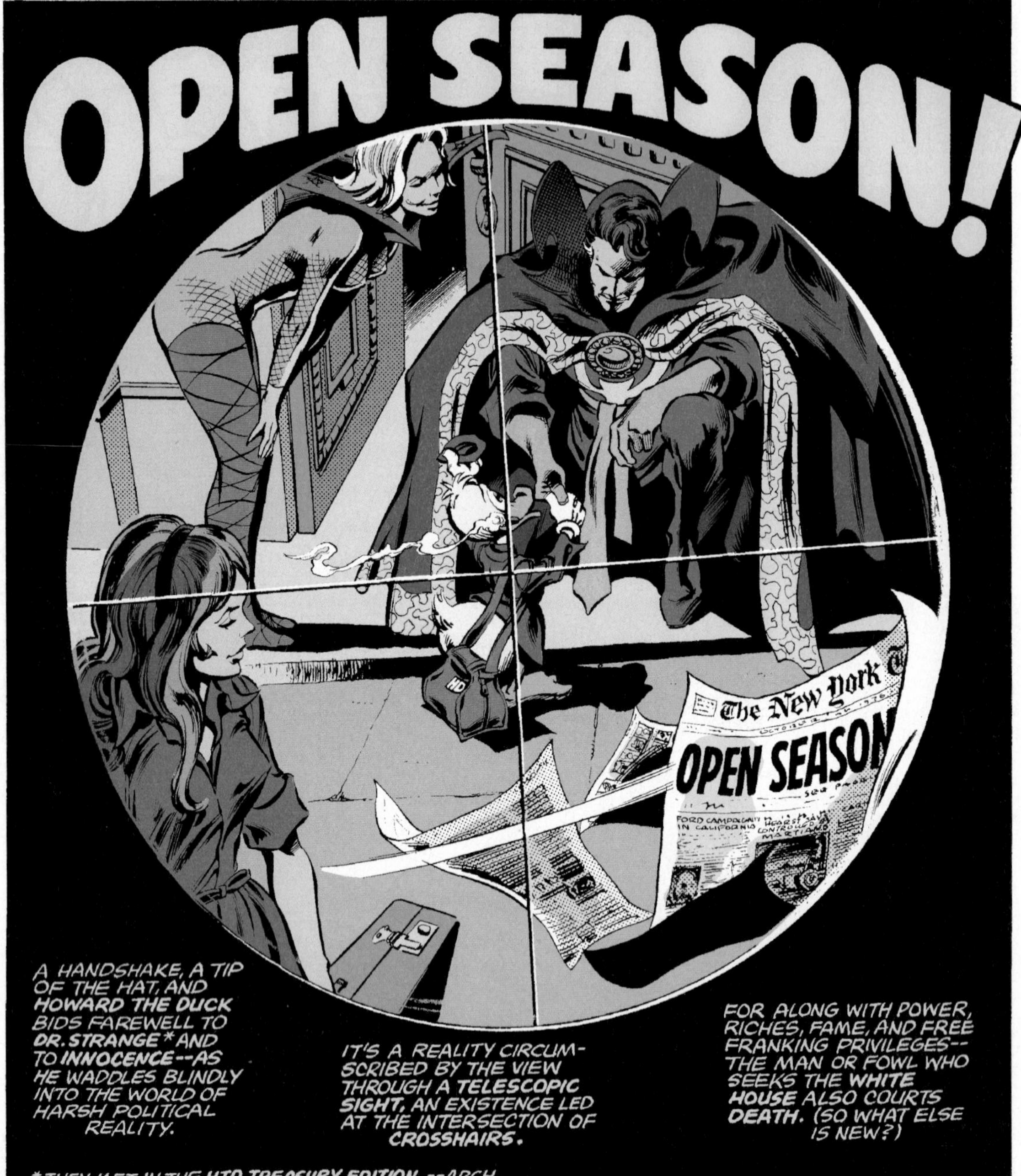

OPEN SEASON!
The New York T
OPEN SEASON
A HANDSHAKE, A TIP OF THE HAT, AND HOWARD THE DUCK BIDS FAREWELL TO DR. STRANGE* AND TO INNOCENCE--AS HE WADDLES BLINDLY INTO THE WORLD OF HARSH POLITICAL REALITY.
IT'S A REALITY CIRCUMSCRIBED BY THE VIEW THROUGH A TELESCOPIC SIGHT, AN EXISTENCE LED AT THE INTERSECTION OF CROSSHAIRS.
FOR ALONG WITH POWER, RICHES, FAME, AND FREE FRANKING PRIVILEGES-- THE MAN OR FOWL WHO SEEKS THE WHITE HOUSE ALSO COURTS DEATH. (SO WHAT ELSE IS NEW?)
*THEY MET IN THE HTD TREASURY EDITION. --ARCH.

BUT WHY COULDN'T WE ACCEPT DOC'S INVITATION TO SPEND THE NIGHT?
DO YOU WANNA SLEEP IN CENTRAL PARK?
WE'RE BROKE, DUCKY. WE HAVEN'T HEARD FROM THE PARTY SINCE THE CONVENTION.

WE DON'T EVEN KNOW IF YOU'RE STILL A CANDIDA--
BLAM

HOWARD? WHAT WAS THAT?
HOWARD??

OH! THERE YOU ARE!
BUT WHO'S THAT?
JUST SOME SLOB WHO FELL OFF THE ROOF, BEY. C'MON!

BUT HOWARD, HE NEEDS HELP. I THINK HE'S DEAD!
YEAH. PROB'LY!
I THINK SOMEBODY PUT A BULLET RIGHT THROUGH HIM!

BUT WHO? WHY?
I DON'T KNOW, AND I DON'T CARE.
WHOEVER OLE DEADEYE WAS, HE'S GETTIN' AWAY--

--HEADING EAST OVER THE ROOFTOPS! SO GUESS WHAT DIRECTION WE'RE TAKING?
IT STARTS WITH "W".
LEAPING FROM PARAPET TO PARAPET PERIPATETICALLY, THE DARING ASSASSIN FLEES THE SCENE.

BUT HIS FLIGHT ENCOUNTERS TURBULENCE IN A NEARBY ALLEY...
WHAT THE--?!
ANOTHER HUMAN AMMUNITION DEPOT.

SO! A SET-UP, HUH?
WELL, YOU'RE NOT RUNNIN' ME IN, YA DIRTY ROTTEN--

HEY! YOU'RE NOT A COP! YOU'RE--!
AND YOU'RE--!

ARE YOU HERE TA KILL 'IM, TOO?
YOU KIDDIN'? EVERY HIT MAN IN THE CITY'S AFTER THAT BIRD!

WELL! IF COMPETITION'S THAT STIFF--COUNT ME OUT! EVEN 10 MILLION AIN'T WORTH DYIN' FOR.
RIGHT ON, MAN. SEE YA!

BLAM
NOT IF I SEE YOU FIRST!!
BAM
WHY YOU--!!

HOWARD, YOU DON'T SUPPOSE--WITH YOU RUNNING FOR PRESIDENT AND ALL--I MEAN, COULD THEY BE--
--SHOOTING AT US?
IT IS POSSIBLE, BEV.

SUDDENLY, FROM AROUND THE CORNER... THE SCREECH OF TIRES, THE ROAR OF A POWERFUL ROLLS ENGINE...
ONE WAY
D★G
...AND THE FAMILIAR, IF ABOMINABLE, SIGHT OF COUNTRY SINGER DREYFUSS GULTCH'S LIMOUSINE.

HURRY, Y'ALL! MUH BULLET-PROOF GLASS WILL PROTECT YA!
IT'S BEEN TESTED BY NORTH CAROLINA WOMEN!
SCRREEEEEECH

THE DOOR SLAMS SHUT... AND CHRISTOPHER STREET BECOMES A WAR ZONE! ASSASSINS WHO MIGHT OTHERWISE HAVE WAITED THEIR TURNS EMERGE, GUNS BLAZING, FROM EVERY NOOK, CRANNY, AND MANHOLE!
WHERE'D YA' ALL RUN OFF TO, HOWIE? IT AIN'T SAFE FOR YA TO TO BE WALKIN' THE STREETS!
BRRRP
PINNNG
POW POW
BAM

YEAH. I GATHERED. GOT ANY SPARE HYPOTHESES WHY?
SHORE. I KNOW WHY! IT'S THEM WILD-EYED POLITICAL PROMISES YOU BEEN MAKIN'!
WHAT PROMISES?! I HAVEN'T--

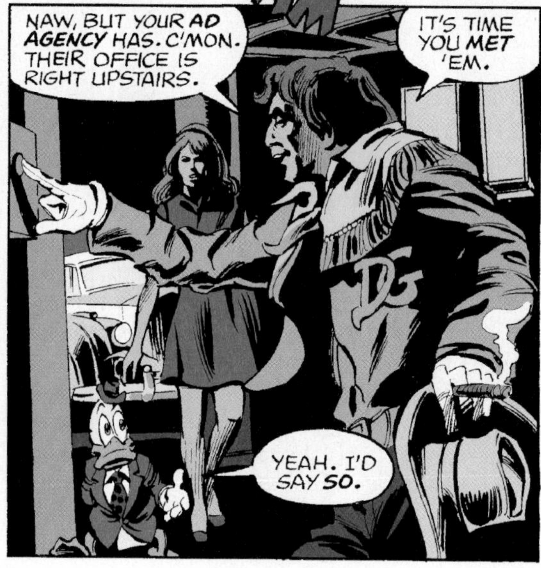
NAW, BUT YOUR AD AGENCY HAS. C'MON. THEIR OFFICE IS RIGHT UPSTAIRS.
IT'S TIME YOU MET 'EM.
YEAH. I'D SAY SO.

UPSTAIRS...
WOW. HEY, DUCKY, I'M **IMPRESSED.**
I USED TO THINK **I** WAS ALL THINGS TO ALL MEN... BUT EVEN IN MY **DEVIL-MAY-CARE** DAYS, I COULDN'T BEAT **THIS!**
OWARD · PRE
STAND UP, AMERICA — VOTE HOWARD THE DUCK IN '76
I DON'T BELIEVE IT.
HOWARD FOR PRESIDENT
WHOSE WARPED MIND IS **RESPONSIBLE** FOR THIS HOKUM?

BOSS! MR. STUDLEY! OH, DARLING--HELP ME!
MAD DUCK! MAD DUCK!

WELL, WELL... COME OUT OF SECLUSION AT LAST! ALL RIGHT, MEN--
--TAKE HIM!
RIGHT, MR. STUDLEY.

NOW, NOW... COME ALONG. IT'S FOR YOUR OWN GOOD. YOU'LL SEE.
WAIT! WHAT ARE YOU DOING?!
OUR JOB, LADY. DON'T INTERFERE.

YOU! YOU'RE IN CHARGE HERE! WHERE ARE THEY TAKING HIM?!
THUMP
HE COMMITTED HIMSELF, MS. SWITZLER--

--TO WINNING THIS ELECTION, I MEAN. NOW IT'S MY JOB--AND THAT OF OUR MAKE-UP MEN--
--TO INSURE HE FULFILLS THAT COMMITMENT, OR DIES TRYING.
FOR THAT, WE NEED HIS--AND YOUR--TOTAL CO-OPERATION.

NOT THAT WE HAVEN'T MADE REMARKABLE STRIDES ALREADY. OF THE THREE MAJOR CANDIDATES--
--HOWARD'S ASSASSINATION QUOTIENT IS BY FAR THE HIGHEST--AN UNPRECEDENTED 7.97.
HTD FORD CARTER
TH-THAT'S GOOD??

GOOD? IT'S GREAT!
IT MEANS PEOPLE CARE!

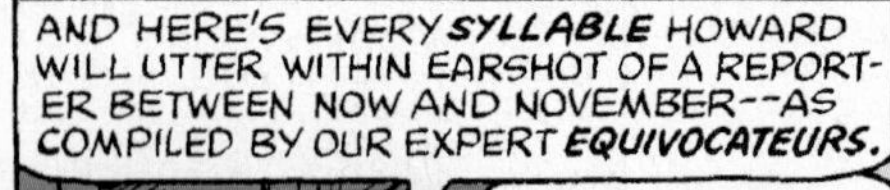
AND HERE'S EVERY SYLLABLE HOWARD WILL UTTER WITHIN EARSHOT OF A REPORTER BETWEEN NOW AND NOVEMBER--AS COMPILED BY OUR EXPERT EQUIVOCATEURS.

BUT--HOW DO YOUR SPEECHWRITERS KNOW WHAT HOWARD THINKS ABOUT--

TODAY'S CANDIDATE DOESN'T THINK, MS. SWITZLER. HE RECITES--
--NICE, SAFE, PRE-TESTED BROMIDIC BOMBASTS LIKE THIS:
AHEM

"I'M TIRED OF HEARING PEOPLE RUN DOWN THIS COUNTRY! SURE, WE'VE GOT PROBLEMS--
"--POLLUTION, INFLATION, RECESSION, CRIME, PERVASIVE MORAL DECAY--JUST TO NAME A FEW.
"BUT WHAT NATION DOESN'T HAVE ITS TROUBLES?"

ARE YOU SERIOUS? YOU EXPECT HOWARD TO SPOUT THAT STUFF?
WITH A STRAIGHT FACE?!
EH? WHATEVER DO YOU ME--
WAAAUGH

WE HADDA WORK FAST, MR. STUDLEY. HE WOULDN'T STOP SQUIRMIN'! BUT--

"BUT" NOTHING! HE'S MAGNIFICENT!!
DISTINGUISHED. SUBTLE. RAZOR-SHARP LINES--YET TASTEFULLY UNDERSTATED.

AND EXUDING UNMISTAKABLE SEX APPEAL! AND LORD A'MIGHTY, THAT WINNING SMILE!!

YEAH? WELL, IF YA LIKE IT SO MUCH--
CHOMP

--YA CAN KEEP IT, YA POMPOUS, PRESUMPTUOUS, PLASTICIZED FASHION PLATE!

STOP!!
YOU'RE COMMITTING POLITICAL SUICIDE!
YOU CAN'T WADDLE OUT ON US! WHO'LL PACKAGE YOU?!

YOU'RE A THIRD-PARTY CANDIDATE AND A DUCK!
YOU EXPECT TO SURMOUNT THOSE IMAGE PROBLEMS ALONE?!

NYAAH
JUST WATCH ME, LAUGHING BOY!

OUTSIDE...
YOU FIGGER EVERY CANDIDATE GOES THRU THIS DEBASEMENT?
NAH. BY THE TIME MOST OF 'EM GET THIS FAR, HUMILIATING COMPROMISE COMES EASY.

WHAT ARE YOU GONNA DO ABOUT AN AD REP, THOUGH?
WE'LL PICK OUR OWN--THE SCIENTIFIC WAY!

AT RANDOM--FROM THE YELLOW PAGES!
TEL EPH
AH-HA!

NOW THAT'S OUR KINDA PEOPLE!
WELL...YOUR KIND, ANYWAY.
MAD GENIUS
ASS ATES
H AVENUE
OOM 806...

CAMPAIGN LOG: SEPTEMBER

AND NOW THE QBS EVENING NEWS WITH WALTER KLONDIKE:
"GOOD MORNING. ONE MONTH AGO, MOST AMERICANS HAD NEVER HEARD OF MAD GENIUS ASSOCIATES--OR THEIR MOST UN-USUAL CLIENT. BUT FOR THE PAST THIRTY DAYS...

5 4 3 2

"...THE ATTENTION OF THE ELECTORATE HAS BEEN **RIVETED** ON THAT DIMINUTIVE FIGURE, PERHAPS THE MOST **EXTRAORDINARY** NEW FACE IN POLITICS.

"HIS CAMPAIGN BEGAN IN-AUSPICIOUSLY ENOUGH--JUST A **SOAPBOX** AND PLAIN TALK. YET HIS DEMEANOR, HIS RAW, THROATY VOICE, HIS RELENTLESS **CANDOR** SET HIM APART AT ONCE.

"IN THE WORDS OF ONE ASTONISHED LISTENER: 'MY GOD, HE'S TELLING THE TRUTH! HE'LL BE DEAD IN A WEEK!'"

"WHY A DUCK?" YOU ASK! I SAY, WHY NOT A DUCK? YOU'VE HAD TURKEYS RUNNING THIS COUNTRY FOR 200 YEARS!
I'M GONNA RUN AN ACTIVIST CAMPAIGN! EVEN THE BOZOS WHO JUST LOOK AT THE PICTURES WILL WILL KNOW WHAT I STAND FOR!
"TO THE SURPRISE OF A JADED CITIZENRY, THIS CURIOUS LITTLE CREATURE KEPT HIS PROMISE--BEGINNING WITH A VISUAL STATEMENT ON POLLUTION.
"FROM ONE SQUARE BLOCK IN NEW YORK, HTD COLLECTED A STEAM-SHOVELFUL OF NON-RETURNABLE CONTAINERS--AND BROUGHT THEM HOME TO ROOST ON THE MANUFACTURER'S IMMACULATE INDUSTRIAL MALL.
PRODIGAL CAN CO.
INDUSTRIAL PARK
"ON BUSING: 'SEND THE PARENTS FOR A RIDE! IF THEY STOPPED YELLING, MAYBE THE KIDS COULD HEAR THEIR TEACHERS!'
SCHOOL BU
UNLAWFUL TO PA
"'AS IT IS, ALL THEY'RE LEARNING IS ARSON AND BAD MANNERS!
"ON THE MILITARY BUDGET: 'YOU GUYS WANT BIGGER, DEADLIER, MORE EXPENSIVE WEAPONS? SWELL! BUT WE GOTTA CUT SOMETHING!'
UNITED STATES OF AMERICA
FORT NEANDERTHAL
NO TRESSPASSING
"'HOW 'BOUT HOUSING? YOU CAN ROUGH IT--IN CAVES. IT'LL SUIT YOUR TEMPERAMENT!'

"NONE OF THOSE POSITIONS PROVED POPULAR, HOWEVER, WITH VARIOUS POWERFUL INTEREST GROUPS--OR WITH THE DUCK'S OPPONENTS.

OUR FOWL MAY FIND THAT EVEN FORTH-RIGHTNESS, CARRIED TO ITS EXTREME, MAY BE DELETERIOUS IN THE LONG VIEW.
MAYBE NOT, THOUGH.

I, UH, AM NOT QUITE CERTAIN HOW TO INTERPRET OR RESPOND TO THIS DUCK'S THEATRICS. BUT IF IT'S SUPPOSED TO BE FUNNY, I DON'T GET THE JOKE.
IS IT DIRTY, OR WHAT?

"BUT MILLIONS OF AMERICANS DO UNDERSTAND AND HAVE RE-SPONDED. AND THEY'RE WEARING THIS NOW-FAMOUS BUTTON TO PROVE IT.
GET DOWN, AMERICA!
★VOTE HOWARD THE DUCK IN '76★

"NOW THE WORLD WONDERS--CAN HE WIN? WILL HE LIVE LONG ENOUGH TO WIN?
"BY THE SIMPLE ACT OF TELLING THE TRUTH AS HE SEES IT, HOWARD THE DUCK HAS MANAGED TO ANTAGONIZE ALMOST EVERY-BODY.

"ACCORDING TO THE POLLS, SOME 48% OF THE POPULATION WANT HIM DEAD--30% INTEND TO GIVE HIM THEIR VOTE--AND 22% ARE UNDECIDED.

"AND THAT'S THE WAY IT IS--TAKE IT OR LEAVE IT."

INTER-LUDE
A CHILL OCTOBER MORN IN CENTRAL PARK!
C'MON, BEV-- THINK! THAT'S WHY YOU RISKED DEATH TO WALK AROUND HERE ALL NIGHT!
JEEZ--HEY, BRAIN, WHERE ARE YA, GUY? WHERE ARE ALL THOSE THOUGHTS I WANTED TO BE ALONE WITH, HUH?
I FEEL LIKE I WANNA TAKE OFF ALL MY CLOTHES AND GET ARRESTED!

LIFE USEDTA BE SO SIMPLE--BEFORE POLITICS, BEFORE FAME, BEFORE--!
DUCKS USEDTA BE SO SIMPLE! JEEZ!

NOW ALL I CAN THINK ABOUT ARE THE POLLS, THE GNP, THE RATE OF INFLATION, THE--ULP!

FREEZE, CHARLIE. I TOOK PRIVATE LESSONS FROM DIANA RIGG!
S-SORRY! I DIDN'T MEAN TO STARTLE YOU!

I--JUST WANTED TO FEED THE DUCKS--AN' THINK, Y'KNOW? I COME HERE A LOT.
S-SURE. I JUST KINDA--OVER-REACTED.

WELL--SEE YA. HAVE FUN WITH THE DUCKS.
OH, I WILL. I REALLY LOVE DUCKS. IN FACT--

WAAAUGH
--I MAKE IT A POINT TO THROTTLE ONE EVERY DAY!

IS THIS REALLY MINK--?!

WE CAN MAKE MAKE IT, EH--WORTH YOUR WHILE TO BE SUPPORTIVE OF US, TOO.

IN OTHER WORDS, YOU YO-YO'S WANNA DO BUSINESS.

I VETO A BILL--THEN BILL YOU FOR A COUPLE HUNDRED GRAND, RIGHT?

WELL OF COURSE, THERE'S NO NEED TO TALK FIGURES JUST YET...!

PSSST
I S'POZE YOU KNOW I'VE BEEN RUNNING AS A PEOPLE'S CANDIDATE...?
CLEAN GOVERNMENT WITH NO WAXY YELLOW BUILD-UP AN' ALL THAT...?
GOTTA HAVE A LINE TO GET ELECTED, I GUESS...!
WELL, S'POZE I TOLDJA I DON'T CARE IF I'M ELECTED?
THAT I'D RATHER LOSE THAN SELL OUT TO YOU OILY GUYS WITH STEEL BRAINS AND EXHAUST PIPE MOUTHS? HUH?
IN THAT CASE, MR. DUCK...

...WE HAVE NOTHING MORE TO DISCUSS.
YOU'LL HAVETA KISS A LOT OF BABIES TO COUNTERVAIL THE DAMAGE YOU'VE DONE TO YOURSELF.
AND I HAVETA BUY MY OWN WINTER COAT, TOO, HUH?

THE MANGY MAGNATES WHO RULE THE WORLD!
THOSE GUYS KILL ME!
YUP, HOWIE-- THEY JUST MIGHT.
SLAM

NOT WITHOUT AN APPOINTMENT. OUR SCHEDULE'S FULL BETWEEN NOW AND ELECTION DAY.
ANOTHER WEEK OF BARNSTORMING--THEN BACK TO NEW YORK FOR YOUR LAST NATIONALLY TELEVISED PRESS CONFERENCE.

PARTIAL TRANSCRIPT OF NATIONALLY TELEVISED PRESS CONFERENCE:
Hotel Rykrisp, New York City, November 1, 1976

HOWARD: Ladies an' germs, I'll keep my opening smart remarks brief. I didn't particularly wanna be president of this coast-to-coast funny farm you hairless apes have set up. When they asked me to run, I'd just been hit on the head an' didn't really understand what I was agreein' to. But I've reached the conclusion that most o' the American public is in the same condition most o' the time, so just maybe I'm the ideal candidate. You meatbrains willingly subject yourselves to more abuse, physical and psychological, than any nation in history! You allow your eyes and lungs to be eaten away by pollution. You fill your digestive tracts with chemicals. Your ears are barraged by the sounds of jackhammer progress. All this while politicians and Madison Avenue bang away at your minds. You all wanna be happy an' secure, yet you open yourselves to the constant tension an' pressure of a society that claims to be free, but refuses to let you make a move without first filing forms in triplicate. You wonder why you got violence? Why your young are either dissident, empty-headed, or drugged into a stupor? It's because you've fashioned an emotionally and intellectually sterile culture, that's why! If an individual is unwilling to spend his life in the plodding pursuit of possessions, there's nothing for 'im to *do!* The United States is one big dateless Saturday night! If I'm elected, I'm gonna inject a little *life* back into you anesthetized Americans! For four years, this country's gonna get down an' boogie, see?! Ungawa! Okay! Now anybody got any brilliant questions?

(Stunned silence, interrupted only by an occasional nervous cough; then...)

RAMSEY KLEP (Devil's Tongue, N.M., *Daily Lick)*: Mr. Duck, which do you favor--- conditional amnesty or a blanket pardon for Vietnam draft evaders?

HOWARD: Neither. I favor education.

KLEP: Beg pardon?

HOWARD: Look, as nearly as I can tell, everybody is still reacting on this question with his gut, not his head. It's still "my country right or wrong" versus "make love not war". I figure the answer is a debate, on television, between proponents of each position. The government would buy time on all three networks and the yelling could go on for days. Then, the country could decide in a national referendum, based on each individual's judgment of the facts. Revolutionary, huh? Next!

DUNSTAN QUOBROX (Lima, OH., *Daily Bean*): What's your opinion of the recent Washington scandals? Should elected officials be held accountable for their private morality?

HOWARD: Nah. As long as the taxpayers aren't financin' their little romps, senators an' congressmen deserve to have a little fun. Heck, we oughtta be heartened to know some o' those old prunes have still got it in 'em.

SAM QUENTIN (Dubious, NJ, *Daily Dunno)*; How do you feel, sir, about violence in movies, television programs, and comic books?

HOWARD: I'm all for it.

QUENTIN: What?

HOWARD: As long as it's never presented as cathartic—as a release, as a solution. A kid oughtta know what he's gettin' into if he's contemplatin' stabbing or shootin' somebody. It's messy. The blood gets all over the floor. It smells bad. It's ugly to look at. I think violence should be presented honestly—as disgustingly and offensively as possible. There's no such thing as tasteful violence.

(Beverly Switzler leaps up on the table, does a little dance, blows a whistle, and chirps "Th-th-that's all, folks!" into a microphone. The auditorium explodes in applause, and the press conference concludes.)

OUTSIDE...
SMILE, MR. DUCK! YOU LOOK LIKE A WINNER!
OKAY--BUT NO MORE QUESTIONS. I'M POOPED!
BUT YOU'LL PUCKER UP FOR MY BABY-DOLL, WON'T YOU?

I BOUGHT HER FOR $5.95 ON SALE. HER NAME IS--
CLUMP

--MUNITIONS!
AND SHE LOVES YOU TO BITS, MR. DUCK--TO BITS!!
BLAMM
WAAUGH

GREER
CONSTRU
WHUMP

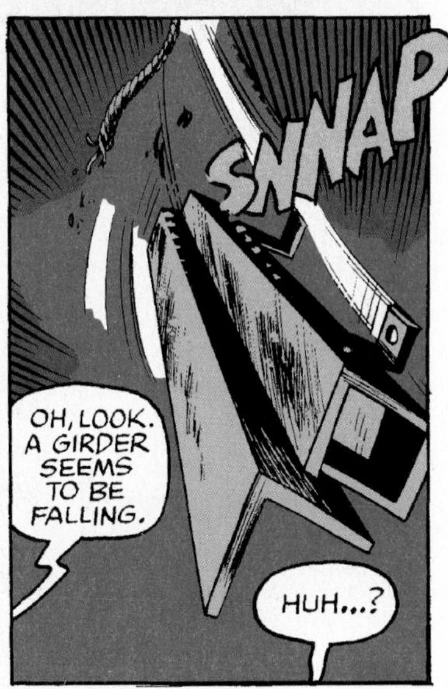
SNNAP
OH, LOOK. A GIRDER SEEMS TO BE FALLING.
HUH...?

HOWARD-- LOOK OUT!!
WAAAUK
CRRASH
DON'T YOU SEE WHAT'S HAPPENING? WE'RE RUNNING A GAUNTLET OF SPECIAL INTERESTS!!
THIS IS THEIR LAST-DITCH EFFORT TO BUMP YOU OFF! THEY'RE SO DESPERATE-- THEY DON'T CARE WHO SEES, WHO KNOWS--!
WE'VE GOTTA GET OUTTA H--
WAIT-- WHAT'S THAT?
A DRIVERLESS CAR! OH, JEEZ,-- WE'RE DOOMED!
UH-UH! ON MY SIGNAL--
CRRASHH
--JUMP!!
WE'LL RIDE IT RIGHT THROUGH THE BARRICADES!!
W-WE'RE STILL ALIVE! WE'VE SURVIVED THREE MAJOR INDUSTRIES!
CAN I HELP YA'S--?
FILL 'ER UP??

NEXT THE BITE OF THE BEAVER! CHOMP!

HOWARD THE DUCK

MARVEL® COMICS GROUP

APPROVED BY THE COMICS CODE AUTHORITY

30¢ CC

9 FEB 02415

TRAPPED IN A WORLD HE NEVER MADE!

HOWARD THE DUCK™

TM

THUNDER OVER NIAGRA FALLS!

WHEN BITES THE BEAVER!

From the time of his hatching, he was...different. A potentially brilliant scholar who dreaded the structured environment of school, he educated himself in the streets, taking whatever work was available, formulating his philosophy of self from what he learned of the world about him. And then the Cosmic Axis shifted...and that world *changed.* Suddenly, he was stranded in a universe he could not fathom. Without warning, he became a strange fowl in an even stranger land.

Stan Lee Presents: HOWARD THE DUCK!™

STEVE GERBER WRITER/EDITOR / GENE COLAN ARTIST / STEVE LEIALOHA INKER / JOHN COSTANZA, letterer MICHELE WOLFMAN, colorist
NOVEMBER 3, 1976: THE PRESIDENTIAL ELECTION IS PAST, AND YESTERDAY'S PAPERS TELL THE TALE-- THE ONLY PART THAT MATTERS, ANYWAY.
HTD L-O-S-T.
AND HE LOST BIG!
DAILY BUGLE
FINAL
NEW YORK, TUESDAY, NOV. 2, 1976, 63rd YEAR
A Tight Family? P. 6
NIGHT OWL
SCANDAL PLUCKS DUCK
EXCELLENT, MON AMI-- TRES NIFTY! A MOST EXTRAORDINARY FEAT OF PUBLIC RELATIONS-- FOR A BELLBOY.
HOWEVER, AS YOU KNOW, WE RECEIVE YOUR NEWS ON A DELAY UP HERE.
PART OF THE PLOT TO KEEP US BACKWARD, EH?
BUT YOU'RE A U.S. CITIZEN... THEY WOULD'VE TOLD YOU. WHAT WAS THE OUTCOME OF THE ELECTION?
POLLSTERS SAY HE'S FINISHE
ATTY HEARST-- GIRL OR AUTOMOBILE? SEE PG. 1
GARINE-- OLEO OR BUST? SEE PG. 12
--EX-PREXY OR LIVE BAIT? SEE PG. 12

I TOLD YOU-- HOWARD DIDN'T WIN. EVEN BACK HOME, NOBODY CARES WHO DID.
NOW WHEN DO I GET MY MONEY?
SIGH I THOUGHT WE'D SETTLED THAT. YOU DID IT ALL FOR AMERICA, NON?
AND TO AVENGE YOUR BELOVED BROTHER?

OH--OH, YEAH! I ALMOST FORGOT! MY BROTHER TOMMY! THE ONLY AMERICAN KILLED IN VIETNAM--
--BY A DUCK!

HE WAS AN ANTI-AIRCRAFT GUNNER, TOMMY WAS-- BRAVEST MAN I EVER KNEW!
HE SIGHTED A CHARLIE MIG OVER-HEAD!
HE FIRED!!

BUT HE MISSED--
--AND HIT A WILD DUCK INSTEAD!

DOWN SPUN THE DIRTY COMMIE FOWL--
--IN A SPECTACULAR DEATH-DIVE FROM HUNDREDS OF FEET IN THE AIR--

--ONLY TO LAND ON A VIETCONG LAND MINE SIX INCHES FROM TOMMY'S FACE!
BOOM!

I'VE HATED DUCKS EVER SINCE! TO LET ONE BE ELECTED PRESIDENT OF THE COUNTRY TOMMY DIED FOR--!
YEAH, THAT'S WHY I DID IT! BUT WHAT ABOUT YOU? YOU'RE NOT AN AMERICAN! WHY'D YOU DO IT?
OH, JUST FOR GIGGLES.
HEE. HEE. HEE.

NEW YORK: AMID THE RUBBLE OF HTD CAMPAIGN HQ, THE DUCK, HIS COMPANION BEVERLY SWITZLER, AND COUNTRY WESTERN SINGER DREYFUSS GULTCH PONDER THE EXISTENTIAL CONSEQUENCES OF COAST-TO-COAST PUBLIC HUMILIATION.
HOWARD THE DUCK HQ
VOTE HOW
AAAH--WHAT DIFFERENCE DOES IT MAKE? I MEAN, IT'S NOT LIKE I THIRSTED AFTER THE PRESIDENCY!
I JUST WANTED A PROJECT TO OCCUPY MY TIME 'TIL NOVEMBER!
DOWN AMER
WELL, NOVEMBER'S HERE, DUCKY-- AND AS USUAL, YOU'RE STILL THINKING ONLY OF YOURSELF!
GET DOWN AMERICA · VOTE HOWARD
WHAT ABOUT MY REPUTATION?? DO YOU KNOW HOW LONG AND HARD I WORKED TO CONVINCE EVERYBODY IN CLEVELAND I WAS A GOOD GIRL??
FOR

AWRIGHT, Y'ALL--QUIT FANNIN' THE BREEZE AN' LISTEN TA SOME SENSE!
AH' JEST GOT OFF THE PHONE WITH A PAL O' MINE AT CIA!
HE SAYS THAR'S MORE HERE 'N MEETS THE EYE! THET PHOTO'S QUEER AS A THREE-DOLLAR BILL!
:WAAUGH:

WE KNOW IT'S A PHONY, YA TWO-BIT TINHORN TROUBADOUR!! BEV AN' I NEVER BATHE TOGETHER!
SHE HATES THE SMELL OF WET FEATHERS!!

WHAT CHANGED THEIR MINDS--NOW THAT I'M BRANDED NATION-WIDE AS A SHAMELESS HUSSY?
THAR WAS NO WATER FAUCET ON EITHER END O' THE TUB!
THEY REALIZED IT HADDA BE HALVES O' TWO PIX PASTED TOGETHER!

AN' THET AIN'T THE HALF OF IT, HOWIE--
MUH BUDDY FIGGERS YO'RE THE VICTIM OF AN INTERNATION-AL INTRIGUE! THET PHOTO WAS TRACED TO A FOREIGN POWER!
SMACK
COME AGAIN?

WHO?? I DEMAND TO KNOW WHAT COUNTRY WRECKED MY LIFE!!
WAS IT RUSSIA--RED CHINA--?

NOPE.
CANADA.
CANADA?!?

'COURSE, THE INTELLIGENCE BOYS WON'T INVESTIGATE. THEY'RE GLAD Y'ALL LOST! BUT--
EXIT
IT'S OKAY, GULTCH. TELL 'EM I APPRECIATE THEIR CANDOR --AND THEIR UTTER LUNACY.
SEE YA.

WHOA UP, BOY! WHAR'S YORE CONSCIENCE FLOWN?
THIS BLAMED SCANDAL DISCREDITS THE WHOLE ALL-NIGHT PARTY-- NOT JES' YOU!
DON'T FORGET ME! I'M TAINTED, TOO!
AW, C'MON-- LAY OFF, WILLYA?!

WHADDAYA THINK--THE PAPERS'LL RETRACT THAT PHOTO AN' WE'LL HOLD THE ELECTION AGAIN?!

YUP--AN' NOPE.
SEE, WE FIGGER THE ONLY SKUNK COULDA TOOK THEM PICTURES WAS THE BELL BOY AT YORE HOTEL.

AN' MUH CIA PARD TELLS ME HE FLED THE COUNTRY-- AN' LEFT A FORWARDIN' ADDRESS IN ONTARIO.
GULTCH--PEOPLE DON'T FLEE AND LEAVE A FORWARDING ADDRESS.!!

MEBBE NOT-- BUT THE PARTY FIGGERS IT'S WORTH CHECKIN' OUT.
AN' HERE'S YORE AIRLINE TICKETS TO PROVE IT!
YOU WANT ME TO INVESTIGATE IT-- PERSONALLY?

SHORE 'NUFF! WE'LL ANNOUNCE TO THE WORLD YO'RE FLYIN' NORTH TA CLEAR YORE NAME! IT'LL MAKE HEADLINES!
HMMM... IT'D PROBABLY SQUARE ME WITH MY PARENTS, TOO.
AN' WHEN YA ALL RETURN, THE CONQUERIN' HERO-- WELL, BY 1980-- YOU COULD BE IN THE RUNNIN' AGAIN, BOY!
OVER MY DEAD BODY.
I'VE BLED ENOUGH FOR THE CAUSE.

WELL, I'M NOT READY TO JOIN THE WADDLING WOUNDED, HOWARD! MY METICULOUSLY FABRICATED REP IS AT STAKE!
EITHER WE BOARD THAT PLANE TOGETHER --OR I NEVER SPEAK TO YOU AGAIN!
WHAT'LL IT BE??

TWO NIGHTS LATER...
I JUST DON'T SEE HOW YOU COULD MISPLACE YOUR TOOTH-BRUSH, YOUR CIGARS, AND YOUR HAT...!
FLY-BY-NIGHT AIRWAYS
WE ALMOST MISSED THE PLANE!
YEAH, HORRORS.

BUT IT LOOKS LIKE WE'RE RIGHT ON TIME.
WE HELD THE FLIGHT JUST FOR YOU, MA'AM.

SLAM
WELCOME ABOARD-- SUCKERS!!

THE RICKETY TWIN ENGINES COUGH SUDDENLY TO EMPHY-SEMATOUS LIFE.
THE PLANE TAXIS BUMPILY DOWN THE RUNWAY... AS THE ONE-MAN GROUND CREW HASTENS INTO THE SHADOWS, THERE TO EFFECT...

TAKE-OFF!
THE REMOTE TRANSMITTER WORKED PERFECTLY-- JUST AS PIERRE PROMISED!

"THEY'RE DOOMED!!"
HEY--WHAT'S GOIN' ON HERE?!
HOW COME WE'RE THE ONLY PASSENGERS ON THIS CRATE??

YOO-HOO! FLYBOY! WHERE'D YA GET YER PILOT'S LICENSE --AT SEARS??
WHAT'RE YA--;ULP;
NOBODY HOME.

AND THE CONTROLS ARE LOCKED IN ONE SETTING...
...NATURALLY.

I COULDN'T FIND ANY PARACHUTES IN BACK. SO WE'RE TRAPPED, HUH?
WHAT MAKES YA SAY THAT?

CANADA, SOME SEVEN HOURS AND 44 MINUTES LATER:
FROM THE SHORE OF YOUR BASIC CRYSTAL BLUE LAKE...
...OVERLOOKING THE SNOW-CAPPED PEAKS AND THICK PINE WOODS COMMONLY BELIEVED TO ENCIRCLE DOWN-TOWN TORONTO...
ARF!

I SAY...!
...A PAINFULLY EARNEST PAIR OF EYES TRACKS THE PLANE'S PERILOUS DESCENT.
FROM THE SOUND OF IT, CHAPS, I'D WAGER THAT CRAFT'S IN TROUBLE.
CRASH
WEEEEEEE
LET'S HAVE A LOOK, SHALL WE, OLD FELLOW?
GIDYAP!

THE SPIRITED STEED RESPONDS-- WITH PERHAPS A SLIGHT SUPERABUNDANCE OF GUSTO.
NO! PRINCE! WHOA, BOY! COME BACK!!
LOOOOO
ARF
WUMP
LARF

WHILE, ON THE OPPOSITE SHORE...
FLY BY NIGHT
WHEW
"FLUSH" WOULD BE MORE LIKE IT.
A FLUSH CALL.
THAT WAS A CLOSE CALL, HUH?
OR AN ABUTTED CALL, MAYBE.

CHEEZ-- CAN'T SEE THE FOREST FOR THE SPLIT HAIRS, CAN YA?
OPEN YOUR EYES, DUCKY! CATCH THAT HAT! WE MADE IT! WE'RE IN CANADA!
GREAT.

'EVENING, FOLKS. BIT OF A NASTY SPILL YOU TOOK THERE, EH?
SGT. PRESTON DUDLEY, RCMP, AT YOUR SERVICE-- MY HORSE PRINCE--
--AND MY TRUSTY HUSKIE ELIZABETH.

YEAH, WELL--CHARMED, I'M SURE.
WE'RE THE PAIN-WRACKED SURVIVORS.
FIGGER YOU COULD GIVE US A LIFT TO CIVILIZATION?

I'M CERTAIN PRINCE WOULDN'T OBJECT.
HE APPRECIATES A LOVELY LADY ON HIS BACK AS MUCH AS I.
CLIMB ABOARD.
SIGH

SHORTLY, AT THE NEIGHBORHOOD RCMP OUTPOST...
FROM WHAT YOU'VE TOLD ME, I'D DEDUCE YOU'RE VICTIMS OF THE INFAMOUS PIERRE DENTIFRIS, CANADA'S ONLY SUPER-PATRIOT!
H-HOW CAN YOU KNOW THAT?

HIS MODUS OPERANDI, MA'AM. PIERRE ALWAYS USES BELLBOYS AND ROBOT PLANES.
ALAS, HE'S USUALLY MORE SUCCESSFUL AT ELIMINATING THE TARGETS OF HIS MAD HATRED.
WE'VE NEVER QUITE MANAGED TO MAKE A CHARGE STICK.
BUT WHY DOES HE DO THESE THINGS...?!

LOVE OF COUNTRY, I EXPECT... RATHER A FANATIC SEEKER AFTER THE CANADIAN IDENTITY, PIERRE IS.

LISTEN, I'M SURE THE SUBTLE COMPLEXITIES OF THE CRIMINAL MIND ARE A SOURCE OF BOUNDLESS FASCINATION...
BUT ARE WE GONNA NAIL THE BUM, OR NOT?!

I BEG YOUR PARDON, SIR! THE MOUNTIES ALWAYS GET THEIR MAN!
REALLY? ALWAYS?? THE COPS BACK HOME CAN'T EVEN CATCH A COLD!
I SUGGEST, IF YOU HARBOR DOUBTS...

...YOU OBSERVE ME IN ACTION. COME ALONG.
WE SHALL SMOKE OUT PIERRE AT ONCE!

A BRIEF RIDE LATER...
PIERRE DENTIFRIS
CANADA'S ONLY SUPER PATRIOT
YOU SEE! I TOLD YOU HE COULDN'T ELUDE ME FOR LONG!
GEE, THAT'S AMAZING!
NO OFFENSE, TOOTS--BUT YOU'RE TOO EASILY IMPRESSED.
MP
MP
SACRE BLEU! PRESTON DUDLEY OF THE MOUNTIES!

AND TO WHAT DO I OWE ZIS ODIOUS INTRUSION?
I WANT YOU TO MEET SOME FRIENDS OF MINE, PIERRE--FROM SOUTH OF THE BORDER.

AMERICANS?! I WEESH A BELLBOY WOULD DROP LUGGAGE ON YOUR HEADS!!
I WEESH YOU WOULD DIE IN ZE CRASH OF A ROBOT PLANE!!
I DESPISE VOUS!

CAREFUL, YOUNG MAN. YOU'LL INCRIMINATE YOURSELF.
THIS GEEZER?! ARE YOU SERIOUS? HE COULDN'T HURT A GNAT!

I COULD--IF IT WERE AN AMERICAN GNAT, DUCKEE!
I WAS ONCE A POWERFUL MAN IN CANADA--A HOTEL AND AIRLINE MAGNATE!

I LOVED CANADA--AND GREW SICK AT ZE WAY YOU BARBARIANS INVADED AND POLLUTED US WITH YOUR INDUSTRY, YOUR SO-CALLED CULTURE--!

"I TURNED MY RESOURCES TO A DARING PLAN-- TO TEACH YOU ARROGANT FOOLS A LESSON! I AIRLIFTED A MILLION BEAVERS TO CONSTRUCT A DAM ACROSS NIAGARA--
"--TO MAKE IT FALL ZE OTHER WAY!!

"AND I SUCCEEDED! MY PETS AND I SLOWED ZE FALLS TO A TRICKLE!
ZUT ALORS! ZAT SOUND IN ZE SKY! QUEL--?

"I SHOULD HAVE KNOWN YOUR MILITARY WOULD NOT ALLOW A CANADIAN MORE THAN A MOMENT OF NATIONAL PRIDE!
"I HAD BARELY ZE TIME TO GLOAT...

"...WHEN ZE BOMBS BEGAN FALLING!"
BLAAMMMM

IT ALL HAPPENED BACK IN FEBRUARY. IT WAS KEPT VERY HUSH-HUSH, OF COURSE.
SINCE THEN, I'VE AGED NEARLY 73 YEARS AND LOST THE USE OF ALL MY LIMBS EXCEPT ZE TEETH!

WOW... WHAT A SAD STORY.
DOWNRIGHT PATHETIC.

LISTEN... IT'S BEEN FUN TALKIN' TO YA, OLD-TIMER... BUT WE GOTTA RUN.
TRY NOT TO BE BITTER. WE'LL PROB'LY DESTROY OURSELVES AN' SAVE YA THE BOTHER.

WAIT, YOU TWO! I THOUGHT YOU WANTED TO HAMMER THE SCOUNDREL!

OR HAVE YOU CHOSEN NOT TO BECOME... INVOLVED?
AW, COME OFF IT, DUDLEY! THIS OLD COOT'S OUTTA HIS MAPLE TREE!
AN' WE NEED SOME SLEEP!

VERY WELL... BUT YOU MAY LIVE TO RE-GRET THIS DECISION.
OH NO, HE WON'T! I SHALL SEE TO ZAT!
BELLHOP!

HE SURVIVED. I FAILED YOU-- AND TOMMY.
PLEASE LET ME KILL HIM AGAIN! I BEG YOU!
NATUREL-MENT.

BUT SINCE YOU BUN-GLED ZE ROBOT PLANE, I SUGGEST YOU EMPLOY MORE COMPLEX, SUBTLE MEANS ZIS TIME.
I WILL! I WILL!

"I'LL BE SO SUBTLE, HE'LL BARELY KNOW HE'S DEAD!"
THIS IS THE LIFE, EH? ROUGHING IT--IN A GOOD NEIGHBORHOOD!
SLEEP WELL, YOU TWO! AND BE UP AT THE CRACK OF DAWN!

HE'S NICE, ISN'T HE, HOWARD? EVEN IF HE DOES LIKE TO LIVE IN THE PAST A LITTLE.
HOW SO?
OH, YOU KNOW... HE WANTS TO BELIEVE THIS IS THE SAVAGE YUKON...

...WHEN WE'RE 60 MILES FROM LONDON, ONTARIO, AND 200,000 PEOPLE!
WE'VE ALL GOT OUR ILLUSIONS, TOOTS--YOU, ME, PRESTON, PIERRE...
IN FACT, I KEEP WONDERIN' IF ANYBODY'S GOT A LINE ON REALITY ANYMORE.

I'LL SHOW YOU REALITY, FOOL-- THE AMERICAN DREAM COME TRUE!
AN EYE FOR AN EYE--A DUCK FOR A BROTHER!
DIE, FEATHERED FIEND!!
HOWARD-- DON'T NOD OUT YET.
THERE'S A MADMAN IN OUR ROOM!
SO? YA WANNA TAKE 'IM--OR TALK 'IM INTA SUBMISSION?
ARF!
FOOLS!
YOU CAN'T STOP ME! I'VE THE STRENGTH OF TEN--
GRRRR
--FOR I'M HATE-CRAZED! MADDENED!
OWCH!
EH?
HOWARD--IT'S THE BELLBOY FROM THE PLAZA HOTEL--!
OKAY, HATE-CRAZED AND MADDENED -- DOCILE YOURSELF AN' SPILL! THE WHOLE STORY!!
HUH? "DOCILE" ISN'T A VERB...!
AND WHEN THE TALE HAS BEEN TOLD...
SORRY I MISSED THE ACTION, FOLKS.
BUT AT LEAST WE NABBED THE ROGUE, EH?
YEAH... AN' MUCH AS I HATE TO ADMIT IT, PRES, YOU WERE RIGHT. HE'S PIERRE'S FLUNKIE.
HIS MOTIVATION'S STILL A LITTLE FUZZY FOR MY TASTE, BUT...!

NO MATTER. I'LL RUN HIM IN POST-HASTE.
AND COME DAWN--WE STALK PIERRE HIMSELF!

DIDJA HEAR THAT, TOOTS? TOMORROW, WE--
TOOTS...?

I SHOULD'A KNOWN. NOTHIN'S EVER THAT EASY.
SHE'S GONE--AN' THE WINDOW'S THE ONLY EGRESS.

TOO DARK TO SEE MUCH-- EXCEPT ANIMAL TRACKS.
BUT THAT'S ENOUGH.

"SHE DIDN'T LEAVE UNDER HER OWN POWER. SOMEHOW, SHE WAS BORNE AWAY--
"--ON THE BACK OR BACKS OF SOME CRAWLING THING OR ANOTHER.
"NUTS!!"

HERE I GO A'FOLLOWIN' AGAIN--NO DOUBT DIRECTLY INTO THE EAR, NOSE, OR THROAT OF DEATH.
MY HEAD IS STARTIN' TO ACHE.
THE TRAIL LEADS INTO THE DEEP WOODS, EAST-WARD TOWARD THE DAWN...

...AND TERMINATES HERE, MANY HOURS AND MILES LATER, AT...
...NIAGARA FALLS!

MONSIEUR DUCK!!
SLOWLY HE TURNS...
AW, NO...!
AW, OUI, MONSIEUR! IT IS I--PIERRE DENTIFRIS--IN ZE MOST FORMIDABLE EXOSKELETON EVER DEVISED BY MAN!!
VOUS THOUGHT I WAS A HELPLESS CRIPPLE--ZE WAY ALL YOU AMERICANS THINK OF CANADA ITSELF!
WELL, IT IS NOT VRAI! I AM--LE BEAVER!
AND IF YOU WISH TO SEE YOUR JEUNE FILLE IN UNE PIECE AGAIN--
--YOU MUST FIGHT ME TO LE MORT--
--AND DON'T DALLY ABOUT IT!
HOWARD... HE'S NOT KIDDING! THE TREE'S WOBBLING ALREADY!
CHEW CHEW
CHOMP CHOMP CHOMP

MY PETS WILL STOP GNAWING ONLY WHEN I COMMAND ZEM--
--OR IF I DIE AND ZEY HAVE NOTHING TO LIVE FOR.
B-BUT...
JE SAIS! VOUS ARE ASKING YOURSELF... WHAT HAS ZIS TO DO FROM AMERICAN PRESIDENTIAL ELECTIONS, NON?
WELL, YEAH... THE QUESTION DID CROSS MY MIND...!
IT HAS TO DO WITH SHADOWS, DUCKEE! CANADA HAS WILTED IN AMERICA'S FOR TOO LONG!
WE HAVE WATCHED WHILE VOUS SQUANDERED YOUR NATURAL RESOURCES... WAITING FEARFULLY FOR YOUR APPETITES TO TURN NORTHWARD WHEN YOUR OWN TERRITORY WAS GUTTED!
SO I ARRANGED FOR VOUS TO BE NOMINATED BY THE ALL-NIGHT PARTY!
I WANTED TO OFFER A COMPLETELY HONEST CANDIDATE-- THEN RUIN HIM IN ZE PUBLIC EYEBALL!
HAH...?
LOOK, BUCK-TOOTH, MAYBE I'M A LITTLE DENSE, BUT--
FOOL! YOUR DEFEAT WOULD LAY BARE ZE UTTER ROTTENNESS OF YOUR NATION'S POLITICAL PROCESS!
I WOULD HAVE ENGINEERED ZE DISPIRIT OF '76!!
THEN, YOUR ALREADY APATHETIC COUNTRYMEN CONSUMED WITH DESPAIR, MY PETS AND I COULD INVADE ZE U.S.--
--AND BE WELCOMED AS HEROES! MY COUNTRY WOULD BE REDEEMED, OUR PARANOIA TURNED UPSIDE-DOWN!
CANADA COULD ANNEX THE UNITED STATES!!

NOW YOU SEE, DUCK--WHY YOU MUST NOT RETURN ALIVE!
IF VOUS EXONERATE YOURSELF--!
AH! OUI! TRES BON! ZIS WAY, FOWL!
HEAD FEELS LIKE AN ELEPHANT'S PLAYIN' SOCCER WITH IT, BUT--!
KEEP YER HAIRSHIRT ON, PAL! I'M COM--
I'M C--
I'M--
THE HELL I AM!!
COWARD!! HOW DARE VOUS TURN BACK?!
AAH--CHEW IT, PIERRE!
I JUST FIGGERED OUT WHAT THIS HEAD-ACHE WAS TRYIN' TA TELL ME!
AN' AS FAR AS I'M CONCERNED --YOU AN' YER POLITICS--
--CAN GO JUMP!
HOWARD--LOOK WHO JUST ARRIVED!
WE SAW IT ALL! YOU WERE BRILLIANT!
FEH!
HOWARD--WAIT! WHAT'S WRONG?
COME BACK!!
WELL, ELIZABETH...
I GUESS THIS BASKET CASE IS CLOSED.
NEXT
SWAN-SONG OF THE LIVING DEAD DUCK!
(A SURREALISTIC CHEAP SHOT)

HOWARD THE DUCK

MARVEL® COMICS GROUP

APPROVED BY THE COMICS CODE AUTHORITY

30¢ 10 MAR 02415

TRAPPED IN A WORLD HE NEVER MADE!

© 1976 MARVEL COMICS GROUP

HOWARD THE DUCK™

OUT OF THE EGG...

...INTO THE FRYING PAN!

WAAAAUGH

"DOOM IN A DARK DIMENSION!"

COLAN-LEIALOHA

From the time of his hatching, he was...different. A potentially brilliant scholar who dreaded the structured environment of school, he educated himself in the streets, taking whatever work was available, formulating his philosophy of self from what he learned of the world about him. And then the Cosmic Axis shifted...and that world *changed.* Suddenly, he was stranded in a universe he could not fathom. Without warning, he became a strange fowl in an even stranger land.

Stan Lee PRESENTS: HOWARD THE DUCK!™

STEVE GERBER WRITER/EDITOR — GENE COLAN ARTIST — STEVE LEIALOHA INKER — JIM NOVAK, LETTERER — JAN COHEN, COLORIST — TED SALLIS CONSULTING SCHIZO

"IN THE BEGINNING WAS THE SAFE DARK AND COZY WARM AND THE NESTLED UP AGAINST MYSELF...
"AND ALL THAT PSEUDO-POETIC VERBAL GARBAGE.
"THEN--AND I'LL NEVER FORGIVE 'ER FOR THIS--! NATURE DECREED THAT TRANQUILITY WAS NOT ENOUGH!
"THUS, FOR NO APPARENT REASON, I S-T-R-E-T-C-H-E-D.
"HUZZAH! EMERGENCE! BIG CLUCKING DEAL! THERE I WAS IN A BIGGER, MORE TEPID BLACKNESS. SO WHAT?
SWAN-SONG
"SO HERE'S WHAT: ONCE YA TAKE THAT FIRST STUPID STEP-- YA CAN NEVER GO HOME AGAIN!
...OF THE LIVING DEAD DUCK!
KRAMM

"NOW WATCH CLOSELY, KIDS. YOU'RE ABOUT TO OBSERVE...
"...THE PROCESS OF SOCIALIZATION IN ACTION!
"...ACTION!
"...ACTION!
"NOTE: THIS ISN'T SOCIALIZATION AS IN 'SOCIALISM'. IT'S A TECHNIQUE THAT EVERY CULTURE HAS MASTERED, ALMOST BY DEFINITION.
SLAM!
"MOSTLY IT'S SIMPLE INDOCTRINATION, SEE?
"YOU'RE EDUCATED--LARGELY INFORMALLY, BUT NONETHELESS EFFECTIVELY--IN A BODY OF CUSTOMS, MORES, TABOOS.
"AND ANY IDEOLOGY CAN PLAY. (LISTEN, IF THIS'S GETTIN' TOO PEDANTIC FOR YA, JUST HOLLER. I'LL TRY TA TONE IT DOWN.) ANYWAY...

"YA LEARN NOT TA YELL 'FIRE' IN A CROWDED THEATRE--NOT TA GO 'HUBBA-HUBBA' AT PICTURES OF ELEANOR ROOSEVELT--
"--AN' MOST OF ALL--
"--YA LEARN THERE'S CERTAIN PLACES YER SUPPOSED TA TREAD LIGHTLY!"
ULP
YEOWTCH!
THIS IS AN OUTRAGE!
WHO DO YOU THINK YOU ARE?!
M-MY GOD... YOU'RE A DUCK! AND YOU'RE BIGGER THAN ALL OF US--!
WHO LET YOU INTO OUR ROOM?
YOUR--?! BUT WHAT DO YOU DO IN HERE? THERE'S NO FURNITURE, NO NOURISHMENT, NO WAY OUT--!
WE--ENTERTAIN GUESTS. WE PROVIDE--ESCAPE.
OH. OH! SURE, I GET IT! I ESCAPED INTA--
INDEED. AND HERE YOU'LL STAY.
YOUR VERY EXISTENCE POSES TOO MANY QUESTIONS, DUCK!
WE'VE NO ROOM FOR A FLUKE LIKE YOURSELF! THEREFORE--
OH, YEAH??
"ONE THING ABOUT INDOCTRINATION: SOME OF US JUST DON'T TAKE TO IT NATURALLY.

"SO THERE'S GOTTA BE A MEANS OF ENFORCEMENT--AN' SOME DUDE HEAVY ENOUGH TA MAKE IT BELIEVABLE."
DESIST, DUCK!!
I AM KONG LOMERATE--AND AND I OWN THOSE PEOPLE YOU'RE TRAMPLING!
UH-OH.
BUT... Y'YOU'RE A HIRSUTE APE! ON THIS WORLD YOU CAN'T--
WRONG! IT'S BECAUSE I'M NOT HUMAN THAT MY WORD IS LAW! I ONLY EXIST ON PAPER!
AND YOU, TOO, MUST OBEY ME, OR...
AAAH--GO SUCK A BEEF JERKY! I'M MY OWN DUCK! I GO WHERE I WANT, SAY WHAT I WANT--!
AN' I BEEN THUMBIN' MY BEAK AT GORILLAS LIKE YOU MY WHOLE LIFE!
BUT THEY NEVER POSSESSED MY POWER, FEATHERED UPSTART! THEY COULD MERELY BERATE YOU--!
I CAN WIPE EVERY TRACE OF YOU FROM THE FACE OF THIS "WORLD YOU NEVER MADE!"
WHAM
WAAAUGH
CANCELLED

"OVER TIME, OF COURSE, AND AFTER A SUCCESSION OF FEATHER'S-BREADTH ESCAPES FROM THE SYSTEM, THE STRAIN BEGINS TO TELL.
"IN SOME, IT EVINCES ITSELF AS ANGER, IN OTHERS AS SELF-DOUBT. FOR ME, IT WAS AN OVERWHELMING SADNESS...
GURU'S HOUSE 10 MI
"...AND UTTER APATHY TOWARD THE VERY BUSINESS OF LIVING.
"OUTWARDLY, I'M SURE IT LOOKED LIKE CYNICISM--BUT A CYNIC'S JUST A FALLEN IDEALIST, RIGHT?
"JUST A POOR SLOB LOOKING FOR ANY MORSEL OF INFO THAT'LL MOTIVATE 'IM AGAIN."
YOO-HOO! GURU? ANYBODY HOME?
"THE CAPED MAN ANSWERED WITH HIS EYES, INVITING ME IN."
YOU GOTTA HELP ME--YA GOTTA GIMME THE ANSWER! WHAT'S IT ALL ABOUT? WHAT'S THE MEANING OF LIFE?
GIMME IT STRAIGHT! WHY AM I?
WHY NOT?

WE'RE IN THE SAME BOAT, THEN, HUH? BUT AT LEAST I'VE GOT SOME CONTROL OVER MY DESTINY. I'VE GOT A FEW FACTS.
TWO AN' TWO IS STILL FOUR...!
AN' THEN THERE'S THE LAW OF--
--GRAVITY.
"I FIGGER THAT'S WHEN MY MOST CHERISHED NOTION--THAT 'FACTS' WERE MORE THAN ASSUMPTIONS BASED ON PAST OBSERVATIONS --DIED.
"THERE WAS NOTHIN' OUT THERE--OR IN HERE, FOR THAT MATTER-- BUT THE VORTEX AT THE CENTER OF THE VOID."
GOO.
"SUDDENLY, I WAS SPOUTIN' DUCKLING TALK. NOTHIN' ELSE MADE SENSE. GOO. GWAK. GWAAAW. PEEP. DIDJA EVER GET THE FEELING YER WORDS WERE JUST FILLIN' DEAD AIR?
SPLAT
"PRATTLE AND TWATTLE AND SPLAT ON YER GUT! HERE'S SOMETHIN' TA LIFT YA OUTTA THAT RUT:

BEV!
N
P
Y
Z
C'MERE, DUCKY! I HAVE SOMETHING TO **SHOW** YOU!

FOR **REAL?** SOMETHIN' **NEW?**

UH-**HUH!** THE TRUTH IS **ALWAYS** NEW!

PEEK-A-BOO!

WELL...?
URP CAN I **GO** NOW?

SQUIT
NOT YET.

OKAY. **NOW** YOU CAN GO.
SNAP
THANKS-- TWO **HEAPS.**

"THE **EGG.**
T
R
G
"BACK TO THE EGG. BACK TO THE EGG. BACK TO THE **EGG.**

"THAT'S ALL MY MIND WOULD **SAY**-- ERGO, BACK TO THE EGG.
"HOWEVER, AS PREVIOUSLY NOTED, YA CAN'T GO HOME **AGAIN.**

"SO, IN THE END...
CLAMP
"...THERE WAS THE MENACING DARK AND STUFFY WARM AND THE CHAFING OF BONE AGAINST WEARY BONE.

"AND, THEN I WOKE UP-- TOTALLY DISORIENTED, IN A COLD SWEAT, AN' WITH A HEADACHE THAT FELT LIKE MY SKULL HAD JUST RETURNED FROM TWO WEEKS IN NEW JERSEY."
HLP

WH-WHERE AM I?! LAST I REMEMBER, I'D JUST WALKED OUT ON THE FIGHT WITH THE BEAVER OVER NIAGARA FALLS! AN' NOW--NO! WAITAMINIT!
SOMETHIN' DID HAPPEN AFTER THAT--I THINK-- I COLLAPSED!
I SUDDENLY FELT SO TIRED--AN' I HAD THIS SAME HEADACHE--!
I SAW THE GROUND RUSHIN' UP AT ME--
--THEN, POOF!

PRESTON DUDLEY-- THE PRIDE O' THE MOUNTIES--MUST'A GIVEN US A LIFT HERE-- WHEREVER HERE IS! A MOTEL, I GUESS.
ANYWAY, BEV SOUNDS OKAY--SNORIN' UP A STORM, AS USUAL.

YEP--THE WORLD'S LOOKIN' GOOD-- LIKE A CHOPPIN' BLOCK SHOULD.
WHAT?
WHY'M I THINKIN' BERSERK CHIMNEY'S LIKE THAT??
HUH?

OH, WELL... A COUPLE'A ASPIRIN AN' SOME CLOUD JUICE OUGHTTA--
"CLOUD JUICE??"
RATS! NO PENNIES!

GUESS I'LL JUST HAVETA SETTLE FOR A GLASS OF PIANO, THEN.

WAAAUGH! THAT AIN'T IVORY! IT'S--SPIDER WEBS!

M-MUSTA TURNED THE WRONG HANDLE! I WANTED COLD--!
NOW I'VE GONE AND SCALDED MY MIND--!
HOW'S IT HANGIN! DUCK-O?
AW, NO--I GET IT NOW! I NEVER REALLY AWAKENED AT ALL! I ONLY DREAMED I WOKE UP!!
WELCOME TO MY NIGHTMARE--PART TWO!
BY THE NECK UNTIL DEAD--WHICHEVER COMES FIRST.
HUH? WHAT ARE YOU CRINGING ABOUT? YOU KNOW ME--YOUR FRIENDLY NEIGHBORHOOD PIANO?
LISTEN, I BROUGHT YOU A PRESENT! BURY YOUR BEAK IN THIS, FELLA.
IF SOMEBODY'D GIVEN ME A COPY, I WOULDN'T BE THE WALL-CRAWLING MASS OF GUILT I AM TODAY.
WHAT IS IT--"ADAM BEDE" OR "THE IDIOT"?
NEITHER--EXACTLY!
AW, G'WAN--
WHEN I SAY NO I FEEL GUILTY
A GUIDE TO ASSERTIVE BEHAVIOR
THE LAST THING I NEED NOW IS POP PSYCHOLOGY--EVEN IF THE TITLE IS GERMANE TO MY SITUATION!
BEAT IT!
WHAM
OKAY, FEATHER-BRAIN--WHATEVER YOU SAY!

CAN'T BLAME ME FOR TRYING!
HAVE A NICE LIFE! SEE YA!
POOFF
AWP
THIS'S GOTTA STOP! I GOTTA SHAKE LOOSE THAT GLOB O' FROZEN CHILI TRYIN' TO PASS FOR MY BRAIN!
MAYBE IF I SNEAK BACK TO BED, I CAN RISE AN' SHINE ALL OVER AGAIN-- FOR ACTUAL, THIS TIME!
NUTS! NO ROOM FOR ME-- I'M STILL HERE!
WAITAMINIT! MAYBE I CAN ROUSE MYSELF!
C'MON, KILLER! UP 'N' AT 'EM! SLEEPYTIME'S OVER!
LET'S GO, HANDSOME! THERE'S A NEW DAY WAITIN' OUT THERE!
NO DICE! HE WON'T BUDGE!
WELL... MAYBE IT'S FOR THE BEST.
AFTER ALL, IF HE WOKE UP, I'D PROB'LY CEASE TO EXIST!
AN' WHAT IF I'M THE REAL DUCK AN' HE'S THE DREAM??
I'D BE DEAD, AN' THERE'D BE A BOGUS CANARD WADDLIN' AROUND IN MY PLACE!
NO, WAIT-- IF I WERE DEAD, I COULDN'T DREAM. SO HE'D DIE, TOO.
NIAGARA FALLS INN
SO THAT'S WHY I'VE BEEN GREETING EACH NEW DAY WITH NAUSEA LATELY.
OFFICE & COFFEE SHOP
ANYHOW, BEFORE I MAKE ANY MORE RASH MOVES, I BETTER ANALYZE THE PROBLEM OVER COFFEE!

"MY SELF-IMAGE HAS ALWAYS BEEN THAT OF AN IRASCIBLE, SOMEWHAT HIGH-STRUNG, BUT EMINENTLY LIKABLE DUCK. STUBBORN, BUT ABLE TO TAKE CRITISISM AND EVALUATE IT DISPASSIONATELY. OPINIONATED, BUT RECEPTIVE TO NEW IDEAS. HOWEVER--
"I CAN'T STAND IT WHEN PEOPLE CALL ME NAMES!!"
KNOW-IT-ALL!
HEY, GUYS--LOOK! IT'S--
COWARD THE DUCK!
YOU GLUTTON!
YOU PAUPER!
STUFFED SHIRT!
PESSIMIST!
WAAAUGH
OKAY, GUYS--RELAX! I CAN TAKE A HINT! I KNOW WHEN I'M NOT WELCOME!
"THE BEAVER'S BELLHOP--THE GIANT GINGER-BREAD MAN--THE FINANCIAL WIZARD, PRO-RATA--TURNIP-MAN--GONZO THE CLOWN--WINKY-MAN--AND THEY WEREN'T EVEN TAKING ME SERIOUSLY!!

SEE? I'LL JUST BACK RIGHT OUT ON YA-- LIKE I SHOULD'A DONE WHEN I FIRST MET YA!
SLAM
AN' I'LL JUST KEEP BACKIN' AWAY--
--'TIL I'M LIGHT YEARS FROM--
WAAUGH
SO! A SET-UP, EH? THOUGHT I'D BE OFF-GUARD, EH? THE OLD SQUEEZE-PLAY, EH?
WELL, SURPRISE! I KNOW QUAK-FU, SEE, AN'--
I WOULD ADVISE, MY FRIEND...
...THAT YOU RESERVE YOUR MARTIAL ARTS EXPERTISE FOR A SITUATION WHICH DEMANDS IT.
OPEN YOUR EYES, AND BEHOLD AN ALLY, HOWARD--I, DR. PIANO.
YOU SEEM TENSE, MY FRIEND. WHAT TROUBLES YOU?
EVERYTHING IN GENERAL --AN EVERYTHING IN PARTI-CULAR.
OH. THAT.
IF YOU'D CARE TO DISCUSS IT, MINE ARE SYMPATHETIC EARS.
WHAT'S TO DISCUSS? I'M NOT AS DUMB AS I LOOK, CHUM. I KNOW WHAT THE PROBLEM IS.
TO THE FALLS
STATE IT, THEN. PERHAPS TOGETHER WE MIGHT FORMULATE A SOLUTION.
OKAY: SINCE I CAME TO THIS IDIOT WORLD, I'VE BEEN BEHAVING COMPLETELY CONTRARY TO MY TRUE NATURE.

COULD YOU ELABORATE--?
I KEEP GETTIN' MYSELF STUCK IN THE HERO'S ROLE, FOR ONE THING.
I'M TEARIN' MY FEATHERS OUT OVER MONEY FOR THE FIRST TIME IN MY LIFE--!

AN' I CAN'T FIGURE OUT WHY...!
PERHAPS YOU'VE OBEYED THE DICTATES OF YOUR CONSCIENCE, RATHER THAN--

BULL!!
I'VE OBEYED THE "DICTATES" OF MY CULTURAL CONDITIONING, THAT'S WHAT!

I'M BEGINNING... TO UNDERSTAND.
AW, DOC-- GET OFF!!
AFTER RESISTIN' IT FOR ALL THOSE YEARS BACK HOME--
BUT SURELY SOMETHING MOTIVATED YOUR SELF-SACRIFICE. PERHAPS IN YOUR UNCONSCIOUS, YOU--
I'VE FALLEN VICTIM TO MY PROGRAMMING! SUDDENLY, I'M RIDIN' THEIR MERRY-GO-ROUND, GRABBIN' FOR THEIR BRASS-RING!
"THEY"--?
THE ARMY OF THE STATUS QUO! THE TURKEYS WHO MAKE THE RULES, DEFINE SOCIETY'S VALUES!
I MEAN-- IT'S HERESY IN THESE PARTS NOT TA WANNA BE YER BROTHER'S KEEPER. BUT IT'S MY BURNIN' AMBITION TA BE AN ONLY CHILD!!

I KNOW IT DOESN'T SIT WELL WITH YOU MYSTIC TYPES--BUT I'M BY NATURE A PRAGMATIST! I TAKE THE ROUTE THAT WORKS!
BUT I'M SUSCEPTIBLE TO PRESSURE --ESPECIALLY IF IT PLAYS ON MY ACHILLES WEB-- COMPASSION FOR THE UNDER-DOG!

BUT I GOT NO ULTERIOR MOTIVES! I'M THE ONLY UP-FRONT CHARACTER IN THIS DREAM! I--
YOU LIE, BEAST!!
DOC...?

YOUR PRESIDENTIAL CANDIDACY-- YOUR FEIGNED ROLE AS OUTCAST -- YOUR WHOLE LIFE HAS BEEN A SORDID PLOT--
--TO ROB THE WORLD OF ITS HEALTHY KIDNEYS!!
CHOOM
"I MANAGED TO DODGE THE BLOW-- BUT THE KIDNEY LADY'S CANE STRUCK THE CLIFFSIDE SO HARD--
"--IT FISSURED! AND UP FROM THE STEAMY BOWELS OF THE EARTH CLAWED LE BEAVER, THE CRAZY OLD CANADIAN IN THE SUPER-POWERED EXOSKELETON WHO SABATOGED MY PRESIDENTIAL CAMPAIGN AND BLACKENED MY NAME!
"LE BEAVER -- THE ONLY FIGHT I'D EVER WALKED OUT ON --'CAUSE IT WAS JUST TOO LUDICROUS!
"AN' NOW THE MOMENT OF DECISION HAD ARRIVED AGAIN!"

HE EMBARRASSED ME. IS THAT WORTH RISKIN' MY LIFE OVER?
NO!
ON THE OTHER HAND-- TAKIN' THE SENSIBLE ROUTE LAST TIME SAVED MY TAIL AT THE EXPENSE OF MY NERVES.
IF I SKIP OUT, I FLIP OUT... THAT MUCH I KNOW.
SO MAYBE THIS'S THE ONE TIME I SHOULD'A STOOD MY GROUND-- WHEN MY HONOR WAS AT STAKE.
OKAY, UGLY... THIS TIME WE DO IT YOUR WAY! THIS TIME, I--
--FIGHT!
OWCH.
BOOOING
"HIS RODENT SUIT WAS FASHIONED OF TRIPLE-THICK TITANIUM STEEL.
"BUT DID THAT STOP ME?!
RAT TAT TAT TAT
"NO! I PULLED A THOMPSON SUB-MACHINE GUN FROM MY COAT!
SPANNG
"I PELTED HIS PELT WITH COLD LEAD!
PING
"ALL OF WHICH RICOCHETED RIGHT BACK AT ME.

CRUNCH
"THEN--
"GLOVE-TO-PAW, I WAS NO MATCH FOR 'IM. MY WEAPON HAD FAILED ME MISERABLY.
"I NEEDED AN AVENUE OF RETREAT! AN' THERE IT WAS-- THE TIGHTROPE HE'D STRUNG OVER THE FALLS.
"IT SHOULD'A WORKED. I SHOULD'A BEEN ABLE TO MAKE IT BACK TO CANADA, CATCH MY BREATH, AN' DEVISE A NEW PLAN OF ATTACK.
"BUT--"
ONE MOMENT, SIR. A FEW QUESTIONS.
CARRYING ANY FIREARMS? LIQUOR? HOW LONG WILL YOU BE STAYING IN CANADA? WHAT--
"--I FORGOT I'D HAVE'TA PASS CUSTOMS!
"SO I LEARNED A VERY SIMPLE LESSON THE HARD WAY.
WAAUGH
"SEE--
"MY HEAD WAS THROBBIN', MY NERVES WERE SHOT BECAUSE FOR ONCE I'D HEEDED MY BETTER JUDGMENT --AN RUN AWAY.

"SOME FOLKS WOULD HAVE YA BELIEVE THAT'S NOT THE DRAKELY THING TO DO.
"WHAT THEY DON'T TELL YA, THOUGH--
"THERE'S REALLY NOTHIN' GLAMOROUS OR HONORABLE ABOUT GETTIN' KILLED TO PERPETUATE THEIR MASCULINE STEREOTYPE.
WAAAAAUGH
"RIGHT. I WAS BRAVE. I WAS HEROIC. I ACTED IN THE BEST MACHO TRADITION OF UNTHINKING PUGNACITY. AN' I DIED... FOR HONOR.
"AN' MY ETERNAL REWARD? TO BE LAUGHED AT FOR ALL TIME -- BY THE BUMS. WHO PUT ME THERE!
"I JUST HOPE I'M STILL DREAMIN'-- CAUSE IF THIS IS FOR REAL, I'M GONNA GET VERY DEPRESSED."
NEXT
QUACK-UP!!

HOWARD THE DUCK

MARVEL® COMICS GROUP

30¢ 11 APR 02415

TRAPPED IN A WORLD HE NEVER MADE!

HOWARD THE DUCK™

IT BEGAN AS CHEAP TRANSPOR-TATION--

--BUT IT ENDED IN DISASTER!!

COLON • LEIALOHA

BUS TO OBLIVION!

From the time of his hatching, he was...different. A potentially brilliant scholar who dreaded the structured environment of school, he educated himself in the streets, taking whatever work was available, formulating his philosophy of self from what he learned of the world about him. And then the Cosmic Axis shifted...and that world *changed.* Suddenly, he was stranded in a universe he could not fathom. Without warning, he became a strange fowl in an even stranger land.

Stan Lee PRESENTS: HOWARD THE DUCK!™

STEVE GERBER WRITER/EDITOR GENE COLAN ARTIST STEVE LEIALOHA INKER JIM NOVAK, LETTERER JAN COHEN, COLORIST

WELCOME TO THE PITS OF HECK...
...TO WHICH "H" THE "D"...
...HAS BEEN DARNED FOR ALL TIME.
OF COURSE, IT'S ALL JUST A DREAM... HENCE THE UNGAINLY EUPHEMISMS.
THE MEPHISTO YOU SAY, SPACE TURNIP! IT'S ALL REAL--THE HEAT, THE HUMILIATION, THE PRICK OF MY PITCHFORK!
"DREAM" IS THE MISNOMER. WHAT WE'VE GOT HERE IS A BONA FIDE--
QUACK-UP!
ISN'T THAT SO, HOWARD?
OUCH

B-BUT, DOCTOR -- WHAT'S WRONG WITH HIM? HE'S BEEN LIKE THIS FOR DAYS-- EVER SINCE WE CROSSED THE BORDER BACK INTO THE STATES FROM CANADA-- AFTER HIS FIGHT WITH LE BEAVER.*
WE WALKED INTO THIS MOTEL ROOM-- HE COLLAPSED ON THE BED--
--AND JUST NEVER WOKE UP! HE TOSSES AND SCREAMS, THEN LIES PEACEFULLY FOR A WHILE, THEN IT ALL BEGINS AGAIN. WHY??
WHAT'S WRONG WITH HIM??
ouch
PLEASE UNDERSTAND, MS. SWITZLER, I'VE NEVER TREATED A PATIENT QUITE LIKE HIM BEFORE--SO THIS DIAGNOSIS ISN'T 100% RELIABLE--!
BUT IF HE WERE HUMAN, I'D CALL IT A CLEAR CASE OF ACUTE EXHAUSTION.

*HTD #9.--STEVE.

YOU DON'T MEAN-- A NERVOUS BREAKDOWN?!
LET'S HOPE NOT. WE'LL KNOW MORE WHEN HE AWAKENS. MEANTIME...

I'VE ADMINISTERED A MEGAVITAMIN INJECTION, AND--
B-BUT... WHAT IF HE HAS TO GO TO A HOSPITAL? WE'RE sob BROKE--
--AND FOR YOU, I'M PRESCRIBING HOT TEA AND SOMETHING TO EAT.
NOW! UNDER MY SUPER-VISION.

THEN WE CAN DISCUSS THE MATTER-- CALMLY. AGREED?

Y-YES... THANK YOU... THANK YOU SO MUCH...
SLAM
...eh?

BONGA BONGA!
WHAM.
WHIM.
WAAUGH

WAKE UP.
NO.
WHY NOT?
BECAUSE THE WORLD SUCKS BEEF JERKIES.
RIGHT. BUT BEV WILL MAKE IT A-A-A-A-ALL BETTER.
BEV?

BEV!
OH! YEAH! BEV!
BEV?
BEV?

YOO-HOO!
BEV-
-ER-
-LY?
BEV?

PFFFFFT
NO BEV.
YOU'RE ALL ALONE.
NOBODY CARES.
AND THE SHEETS ARE ALL SWEATY.
PIANO.
EPOXY.

HOT TEA.
MY SUPER-VISION.
GET DRESSED.
FOR TEA.
I DARE YOU TO GET UP!
OKAY, SO YOU DID IT. BIG DEAL.
YOU'RE STILL WASTED.
KLUNK

YOU'LL NEVER PUT ALL THE PIECES TO--
CLICK
OFFICE & COFFEE SHOP
OH, WHIZ KID, HUH? FIGGERED IT ALL OUT, DIDJA?
WELL, BRACE THYSELF, THUCKER--
THUD
--FOR A REAL KICK IN THE HEAD.
HERE YOU ARE --ALONE, DISORIENTED, UNABLE TO THINK RATIONALLY-- AND SHE'S OUT HAVIN' A GOOD TIME--
--WITH A HANDSOME HAIRLESS APE!
SOME PAL.

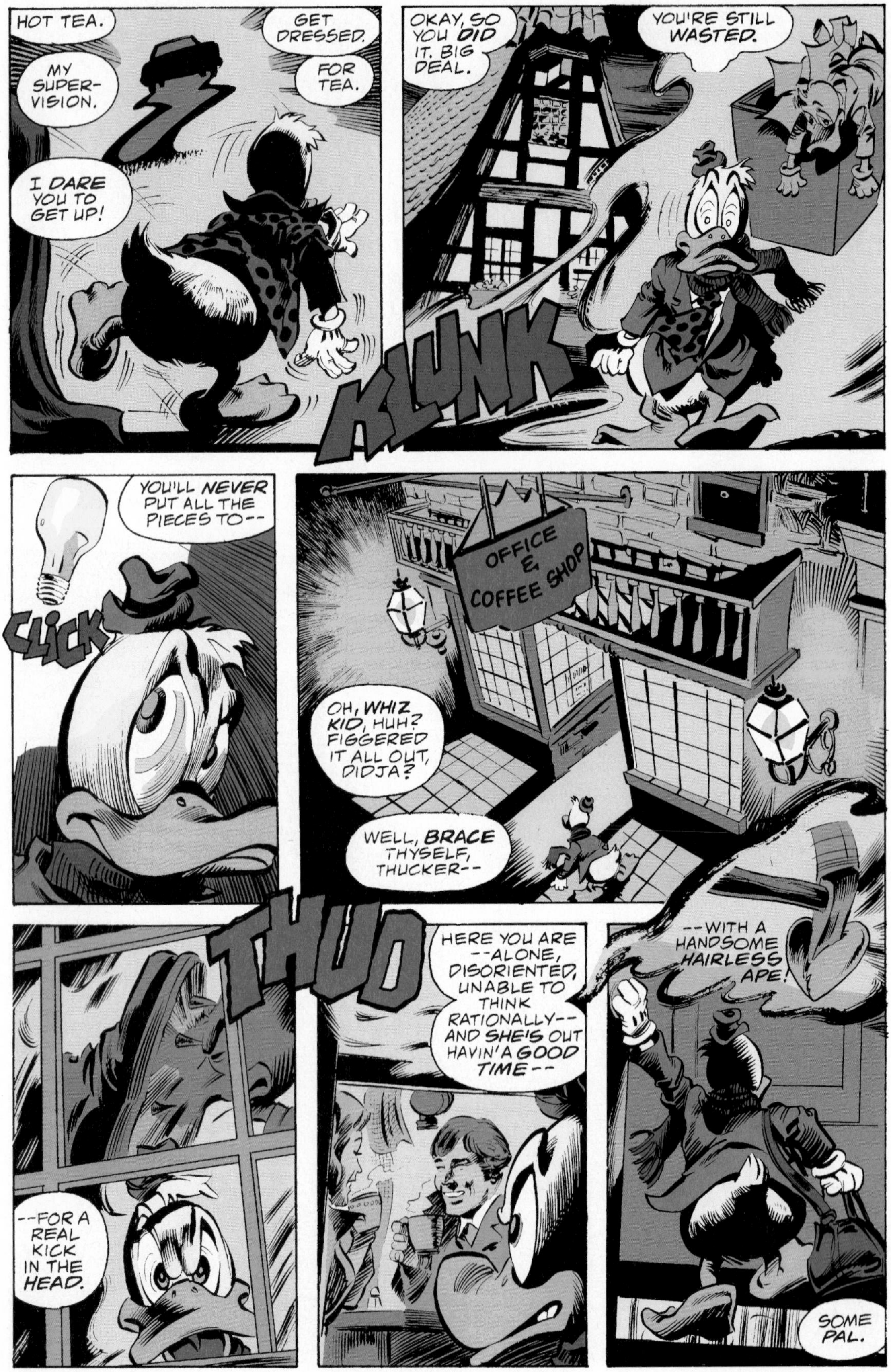

HEEEYY! THAT'S GOOD! GET ANGRY! GIVE US ONE O' THOSE FAMOUS H.T.D. TANTRUMS!
BLACK DOG BUS TICKETS SOLD HERE
DING DING DING
AAH, SHUDDUP!
HEY, CONCIERGE! WHEN'S THE NEXT BUS OUTTA HERE?
IT'S DUE ANY TIME NOW. BUT, SIR, YOU REALLY DON'T WANT TO...
SEZ WHO???

HERE'S THE LAST O' MY PRESIDENTIAL CAMPAIGN TREASURY! HOW FAR'LL IT GET ME?
I--I DON'T KNOW. I'LL HAVE TO COUNT IT--

WELL??
YOU COULD RIDE TO THE END OF THE LINE ON THIS, SIR, BUT--
NO "BUTS!" JUST GIMME THE TICKET!
ALL RIGHT --IF YOU INSIST.

HERE YOU ARE-- AND THERE'S YOUR BUS. BUT ARE YOU SURE YOU'D RATHER NOT WAIT FOR THE NEXT--?
JUST MIND YER OWN BIZNESS, MAC. YOU RUN YER MOTEL, AN' I'LL RUN MY LIFE, OKAY?

WHATEVER YOU SAY. HOPE YOU WON'T BE SORRY.
YEAH, WELL--I APPRECIATE THE DEEP CONCERN.

CLEVELAND
"BUT I CAN'T IMAGINE ANY SORRIER SPOT THAN THE ONE I'M IN RIGHT NOW."

BETTER, HUH? QUIET. DARK. ALMOST EVERY-BODY'S ASLEEP. NO ONE TO HARRASS YOU.
YEAH. THIS'S THE LIFE.
SO THEN WHY'VE YOU BEEN SITTING RIGID LIKE THAT FOR AN HOUR AND A HALF?
HAH?

CAN'T GET COMFY, CAN YA?
JACKET BUNCHES UP IN BACK.

SLEEVES RIDE UP.
MUFF IS CHOKING YA, HUH?

SEAT BACK
AH! CLEVER FELLOW!

PITY, THOUGH--HOW YOU AND MACHINES HAVE NEVER GOTTEN ALONG.
THEY HATE YOU.
YOU HATE THEM.
ZZUNNG

BOOiiiNG
WAUK
THEY WORK FOR EVERYONE ELSE-- BUT YOU THEY WANT TO KILL.

'SCUSE ME-- D'YOU KNOW HOW TA WORK THIS THING?
ARE YOU ADDWESSING ME?
YEAH.

NO. THIS IS MY FIRST TWIP ON A BUS.
MY NAME IS WINDA.
HI!
MY PAWENTS SAY I'M POSSESSED BY THE DEVIL.
I'M ON MY WAY TO CWEVEWAND TO BE EXORCISED.

OKAY.
FORGET I ASKED.
I SHOULD'A KNOWN-- 139 SEATS, 139 STORIES.
I--

CLEVE-LAND?!

IS THIS BUS GOING TO--
EXCUSE ME--

I'M TAKING A SURVEY, SIR, AND I WONDER IF YOU'D PARTICIPATE.
ARE YOU INTERESTED IN ...THE MIND?
ARE YOUR INNERMOST THOUGHTS INACCESSIBLE TO YOU? IS YOUR HIGHER CONSCIOUSNESS PADLOCKED?
ARE YOUR EMOTIONS IN DEEP-FREEZE STORAGE?
IS YOUR BRAIN A MUSTY ATTIC, CLUTTERED WITH INTELLECTUAL NOSTALGIA?
WHO WANTS TA KNOW?

MY NAME IS ALVIN, SIR, BUT THAT'S COMPLETELY IRRELEVANT.
WRONG! IT JUST SO HAPPENS NOBODY NAMED "ALVIN" IS ALLOWED TO INQUIRE ABOUT MY MIND.
SO CHANGE YOUR NAME, OR BUG OFF!
JUST ONE MORE QUESTION, SIR: ARE YOU FAMILIAR WITH GNOSTICOLOGY?

NO? THEN LET LET ME GIVE YOU THE MOST IMPORTANT GIFT OF YOUR LIFE.

NATURALLY. A SALES PITCH. IT HADDA BE.
THE NEW SCIENCE OF BRAIN LOCKSMITHING

SORRY. GONNA HAVETA PASS THIS TIME, ALVIN.

BUT YOU DON'T HAVE TO PAY FOR IT NOW. READ IT WHILE YOU SLEEP.
AND IF YOU LIKE IT, CHECK OUT OUR OPERATION WHEN WE REACH CLEVELAND.
UH...

NAH. HONEST. FERGET IT. I'M NOT UP TO A NEW RELIGION THIS WEEK. PLEASE--!

GNOSTICOLOGY ISN'T A RELIGION, SIR--
RIGHT--IT'S A SCAM! AN' I'M NOT BUYIN'-- GOT THAT, ALVIN?
BUT--
RIGHT ON, BROTHER DUCK!
LET NOT THE DEVIL TEMPT THEE ASTRAY WITH HIP RHETORIC!

THERE IS BUT ONE WAY--
--ONE PATH TO GLORY, ONE ROAD TO HEAVEN, ONE SUPERHIGHWAY TO SALVATION!
THERE'S GOOD NEWS FOR ONE AND ALL, BELIEVE ME, BRETHREN--
HE LOOKS SO FAMILIAR--I THINK I'VE SEEN HIM ON TELEVISION!

AND IT'S ALL RIGHT HERE--
--JAM-PACKED WITH INFO AND COLOR PHOTOGRAPH'S!
MARTYRDOM FOR THE MILLIONS
TELL HIM TO BACK OFF.
YOU'RE SUFFO-CATING.
YOUR NERVES CAN'T TAKE THIS.
WHIM.
WHAM.
FUNGA.

HARE!
HARE!
KRISHNU! KRISHNU!
WAITAMINIT! I SAW 'IM FIRST!
WHAT NEW BLASPHEMY IS THIS HERE??
NO! PLEASE! NOT ANOTHER ONE! AREN'T THERE ANY NON-BELIEVERS ON THIS BUS??

HARE! HARE! HARE! STEP RIGHT THIS WAY--!
TO SRI WITH LOVE
LOSE YOUR ILLUSION OF SEPAR-ATENESS-- YOUR EGO-- YOUR--

STOP!!
I DON'T WANNA THAW MY BRAIN--
I DON'T WANT A ROADMAP TO HEAVEN--AN' I DON'T WANNA FORGET WHO I AM!
I JUST WANNA BE LEFT ALONE! THAT'S ALL I EVER WANTED MY WHOLE LIFE!
IS THAT TOO MUCH TO ASK? HUH? IS IT??

ANYWAY, YOU'RE NEVER REALLY ALONE.
YES.
OBVIOUSLY.
NO DUCK IS AN ISLAND.
NOR EVEN A PENINSULA.
AND BESIDES, IT'S NOT NORMAL.
WE'RE WITH YOU.
ALWAYS.
FOR THE WHOLE RIDE.

FOUR HOURS, 21 MINUTES LATER; 5:06 A.M.:
"HEY!" A PASSENGER CRIES. "WE JUST CROSSED THE OHIO BORDER!"
YIPPEE.

MR. DUCK...?

YOU WOOK VEWY AGITATED.
I BET YOU'RE JUST WIKE ME--
YOU WISTEN MUCH TOO MUCH TO OTHER PEOPLE'S NONSENSE.
F'WINSTANCE...

THEY SAY I'M POSSESSED... BUT WEAWWY, I JUST MAKE FUNNY FACES...
--AND SIWWY NOISES.
NURRRG

IT'S VEWY THEWAPEUTIC.
AND IT KEEPS PEOPLE AWAY IN DWOVES.
WHY DON'T YOU TWY IT?

VEWY GOOD!
YOU'RE A NATUWAL!

NOW TWY ADDING SOUND!
YUBBA-WAB-HOOP-DIBBY!

GUMF! GUMF!

SEE? ISN'T IT A TEWWIFIC WEWEASE? HMMM?
YOU'RE THE ONLY PEWSON WHO EVEW TOOK MY ADVICE SEWIOUSLY.
YOU'VE GWEATLY BUTTWESSED MY SAGGING SEWF-CONCEPT, YES YOU HAVE.

AND NOW, IT'S TIME FOR SOME WEST AND WEWAXATION. SWEEP GOOD. SEE YOU IN CWEVEWAND.
YEAH...

SLEEP...
...DEEP, DREAMLESS SLEEP...
YEAH...YEAH... I COULD GO FOR SOME O' THAT...
TAKE YOUR HANDS OFF HER. YOU ANIMAL!!
EEEEEK
MUNCHIES.
THE GRIPPE.
BROKEN DREAMS.
THUNK
PIANO WIRE.
DEAD HORSES.
RESOLVED.
REPUG.
ATAVISM.
LAVE.
GOOZ.
FEDERAL RESERVE NOTE.
INEFFABILITY.

I KNEW OUR PATHS WOULD CROSS AGAIN IF I STAYED ON THE STRAIGHT AND NARROW AND YOU WADDLED YOUR WARPED AND CROOKED WAY!
LOOK, WORLD, ON THE HATEFUL, TWISTED, LEERING, LASCIVIOUS VISAGE OF FILTHY NASTINESS INCARNATE--
THE OVERALL HEAD OF THE MASSIVE INTERNATIONAL KIDNEY-POISONING CONSPIRACY!
waaaugh
HE USES SWEET, INNOCENT GIRLS LIKE THIS--SUBVERTS THEIR INNATE NICENESS--
--HOOKS THEM ON FRIED FOODS, TOBACCO AND FAST LIVING--
--JUST TO GET AT THEIR KIDNEYS!!
OH, THAT IS WIDICUWOUS!
I DON'T BEWIEVE YOU! SO THEWE!
OH, YEAH? WELL, MAYBE YOU SHOULD TELL HER ABOUT YOUR LAST CONQUEST, EH? THE REDHEAD?
WED-HEAD?
THAT DOES IT.
WHERE'D YOU DUMP HER--ONCE YOU GOT WHAT YOU WANTED?
WHAP
YA FINALLY HIT A NERVE!!

LOOK, WORLD! THE VOICE OF TRUTH HAS DRIVEN HIM TO DESPERATION AND VIOLENCE!
ME?! TAILIN' YOU?? HA! THAT'S FUNNY, BEEFCAKES! I'M ROLLIN' IN THE AISLE!
HE'S BEEN FOLLOWING ME-- FROM CITY TO CITY--BUS TERMINAL TO BUS TERMINAL--
--HOPING TO CATCH ME OFF-GUARD, HARM ME BEFORE I COULD EXPOSE HIS HEINOUS MISDEEDS!

RIDICULE AND DENIAL-- THE FIRST REFUGE OF THE HOPELESSLY GUILT-RIDDEN!
BUT YOU CAN'T DENY THE EVIDENCE OF YOUR EYES, CAN YOU WORLD?

WOULD A DECENT, HONORABLE, MORAL CREATURE--
--WHUP THE TAR OUT OF A HELPLESS OLD WOMAN IN PUBLIC?!?

INDEED. YOU SHOULD LOVE THY NEIGHBOR AND BE TRUE TO THY SCHOOL.
LET HIM WHO IS WITHOUT SIN CAST THE--

THUD
YOU STAY OUTTA THIS, YOU DIRTY HIPPIE--THE FORCES OF GOODNESS CAN DO WITHOUT YOU!

CEASE THESE HOSTILITIES! I HAVE BERRIES AND NUTS AND ***THREE WORLDS*** TO SHARE!

HARE! HARE! GOO-GOO-GOO-***JOOB!***

DIDJA ***HEAR*** THAT, KIDNEY? THAT "GOO-GOO"? I CAN'T TAKE IT. I CAN'T ***STAND*** IT ANYMORE.

I REALLY CAN'T. I'M GOIN' ***BERSERK.***

EXCUSES, BIRD OF PREY--MERE ***EXCUSES!***

<hmph> TYPICALLY UNENLIGHTENED...!

SOCK

SMACK

I SHALL ABORT THIS BRAWL BY FORCE OF ***MIND!***

YES... YES... I'M ***GETTING*** IT... I'M ALL THE WAY TO ***TRANS-PARENT...!***

HEY! WHAT'S THAT ***BROUHAHA*** BACK THERE? ***QUIET!!***

--I'M TRYIN' TA ***DRIVE*** THIS--

BAMM

THE BUS! ITS ***KIDNEYS*** HAVE BURST!!

BUSES DON'T ***HAVE--***

NO! ***NO!*** MY MIND ***BLEW*** IT! FORGIVE ME.

SKREEEEEEEEE

HARE REASONER! HARE REASONER!

ONLY ASK FOR FORGIVENESS, AND IT IS ***THINE!***

"***THINE?!***" NOBODY TALKS WIKE THAT ANYMOWE!

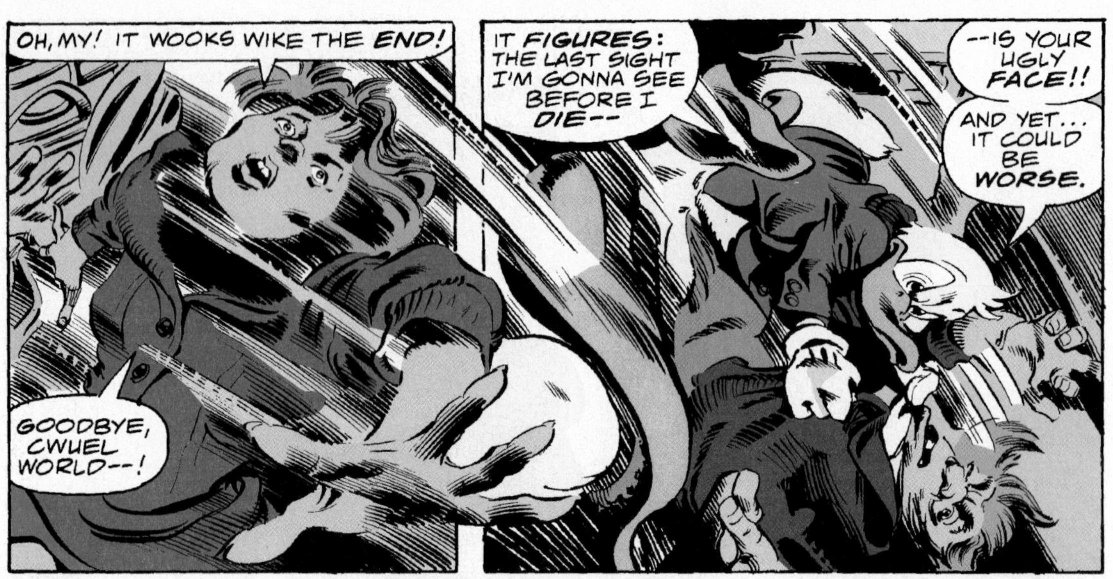
OH, MY! IT WOOKS WIKE THE END!
GOODBYE, CWUEL WORLD--!
IT FIGURES: THE LAST SIGHT I'M GONNA SEE BEFORE I DIE--
--IS YOUR UGLY FACE!!
AND YET... IT COULD BE WORSE.
I MEAN... WHAT IF I'D HADDA WATCH MY WHOLE LIFE FLASH BEFORE ME?
NOW THAT WOULD B--
DOES A BUS SCUDDING OFF THE INTERSTATE AMID BILLOWS OF DUST AND SMOKE MAKE A SOUND IF NO ONE IS PRESENT TO HEAR IT?
CRASHH!
YES.
AND IT'S DISGUSTING.
HOWEVER, WHEN THE CLOUDS OF VAPOR DISPERSE, ALL IS OMINOUS SILENCE...
...BUT THE SMELL MAKES UP FOR IT.

NEXT: NIGHTSHIRT CITY!

HOWARD THE DUCK

MARVEL® COMICS GROUP

APPROVED BY THE COMICS CODE AUTHORITY

30¢ 12 MAY 02415

TRAPPED IN A WORLD HE NEVER MADE!

HOWARD THE DUCK™

From the time of his hatching, he was...different. A potentially brilliant scholar who dreaded the structured environment of school, he educated himself in the streets, taking whatever work was available, formulating his philosophy of self from what he learned of the world about him. And then the Cosmic Axis shifted...and that world *changed.* Suddenly, he was stranded in a universe he could not fathom. Without warning, he became a strange fowl in an even stranger land.

Stan Lee PRESENTS: HOWARD THE DUCK!™

STEVE GERBER, WRITER/EDITOR • GENE COLAN, ARTIST • STEVE LEIALOHA, INKER • JIM NOVAK, LETTERER • JANICE COHEN, COLORIST

IT'S A CRISP, SUNSHINY MORNING IN SAUERBRATEN COUNTY, OHIO...
CHOOMBAH PAPA-AH GOOMBAH!
...BUT NOT IN THIS WEARY WATER-FOWL'S HEAD.
OOOOOO
BEHIND THOSE DROOPY EYELIDS, IT'S ARMAGEDDON IN AN ECHO CHAMBER.
INEPTITUDE.
FORTUNE.
LUNCH.
REEK.
BUSY.
DUTY-BOUND.
MALARKEY.
SWIRLING PLASMA, HURTLING COMETS, WOBBLING WORLDS, DISEMBODIED VOICES--THIS IS THE WAY TO START A NEW DAY?!
MIND-MUSH!

RISE!
SHINE!
YEAH, YEAH... I HEAR YA...!

I...
I...
I...

...THINK I BROKE SOMETHIN'...!
NAH. IT BROKE ME.
WUMP
HEE-HEE-HEE.

HYUK! WHADDAYA KNOW! YO'RE A GOLDANGED DUCK!
AN' THIS...IS A JAIL CELL?

YUP! HERE, LEMME GIVE YA A HAND...!
I DIDN'T FIGGER YOU WAS EVER GONNA WAKE UP-- THE WAY YOU LOOKED LAST NIGHT.
ALL TRANKILIZED AN' STUFFED INTA THET STRAIT JACKET --HOO-EEE!

I DON'T SUPPOSE YOU'VE GOT A SPARE CIGAR ON YAH, HUH...?
NOPE. SORRY.

GUESS I CAN SPOT YA A SLIGHTLY DENTED COFFIN NAIL, THOUGH, IF YUH WANT...

SORRY 'BOUT THE SHAPE IT'S IN. THET CRUSH-PROOF BOX AIN'T NO PROTECTION--
--WHEN A FELLA'S FALLIN'-DOWN DRUNK.

SNIF YA MUST'A SQUASHED THE FLAVOR OUT OF 'EM, TOO...!

TASTES LIKE PENCIL SHAVINGS WRAPPED IN BATHROOM TISSUE...!
'COURSE IT DOES...

...IF YA DON'T INHALE IT!

OH. YEAH. RIGHT HERE G--

COFF WAAAAUGH COFF
Y-YOU CALL THAT A SMOKE?! GASP MY GOD...!
TELL IT TO THE JUDGE, PAL. MAYBE HE'LL SYMPATHIZE. HE WAS BORN THERE.
YOU CAN CLEAR OUT, TOO, GUMPY. SEEYA TONIGHT.
I F-FEEL LIKE I JUST SUCKED IN HALF OF NEW JERSEY!
PROB'LY, FRED. THANKS.

THE PAUNCHY PATROLMAN ESCORTS HOWARD UP THREE FLIGHTS OF COLD CONCRETE STAIRS--TO THE BENCH OF THE HONORABLE HIRAM "DON'T-GIMME-NO" BALOGNA, HANGIN' JUDGE OF THE COUNTY'S TRAFFIC COURT.
GOOD HEAVENS!
UH-OH.
ASKANCE
AFOUL.
REPROBATE.
ADJUDICATE.
RELEGATE.
NUG.

GOODNESS GWACIOUS! MR. DUCK! HOW DWAWN AND BEDWAGGLED YOU WOOK!
WHAT HAVE THEY DONE TO YOU?
YOU KIDDIN', LADY?
ALL WE DID WAS CLEAN 'IM UP--
--AN TRY TA GET THAT BLAMED COSTUME OFF 'IM!

WELL, I THINK THEY SHOULD'VE TRIED HARDER-- SKINNED THE BEAST ALIVE, IF NECESSARY.
HUH? WHA--NO! YOU CAN'T BE--
YOU!
I CALL IT THE "MAMIE EISENHOWER LOOK" DO YOU APPROVE--
--KIDNEY THIEF?

OKAY, CAN THE GAB! COURT'S IN SESSION!
FIRST CASE-- COUNTY VERSUS H. DUCK, W. WESTER, AND S. BLOTTE!
RAP

YOU THREE ARE CHARGED WITH DISTURBING THE PEACE ABOARD A BLACK DOG BUS EN ROUTE TO CLEVELAND, THUS DISTRACTING THE DRIVER AND ENDANGERING YOUR FELLOW PASSENGER'S LIVES!
THESE ARE SWORN DEPOSITIONS TO THAT EFFECT FROM EYEWITNESSES.

H. DUCK IS FURTHER CHARGED WITH RESISTING ARREST. SAYS HERE THEY HADDA STRAIT-JACKET AND SEDATE YOU. MY, MY!
HEH
SHHH-- DON'T... DON'T... WOSE YOUR TEMPER.

FRANKLY, I'M MIGHTY ANXIOUS TO HEAR YOUR SIDE O' THE STORY. WHO'D CARE TO SPEAK FIRST?
WELL...
ME!!

I WAS ONLY TWYING TO STOP THE HOSTIWITIES! YOU SEE, I MUST GET TO CWEVE-WAND IN A HUWWY--
--TO BE EXOWCISED. MY PAWENTS SAY I'M POSSESSED BY THE DEVIL, AND--
waaaugh
AHEM THAT WILL DO, MISS WESTER. YOU MAY BE SEATED. MISS BLOTTE, HAVE YOU ANYTHING TO SAY IN YOUR DEFENSE?

YEAH, BEEF-CAKES --GO TO IT!
TELL 'IM ABOUT THE KIDNEY-POISONING CONSPIRACY--
--SO US INNO-CENT TYPES CAN BE ON OUR WAY!

YOUR HONOR... LOOK AT ME.
I ASK YOU: COULD THIS FRAIL OLD WOMAN POSSIBLY HAVE INSTIGATED A BRAWL IN THE AISLE OF A BUS?
WELL...
PURELY A RHETORICAL QUESTION, YOUR HONOR.

THE ANSWER IS NO. I'M TOO SICKLY, TOO WEAK, AND BY NATURE TOO GENTEEL. RUFFIANISM REPELS ME.
I SHRINK AT THE VERY THOUGHT OF GOUGING, MAIMING, OR MANGLING MY FELLOW MAN.

NOT THAT MINE HAS BEEN AN EASY LIFE, YOUR HONOR. OH, YES... I'VE HAD MY SHARE OF SORROW!
1941

"I'M A POOR FARMGIRL AT HEART, YOUR HONOR, THE SAME, NAIVE IMPRESSION-ABLE LASS--
"--WHO ANSWERED THE DOOR--
"--ON THAT FATEFUL DAY THE META-PHYSICAL BOOK SALESMAN CAME TO CALL.
MR. BLOTTE, I REPRESENT --OH! 'SCUZE ME! YOUR DADDY HOME?
WHY-- NO.
GOOD! I THINK I'M IN LOVE!
OOOOH! I BEG YOUR--
I...
I'M NOT THAT KIND OF--
AW, WHAT THE HEY--!
"BEFORE MY HEAD COULD STOP SPINNING, HE'D SOLD ME A BOOK--AT A GENEROUS DISCOUNT--
CLEVELAND
"--AND APPLIED THE PURCHASE PRICE TO OUR 'TICKET TO FREE-DOM' AS ELMER CALLED IT.
"CLEVELAND-- THE BIG CITY! BRIGHT LIGHTS, GLAMOR, THE THRILL OF ROMANCE!
"HE DRAPED ME IN SILKS, PLIED ME WITH FINE WINE...!
"WE CAVORTED ALL DAY AND DANCED 'TIL DAWN! PLUSH NIGHTCLUBS, GOURMET CUISINE...

"...AND ONLY THE BEST HOTELS.
Com-o-Hotel
Com-o-Hotel
"I WAS HIS QUEEN IN A WONDERLAND OF LOVE!
"AND THEN--MY WORLD COLLAPSED!

ELMER... DARLING...?
"I AWOKE ONE MORNING --AND MY LOVE HAD FLED--
"...LEAVING ONLY A NOTE, MY BOOK--

"...AND OUR UNPAID BILL.
Sorry sweets I've been drafted. See to the tab. -E.
OH SOB NO!

"SUDDENLY, I WAS ALONE, ADRIFT, AND HELPLESS-- IN A BLEAK, UNCARING WORLD!"
SOB
SOB
ELMER, MY ELMER, YOU-- SOB
SOB
SOB FORGIVE ME, YOUR HONOR. I'M AFRAID... I STILL MISS HIM SO.

I STILL HAVE HIS FAREWELL NOTE, YOUR HONOR.

AND I STILL CARRY THAT BOOK ON MY PERSON AT ALL TIMES.
I'VE TRIED TO LIVE MY LIFE BY IT...!

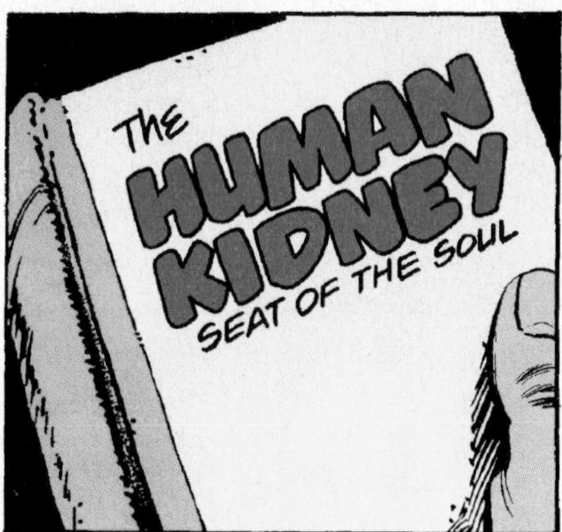
THE HUMAN KIDNEY SEAT OF THE SOUL

HAVE MERCY, YOUR HONOR!
SOB COULD A WOMAN WHO'S WAITED 36 YEARS FOR HER MAN TO RETURN FROM WORLD WAR II...
...COMMIT THE CRIME OF WHICH I AM ACCUSED?
SOB

NO, NO, NO... OF COURSE NOT, DEAR LADY!
WHY... I'M ASHAMED TO HAVE PUT YOU THROUGH THIS DREADFUL ORDEAL.
ALLOW ME TO ASSIST YOU TO THE DOOR...!
SOB
SOB
BOO HOO
NO!!

STOP!! WHAT'RE YA DOIN'?! SHE STARTED IT ALL!!
STRAP 'ER DOWN! RUBBER-HOSE 'ER!! MAKE 'ER TALK!! DON'T--
WAAAUGH

POOR, DELUDED CREATURE!
HE DESERVES OUR COMPASSION, NOT OUR HATRED. TRY TO... HELP HIM.

AND SO, WHEN THE JUDGE RETURNS TO THE BENCH...
WRAP
WRAP
SILENCE! ORDER IN THE COURT! I'VE REACHED MY JUDGEMENT!

"THIS VIOLENT OUTBURST, YOUR REFUSAL TO REMOVE THAT FARCICAL DUCK GARB, AND MISS WESTER'S APPARENT BELIEF IN HER OWN POSSESSION BY DEMONS--
"--IMPEL ME TO CONCUR WITH THE ARRESTING OFFICERS THAT YOU BOTH MAY BE DANGEROUSLY UNBALANCED!
"ACCORDINGLY, I SENTENCE YOU EACH TO NINETY DAYS' CONFINEMENT...

"... SAID TERMS TO BE SERVED UNDER OBSERVATION IN THIS COUNTY'S **MENTAL FACILITY**."
AND THERE THEY **GO...** FURTHER PROOF, IF ANY WERE **NECESSARY...**

...THAT WHOLESOME NICENESS ALWAYS... **ALWAYS!**--TRIUMPHS OVER DEPRAVED NASTINESS.
WATCH OUT FOR **YOUR** KIDNEYS, BOYS 'N' GIRLS!

⋮SIGH⋮ MAYBE IT WON'T BE SO BAD. YOU WOOK WIKE YOU COULD **USE** A WONG WEST.
WATCHA THINK? HMMM...?

QUACKER OATS
OATMEAL
MUSH.
OVER.
RUNNETH.
GOOZ.
NOOP.
ATROCITY.

IT'S SO CONFUSING... **WIFE**, I MEAN.
NOW IT JUST PWOCEEDS ON ITS **OWN...** WITHOUT WHYME OR WEASON.

SAUERBRATEN COUNTY MENTAL FACILITY
I WONDEW... WILL THEY **EXOWCISE** ME... OR JUST WOCK US AWAY?
⋮waaaugh⋮
MISS.
CUMBERSOME.
HIT.
STALINIST.
HOKUM.
HI-DE-HI-DE-HO.
NEWT.
POLICE

SHORTLY, INSIDE...

LOOKIT, BARBARA-- HE'S A **DUCK!!**

A **DRAKE**, TECHNICALLY-- A MALE OF THE SPECIES--SO THANKFULLY HE'S **YOUR** CHARGE.

YOU'LL BE UNDER **MY** CARE, WINDA. I'M ***NURSE BARBARA.***

AND LET'S UNDERSTAND ONE ANOTHER FROM THE START. I'M A STRICT DISCIPLINARIAN.
PROCESSING MEN
ME TOO, DUCK.
PROCESSING WOMEN
"PWOCESSING?" ISN'T THAT WHAT THEY DO TO CHEESE?
HMMM?
OH, I SEE-- YES I DO!
AND FORBEARANCE IS NOT ONE OF MY VIRTUES!
I SHOULD KEEP MY TWAP SHUT, HUH?

BEHIND THE SCREEN, JACK.
YOU'LL FIND YOUR NEW WEARING APPAREL READY AND WAITING!
WALTZ
DISCOMFIT.
BUT YOU'D BE AN IDIOT TO RESIST.
OKAY...BUT CALL ME "HOWARD"-- PLEASE?

WHY-- THAT YOUR NAME?
YEAH... I THINK, SO, ANYWAY.
I'M PRETTY FUZZY ON JUST ABOUT EVERYTHING THOUGH, THESE DAYS.

THAT'S WHY WE GOT RULES AROUND HERE, HOWARD--WE DO THE THINKING SO YOU DON'T HAVETA.
JUST REMEMBER-- NO NOISE, NO VISITORS, NO SMOKING--

NO SMOKING?!
--EXCEPT AT DESIGNATED TIMES... NO UNAUTHORIZED PHONE CALLS... NO LEAVING THE COMPOUND...

UH-HUH... ANY YESSES IN YOUR REPERTOIRE, PAL?
NO.
AND MY HANDLE'S CECIL-- GOT THAT?
DEPENDS. IS THERE A "NO HILARITY" RULE?

DON'T GET WISE, HOWARD. I WANNA TREAT YOU GOOD. BUT WE'RE UNDER-STAFFED, SEE?
I GOT LOTS O' PATIENTS TO LOOK AFTER. AND FRANKLY...
BUMP BUMP

I PLAY FAVOR-ITES!
WELL. I MEAN...
THAT'S ONLY HUMAN, RIGHT?

RIGHT ON.
SO I DON'T WANNA HEAR NO ARGUMENTS...
...WHEN I TELL YOU TO STEP INSIDE THIS ROOM...

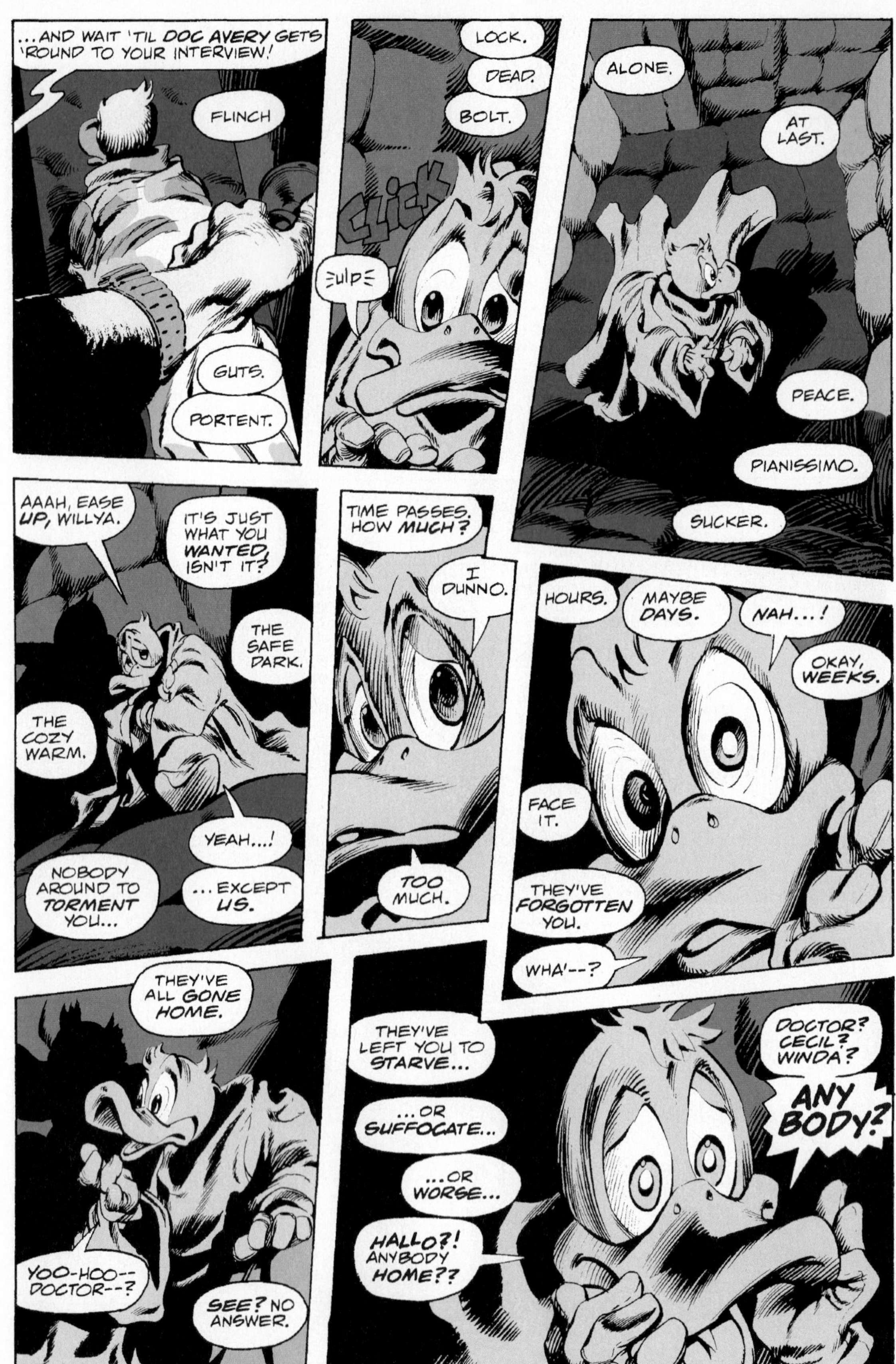
...AND WAIT 'TIL DOC AVERY GETS 'ROUND TO YOUR INTERVIEW!
FLINCH
GUTS.
PORTENT.
LOCK.
DEAD.
BOLT.
CLICK
ULP
ALONE.
AT LAST.
PEACE.
PIANISSIMO.
SUCKER.
AAAH, EASE UP, WILLYA.
IT'S JUST WHAT YOU WANTED, ISN'T IT?
THE SAFE DARK.
THE COZY WARM.
YEAH...!
NOBODY AROUND TO TORMENT YOU...
...EXCEPT US.
TIME PASSES. HOW MUCH?
I DUNNO.
TOO MUCH.
HOURS.
MAYBE DAYS.
NAH...!
OKAY, WEEKS.
FACE IT.
THEY'VE FORGOTTEN YOU.
WHA'--?
THEY'VE ALL GONE HOME.
YOO-HOO-- DOCTOR--?
SEE? NO ANSWER.
THEY'VE LEFT YOU TO STARVE...
...OR SUFFOCATE...
...OR WORSE...
HALLO?! ANYBODY HOME??
DOCTOR? CECIL? WINDA?
ANY BODY?

THUMP
THUMP
NOW, NOW... LET'S NOT PANIC.
EPOXY! EPOXY!
HALP!
HISTRIONICS WILL AVAIL US NAUGHT.
YEAH--RIGHT --GOTTA STAY CALM-- RATIONAL--!
MAYBE I COULD CLAW MY WAY OUT--!
HOWARD, IT'S--OH! EXCUSE ME!
I'VE BROUGHT SOMETHING TO CALM YOU. JUST GULP THESE DOWN, AND--
WHUMP
PILLS?
UH-UH! NOPE! NO WAY! SORRY! I HATE THE WRETCHED THINGS!
YOU GOTTA TWIST MY ARM TO GET ME TO TAKE ASPIRIN!
SIGH OKAY... I CAN'T FORCE YOU!..
BUT YOU CAN'T SEE THE DOCTOR 'TIL YOU'VE HAD YOUR MEDICATION.
WHA'--?
WAIT-- DON'T LEAVE ME --NOT AGAIN--
--NOT AGAIN--!
CECIL--?
PLEASE--?
I'LL GO--
CLICK
--CRAZY.

STUBBORN ONE, EH?
NAH... NOTHIN' OUTTA THE ORDINARY.
WATCH: 9--8-- 7--6--

5--4-3--
--2 --1.

WAAAAAAUGH
--ZERO.
THERE. DIDN'T I TELL YOU?

READY FOR YOUR MEDICATION NOW, HOWARD?
YEAH-- YEAH--

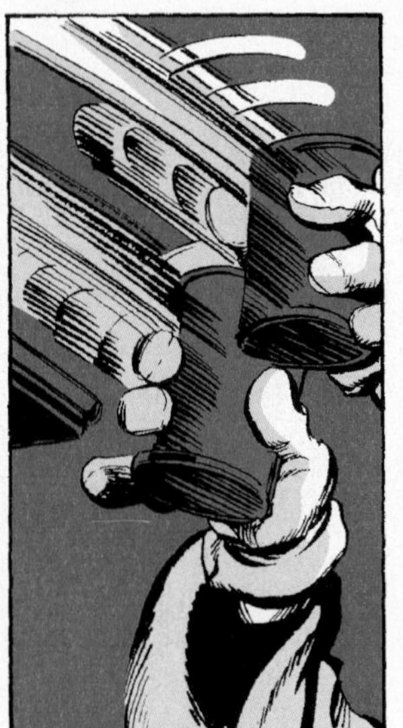

VERY GOOD.
NOW, COME ALONG.
THE DOC-TOR'S WAIT-ING.
SEE HOW EASY IT IS IF YOU CO-OP-ERATE?

MEANWHILE--
SO YOUR PARENTS BELIEVED YOU POS-SESSED BY THE DEVIL.
AND YOU AGREED WITH THEM, DID YOU?
OH, NO, DR. AVEWY!
I JUST WIKE TO MAKE FUNNY FACES AND SIWWY NOISES!
IT'S VEWY THEWAPEUTIC, YOU KNOW.

BUT YOU DID CONSENT TO THE TRIP TO CLEVELAND TO BE EXORCISED, DID YOU N--
RING
EXCUSE ME A MOMENT...

YES, THIS IS HE-- OH! HELLO, PHIL-- YOU DID?--I SEE!
NO, THAT WON'T BE NECESSARY. THANK YOU.

WELL, WINDA-- WE'VE CHECKED ON THE HOME ADDRESS YOU GAVE US.
IT'S A VACANT LOT.
OH, NO!!

THEY PUT ME ON THE BUS--PACKED UP EVEWYTHING--EVEN THE HOUSE--
--AND MOVED AWAY!! I'M AWONE! FOWSAKEN! MAWOONED!
NOW, WINDA, ARE YOU SURE?

MIGHTN'T YOU HAVE GIVEN US AN INCORRECT ADDRESS, OR--?
NO! NO! THE DEVIL POSSESSED ME AND MY EMBAWWASSED PAWENTS HAVE FWED--DISOWNED ME!!
WHERE CAN I GO? WHAT CAN I DO?? OH, WOE!

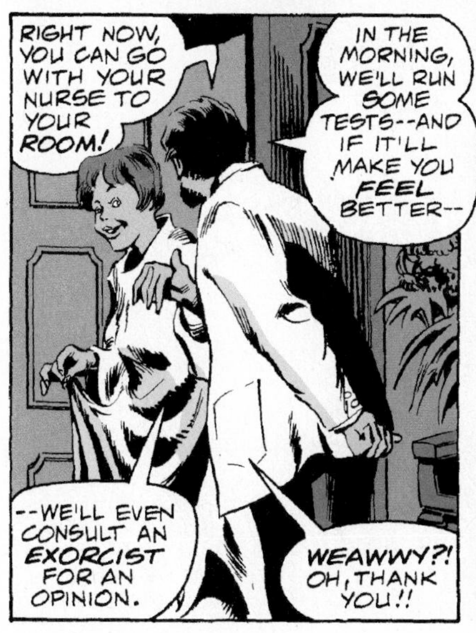
RIGHT NOW, YOU CAN GO WITH YOUR NURSE TO YOUR ROOM!
IN THE MORNING, WE'LL RUN SOME TESTS--AND IF IT'LL MAKE YOU FEEL BETTER--
--WE'LL EVEN CONSULT AN EXORCIST FOR AN OPINION.
WEAWWY?! OH, THANK YOU!!

OUTSIDE, IN AVERY'S WAITING ROOM...
HOWARD! HOW WOVEWY TO SEE YOU!
IT'S YOUR FRIEND, HOWARD. SAY "HELLO."
HAH...?

THEY'WE GOING TO HEWP ME! THEY'WE GOING TO GIVE ME TESTS AND EXOWCISE ME!
ISN'T IT WONDEWFUL?!
HAH...?

GEE! WHAT'S WONG WITH HIM? HE'S TOTAWWY UNWESPONSIVE!
THAT'S DR. AVERY'S CONCERN, WINDA-- NOT YOURS! COME!

PLEASE BE SEATED--"MR. DUCK!"
I SUPPOSE YOU'LL EXPECT SOME REACTION, WHEN I TURN TO FACE YOU, EH?
HAH...?

WELL, MY FRIEND--SORRY TO DISAPPOINT YOU...
BUT MY SON RONALD WORE THE SAME COSTUME LAST HALLOWEEN.
VERY REALISTIC!

...BUT IT'LL HAVE NO SHOCK VALUE IN THIS OFFICE. CLEAR?
HAH...?

GOOD! NOW THAT THAT'S OUT OF THE WAY, LET'S DISCUSS SOMETHING MORE INTERESTING.
WERE YOUR PARENTS AS SHORT AS YOU ARE, HOWARD?

HAH...?

I JUST WONDERED WHETHER YOU WERE SELF-CONSCIOUS ABOUT YOUR HEIGHT. MANY PATIENTS COMPENSATE BY ADOPTING A FLAMBOYANT STYLE OF--

AIIIEEEEEEEEEEEE
GOOD HEAVENS!
HAH...?
IT CAME FROM THE HALLWAY-- OUT HERE--!

DR. MORTON AVERY IS A GOOD PSYCHIATRIST. HE STUDIED THE FREUDIANS, THE BEHAVORISTS, AND THE SO-CALLED "THIRD FORCE" IN DEPTH. HE'S EVEN SCANNED CASTENEDA. AND HE'S CURRENT ON ALL THE MAJOR JOURNALS.
BUT AWARE AS HE IS OF ALL THE NEW THERAPIES OF THE COLLECTIVE UNCONSCIOUS, OF ARCHETYPES, OF NONORDINARY REALITIES--
NOTHING IN HIS READING HAS PREPARED HIM TO DEAL WITH THE SWIRLING, SEETHING, SAVAGE NIGHTMARE RISING IN BILLOWS FROM WINDA'S SKULL!
HALLO...?
HAH...?
NEXT CHAINS, LEATHER, AND PETUNIAS!

HOWARD THE DUCK™

MARVEL® COMICS GROUP

APPROVED BY THE COMICS CODE AUTHORITY

30¢ 13 JUNE 02415

TRAPPED IN A WORLD HE NEVER MADE!

HOWARD THE DUCK™

KISS AND TELL IN THE PSYCHO-WARD!

OMEN OF AN EXORCIST!

From the time of his hatching, he was...different. A potentially brilliant scholar who dreaded the structured environment of school, he educated himself in the streets, taking whatever work was available, formulating his philosophy of self from what he learned of the world about him. And then the Cosmic Axis shifted...and that world *changed.* Suddenly, he was stranded in a universe he could not fathom. Without warning, he became a strange fowl in an even stranger land.

Stan Lee PRESENTS: HOWARD THE DUCK!™

STEVE GERBER WRITER/EDITOR
GENE COLAN ARTIST
STEVE LEIALOHA INKER
JIM NOVAK, LETTERER
JAN COHEN, COLORIST

WELCOME TO THE CORRIDORS OF THE LOCAL **MENTAL FACILITY!** ORDINARILY, THE AMBIENCE IN THESE HALLWAYS IS AS HEAVILY **SEDATED** AS THE PATIENTS.

BUT NOT TODAY.

TODAY, IT'S **PARTY TIME!** THE RIGIDLY-ENFORCED TRANQUILITY HAS BEEN **SHATTERED** BY THE EMERGENCE OF FOUR SILVER-AND-BLACK **BAROQUES** FROM WINDA WESTER'S **HEAD!**

HAH...?

AW-**RIIIGHT!** SAUERBRATEN COUNTY, **OHIO**-- LET THIS OLD **COS**MOS...

ROCK, ROLL OVER, AND WRITHE!

THAT SOMEWHAT ABSTRUSE, IF UN-SUBTLE, PRONOUNCEMENT IS THEIR FIRST AND LAST BEFORE ASSUMING SINGLE-FILE FORMATION AND COM-MENCING THEIR MARCH ON... THE DUCK!
JEEZ... LOOKIT THIS!
OKAY, YOU GUYS --FREEZE!

HOLD IT RIGHT WHERE YA ARE OR WE'LL SH--

--UCKS.
THE SECURITY GUARDS FREEZE IN THEIR TRACKS... EYES OPEN, MINDS AWAKE BUT SOMEHOW UNABLE TO ISSUE COMMANDS TO THEIR NUMB, STIFFENED BODIES.

HOWARD, MEANWHILE, WATCHES WITH DRUG-INDUCED APATHY...
...AS THE CATMAN, THE DEMON, THE STARCHILD, AND THE SPACE-ACE MOVE IN FOR--

--THE WORD!
WHEN YOU MEET REALITY HEAD-ON --KISS IT, SMACK IN THE FACE!
THAT'S THE WORD! PASS IT ON!
HAH...?

MESSAGE CONCLUDED, THE FOUR PHANTASMS RETREAT INTO THE COILS OF SMOKE. "REMEMBER THE WORD," THE STARCHILD'S JABBING FINGER SEEMS TO SAY. "KISS IT, YOU'RE THE TARGET, BUT YOU DON'T HAVE TO BE A SITTING DUCK!"
THE DEMON SNARLS AND ROARS IN AFFIRMATION!

AND THEN, WITH ONE AWFUL WHOOSH, THEY ARE DRAWN BACK INTO WINDA'S BRAIN.

THE STORM SUBSIDES.
HOWARD IS LEFT WITH HIS STUPOR AND A SEQUIN OF QUESTION-ABLE WISDOM.
HAH...?

THE HOSPITAL PERSONNEL STRAIN TO RECOVER FROM SHOCK, WONDERMENT, AND SMOKE INHALATION.
SNAP
ONE INTREPID INTERN FARES BETTER THAN MOST, GATHER-ING ENOUGH OF HIS WITS ABOUT HIM TO SNATCH A NIKON FROM THE RESEARCH SECTION...
...AND RECORD THE EVENT FOR POSTERITY.

NOT THAT POSTERITY IS THE ONLY FELLOW INTERESTED:
SO! ZIS OCCURRED SREE DAYS AGO, DURING MEIN ABSENCE. UND SINCE...?

NOTHING, DR. REICH. WE HAVE SUBJECTED MISS WESTER TO EXHAUSTIVE EXAMINATION...
...AND FOUND NO PHYSIOLOGICAL EXPLANATION FOR THE PHENOMENON.
AH, BUT YOU'VE UNCOVERED ZOME JUICY TIDBIT, HAVEN'T YOU?

I CAN TELL BY YOUR ZMIRK!
MAY I HAVE DER ENVELOPE, PLEASE?
X-RAYS
#62 H.D.
ROOM 14-A

ACH DU LIEBER! ZIS IS DER X-RAY OF DER DUMMKOPF IN ZE DUCK SUIT?

CORRECT. WHAT WE ASSUMED TO BE A DWARF MASQUERADING AS A DUCK APPEARS IN FACT TO BE--
QVIET YOUR VERDAMMT VERBOSE MOUTH! VHERE ARE ZEY NOW-- DER FRAULEIN UND DER DUCK?
IN ISOLATION-- TOGETHER.

DR. AVERY--AGAINST MY ADVICE--HAS SUMMONED AN AUTHORITY ON DEMONOLOGY TO DETERMINE IF WINDA IS POSSESSED, AS SHE ASSERTS.
I FELT YOU, AS DIRECTOR OF THIS FACILITY SHOULD BE CONSULTED FIRST.

MOST COMMENDABLE, NURSE. BUT REMOVE YOUR PERSON FROM ZIS DESK--SCHNELL!!
=GASP= YES, HERR DOCTOR! FORGIVE ME!

UND NEVER ASK FORGIVENESS! NEVER!! BE STRONG! MIGHT MEANS RIGHT--
--UND RIGHT MEANS NEVER HAVING TO SAY YOU'RE SORRY!
YES, HERR DOKTOR!

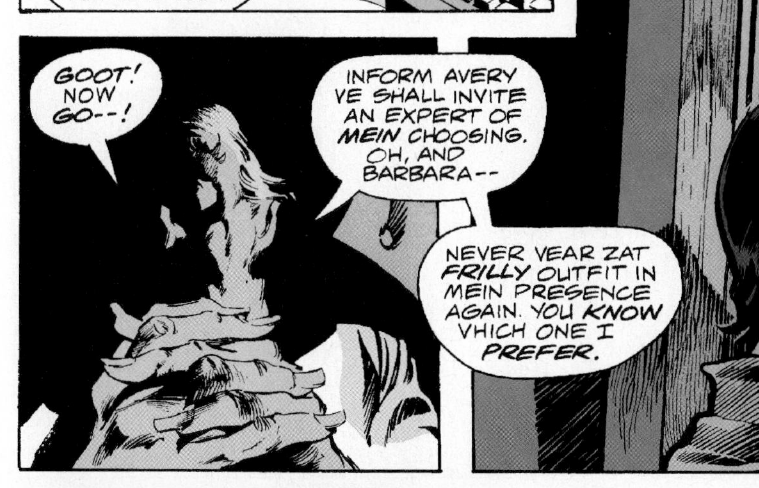
GOOT! NOW GO--!
INFORM AVERY VE SHALL INVITE AN EXPERT OF MEIN CHOOSING. OH, AND BARBARA--
NEVER VEAR ZAT FRILLY OUTFIT IN MEIN PRESENCE AGAIN. YOU KNOW VHICH ONE I PREFER.
YES, HERR DOKTOR. I KNOW.

GOOT! NOW, RAUSE MIT YOU! UND DON'T DISAPPOINT ME!

I WON'T, MY DARLING--FEAR NOT! UNLIKE THE OTHERS, I SHALL EARN YOUR ADORATION!
OUR IMPUDENT DR. AVERY WILL BE TAUGHT THE PRICE OF DEFYING THE FUTURE MASTER OF THE WORLD!

MEANWHILE, SEVERAL STORIES BELOW...
YOUR TWANQUIWIZER MUST BE WEARING OFF, HOWARD. YOU'WE A NEWVOUS WECK!
CLAM DIG.
MORDANT.
INFIRM.
THREAD.
GARNISH.
STIMULUS.

SHIN.
DIG.
IMP.
PALE.
WAN.
WAAAUGH

AND YOU'WE MAKING ME NEWVOUS, TOO. YOU'WE A'WAYS SO DISTWACTED! SIT DOWN! TALK TO ME!!
CLUMP
REAP.
SOW.
KISS IT.
TRIP.

I'M SOWNNY-- I CAN'T HEWP IT--I'M VEWY, VEWY AFWAID--!
BESIDES--THE FWICTION OF YOUR FEET IS EWODING THE PADDING IN THIS CELL!
THAT WAS A JOKE... SUPPOS-EDWY.
COULD YOU JUST GWOAN A WITTLE, HUH? WET ME KNOW I EXIST? HMMMMM?

GROAN
HOWZAT?
PATHETIC, RIGHT?
AT WEAST IT'S A WESPONSE! NOW, WET'S HAVE SOME CHIT-CHAT!
MUST I WESORT TO VIOWENCE BEFORE YOU TALK TO ME? IS MY CWAVING FOR COMPANION-SHIP TOO BWATENT, OR WHAT?
NAH--IT'S JUST--THERE'S THESE OTHER VOICES, SEE?
AND THIS RUNNING VISUAL COMMENTARY IN MY MIND...!

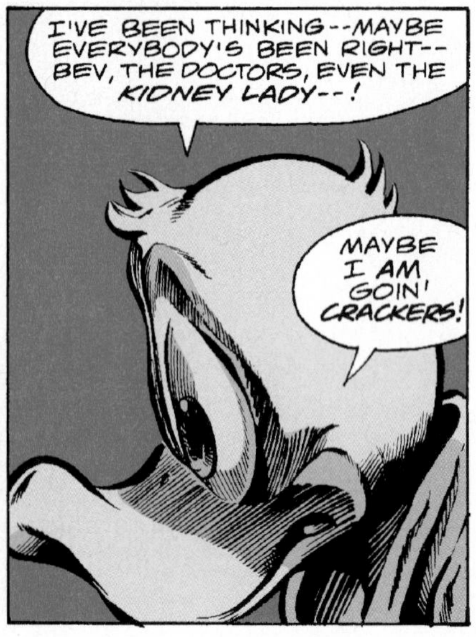
I'VE BEEN THINKING--MAYBE EVERYBODY'S BEEN RIGHT-- BEV, THE DOCTORS, EVEN THE KIDNEY LADY--!
MAYBE I AM GOIN' CRACKERS!

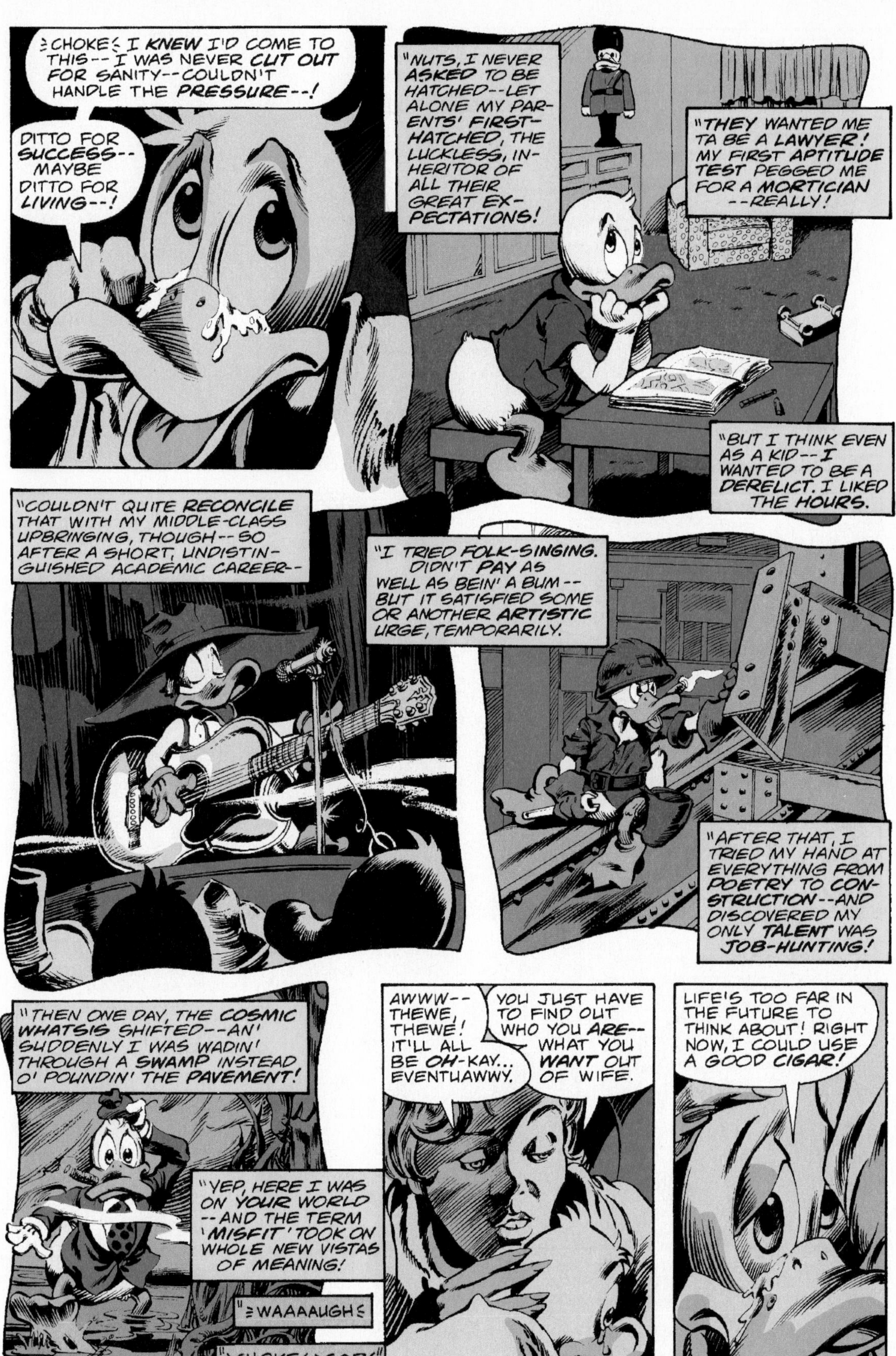

≷CHOKE≶ I KNEW I'D COME TO THIS-- I WAS NEVER CUT OUT FOR SANITY--COULDN'T HANDLE THE PRESSURE--!
DITTO FOR SUCCESS-- MAYBE DITTO FOR LIVING--!
"NUTS, I NEVER ASKED TO BE HATCHED--LET ALONE MY PARENTS' FIRST-HATCHED, THE LUCKLESS, INHERITOR OF ALL THEIR GREAT EXPECTATIONS!
"THEY WANTED ME TA BE A LAWYER! MY FIRST APTITUDE TEST PEGGED ME FOR A MORTICIAN --REALLY!
"BUT I THINK EVEN AS A KID--I WANTED TO BE A DERELICT. I LIKED THE HOURS.
"COULDN'T QUITE RECONCILE THAT WITH MY MIDDLE-CLASS UPBRINGING, THOUGH--SO AFTER A SHORT, UNDISTINGUISHED ACADEMIC CAREER--
"I TRIED FOLK-SINGING. DIDN'T PAY AS WELL AS BEIN' A BUM--BUT IT SATISFIED SOME OR ANOTHER ARTISTIC URGE, TEMPORARILY.
"AFTER THAT, I TRIED MY HAND AT EVERYTHING FROM POETRY TO CONSTRUCTION--AND DISCOVERED MY ONLY TALENT WAS JOB-HUNTING!
"THEN ONE DAY, THE COSMIC WHATSIS SHIFTED--AN' SUDDENLY I WAS WADIN' THROUGH A SWAMP INSTEAD O' POUNDIN' THE PAVEMENT!
"YEP, HERE I WAS ON YOUR WORLD --AND THE TERM 'MISFIT' TOOK ON WHOLE NEW VISTAS OF MEANING!
"≷WAAAAUGH≶
"≷CHOKE≶ ≷SOB≶"
AWWW-- THEWE, THEWE! IT'LL ALL BE OH-KAY... EVENTUAWWY.
YOU JUST HAVE TO FIND OUT WHO YOU ARE-- WHAT YOU WANT OUT OF WIFE.
LIFE'S TOO FAR IN THE FUTURE TO THINK ABOUT! RIGHT NOW, I COULD USE A GOOD CIGAR!

WHILE, ON A FLOOR SOMEWHERE BETWEEN THE DEVILISH DIRECTOR AND THE DEEP BLUE DUCK...
I'LL THANK YOU TO KNOCK BEFORE ENTERING THIS OFFICE, NURSE!
I'M ENGAGED IN A PRIVATE CONVERSATION, AND I WILL NOT TOLERATE--
ORDERS FROM THE DIRECTOR, DR. AVERY --URGENT!
YOU'RE TO CANCEL ANY INVITATION YOU MAY HAVE PROFFERED TO ANY EXORCIST, OR RISK--

I'M AFRAID THE COUNTERMAND COMES TOO LATE, BARBARA.
MEET MY FRIEND AND FORMER COLLEAGUE AT GATEWAY UNIVERSITY...
...MR. DAIMON HELLSTROM!

MY PLEASURE, NURSE.
SURELY YOUR DIRECTOR WOULD NOT OBJECT TO MY MERELY EXAMINING THE GIRL.
NO CHARGE, NO OBLIGATION, I SUPPOSE?

NATURALLY. AND HE IS FREE, OF COURSE, TO OBTAIN ANOTHER OPINION.
OH, VERY WELL, THEN--AS LONG AS YOU'RE ALREADY HERE.
GOOD!

OH, DAIMON-- SOMETHING ELSE YOU SHOULD KNOW.
WE'VE ANOTHER RATHER UNUSUAL PATIENT WITH MISS. WESTER. HE--
NO, YOU'D BEST SEE FOR YOURSELF.

YOU WON'T GET AWAY WITH THIS, AVERY. THE DIRECTOR KNOWS ALL ABOUT YOU--
--AND YOUR AMBITIONS!
DO TELL...?

PRESENTLY...
WINDA, HOWARD-- THIS IS--
BY THE SEVEN CIRCLES!
Y-YOU ARE-- A DUCK!!
YEAH. AIN'T IT GREAT HOW SOME THINGS IN THE UNIVERSE REMAIN CONSTANT.

DAIMON IS AN AUTHORITY ON DEMONOLOGY AND EXORCISM, WINDA.
HE'S HERE TO EXAMINE YOU.
WEAWWY?!

YOU'WE GOING TO DISPOSSESS ME?
DID DR. AVEWY TELL YOU HOW I GOT POSSESSED AND MY TEWWIFIED PAWENTS PUT ME ON A BUS TO CWEVEWAND TO BE EXOWCISED...
...AND HOW I JUST WIKE TO MAKE FUNNY FACES AND SIWWY NOISES...
...ONWY MY PAWENTS THOUGHT IT WAS THE DEVIL, MM-HM, AND THE BUS CWASHED, AND--AND--

NO. HE DID NOT. PERHAPS YOU CAN TELL ME... LATER.
BUT FOR NOW, WINDA, PLEASE REMAIN ABSOLUTELY SILENT. THE EXAMINATION REQUIRES ONLY A MOMENT...

...BUT A DELICATE MOMENT, IN WHICH I MUST REACH BEHIND YOUR EYES AND TOUCH YOUR VERY SOUL.
OH, MY GOODNESS!

PRECISELY 33 HEARTBEATS LATER...
IT IS DONE.
SNAP

AND BY NO MEANS IS MS. WESTER UNDER DEMONIC INFLUENCE, DOCTOR.
SHE DOES POSSESS CERTAIN LATENT PSYCHIC TALENTS, HOWEVER... WHICH LIKELY ACCOUNT FOR THE EPISODE IN THE CORRIDOR.
I WOULD HYPOTHESIZE THAT IN A MOMENT OF EXTREME STRESS HER MIND REACHED OUT...

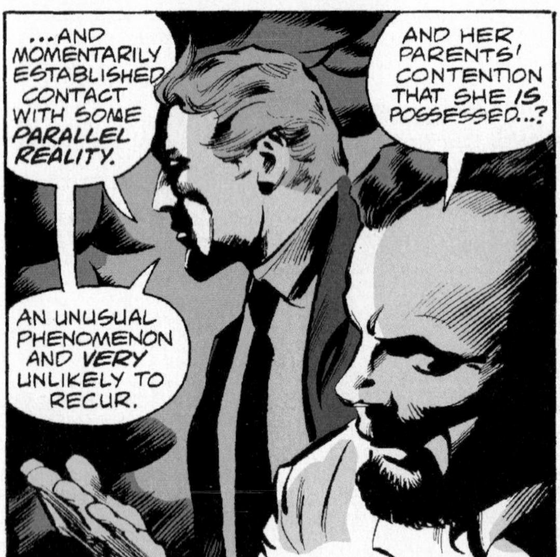
...AND MOMENTARILY ESTABLISHED CONTACT WITH SOME PARALLEL REALITY.
AND HER PARENTS' CONTENTION THAT SHE IS POSSESSED...?
AN UNUSUAL PHENOMENON AND VERY UNLIKELY TO RECUR.

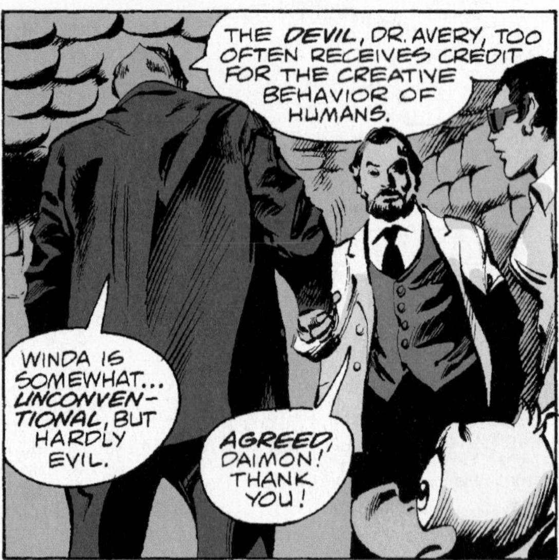
THE DEVIL, DR. AVERY, TOO OFTEN RECEIVES CREDIT FOR THE CREATIVE BEHAVIOR OF HUMANS.
WINDA IS SOMEWHAT... UNCONVENTIONAL, BUT HARDLY EVIL.
AGREED, DAIMON! THANK YOU!

WINDA, I'LL GET PROCEDURES UNDERWAY IMMEDIATELY TO SECURE YOUR RELEASE.
CLAP
CLAP
OH, HOOWAY, HOOWAY!!

UH, DOC--WAITAMINIT--WHAT ABOUT ME?
I DON'T WANNA SPEND THE REST O' MY LIFE IN HERE, EITHER.
DOC...?
WE'LL SEE...!

I'M MORE THAN MILDLY CURIOUS ABOUT WINDA'S **COMPANION,** DR. AVERY.
WHAT DO YOU KNOW OF HIS-- **ITS**-- ORIGINS?
DID YOU FOLLOW LAST YEAR'S **PRESIDENTIAL CAMPAIGN** AT ALL, DAIMON?

NO, NOT CLOSELY--!
WELL, THERE WAS A MINOR CANDIDATE WHO RAN UNDER THE NAME "HOWARD THE DUCK"...!
HE GOT A FEW WRITE-UPS --EVEN A SPOT ON WALTER KLONDIKE'S NEWS--
BUT, LIKE **MOST** OF THE PUBLIC I ASSUMED IT WAS ALL AN ELABORATE **GAG**--

--RATHER LIKE THE **FIRESIGN THEATRE'S** "PAPOON FOR PRESIDENT", OR THE YIPPIES RUNNING A **PIG** FOR OFFICE BACK IN '68.
THEN I SAW **OUR** DUCK'S **X-RAYS**--!
NOW I DON'T KNOW **WHAT** TO THINK.
QUITE A **DILEMMA**.
I SUGGEST-- ONE MOMENT, DOCTOR.

YOU MAY HAVE A FAR MORE **SERIOUS** PROBLEM TO COPE WITH--
--IF I'VE CORRECTLY IDENTIFIED THE **SUN SYMBOL** ON THESE YOUNG PERSON'S SHIRTS!
I'M AFRAID I DON'T FOLLOW YOU--!
C'MON GANG--LET'S **CLEAN UP** THIS PARKING LOT!!
LET'S ALL PITCH IN AND SCRUB AND SURPRISE THE **MASTER** WITH OUR GOOD WORKS!!

IF YOU QUESTION THEM, DOCTOR, I BELIEVE YOU'LL FIND THEM TO BE "YUCCIES"--DISCIPLES OF THE REVERAND JOON MOON YUC-- A RATHER CONTROVERSIAL EVANGELIST--
--WHO'S BEEN ACCUSED OF BRAINWASHING HIS YOUTHFUL FOLLOWERS AND USING THEM TO HIS OWN, OFTEN LUCRATIVE ENDS.
AW, C'MON--DO WE LOOK BRAINWASHED TO YOU??
WE'RE JUST HIGH ON LIFE, THE LORD, AND THE MASTER!
THEN YOU ARE MEMBERS OF THIS GROUP. BUT--WHAT ARE YOU DOING HERE?
HOW DID YOU GET PAST THE GUARD AT THE GATE? WE HAVE A POLICY OF "NO ADMITTANCE" UNLESS--

OH, IT'S OKAY! WE CAME WITH THE MASTER!
I'M QUITE AS CONFUSED AS YOU ARE, DOCTOR.
OH, BUT OF COURSE--THAT EXPLAINS EVERY-THING! THEY CAME WITH THE MASTER!
WHAT BUSINESS WOULD THE YUCCIES HAVE H--

WINDA!
BLAST! THIS MUST BE REICH'S IDEA! NATURALLY, HE'D NEVER TRUST ME--!
DOCTOR--CALM YOUR-SELF! I NEGLECTED TO MENTION THAT REV. YUC IS--DEAD!
A HOUSE EXPLODED IN PENNSYLVANIA--HE WAS TRAPPED INSIDE--!*
SURELY HIS FOLLOWERS ARE SUFFERING SOME MASS-DELUSION, BORN OF GRIEF!
*AS SEEN IN HTD #5--STEVE.

HOWEVER, BACK IN THE VINYL-UPHOLSTERED CELL...
I DON'T CARE WHAT AVERY SAID! DR. REICH WISHES TO CONDUCT HIS OWN TESTS!
NO! NO!! OH, HEWP ME!! SOME-BODY!!
IT'S OKAY, BARBARA. YA WON'T GET NO TROUBLE FROM THIS BIRD.

RIGHT, HOWARD?
NOW YOU STAY HERE AND BE-HAVE YOURSELF --OR YOU COULD GET HURT!
THUN

YOU 'N' ME WERE SUPPOSED TO BE FRIENDS, CECIL.
PALS! CHUMS! WAR BUDDIES IN THE BATTLE AGAINST MENTAL ILLNESS!

WHAP
AN' YOU SOLD ME OUT!!
RIGHT DOWN THE RIVER-- IN EXCHANGE FOR ONE FRIGID SMILE FROM ≷SIGH≶ BARBARA!

≷tsk tsk≶ HOWARD, YOU COULDN'T PUNCH OUT AN ANGEL FOOD CAKE!
DIDN'T EVEN FEEL IT, HUH...?

UH-UH.
THWIP
WHUMP

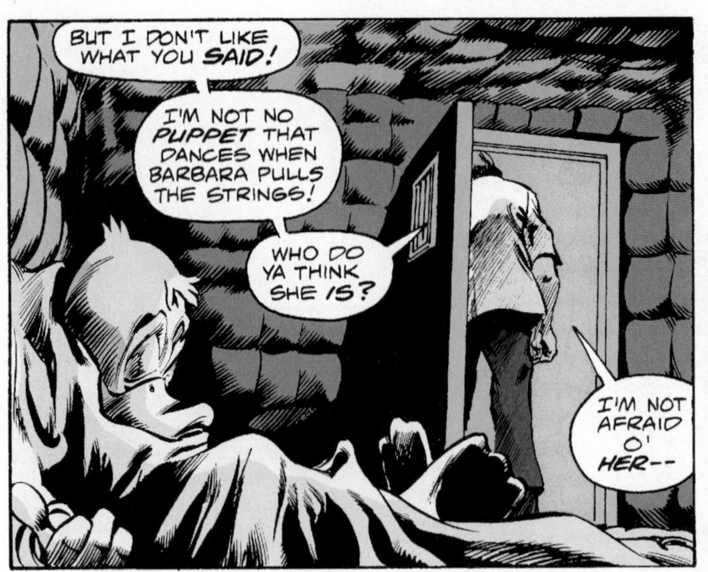
BUT I DON'T LIKE WHAT YOU SAID!
I'M NOT NO PUPPET THAT DANCES WHEN BARBARA PULLS THE STRINGS!
WHO DO YA THINK SHE IS?
I'M NOT AFRAID O' HER--

"--JUST THE DIRECTOR!"
...UND YOU LANDED IN A TREETOP IN DELAWARE?
AMAZING.

UND VER-R-RY FORTUNATE! I FEEL OUR COLLABORATION VILL BE A LONG UND FRUITFUL ONE--
--REVEREND YUC!!
PERHAPS SO. WE SEEM TO SHARE A COMMON VISION, DR. REICH.

BEGGING THE DIRECTOR'S PARDON... WE ARE READY FOR THE RITUAL.
SANK YOU, BARBARA-- UND JAH, YOU LOOK MUCH BETTER IN BLACK LEATHER!
I VOULD SUGGEST YOU TAKE IN DER COAT AT DER WAIST, HOWEVER.
YES, HERR DOCTOR.

I GO NOW--TO THE DUNGEON!
FOR THE GREATER GLORY OF THE ALMIGHTY!
NEIN, HERR REVEREND --TO DEMONSTRATE A TECHNIQUE.

A GREAT DEAL IS RIDING ON DER OUTCOME OF ZIS RITUAL ...FOR US BOTH!
DO NOT ALLOW DER ALMIGHTY TO DISTRACT YOU FROM DER PURPOSE, eh?

GOOD HEAVENS!! HOWARD--WHAT'S HAPPENED?! WHERE'S WINDA?
I... DUNNO...
"BARBARA... SAID SOMETHIN'... ABOUT... THE SUB-CELLAR!... MAYBE THEY RAN OUTTA COAL... FIGGERED THEY'D BURN 'ER... FOR FUEL...!"
AS YOU CAN SEE, REVEREND, POOR, POOR WINDA IS DEFINITELY POSSESSED.
OH, YES, UNQUESTIONABLY.
AND YOU MUST UNDERSTAND, WINDA, THAT THE DEMON MAY ONLY BE DRIVEN FROM YOU THROUGH THE DIVINE APPLICATION OF... SENSATION.
THE DEMON WILL FLEE, YOU SEE--FROM PAIN INFLICTED BY BEAUTY.
YOU MUST LOVE THE LORD AND ALL HIS WORKS AND ME, HIS AGENT--'TIL IT HURTS.

FOR BESIDE THIS EXQUISITE ANGUISH, THE DEMON'S POWER PALES.
BEHOLD--THE HUMBLE PETUNIA!

FIXATE ON ITS BEAUTY, CHILD--FEEL ITS MEMORY OF THE TORMENT AS IT STRAINED TO PIERCE THE SURFACE OF THE EARTH TO MEET THE SUNLIGHT--AS IT WAS LATER TORN FROM THAT EARTH TO SERVE YOU!
IT MUST MAKE YOU CRY, WINDA--AND ADORE IT--AND ADORE ME--AND BELIEVE IN ME WITHOUT QUESTION!

WHAP
ouch
BELIEVE ME, WINDA --CRY AND BELIEVE ME!!

SUDDENLY--
WHAT IN THE NAME OF SANITY--?!
MY APOLOGIES, DOCTOR-- IT IS REVEREND YUC-- ALL TOO ALIVE!
AVERY--AND HELLSTROM!!
HELLST-- DAIMON HELLSTROM?!
REMOVE THEM!! NO ONE MAY INTRUDE ON THIS RITUAL!
WITH PLEASURE, REVEREND! I'VE LONG AWAITED A SATISFYING MATCH WITH THIS FOOL!
BUT BEFORE THE BEHEMOTH NAMED CECIL CAN REACH DAIMON...
YAAARGH
BARBARA-- ARE YOU MAD?!
...THE YOUNG EXORCIST LIFTS HIS HANDS IN THE SIGN OF THE TRIDENT!
INSTANTLY, THE SOULFIRE BLAZES FORTH, AS IF FROM WITHIN HIS PORES, SHEATHING DAIMON IN A COLUMN OF SULFUROUS FLAME!
IT SEEMS, ON SIGHT, TO BE CONSUMING HIM ALIVE! BUT IN TRUTH...
...IT IS THE FIRST STAGE IN A TOTAL AND TERRI-FYING TRANSFORMATION!
IT'S AT THIS CRUCIAL MOMENT...
WINDA...?
HAH...?
...THAT A CONCERNED, BUT STILL GROGGY FOWL CHOOSES TO STUMBLE BACK ONTO THE SCENE.
WHOOP!

DID YOU PRESUME, HELLSTROM, THAT I WOULD NOT BE AWARE OF YOUR PECULIAR TALENTS...
...OR, FOR THAT MATTER, THE RUMORS CONCERNING YOUR LINEAGE?
I'VE BEEN PREPARED TO CONFRONT YOU NOW FOR SOME TIME...
...PREPARED TO UNLEASH THE FURY OF THE WHITE WIND...TO STRIP THE TEMPTER'S FLAME FROM YOUR VERY FLESH...!
YOU SEE, I'VE DABBLED IN DEMONOLOGY, ALSO!
NO!!
WHOOSH!
BY THE HADEAN CHIMES!
THE TRANSFORMATION HAS BEEN ARRESTED!
YET, I FEEL AN ODD BUOYANCY AS THOUGH SOME TERRIBLE BURDEN HAS BEEN LIFTED FROM--
IT HAS, DAIMON--FOR YOUR SECOND SOUL, YOUR DEMONIC SELF--
--HAS FOUND A NEW HOME!!
NEXT
The RETURN OF BEVERLY--The RETURN TO CLEVELAND--and A FEW NEW TURNS of FATE'S CRUEL SCREW IN--
A DUCK POSSESSED!

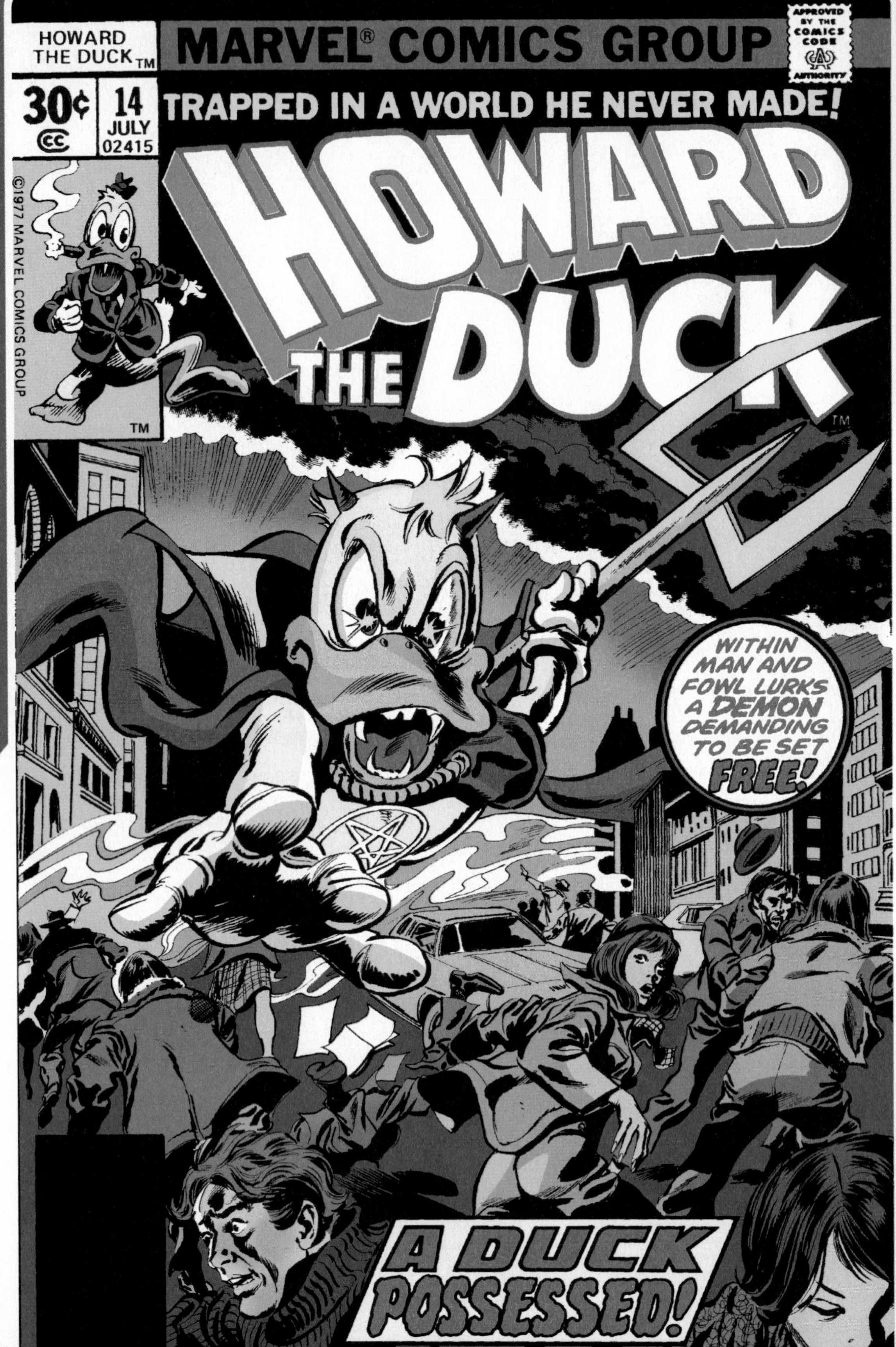
HOWARD THE DUCK TM
MARVEL® COMICS GROUP
APPROVED BY THE COMICS CODE AUTHORITY
30¢
CC
14
JULY
02415
TRAPPED IN A WORLD HE NEVER MADE!
©1977 MARVEL COMICS GROUP
TM
HOWARD THE DUCK
TM
WITHIN MAN AND FOWL LURKS A DEMON DEMANDING TO BE SET FREE!
A DUCK POSSESSED!

From the time of his hatching, he was...different. A potentially brilliant scholar who dreaded the structured environment of school, he educated himself in the streets, taking whatever work was available, formulating his philosophy of self from what he learned of the world about him. And then the Cosmic Axis shifted...and that world *changed.* Suddenly, he was stranded in a universe he could not fathom. Without warning, he became a strange fowl in an even stranger land.

Stan Lee PRESENTS: HOWARD THE DUCK!™

STEVE GERBER WRITER/EDITOR * GENE COLAN PENCILLER * KLAUS JANSON INKER * JIM NOVAK LETTERER * IRENE VARTANOFF COLORIST

IT'S TWO! TWO! TWO DUCKS IN ONE!

DAIMON HELLSTROM'S SECOND SELF--THE IMPLACABLY SAVAGE SON OF SATAN--HAS BEEN TRANSPLANTED FROM THE YOUNG EXORCIST'S BODY INTO HOWARD'S!

AND HOWEVER LUDICROUS THE SITUATION MAY APPEAR, ITS POTENTIAL FOR DISASTER IS MONUMENTAL! FOR DESPITE THE FOWL'S DIMINUTIVE STATURE, HE NOW EMBODIES ALL THE SEETHING POWER, ALL THE VIRULENT RAGE, ALL THE CALLOUS DISDAIN OF MORALITY AND HUMANKINDNESS--OF THE TRUE SCION OF HELL!

HE IS, IN SHORT--

A DUCK Possessed!

THE SUBCELLAR OF SAUERBRATEN COUNTY, OHIO'S, MENTAL FACILITY:
BY THE SEVEN CIRCLES! EVEN THE SOULFIRE IS AT HIS COMMAND!
WAAUGH
ZZZZZZZ
ALL THE ABILITIES OF YOUR FATHER'S SON ARE MINE NOW, HELL-STROM-- FOR NOW I BEAR ON MY CHEST THE INVERTED PENTACLE-- THE MARK OF BAPHO-MET!
SNAP!
YOU'VE TRIUMPHED, DAIMON-- YOU'RE FREE AT LAST OF YOUR SATANIC HERITAGE--!
GWACIOUS!
H-HOWARD--YOU'RE FWYING TOWARD THE CEIWING--!

AYE, DAIMON-- YOU'RE FREE AT LAST--!
NOW ONLY THE WORLD NEED TREMBLE!!
OOOO! I'M GOING TO BE TEWWIBWY, TEWWIBWY ILL--!
THE YOUNG WOMAN'S NAME IS WINDA WESTER, AND UNTIL THIS MOMENT, SHE, LIKE HOWARD, HAD BEEN AN UNWILLING INMATE OF THE ASYLUM... SERVING A 90-DAY TERM AS THE RESULT OF A TRAFFIC VIOLATION.*
IRONICALLY, IT WAS SHE WHO'D BELIEVED HERSELF POSSESSED --AND ON HER BEHALF THAT DR. MORTON AVERY SUMMONED DAIMON HELLSTROM TO OHIO.
* SEE HTD #12.--STEVE.

HOWARD-- PWEASE-- I'M AFWAID OF HEIGHTS!

SILENCE, FEMALE!

OF COURSE, BOTH AVERY AND HELLSTROM RECKONED WITHOUT THE INTERFERENCE OF REVEREND JOON MOON YUC AND THE HOSPITAL'S MYSTERIOUS DIRECTOR IN TREATING WINDA'S CASE.

DAIMON DIAGNOSED WINDA AS NORMAL. THE DIRECTOR DISAGREED. AND THAT, AS THEY SAY IN MED CIRCLES, IS WHEN COMPLICATIONS SET IN.

HOWARD, PWETTY PWEASE-- POINT US DOWN-- I'M FWIGHTENED--!

POINT IT DO-OWWW IT'S HOT!!

NATURALLY, IT'S HOT! THE SCATHING FIRES OF HELL ITSELF COURSE THROUGH THE TRIDENT'S NETHER-METAL STEM!

M-MY HANDS-- I THINK I BURNED THEM--!

KLOMP

BUT I'M SO GWATEFUL TO BE OUT OF THAT HOWWIBLE PWACE-- I DON'T EVEN CARE--!
THANK YOU, HOWARD--
OH, THANK YOU, THANK YOU--

TH--OOOH
SLAP!
STOW IT, SISTER!

:SNIFL: B-BUT, HOWARD--WHAT DID I DO?--WHY DID YOU WAWWOP ME--?!
BECAUSE, YOU INSIPID SNIVELLING FOOL--
YOUR TAMPERING WITH THE TRIDENT IN MID-AIR JEOPARDIZED BOTH OUR LIVES--AND COULD HAVE ABORTED OUR ESCAPE!
HOWARD--WAIT--DON'T FWY OFF IN A SNIT--!
DON'T WEAVE ME ALL AWONE--!
"I CANNOT AFFORD TO BE SADDLED WITH THE LIKES OF YOU, WINDA," THE DEMONIC DUCK SHOUTS BACK. "I'VE CARRIED YOU THIS FAR--
"--THE REST IS UP TO YOU!"
MEANWHILE, BACK IN THE BASEMENT--
REICH AUTHORIZED YOU TO SUSPEND THE GIRL BY HER WRISTS FROM THE PIPES--?!
--TO CONFUSE AND TERRIFY HER WITH TALK OF DEMONS AND TORTURE?! AND YOU COMPLIED??
YOU HAD NO RIGHT TO INTRUDE, DR. AVERY! YUC'S RITUAL WAS SPECIFICALLY ORDERED BY THE DIRECTOR!
MY GOD--I'LL SEE YOU BOTH UP ON CHARGES FOR THIS--!
WOULD THAT I, LIKE YOURSELF, COULD NOT ANTICIPATE THE CONSEQUENCES--
WOULD THAT I COULD REMAIN TO WITNESS IT, DR. AVERY.
--OF MY SATANIC SOUL'S LUST FOR DESTRUCTION UNLEASHED IN THE BODY OF A CREATURE RECENTLY UNABLE TO CONTROL EVEN HIS OWN MIND!*
IN TIME, THE FOWL'S GENUINE PERSONALITY CANNOT HELP BUT SUCCUMB TO ITS SEVERE MENTAL FATIGUE.
*HOWARD SUFFERED A NEAR-NERVOUS BREAKDOWN IN ISH #11.-S.

AND WHEN IT DOES-- WHEN ITS INFLUENCE UPON THE DUCK'S BEHAVIOR IS NEGATED COMPLETELY--
--ONLY I SHALL STAND 'TWIXT THIS HAPLESS WORLD AND THE WRATH OF THE DEVIL'S FIRSTBORN!

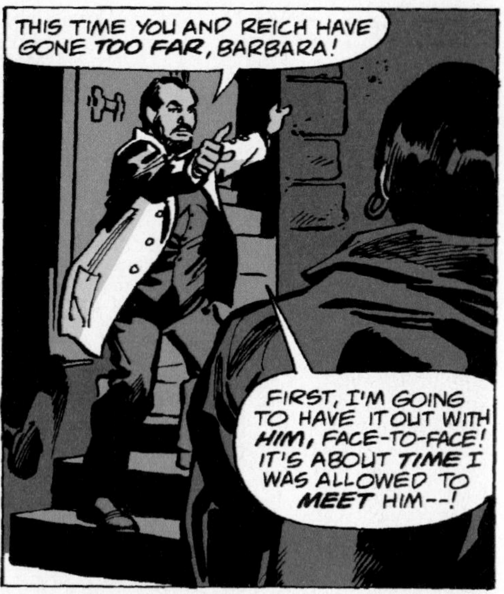

THIS TIME YOU AND REICH HAVE GONE TOO FAR, BARBARA!
FIRST, I'M GOING TO HAVE IT OUT WITH HIM, FACE-TO-FACE! IT'S ABOUT TIME I WAS ALLOWED TO MEET HIM--!

AND THEN, NO DOUBT, YOU'LL NOTIFY THE STATE MENTAL HEALTH COMMISSION, WON'T YOU?

=SIGH= VERY WELL, DOCTOR--DO AS YOU WILL!

YOU'LL PAY IN SPADES FOR YOUR AUDACITY-- WHEN THE PLAN BECOMES THE LAW!

CLEVELAND!

AS THE DEVIL-DUCK DESCENDS UPON THE DECAYING CITY, VENGEANCE FILLS HIS HEART, AND RAGE--OR PERHAPS SMOG-- TINGES HIS EYES WITH CRIMSON!

THERE'S ANOTHER HUMAN HERE TO WHOM HE OWES A DEBT OF ANGER...

...A DEBT HE FULLY INTENDS TO HONOR.

EMPLOYING THE PSYCHO-SENSITIVE PROPERTY OF THE TRIDENT, HE ATTUNES HIMSELF TO HER INDIVIDUAL PSYCHIC WAVELENGTH...

...AND PINPOINTS THE SOURCE OF TRANSMISSION.

AND THEN, HE GRINS... NOT WITH AMUSEMENT, BUT WITH THE PERVERSE DELIGHT...

...OF A GONIF WHO'S JUST SPIED AN EASY MARK!

HER NAME IS BEVERLY SWITZLER.

AND FOR SOME TIME SHE'D BEEN HOWARD'S CLOSEST COMPANION, UNTIL...

THAT NIGHT IN THE MOTEL--I CAN'T GET IT OFF MY MIND, PAUL!

I'VE GONE OVER IT AGAIN AND AGAIN... AND I STILL CAN'T IMAGINE WHY HOWARD DESERTED ME!*

HE'D COLLAPSED WITH EXHAUSTION... I WENT OUT WITH THE DOCTOR TO DISCUSS HIS CONDITION...

*HTD #11.--S.

...AND WHEN I GOT BACK, HE WAS GONE!!
I KNOW, BEV... YOU'VE TOLD ME THE STORY A HUNDR--
UHM... THAT WAS UN-CALLED FOR, WASN'T IT?

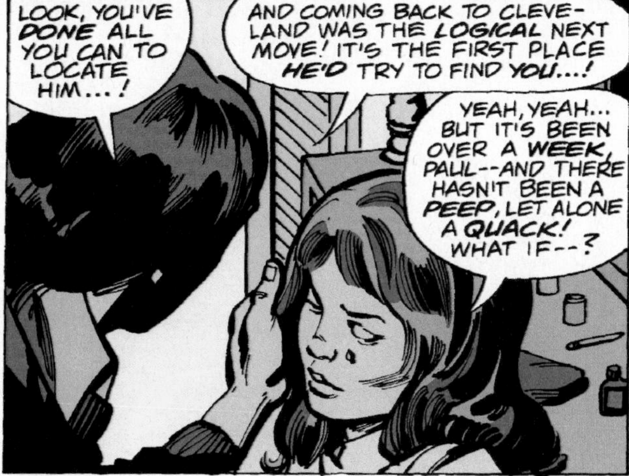

LOOK, YOU'VE DONE ALL YOU CAN TO LOCATE HIM...!
AND COMING BACK TO CLEVELAND WAS THE LOGICAL NEXT MOVE! IT'S THE FIRST PLACE HE'D TRY TO FIND YOU...!
YEAH, YEAH... BUT IT'S BEEN OVER A WEEK, PAUL--AND THERE HASN'T BEEN A PEEP, LET ALONE A QUACK! WHAT IF--?

BUT BEFORE BEV CAN GIVE VOICE TO HER FEARFUL SPECULATION...
HOLY LEAPING--! IT'S HIM!!
CRASH
I'VE COME FOR YOU, BEVERLY!
JEEZ--HE ALWAYS DID KNOW HOW TO RELIEVE ANY GIVEN MONOTONY.

AND YOUR AGONIES HAVE ONLY BEGUN, MY SWEET!
WE'VE MUCH TO SETTLE, YOU AND I-- BUT MOSTLY I!
AND I'VE AN AVERSION TO SPECTATORS!
WAVE "BYE-BYE" TO MR. SAME, DEAR!
JEEZ!
S'LONG, PAUL!
MEANWHILE, ON A LONELY SUB-URBAN ROAD, HEADED TOWARD TOWN...!
...OH, YES, POSITIVE! ESPECIAWWY IF HE HAD THE POWER TO OBWITEWATE IT FWOM THE MAP!
YES, MMM-HMM, CWEVEWAND IS UNDOUBTEDWY WHEWE HE WOULD GO, YES!
THEN, PW-- PLEASE BE SILENT, WINDA, AND ATTENTIVE TO ANY SIGN OF --
WOOK! WOOK UP THEWE--AT THWEE O'CWOCK!
YOU SEEM AGITATED, MY DEAR. ANYTHING AMISS?
SHUCKS, N-NO! I MEAN--HOW MANY GIRLS EVER GET THE THRILL OF DANGLING OVER CLEVELAND--
--BY THE NAPE OF THEIR HONEYBEE BLOUSE?!
THAT'S MOWE THAN A SIGN, MR. HEWWSTWOM-- IT'S PWACTICAWWY SKY-WITING!
STEP ON IT!
VRROOM
AND AS WE WACE TO THE WESCUE, WET ME WEPEAT HOW VEWY KIND IT WAS OF YOU TO OFFER ME A WIFT TO TOWN.
IF YOU HADN'T COME AWONG, I MIGHT'VE SAT AND CWIED FOR DAYS--!

SUNSPOT SLOPE: CLEVELAND'S POPULAR LOVER'S LANE, WHERE ACCORDING TO LEGEND, SOME YOUNG COUPLE IS STRICKEN WITH TERMINAL HICKEYS ONCE EVERY 11 YEARS.
H-HOWARD... WHY DID YOU BRING ME HERE?
SPEAK NO MORE!
BUT HOW'M I SUPPOSED TO LEARN IF I CAN'T ASK QUESTIONS?
BY LISTENING CLOSELY--TO YOUR ANSWERS.
I SHALL BE THE INQUISITOR!
AND OUR FORUM SHALL BE THIS CIRCLE OF HELLFIRE!
NOW, THEN --FIRST QUESTION:
HOW DO YOU FEEL ABOUT ME, BEVERLY?
ANSWER!
UH--GEE, I DUNNO!
GUESS I NEVER REALLY THOUGHT ABOUT IT MUCH--
OUCH!
D-DUCKY, THAT'S MY WRIST--NOT A DOORKNOB--!
ANSWER! HOW DO YOU CONCEIVE OUR RELATIONSHIP?
WHAT DO I MEAN TO YOU?
DO YOU LIKE ME--OR CHERISH ME--OR PERHAPS I MERELY AMUSE YOU?
AM I YOUR OBJECT OF RIDICULE, SWEET?
AM I??
OH, NO, HOWARD--NO!!
THEN WHAT?! TELL ME!! I DEMAND TO --EH?
SCRREEEE

IT IS A CALCULATED RISK. THE SOULFIRE CAN INSTANTLY INCINERATE HUMAN FLESH.
BUT METAL IS SOMEWHAT MORE RESISTANT.
BUMP
TOO, THIS IS A SPIRITUAL RATHER THAN A PHYSICAL FLAME. ITS INTENSITY IS DIRECTLY PROPORTIONATE TO THE STRENGTH OF THE DUCK'S WILL.
GWACIOUS! YOU WAMMED WIGHT INTO HIM!!
NO, WINDA... MY FOOT WAS ON THE BRAKE.
THE INTENT WAS TO ADDLE HIS CONCENTRATION, NOT KILL HIM.
BUT I FEAR I'VE ACHIEVED ONLY MEAGER SUCCESS EVEN AT THAT!
ONCE PROVOKED, THE HELLSPAWN IS NOTORIOUSLY SINGLE-MINDED IN HIS PURSUIT OF RETRIBUTION!
BLAM
MMM-- I SEE WHAT YOU MEAN, YES I DO!
AT LEAST WE MADE POSSIBLE THAT OTHER YOUNG WOMAN'S ESCAPE!
I SUGGEST YOU JOIN HER, WINDA--OUT OF THE LINE OF FIRE!

HENCEFORTH, THE BATTLE MUST BE MINE ALONE!
WHY, HOW NOBLE OF YOU, DAIMON--
--HOW INSIPIDLY NOBLE!
YOU'RE COGNIZANT, THEN, THAT YOU'VE BROUGHT ABOUT PRECISELY WHAT YOU'D HOPED TO AVOID--
--THAT YOUR STUNT-CAR HEROICS HAVE THRUST THE DUCK'S PERSONALITY INTO THE UNCONSCIOUS--
--THAT I AM THE SON OF SATAN!
--AND I FULLY INTEND TO DEVOUR YOUR VERY SOUL??
WHUMP
AYE, HELLSPAWN, I'M AWARE OF ALL THAT--
SSSSSS
--AND MORE!
NO! RELEASE YOUR GRIP ON THE TRIDENT!
I COMMAND YOU!
"NO, DEMON, YOU DO NOT, AND NEVER DID! BUT YOU ARE PART OF ME--MUCH AS I LOATHE THE THOUGHT --AND I MUST RECLAIM YOU--!
"--FOR THE DUCK'S SAKE, FOR THE WORLD'S, AND PERHAPS EVEN MY OWN!"

IT IS DONE. THE DEMON OCCUPIES ITS RIGHTFUL HOST ONCE MORE...
--DRAWN BACK THROUGH THE NETHER-METAL TRIDENT INTO MYSELF!
BUT ALAS, THAT SHIMMERING MIST DISPERSING IN THE BREEZE...!
UH, EXCUSE ME, BUT... ARE YOU?... IS HE?... OKAY, HUH?
IN A WORD:
NO.
NO. HIS BODY FUNCTIONS CONTINUE. BUT UNLESS I CAN GATHER THOSE WIND-SCATTERED PARTICLES OF SPIRIT...
THE FOWL'S SOUL PROVED TOO DEBIL-ITATED...
...TO ENDURE THE RIGORS OF THE DEMON'S VIOLENT DEPARTURE.
THAT CURIOUS MIST--WAS HOWARD'S DISCARNATE SELF.
YOU MEAN--HE'S DEAD?!
...AND RETURN THEM TO THE DUCK'S CORPOREAL FORM...
...WELL, I BELIEVE THE COLLOQUIAL-ISM IS STILL "VEGETABLE," IS IT NOT?
OH, HOW TWAGIC!!

PERHAPS...BUT IT'S ALSO AN EDUCATION FEW BEINGS HAVE BEEN PRIVILEDGED TO EXPERIENCE.
AS DAIMON SOON DISCOVERS, HOWARD'S PSYCHIC MIST, DISSEMINATED ON THE WIND, HAS SETTLED GENTLY, IMPERCEPTIBLY UPON OTHERS IN THE VICINITY, INSINUATING ITSELF INTO THEIR HEARTS AND MINDS!
SUDDENLY, THE DUCK FINDS HIMSELF LEADING A THOUSAND LIVES AT ONCE--PERCEIVING THE UNIVERSE THROUGH SENSES AND SENSIBILITIES NOT HIS OWN!

AND IT'S PRETTY DISCONCERTING AT FIRST -- THIS BEING AT ONE WITH CLEVELAND -- THIS INITIAL INABILITY TO DISCERN SYMBOL FROM PHENOMENON.
THE INFLUX OF DATA IS TOO RAPID, TOO MASSIVE -- AND HIS PRESENCE IS TOO DIFFUSE TO PERMIT COMMUNICATION.
HE MUST CONTENT HIMSELF TO OBSERVE -- AND FEEL -- AND BE -- WITH THESE ACCIDENTAL SOUL-MATES.
THE STREET PUNK, WHO SEES A PREDATOR IN EVERY SHADOW -- WHO KNOWS THE BIG BAD WORLD EXISTS JUST TO EAT HIM ALIVE -- UNLESS HE CHEWS IT UP AND SPITS IT OUT FIRST.
THE ASSEMBLY-LINE WORKER, WHO KNOWS HIS HEAD LONG AGO BECAME A PART OF SOMEBODY'S CAR.
THE HOUSEWIFE, WHOSE GRAVE RESPONSIBILITIES ARE ALL THAT'S KEEPING HER AFLOAT.
THE EX-EXECUTIVE, EJECTED FROM HIS ENCAPSULATED EXISTENCE WITHOUT LIFE-SUPPORT. SORRY. BUDGET CUT!
THE GRANDFATHER WHO KNOWS HE POSSESSES NO WISDOM TO PASS ON TO HIS HEIRS, JUST JOKES. AND THE GRANDSON, WHO KNOWS IT, TOO -- BUT THINKS THEY'RE FUNNY.

NOW, UNDER DAIMON'S GUIDANCE, THE MISTS CONGEAL ONCE MORE...
...SWIRLING IN RIBBONS OF COLOR ABOUT THE WATERFOUL'S SOULLESS SHELL...

...DROPPING SOFTLY, SILENTLY, LIKE A BLANKET OF STARS, WARMING THE DUCK WITH THEIR LIFE-LIGHT...!
UNTIL...

...HE WAKES, SO CONSUMED AT FIRST WITH EMOTION THAT HE CANNOT SEE, CANNOT HEAR, CANNOT SPEAK...

...ONLY WEEP!

BEHOLD, HOWARD-- THE SUNRISE!
≡SNIF≡ FIGURES! YOUR TYPICAL CORNBALL CAPPER TO A STORY LIKE THIS...!
WHAT HAPPENED TO ME, HELLSTROM? I SAW-- SOMETHING--!
AHH-- FORGET IT. MUST'A BEEN A WEATHER BALLOON.

EPILOG:
WELL... WHAT'S THE VERDICT? DO HOWARD AND WINDA GO BACK TO THE ASYLUM--?
OR DO I GET TO KEEP THEM?
WE'RE GONNA BE BOARDERS, PAUL--NOT SLAVES!
TELL 'EM WE PROMISE TO HOLD WEEKLY GROUP THERAPY SESSIONS!
NO NEED, MS. SWITZLER. DR. AVERY HAS ALREADY SIGNED THE NECESSARY PAPERS FOR THEIR DISCHARGE.

WEAWWY?! OH, JOY!! WE'RE FWEE!!
THEN IT'S OFFICIAL! WE'RE REUNITED, DUCKY! THE PARTNERSHIP'S BACK ON!
waaaugh

AND BACK AT THE HOSPITAL...
HE'S DONE IT, HERR DOKTOR-- SIGNED THEIR RELEASES!
IN DIRECT DISOBEDIENCE OF MEIN ORDERS! VERY VELL!
THEN YOU AGREE, HERR DOKTOR?

JAH, YUC! DER TIME HAS COME TO MOBILIZE!
PREPARE TO EVACUATE ZESE PREMISES, BARBARA--
--UND RELOCATE DER OPERATION TO REV. YUC'S PRIVATE UNIVERSITY!
JAWOHL... NOW "DR. REICH" VILL DISAPPEAR MIT-OUT DER TRACE, TO MAKE ROOM FOR--DER VON --DER ONLY--!!
NEXT: THE HTD ANNUAL #1 WITH "BAD NIGHT IN BAGMOM!"
THEN THE ISLAND OF DR. BONG! IN HTD #15 --ON SALE SOON!

HOWARD THE DUCK ANNUAL

1

1977
02990

50¢

MARVEL COMICS GROUP

KING-SIZE ANNUAL!

APPROVED BY THE COMICS CODE AUTHORITY

ALL NEW!

HOWARD THE DUCK™

EVER WONDER WHAT TRANSPIRES ON THE 1,002nd ARABIAN NIGHT?

SINBAD WAS NEVER LIKE THIS!

THE THIEF OF BAGMOM!

From the time of his hatching, he was...different. A potentially brilliant scholar who dreaded the structured environment of school, he educated himself in the streets, taking whatever work was available, formulating his philosophy of self from what he learned of the world about him. And then the Cosmic Axis shifted...and that world *changed.* Suddenly, he was stranded in a universe he could not fathom. Without warning, he became a strange fowl in an even stranger land.

Stan Lee PRESENTS: HOWARD THE DUCK!™

REUNITED AT LAST! THE CREATIVE TEAM WHO HATCHED THE WONDROUS WATERFOWL BACK IN (GASP!) 1973:

VAL MAYERIK, ARTIST and STEVE GERBER, WRITER / EDITOR

JOE ROSEN, LETTERER | JAN COHEN, COLORIST | M. SKRENES, CO-SCENARIST

THIEF OF BAGMOM!

"DIDN'T WANT TO WAKE YOU," THE NOTE READ. "WENT SHOPPING. HOME BY SIX. -- BEV, PAUL, & WINDA."

AND THAT'S HOW A DUCK FINDS HIMSELF ALONE IN THE WANING LIGHT OF A CLEVELAND SATURDAY...

...AMID THE DEBRIS OF EIGHT WEEKS' COMMUNAL LIVING IN THE ONE-ROOM APARTMENT HE SHARES WITH THREE HAIRLESS APES.

HIS BLEARY EYES SURVEY THE FLOOR AND FIND IN ITS CLUTTER AN **ANALOGUE** TO HIS STATE OF **MIND.**

AN **OBSTACLE COURSE** OF EMPTY TIN CANS, CANDY WRAPPERS, ASSORTED ARTICLES OF DIRTY LAUNDRY.
REFUSE. RUBBISH. **DROSS.**
MENTAL NOTATION: MUST FIND A **JOB.** MUST GET THE MONEY TOGETHER TO BUY A **WASTE-BASKET...**

...AND CRAWL **IN.**
THESE FEELINGS ARE RUNNING A LITTLE **AMOK,** AREN'T THEY?
NAW. **WAIT!**

ALL THIS EXISTENTIAL **DE-SPAIR** OVER BEING EXCLUDED FROM A **SHOPPING** EXPE-DITION?
DISPROPORTIONATE!

BUT **SLIPPING** ON A STRAY **SOUP CAN...**

...**CAREENING** MADLY ABOUT THE ROOM, OFF-BALANCE, WITH A CUP OF **SCALDING** HOT COFFEE...

WAAAUGH

...NOW **THERE'S** SOMETHING **WORTH** GETTING UPSET ABOUT!

OR PERHAPS IT'S CAUSE FOR **REJOICING!** FOR THE FOWL REGAINS HIS **FOOTING...**
...WITHOUT HAVING SPILLED A **DROP!**

AND AFTER HIS RECENT BOUT WITH NEAR-TOTAL **NERVOUS COLLAPSE...**
...THAT'S AN **ACCOMPLISHMENT!**

YOO-HOO, HOWARD -- WISE AND **SHINE!!**
HOWEVER SHORT-LIVED.

KLUNGE

HOWARD'S **ROOMIES:** WINDA WESTER, PAUL SAME, AND BEVERLY SWITZLER.
HEH HEH
ACCIDENT.
UH...**HIYA**, HOWARD.
TSK TSK

WE, UH...DIDN'T FIGURE YOU'D BE **AWAKE** YET.
YEAH, WELL... I'M AWAKE... I'M **WET**... AN' I'M IN **PAIN.**
NOW WHAT'RE YA GONNA **DO** ABOUT IT?!
OH, YES, MM-HM, YOU'VE BEEN SWEEPING SUCH **WONG** HOURS WATEWY...!

PERSONALLY, DUCKY-- I'D LIKE TO OFFER SOME AID AND COMFORT... IF YOU'LL LET ME NEAR YOU.
C'MON-- WHATCHA SAY?

LET ME PAMPER YOU! YOU KNOW YOU'RE A SUCKER FOR SUCCOR.
SEE! IT FEELS GOOD TO BE TAKEN CARE OF, HUH?

NO...?
BLAST IT, BEV-- DON'T PATRONIZE ME!!

THIS PLACE IS BECOMIN' AS INTOLERABLE AS THE MENTAL HOSPITAL!!
NOT ONLY IS IT JUST AS CRAMPED AN' JUST AS SMELLY--
--BUT YOU'VE BECOME AS CLOYINGLY SOLICITOUS AS ANY WARD NURSE!!
ulp THAT OBVIOUS, HUH?
I'M SORRY, DUCKY... BUT DR. AVERY WARNED US TO HANDLE YOU... WELL, GENTLY.

UH-HUH... AN' IT MIGHT EVEN BE BELIEVABLE IF WE WEREN'T LIVIN' LIKE DEGENERATE PIONEERS!
DON'TCHA SEE, BEV-- YA CAN'T PAMPER SOMEBODY IN A PIGSTY!
OH! WHAT A CWUEL, STUPID THING TO SAY!!

IF YOU'WE SO MISEWABLE-- DO SOMETHING FOR YOURSEWF!
WE TOOK WHAT WITTLE BWEAD HE HAD-- AND BOUGHT SOME STUFF TO MAKE WIFE MORE PWEASANT AWOUND HEWE! SO THEWE!!

"SO THEWE," HUH?
WINDA... YOU OWE ME A CUP OF COFFEE.
WHA--?
TO REPLACE THE ONE I'M **WEARING.**

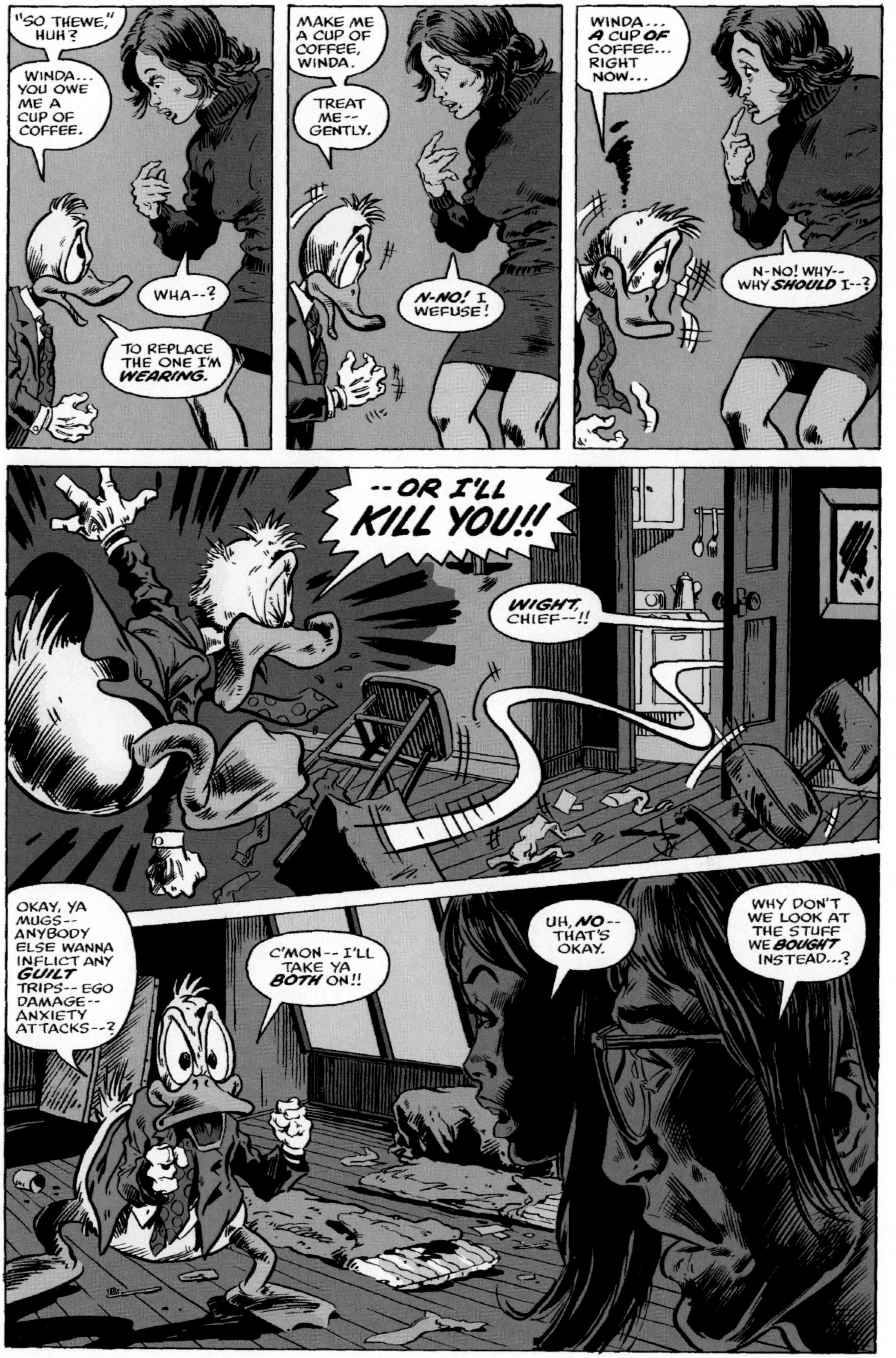

MAKE ME A CUP OF COFFEE, WINDA.
TREAT ME-- GENTLY.
N-NO! I WEFUSE!

WINDA... **A** CUP **OF** COFFEE... RIGHT NOW...
N-NO! WHY-- WHY **SHOULD** I--?

--OR I'LL KILL YOU!!

WIGHT, CHIEF--!!

OKAY, YA MUGS-- ANYBODY ELSE WANNA INFLICT ANY **GUILT** TRIPS-- EGO DAMAGE-- ANXIETY ATTACKS--?

C'MON-- I'LL TAKE YA **BOTH** ON!!

UH, **NO**-- THAT'S OKAY.

WHY DON'T WE LOOK AT THE STUFF WE **BOUGHT** INSTEAD...?

REALLY, HOWARD--WE FOUND SOME NIFTY BARGAINS.
DECORATIVE AND PRACTICAL, DUCKY.

FOR EXAMPLE, THIS LITTLE BEAUTY TO INTERPOSE BETWEEN YOUR SLEEPING BAGS AND THAT COLD, SPLINTERY FLOOR!

C'MERE, HOWARD--TAKE A CLOSE LOOK!
THE PATTERNWORK IN THIS CARPET IS AMAZING! I BET IT WAS WOVEN BY GENUINE PERSIAN HANDS!
SWELL! AT LEAST SOME CLOWN IN PERSIA FOUND A JOB!

OKAY, THEN, IF YOU'RE STILL TOO GROUCHY TO APPRECIATE IT, SEND WINDA IN--!
M-MAY I?
AAAAH, G'WAN--I'LL FEEL SAFER MAKIN' MY OWN COFFEE, ANYWAY.

I KNOW WHAT YOU'RE THINKIN', PAUL--
--BUT IT'S NOT MY LATENT MALE CHAUVINISM SURFACING.
I CONSIDER YOU A HOPELESS CASE, TOO.

OKAY, HOWARD, INSULT ME IF YOU MUST--BUT I WANT YOU TO KNOW I SYMPATHIZE.
I PREFER LIVING ALONE TO THESE CROWDED CONDI-TIONS, ALSO.

NATURALLY! THAT'S THE TROUBLE WITH YOU MEN-- NO ADAPTIVE CAPACITY WHATSOEVER!
YES! YOU'WE SO-- SO-- WIGID!!

WHOOOSH
OH, LORD...!
EEEEK!
HAH...?
UH, C'MON, FELLAS-- UP OFF YOUR THUMBS, HUH?
HELP!!
MMM-HM-- PWEASE! THIS IS TEWWIBWY DISTWESSING!
B-BUT WHAT CAN WE DO??
I DON'T THINK AIR TRAFFIC CONTROLLERS MAKE HOUSE CALLS!

THEN-- WIKE IT OR NOT-- WE'WE GOING ON A TWIP!
WHOOOSH!!
IT-- IT'S PICKING UP SPEED-- ALTITUDE-- PRETTY SOON THEY'LL BE OUT OF SIGHT COMPLETELY!
I HAVEN'T FELT SO STUPIDLY IMPOTENT...
...SINCE THE LAST TIME I TRIED TO FIGHT THE POWER COMPANY OVER MY ELECTRIC BILL!
YEAH, WELL... TRY'N SEE THE BRIGHT SIDE: AT LEAST NOTHIN' ELSE THAT HAPPENS TODAY--
--CAN BE ANY MORE DISORIENTING THAN THIS!
SUDDENLY--
KRAK!
I SHOULD'A KNOWN-- THE MINUTE I EVINCE EVEN A TRACE OF OPTIMISM--!
WE ARE COME TO CLAIM THE CARPET-- OR YOUR HEADS!
UNBEARABLY HACKNEYED... BUT TRUE! SURRENDER WIJID'S RUG-- OR YOUR LIVES ARE FORFEIT!

UH-HUH, WELL, SORRY, EFFENDIS! YA JUST MISSED THE FLIGHT!
MAYBE I CAN BOOK YA ON STANDBY FOR THE NEXT--
BY THE CALIPH'S BEARD--Y-YOU'RE A DUCK!!

SO! THERE IS SORCERY AS WELL AS THIEVERY AFOOT IN THIS LAND!
WHUK
ULP

INDEED! BUT WE HAVE SWORN AN OATH, ABDUL, TO RECOVER THE CARPET--
-- REGARDLESS OF THE RISK TO OURSELVES!
AYE, AND EVEN MAGIC THAT PUTS WORDS IN THE MOUTHS OF FOWL SHALL NOT DETER US!
WHERE IS THE CARPET??
SPEAK-- OR DIE!!

B-BUT HOWARD ALREADY TOLD YOU! IT FLEW AWAY! HONEST!
RIGHT OUT THAT WINDOW!!
NO! HE LIES! HOW COULD THEY HAVE KNOWN THE MAGIC WORD?

MMM... HARD TO SAY. PERHAPS THE WIZARD WHO GAVE VOICE TO THE DUCK?...
BAH! SLIT THAT ONE'S THROAT! THEN THE FOWL WILL SURELY ANSWER...!
GOTTA MOVE FAST-- AND QUIETLY-- WHILE THEY'RE ENGROSSED IN THEIR DEBATE--!

WE'VE NO TIME TO **WASTE** ON IDLE--
OWWWW
WHAP
THE "ELEMENT OF SURPRISE," THEY CALLED IT IN THE OLD PULP NOVELS.
THAT EPHEMERAL **ADVANTAGE**...
...WHICH SOMEHOW, ALMOST MYSTICALLY, IS SAID TO REVERSE THE **ODDS** AND MAKE **WARRIORS** OF CLODS.
UNTIL THIS **MOMENT**...
RUNCH
GNNPH
PASTE 'EM, PAULIE!!
THINK "EXTREME CRUELTY!"
...NEITHER HOWARD NOR PAUL LENT MUCH **CREDENCE** TO ITS REPUTED EFFICACY.
AND YET...
I--I THINK WE'RE **DOING** IT, HOWARD-- WE'RE ACTUALLY--
--**WINNING!!**
KLUDG
YAH-HOO!!
HEY, YOUSE INCONSIDERATE BUMS--**HOLD DOWN THE NOISE THERE!!**
CHUNT
WHAP
AIEEEE
THULK
I'M TRYIN' TA WATCH THE **RASSLIN'** ON TV!

I'LL TELL YA, YOU YOUTHS O' TODAY GOT NO **RESPECT** FOR--

urp

PEARL OF POOGROCH!

THEY'VE **SEEN** US, ABDUL!

WELL I'LL BE! **INJUNS!!**

AYE, ABDUL-- AND NEXT, THEY'LL BE SUMMONING THEIR **AUTHORITIES!**

WE MUST **FLEE!**

NO!! WAIT!! NOT **THAT** WAY!!

PAUL-- SHUT YER **YAP!!**

THERE ARE **LIMITS**--EVEN TO **CHARITY!**

WE HAVE **FAILED** OUR BELOVED **BAGMOM!**

"B-BUT, HOWARD" PAUL STAMMERS, "IT'S A FIVE-STORY **DROP!**

SO?! THESE CLOWNS'RE ARE ALWAYS LEAPIN' OUT OF WINDOWS AN' OVER WALLS IN THE **MOVIES!**

THEY ONLY GET HURT IF DOUGLAS FAIRBANKS **PUSHES** 'EM!

UNFORTUNATELY, THIS BEING REAL LIFE:
DIPIZZO PIZZA
PETE'S BAR & GRILL
PAWN SHOP

THEY'RE **DEAD!**
NOW WE'LL **NEVER** KNOW WHAT HAPPENED TO BEV AND WINDA!
FINISH THE SENTENCE, PAUL: "AN' IT'S ALL YOUR **FAULT!**"

I DIDN'T-- I MEAN, WHO CARES WHOSE FAULT IT IS?!
WE'VE GOTTA THINK, MAN, NOT MOUTH OFF AT--
WHOA! THE LAMP!!

I'M PROBABLY DEMENTED, BUT IF THE RUG WAS A MAGIC CARPET, MAYBE--!
A RUB OR TWO CAN'T HURT, RIGHT?
IF YOU SAY SO...!

SHOOM
H-HOWARD... I F-FEEL FAINT...!

BUT DESPITE THE STEAMY RESPONSE TO PAUL'S MASSAGE NO GENIE APPEARS. ONLY--
GOTCHA
HUH?! I WISHED TO BE TAKEN TO BEV AND WINDA...!
AN' ALL YA GOT WAS A SMOKE-SCREEN OF WORDS.
TOO BAD, PAUL. NICE TRY.

HOWEVER, EVEN AS THE MESSAGE DISPERSES--
RRINNG

YEAH, YEAH--THIS'S THE PAUL SAME RESIDENCE.
I DUNNO-- GRANT, I GUESS!
WHY?
OH.
YEAH. THANKS.

WHAT WAS THAT...?
SOME RADIO STATION! I TOLD 'EM WHO WAS BURIED IN GRANT'S TOMB...
AND...?
WE WON A TRIP FOR TWO TA SOMEPLACE CALLED BAGMOM.

BAGMOM?! THE MAMELUKES SPOKE THAT NAME JUST BEFORE--!
LET'S MOVE!!
waaaugh

CHAPTER II CALLING ALL CARPETS!

MORNING: ATOP A MINARETTED MOSQUE, A PRIEST CALLS THE FAITHFUL TO PRAYER.

HIS FATE IN THE NEXT HALF-SECOND OR SO MAY BE TESTIMONY TO HIS OWN FAITH.

FOR ALLAH SPARES HIM A PAINFUL PLUNGE...

...AND GRANTS TO WINDA AND BEV A GUILT-FREE FIRST VIEW OF THIS STRANGE CITY WALLED OFF FROM TIME FOR SOME 1500 YEARS.

THIS CITY CALLED... BAGMOM!

THE RULER OF THIS PLACE STILL BEARS THE TITLE CALIPH, AND STILL RESIDES IN A PALACE.
AND, LIKE HIS ANCESTORS, HE EMPLOYS A LIVE-IN WIZARD.
TRULY, WIJID, 'TIS A FINE CARVING! YOU HAVE PLEASED ME.
BUT WHEN WILL IT BE DONE, O WIZARD?
ON THE MORROW, MAGNIFICENT ONE--
--IN TIME FOR THE FEAST, AS PROMISED!
BIG DEAL!

I CANNOT FATHOM, FATHER, WHY YOU WASTE YOUR TIME ON SUCH FRIVOLITIES!
THERE IS NO MAGIC IN THIS WOODEN MULE--

--NOR IN YOUR "WIZARD," EITHER!
HASSIM!!
WIJID! IT IS NOT YOUR PLACE...!

OH, I KNOW, I KNOW-- BUT IT'S SUCH A PITY, SIRE!
FOUR YEARS OF COLLEGE IN CLEVELAND--
--AND HASSIM IS READY TO JUNK ALL OUR TRADITIONS!

IT SADDENS ME, THAT IS ALL I--
BY THE PROPHET!!

SIRE-- BEHOLD! 'TIS THE VERY CARPET I BESTOWED UPON HASSIM--
--ON THE OCCASION OF HIS DEPARTURE FOR AMERICA!
THE ONE HE-- HOW DID HE PUT IT--? HOCKED TO BUY A BROOKS BROTHERS SUIT?!

REMARKABLE! AND THESE FEMALES-- SURELY IT MUST BE DIVINE PROVIDENCE--!
WHAT'S HE SAYING?
I DUNNO! I'M ONWY FWUENT IN ENGWISH!

TWO SUCH BEAUTEOUS WESTERNERS DELIVERED TO MY PALACE--
--JUST AS MY SON THREATENS TO DEPART!
AH, YES-- PERFECT! SO FRAGILE, AND YET...

HANDS OFF, BUSTER!!
SMAK

...YET POSSESSED OF SUCH SPUNK!
RASHID-- TAKE THEM TO THE HAREM!

AS YOU WISH, GREAT SIRE!
WHAT THE--?! HEY!! YA BIG GORILLA--!!
IS THIS WISE, CALIPH?
SILENCE, WIZARD! IT IS ALLAH'S WILL!
MOREOVER, SHOULD THESE TWO ASSUAGE MY SON'S APPETITE FOR THINGS WESTERN... IT'S MY WILL, ALSO!
GWACIOUS!
THE AMERICANS ARE... SENSITIVE ABOUT SUCH MATTERS AS ABDUCTION OF NATIONALS.

MIDNIGHT!
AN AIR CASBAH TWIN-ENGINE LUXURY CRATE WHEEZES THROUGH THE SKIES OVER BAGMOM...
...DISCHARGING TWO TERRIFIED PASSENGERS!
THEY MIGHT'VE AT LEAST WARNED US THAT NO PLANES ARE ALLOWED TO LAND IN BAGMOM!
SO BIG DEAL-- THEY DON'T ENCOURAGE TOURISM!
JUST CLAM UP AN' PLUMMET, PAUL!!
WHICH IS PRECISELY WHAT THEY DO-- THEIR CHUTES AFFORDING SOME BRAKE--
--BUT TOO LITTLE AT SO LOW AN ALTITUDE--
--TO MAKE THEIR IMPACT IN A BAGMOM BACK ALLEY ANYTHING RESEMBLING GENTLE.
H-HEY-- WE MADE IT! WE'RE ALIVE!!
waaugh
THUK

WE WON'T BE FOR LONG--UNLESS YOU CAN CONTAIN YOUR EXUBERANCE!
SOMEBODY'S COMIN'--AN' I DON'T THINK WE WANNA BE NOTICED YET!

pssst HOWARD--NEITHER DOES HE! SEE THAT PURSE HE'S CLUTCHING?
A THIEF, YOU FIGURE?
UH-HUH.

LOOK, I'M GONNA TAKE THE CHANCE--ASK FOR HELP.
THE WORST HE CAN DO IS SAY "NO," RIGHT?
TAP TAP

WRONG!
WHAT CRAVEN JACKAL DARES AMBUSH ALI WAZOO?!
FWASH!
ulp

SPEAK, DASTARD!
SPEAK YOUR SERPENTINE NAME FOR THE LAST TIME--
--BEFORE MY BLADE CARVES A HEART-SHAPED HOLE IN YOUR CHEST!
AW, SHOOT! I FORGOT ALL ABOUT THE LANGUAGE BARRIER!
PAUL--THE LAMP?

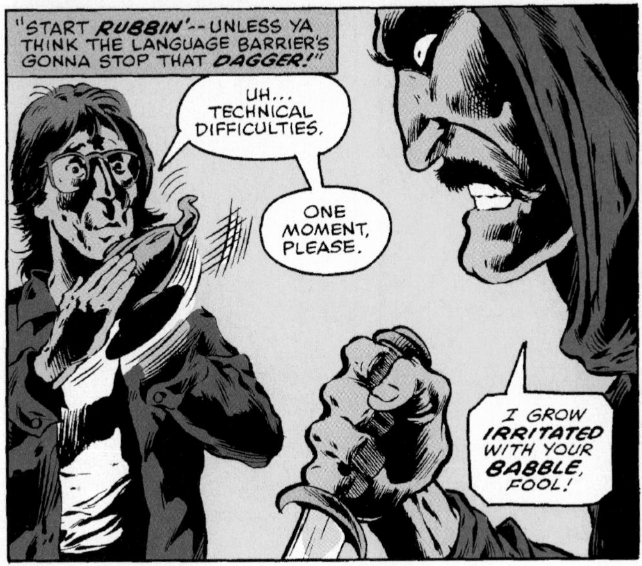
"START RUBBIN'--UNLESS YA THINK THE LANGUAGE BARRIER'S GONNA STOP THAT DAGGER!"
UH... TECHNICAL DIFFICULTIES.
ONE MOMENT, PLEASE.
I GROW IRRITATED WITH YOUR BABBLE, FOOL!

'NUFF SAID!
SPEAK!!
WHO ARE--
gasp

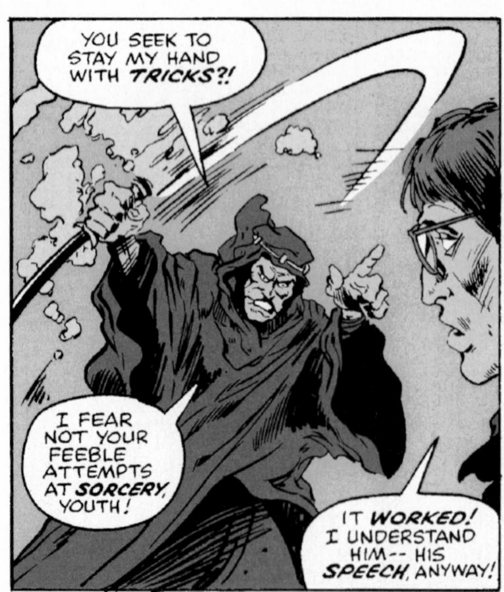
YOU SEEK TO STAY MY HAND WITH TRICKS?!
I FEAR NOT YOUR FEEBLE ATTEMPTS AT SORCERY, YOUTH!
IT WORKED! I UNDERSTAND HIM-- HIS SPEECH, ANYWAY!

LET'S HOPE THE VICE IS VERSA!
LISTEN, FRIEND-- WE'RE NOT LOOKIN' FOR TROUBLE-- JUST FOR A COUPLE O' GIRLS WHO DISAPPEARED FROM CLEVELAND ON A FLYING CARPET!
YEAH-- REALLY! HONEST!
WE WERE HOPING YOU MIGHT HELP US!

LOOK-- YOU CAN SEE FOR YOURSELF WE'RE NOT LOCALS!
THIS... IS TRUE.
AND FROM WHAT OUR PILOT TOLD US, OUTSIDERS ARE AT LEAST AS UNWELCOME AS THIEVES IN BAGMOM!
THERE'S THE SCOUNDREL! WE'VE FOUND HIM!
UH-OH...!

THE CALIPH'S POLICE!
TRULY, WE ARE AS BROTHERS NOW!
HUH...?
GUILT BY ASSOCIATION, PAUL!

CHEESE IT!!

HALT!! HALT IN THE NAME OF THE CALIPH!!
SEZ YOU!

AAEIIIII
THIS WAY, MY FRIENDS!

DOWN THERE?! B-BUT--
TRUST ME!
YOU'VE LITTLE CHOICE.

WE MUST BE CERTAIN WE'VE ELUDED THE POLICE--
--BEFORE WE PRESS ON!
ON WHERE?!
THIS IS A DEAD END!
FOUR WALLS AND ONLY ONE EXIT--

--THE WAY WE CAME IN!
YOU ARE MISTAKEN, COMRADE. YOUR DUCK-SUITED DWARF UNDERSTANDS BETTER.
UHHN
I'LL REFRAIN FROM COMMENT ON THAT LAST REMARK--
--IF I CAN GET AN ASSIST FROM YOU BOZOS!

HOWEVER, EVEN WITH PAUL'S GRUNTING ADDED TO HOWARD'S OWN, THE RING-- AND THE STONE ATTACHED TO IT-- REFUSES TO BUDGE.
ZILCH! IT'S LIKE TRYING TO LIFT THE EARTH BY THE BACK OF ITS NECK!
NATURALLY.

BECAUSE THE DOOR WILL OPEN ONLY FOR ONE WHO KNOWS THE MAGIC WORDS:
TU-AHLBIF-PATIZ--
SPESHULZAWZ-LETTUZ-CHI'IZ--
PEEKLZON-YUNZON-AHSEZME-SEET--
BUHNN!!

WHOOMPH
waaaugh

BEHOLD!
THÜNK
THE PROUDEST ACHIEVEMENT OF ***SEVEN GENERATIONS*** OF BAGMOM'S THIEVING CLASS--
--THE ***UNDERGROUND RAILWAY!***
OASIS EXP 7

SINCE THEN, WE'VE DUG ARTERIES BENEATH ALL THE MAJOR THOROUGH-FARES AND ROBBED BAGMOM BLIND!
WE'RE CURRENTLY TUNNELLING UNDER THE PALACE ITSELF!
OASIS EXP 7
THEN THE POLICE DON'T KNOW--?

NO ONE IN BAGMOM SAVE THE THIEVES THEMSELVES IS AWARE OF THE RAILWAY'S EXISTENCE.
EXCEPT US, YOU MEAN?
AH, YES-- A THOUSAND PARDONS! NO ONE EXCEPT YOURSELVES!
BUT IF YOU VALUE YOUR TONGUES-- WE HAVE NAUGHT TO FEAR.

SHORTLY, JUST OUTSIDE THE CITY WALLS--
PRAISES BE TO THE ALL-MERCIFUL! ABU HO DADI IS AT THE OASIS!
ABU HO DADI-- YOUNGEST, HAND-SOMEST, AND MOST DARING OF ALL THE THIEVES!

ABU HO DADI-- WHOSE EARS, OR THEIR PROXIES, HEAR EVERY WORD SPOKEN IN BAGMOM-- WHOSE LIPS HAVE BRUSHED THOSE OF ALL THE CITY'S MOST EXQUISITE BEAUTIES--

--AND WHOSE EYES CURRENTLY BULGE AT THE SIGHT OF--
INTRUDERS!!
KILL!!

NO, NO, PRINCE OF ROGUES-- I BEG YOU! SPARE THEM-- AND, INCIDENTALLY, MYSELF!
THEY ABETTED MY FLIGHT FROM THE PALACE TROOPS!

ALI WAZOO SAID YOU MIGHT BE ABLE TO HELP US LOCATE TWO AMERICAN WOMEN WHO, AH, FLEW IN THIS MORNING.
HOW DID THESE WOMEN "FLY IN?"
heh WOULDJA BELIEVE-- CARPET?

WHY WOULD I NOT BELIEVE? YOUR WOMEN ARE VERY FORTUNATE, YOU KNOW.
ARRIVING THUS, THEY ARE ALMOST CERTAINLY IN THE CUSTODY OF--
ABU! DO YOU HEAR?!

THE OUTLAW FALLS SILENT, HIS EARS ATTUNED TO THE SHIFTING OF EACH GRAIN OF DESERT SAND.
THEN-- HE DASHES UP THE DUNE!
WHAT DO YOU THINK?
SURE... LET'S GO.

AND, AT THE CREST OF THE WAVE OF GRAINS...
BY ALL THE STARS!!
'TIS MY SWORN ENEMY PRINCE HASSIM-- VILEST OF DESERT RATS--!
LIAR! BLASPHEMER! DISGRACE TO HIS FATHER AND ALL BAGMOM!
tsk YEAH, THEY DON'T MAKE PRINCES LIKE THEY USEDTA.

--AND WE APPRECIATE YOUR EFFORTS IN ROXXON'S BEHALF, PRINCE HASSIM.
YOUR FATHER'S A MIGHTY STUBBORN MAN.
HOW WELL I KNOW!
BUT YOU DO PREDICT HE'LL RELENT--ASSIGN US EXPLORATION RIGHTS?

OIL IS BAGMOM'S FUTURE, MR. PETRIE. YOU, I, AND THE ROXXON CORPORATION ALL KNOW THAT.
MY FATHER, TOO, CAN BE PERSUADED EVENTUALLY. BUT HE MUST BE TAKEN EVERY STEP BY HAND.
WHAT APPROACH DO YOU SUGGEST?
COME TO THE BANQUET TOMORROW EVE. BRING GIFTS.

HE HAS TODAY SEEN TWO FINE SPECIMENS OF AMERICAN WOMANHOOD.
IF HE CAN BE MADE TO ADMIRE YOUR TECHNOLOGY HALF SO MUCH--!
UNDER-STOOD.

AND IF HE CANNOT LOVE COLOR TV AS HE DOES HIS NEWLY-ACQUIRED "BEV" AND "WINDA"--!
WELL, HE'S ON IN YEARS-- THINGS HAPPEN--!
waaaugh

H-HOWARD! NO!! WHAT'RE YOU DOING?!
YOU HEARD 'IM! HE'S GOT BEV AN' WINDA!
B-BUT--!

NOT SO FAST, CHUMS! STICK AROUND A MINUTE!
DIDN'T YOU FINE, UPSTANDIN' AMERICANS HEAR WHAT THIS YOYO SAID?!
IT-- IT'S A DUCK!!

HIS PA JUST "ACQUIRED" TWO O' YOUR COUNTRYWOMEN!
THAT'S A NO-NO, FELLAS!
A TALKING DUCK...!

A TALKING AMERICAN DUCK! AND MY FATHER IS OBSESSED WITH SUCH CURIOSITIES!
DRIVE ME TO THE CITY GATES, WON'T YOU, PETRIE?
HAH?
YOUR LEASES ARE IN THE BAG, I THINK.

WAAAAUGH
BECAUSE I HOPED SOMETHING LIKE THIS MIGHT OCCUR! ALLAH SMILES UPON US.
YOU WILL SEE...IN DUE COURSE.
WE COULD'VE TAKEN THOSE THREE! WHY--?!

CHAPTER III THE DESERT SONG-- AND DANCE!

THE GREAT HALL OF THE PALACE OF BAGMOM IS A MARVEL OF MARBLE AND JADE AND GOLD AND IVORY AND -- TONIGHT -- DRINK, FOOD, AND FLESH!

THE MUSIC, THE DANCERS, THE ARCHITECTURE LEAP AND BEND AND CURL AND SWOOP AND UNDULATE IN CURVILINEAR EXPRESSIONS OF REJOICING.

ARE YOU HAPPY, MY LOVELIES? HAS YOUR LORD AND MASTER, THE CALIPH, WARMED YOUR HEARTS AND FILLED YOUR TAUT BELLIES WITH THIS FEAST OF FEASTS?
OH, YES, GOOD AND MIGHTY ONE! YES! YES!
sigh HOW YOU GUSH, MY SWEET.
STILL... YOU ARE CORRECT.

NOW LET US SEE IF MY MAGICIAN CAN LIKEWISE GRATIFY ME! WIJID...?
NOT LIKEWISE, MAJESTY... BUT EQUALLY, I PRAY! BEHOLD!

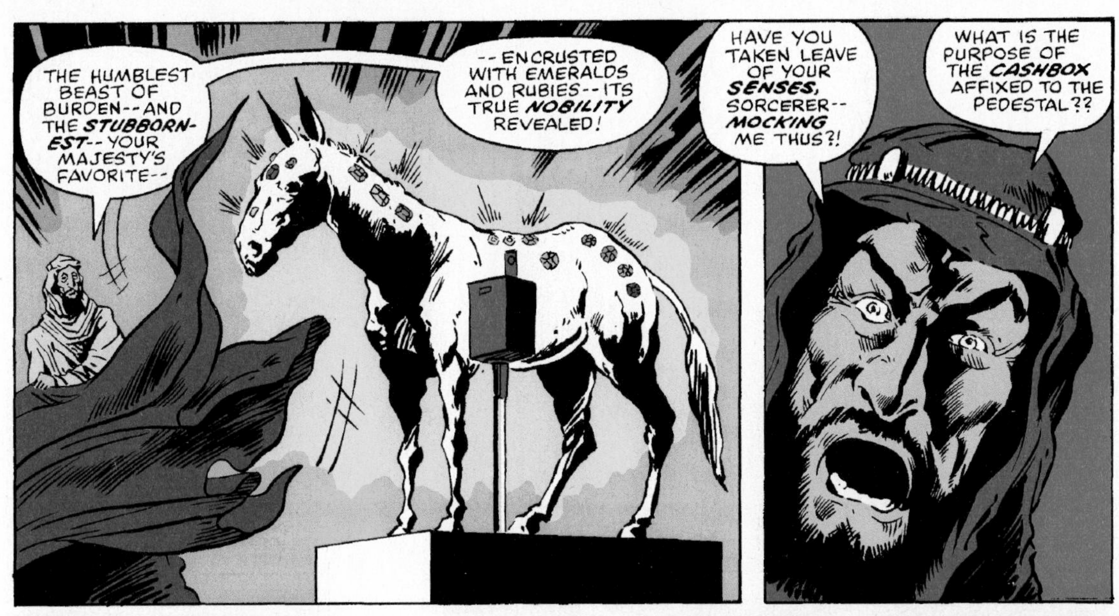
THE HUMBLEST BEAST OF BURDEN--AND THE STUBBORN-EST--YOUR MAJESTY'S FAVORITE--
--ENCRUSTED WITH EMERALDS AND RUBIES--ITS TRUE NOBILITY REVEALED!
HAVE YOU TAKEN LEAVE OF YOUR SENSES, SORCERER--MOCKING ME THUS?!
WHAT IS THE PURPOSE OF THE CASHBOX AFFIXED TO THE PEDESTAL??

EXPLAIN--OR I'LL HAVE YOUR HEAD!!
IT--IT WAS HASSIM'S IDEA, MOST ILLUSTRIOUS MASTER!
HE SUGGESTED WE DISPLAY THE CARVING IN THE FOUNTAIN-SQUARE--
--AND, FOR A PRICE, ALLOW CHILDREN TO SIT ASTRIDE IT WHILE THEIR MOTHERS TENDED TO THE LAUNDRY!

WIJID SPEAKS THE TRUTH, FATHER.
BUT I HUMBLY BEG WE BOTH BE SPARED YOUR TERRIBLE RAGE...

...AND THAT I BE PERMITTED TO BANISH YOUR DISPLEASURE WITH THESE OTHER GIFTS.
LO, FATHER! TELEVISION! STEREO! DIGITAL CLOCKS! BLENDERS! ELECTRIC CAN OPENERS!
ALL THE FRUITS OF PROGRESS, GREAT KING--COURTESY OF ROXXON.

AH, YES-- YOUR OIL FRIENDS!
BUT, HASSIM... WE'VE NO USE FOR SUCH DEVICES IN BAGMOM.
WE LEAD A SIMPLE LIFE HERE... MAKING OUR OWN MUSIC AND MERRIMENT.
BESIDES, WE'VE NO ELECTRICITY, AND--
NOW, NOW, FATHER-- THESE ARE MERE TRINKETS!

PREPARE TO GAZE UPON ONE OF THE WEST'S TRUE WONDERS!
ENTER!!
MASTER OF MERCY! THIS IS A PRESENT?! AN INFANT'S COFFIN?!

HARDLY, SIRE-- SEE FOR YOURSELF!
GREAT HEAVENS!!
choke
waaugh
gasp

NOW THIS IS IMPRESSIVE! I'D HEARD OF PERDUE'S GIANT CHICKENS-- AND OF BUTTER-BALL TURKEYS, BUT--!!

I HOPE THAT MEANS WE'RE GONNA BE PALS! I COULD USE ONE IN THIS BURG!
BY THE WAY... YOU GOT A LIGHT?
gasp IT TALKS?!
TRULY, THIS IS A MAGNIFICENT CREATURE!!

FAR SUPERIOR TO EVEN A JEWELED MULE!
WHICH AIN'T SAYIN' MUCH, BUT--!
AND MY FRIENDS, FATHER...?
I AM SOFTENING, HASSIM. GIVE ME TIME.

FOR THE NONCE, I PREFER DIVERSION FROM THESE MATTERS OF STATE.
BRING ON THE NEW HAREM DUET!
CLAP
CLAP

GO! SING! DANCE! OR HEADS ROLL!
RASHID MAKES A CONVINCING CASE, HUH?
MM-HMM, YES HE DOES!
WET'S GET HOPPING-- OR WE'LL BE DANCING TOPWESS.
FWOM THE CWAVICLES UP!
A-ONE, AN' A-TWO, AN'--

WHAT A CURIOUS MELODY!
DA- DA- DA- DA- DA- DA-- BOOP!
C'MON AWONG AN WISTEN TO TO-- THE WUWWABY OF BWOADWAY!
THAT'S FUNNY-- I DON'T HEAR ANY MELODY.

FATHER, I AM LOATHE TO DISTRACT YOU FROM THE ENTERTAINMENT-- BUT THESE DRILLING PERMITS...
PLEASE, HASSIM, CAN IT NOT WAIT A MOMENT?
YEAH-- BUG OFF, SONNY!

KAWATE KICKS, NUNCHAKU STICKS-- THE WUWWABY OF BWOADWAY--!

FATHER, MY FRIENDS MUST DEPART SHORTLY...!
HASSIM, INDULGE ME! I'M AN OLD MAN--!
YEAH, THINGS HAPPEN WHEN YOU'RE OLD.

PEOPWE SCWEAMING IN HOWWIBLE PAIN-- THE MUGGERS WUNNING WAMPANT--!
ARE THOSE REALLY THE LYRICS??
YOU BEEN TO NEW YORK WATEWY?
YOU WIN.
THE FOWL SEEMS TO THINK YOU MEAN ME HARM, HASSIM!
YOUR OWN FATHER!
YES, HOW AMUSINGLY ABSURD.
SIGN HERE.
THE WUMBLE OF THE SUBWAY TWAINS--!
AND, AS IF ON CUE--
CHOOM
HAIEEEE
PAUL, HO DADI, AND THE THIEVES STAGE THEIR UPRISING FROM THE UNDER-GROUND RAILWAY!
waaaugh

WE COME AS PATRIOTS, GREAT SIRE-- LOYAL SUBJECTS WHO SEEK ONLY TO SAVE BAGMOM-- AND YOU--
--FROM THE GREEDY CLUTCHES OF YOUR SON!!
HO DADI'S ON THE LEVEL, WHISKERS! HASSIM'S BOUGHT OFF YOUR ARMY WITH PETRODOLLARS...!
BUT... TO WHAT PURPOSE?
TO ENRICH HIMSELF, O NOBLE AND LUSTROUS ONE--
--AT YOUR EXPENSE AND THAT OF YOUR PEOPLE!
FIND HIM, SIRE! ASK HIM IF HE OFFERED YOUR SUBJECTS AS CHEAP LABOR--
--IF HE ARRANGED FOR HIM-SELF TO BE THE SOLE RECIPIENT OF BAGMOM'S OIL PROFITS!
HASSIM!
SHOW YOURSELF, DOG OF A TRAITOR!!
THE CUR HAS FLED!
I-- I DON'T SEE BEV AND WINDA, EITHER!
Y-YOU DO NOT THINK HASSIM...?
THE THIEVES HAVE OVER-RUN THE WHOLE PALACE!
WHERE COULD HE--?

VRROOM
WHAT THE--?!
A MOTOR-- IN BAGMOM?!?

IT'S HASSIM!
AND YOU'LL NEVER CATCH ME! HA HA HA
I HAVE ALL THE FRUITS OF U.S. TECHNOLOGY AT MY DISPOSAL!
OH, DARK NIGHT OF THE SOUL!
THE FLESH OF MY FLESH-- A SELL-OUT!

HEWP! HEWP!!
D-DUCKY!!
AND I'VE GOT THE CHICKS, TOO! SO DON'T TRY ANY TRICKS, SEE?
TEN-FOUR, GOOD BUDDIES!
YALE
waaugh C.B. TALK! THAT DOES IT! NOW I'M INSULTED!

FUN-NEE, HOWARD!
BIG TIME YOKS!
DON'T YOU REALIZE-- WE'VE COME ALL THIS WAY JUST TO LOSE THE GIRLS FOREVER??
THERE'S NO OTHER AIR-CRAFT IN BAGMOM! NO WAY TO--
WRONG!!
AS WRONG AS HASSIM, WHEN HE CLAIMED MY CREATIONS HARBOR NO MAGIC!

"BEHOLD-- ONE THIN DINAR!"
AND SUDDENLY--
HEE HAW
HEE HAW
IN AMAZEMENT AND AESTHETIC REVULSION, THE ASSEMBLAGE WATCHES... AS THE MULE TAKES WING!!

NORMALLY, I'D THINK TWICE ABOUT A RIDE ON A MERRY-GO-ROUND!
BUT IF THERE'S ANYTHING NORMAL ABOUT THIS SITUATION--
--I MUST'A BLINKED AN' MISSED IT!
HEE HAW

PADDLING THROUGH THE NIGHT SKY WITH ASTONISHING SPEED-- FOR AN AERODYNAMIC ABSURDITY--THE MULE SOON OVERTAKES THE STUNNED HASSIM!
YOU SLIME!!
CURSES!! BUT YOU CANNOT FORCE ME DOWN!
THE GIRLS-- REMEMBER??
AND THEY'RE NOT WEARING SAFETY BELTS!
HEEHAW
YOU TRY ANY AERO-BATICS, AN' I'LL--

WE WON'T EVEN GIVE 'IM THE CHANCE, ACE!
C-CAREFUL, TOOTS-- IT'S A LONG DROP!
C'MON, WINDA!
OH, GWACIOUS!!
I-- I CAN'T! I'M AFWAID OF HEIGHTS!!
UNFORTU-NATELY, KID-- THERE'S NO CHOICE ANYMORE!
HASSIM'S OUT FOR BLOOD! TAKE MY HAND!
I-- I'LL TWY!!
oooh I CAN'T WOOK...!
NO! NO!! I CAN'T HAVE OUT-WITTED THEM ALL-- ONLY TO BE THWARTED BY A DUCK!!
I'LL KILL YOU FOR THIS-- WEB-FOOTED FREAK!!
BUT BEFORE HASSIM CAN LEAP ASTRIDE THE FLYING STEED...
HOWARD, YOU DID IT! YOU OUT-MANEUVERED HIM -- ON A MULE!
HEEHAW
SO... WHY ARE YOU WOOPING BACK, FOR CWYING OUT WOUD??
TA KNOCK HIM OUTTA THE SKY-- THAT'S WHY!!
NOT LIKELY, FOWL! NOT WHEN YOU AND YOUR MULE--
-- WILL SHORTLY BE RIDDLED WITH LEAD!
THAKOW

HOWWOWS! HE'S FIWING ON US!!
THINK FAST, DUCKY--PLEASE!
DON'T PANIC, LADIES.

WIJID DID OUR THINKIN' FOR US!
BZZZZ
MISSILE LAUNCHER

OH! WOOK AT THAT!
IT'S A WITTLE WOBOT!

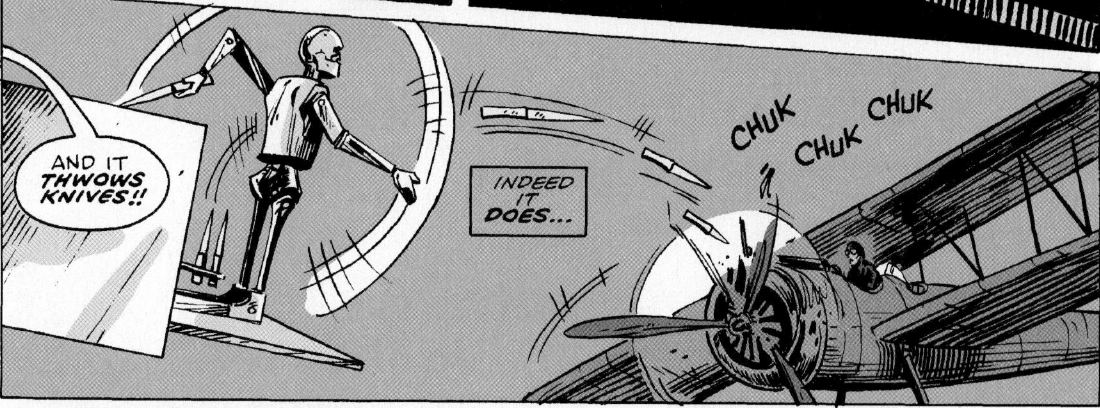
AND IT THWOWS KNIVES!!
INDEED IT DOES...
CHUK
CHUK CHUK

...AND WITH DEADLY ACCURACY!
!

HEE HAW HEE HAW
SAY G'NIGHT, SWEET PRINCE!
IT'S ALL OVER!

OH, DWAT! HE SEEMS TO HAVE SET THE PWANE DOWN SAFEWY!
NOT TO WORRY, KIDDO. IF I KNOW MY GEOGRAPHY, HE'LL GET HIS!
HE LANDED ACROSS THE BORDER FROM BAGMOM...
...IN ISRAEL!
HEE HAW

EPILOG: AFTER THE EXPLANATIONS, THE FEASTING, THE FAREWELLS...
GUESS IT DIDN'T WORK OUT TOO BADLY, ALL IN ALL...!

IT WAS NICE OF THE CALIPH TO ARRANGE FOR OUR PASSAGE HOME, THIS MEDITERRANEAN CRUISE, AND EVERYTHING, HUH?
YEAH, HE WAS DECENT ENOUGH--
--ONCE WE TALKED 'IM OUTTA HAVIN' ME BRONZED, AN'--

HOWARD! BEV! HUWWY! IT'S VEWY UWGENT!
PAUL IS WUBBING THE WAMP AGAIN!!

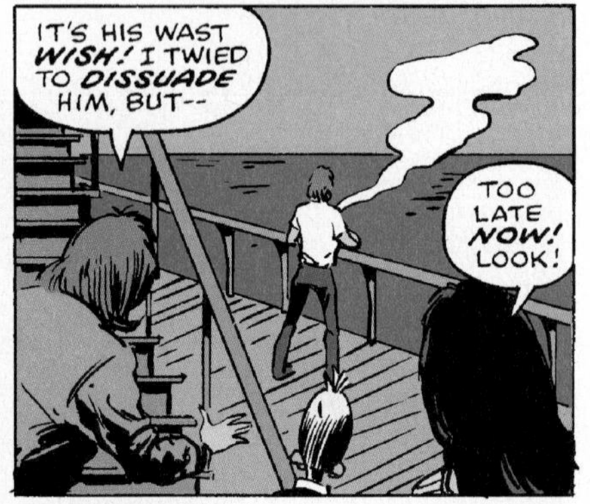
IT'S HIS WAST WISH! I TWIED TO DISSUADE HIM, BUT--
TOO LATE NOW! LOOK!

HOWEVER...
LECHEROUS CUR! NO!
ulp

THIS IS... UH...
TEE HEE
...VERY EM-BARRASSING.
WHAT DID YOU ASK FOR-- THAT COULD OFFEND A GENIE'S SENSIBILITIES

I'D... REALLY RATHER NOT SAY.
OH... DON'T FWET, PAUL.
I'M EXTWA-ORDINAWIWY FWATTERED, ANYHOW.
FIN

BRUNNER

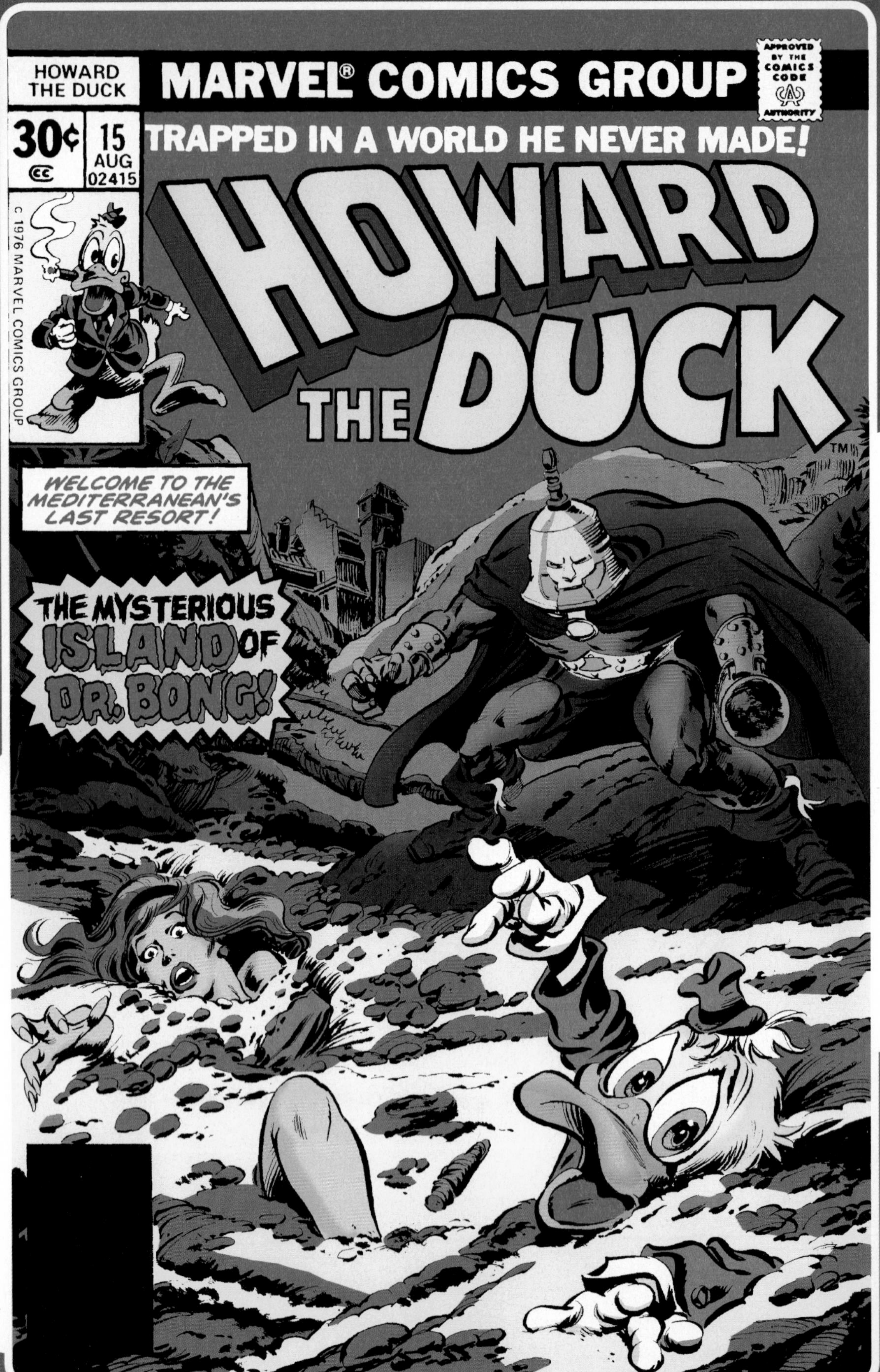

HOWARD THE DUCK

MARVEL® COMICS GROUP

30¢ 15 AUG 02415

TRAPPED IN A WORLD HE NEVER MADE!

HOWARD THE DUCK™

WELCOME TO THE MEDITERRANEAN'S LAST RESORT!

THE MYSTERIOUS ISLAND OF DR. BONG!

From the time of his hatching, he was...different. A potentially brilliant scholar who dreaded the structured environment of school, he educated himself in the streets, taking whatever work was available, formulating his philosophy of self from what he learned of the world about him. And then the Cosmic Axis shifted...and that world *changed.* Suddenly, he was stranded in a universe he could not fathom. Without warning, he became a strange fowl in an even stranger land.

Stan Lee PRESENTS: HOWARD THE DUCK! TM

STEVE GERBER WRITER/EDITOR * GENE COLAN ARTIST * KLAUS JANSON INKER/COLORIST * IRV WATANABE LETTERER

ACTUALLY, I SUPPOSE WE'RE AN ITEM--BUT WHAT OF IT?
I'D RATHER DEVOTE MY ATTENTION TO THE ENDLESS SEA OUT THERE.
YEAH--IT'S BEAUTIFUL, ISN'T IT? CALM, QUIET...
...GENTLY LAPPING AT THE HULL OF THE SHIP.

I NEEDED A CRUISE LIKE THIS TA CLEAR MY HEAD, BEV.
I HAVEN'T HEARD THOSE VOICES IN MY HEAD SINCE WE SET SAIL.

"IT'S DONE US BOTH GOOD, DUCKY. THIS SHIP IS LIKE A FLOATING CITY, BUT DETACHED FROM THE REST OF REALITY.
"ALL THE CONVENIENCES OF HOME, DRUGSTORES, BOUTIQUES, THEATERS-- AND NONE OF THE HASSLES, Y'KNOW?"

YEAH...IN THE EVENT OF NUCLEAR DISASTER THE ENTIRE FREE ENTERPRISE SYSTEM--
--COULD BE PRESERVED ABROAD THIS SHIP FOR FUTURE GENERATIONS.
WHA'--?
NOTHIN'...!

ANYWAY, I PROMISED MYSELF-- NO HEAVY THOUGHTS THIS TRIP.
DITTO! KEEP IT LIGHT-- EVERYTHING MELLOW-- NOTHING--

--DISRUPTIVE.
ZZONK

H-HOWARD, ARE YOU ALL RIGHT?
MELLOW...

HE SIGHS DREAMILY. HIS EYES ROLL UPWARD AS IF IN ECSTATIC CONTEM-PLATION. HE LISTS TO AND FRO.
SPLASH
AND THEN HE TAKES THE PLUNGE!

AND SO IT ARRIVES AT LAST: THAT AWFUL MOMENT HE'S EX-PECTED--AND DREADED-- SINCE HIS CHILDHOOD.
SPLAT
AND THERE'S NOTHING TO DO BUT MAKE THE EMBAR-RASSING ADMISSION.
GLUB B-BEV-- I-- I CAN'T SWIM!

WH-WHAT? BUT THAT'S IMPOSSIBLE! ALL DUCKS CAN--
OH, HOWARD! MY POOR BABY!
OH, GWACIOUS-- THIS IS ALL MY FAULT!
IT WAS MY SHUFFLEBOARD PUCK THAT STWUCK HIM!
SOMEBODY-- HELP!!

I'M SOWWY, HOWARD! I JUST DON'T KNOW MY OWN STWENGTH SOMETIMES!
BUT DON'T WOWWY! WE'LL SAVE YOU!

GET WEADY! HEWE COMES THE WIFE-PWESERVER!
EEEEK!

UH, WINDA-- I CAN APPRECIATE THE IMPULSE TA BUILD DRAMATIC TENSION, AN' ALL...
BUT, SEE, I'M DROWNING.

AN' WHATEVER YOU'RE SCREAMIN' ABOUT, IT CAN'T BE AS URGENT AS--
waaaugh

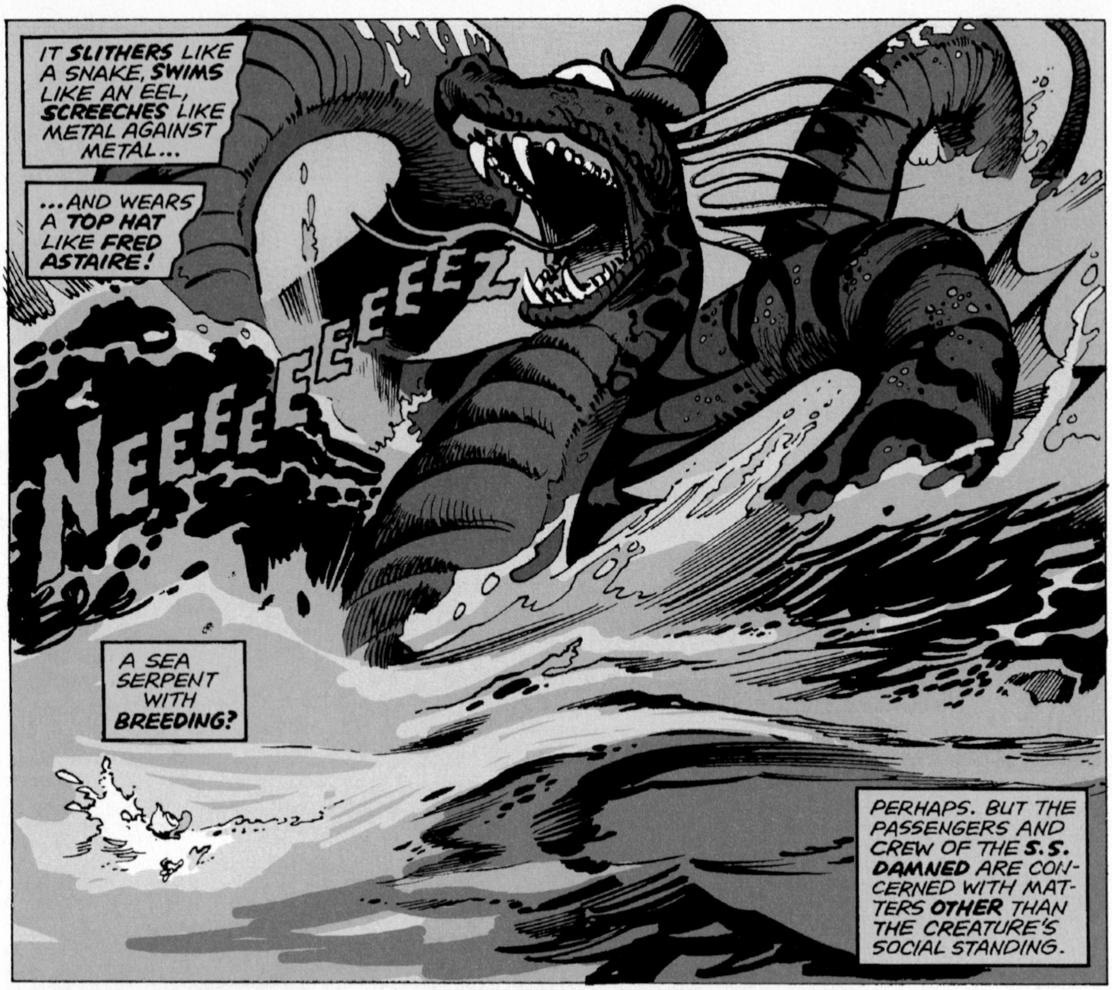

IT SLITHERS LIKE A SNAKE, SWIMS LIKE AN EEL, SCREECHES LIKE METAL AGAINST METAL...
...AND WEARS A TOP HAT LIKE FRED ASTAIRE!
NEEEEEEEEEEZ
A SEA SERPENT WITH BREEDING?
PERHAPS. BUT THE PASSENGERS AND CREW OF THE S.S. DAMNED ARE CONCERNED WITH MATTERS OTHER THAN THE CREATURE'S SOCIAL STANDING.

ITS SIZE, FOR EXAMPLE.
AND THE FACT THAT ITS SCALY BODY SEEMS TO BE ONE LONG, SINUOUS MUSCLE...
NEEEEEEEEEEZ
WINDA-- THE LIFE-PRESERVER-- PLEASE!!
...CAPABLE OF COILING ABOUT THE SHIP AND CRUSHING IT, EFFORTLESSLY.

KLONK
S.S. DAMNED
I MUST BE THE VERY PERSONIFICATION OF THE RAGE TO LIVE.
HIT ME, DUNK ME, INSULT ME--I'LL STILL HANG IN THERE.
I WONDER WHY--?!
DECKSIDE:
BLAM
THIS'S LIKE HUNTING ELEPHANTS WITH A CAP PISTOL!
IT'D TAKE A HOWITZER TO PUT A HOLE IN THAT THAT!
M-MAYBE WE CAN CHARM IT! I USED TO PLAY THE RECORDER--!
THE CHURNING WATERS, MEANWHILE, TOSS HOWARD UP CLOSER TO THE MONSTER, WHERE HIS BEMUSED GAZE FIXES UPON:
A PLAQUE--RIVETTED INTO ITS HIDE--!
TO GIVE SERPENT PLEASURE PRESS HERE
"TO GIVE... PLEASURE... WHAT??
BZZZZZZZZ
NOTHIN' TO LOSE BY TRYIN', I GUESS--!
INSTANTLY, THE CREATURE'S EYES LIGHT UP! AND THE ENDS OF HIS MOUTH CURL INTO A... SMILE!

AND, AS IF THE SHIP HAD NEVER EXISTED, THE MONSTER ABANDONS ITS ATTACK AND PLOWS OFF THROUGH THE WATER, THE ENTIRE LENGTH OF ITS BODY QUIVERING WITH DELIGHT.
NEEZ! NEEZ! NEEZ!
SO... IT MUST BE LIFE'S LITTLE SURPRISES THAT KEEP ME GOING...
GEE! IF I'D DROWNED, I'D NEVER HAVE LEARNED THAT SEA SERPENTS COME EQUIPPED WITH PLEASURE-CENTER STIMULATORS!

HOWARD!! CATCH!!
HUH--?
OH!!
NUTS! ALMOST FORGOT WHERE I WAS!

ATTAWAY, MATE-- JUST STAY LOOSE! WE'LL HAUL YA RIGHT UP!
YOU'RE A HERO, FELLA!
OTHERWISE, YOU'D'A LET ME SINK, HUH, CAP'N?

NOW, NOW... NO NEED FOR SARCASM, SON. WE'RE GLAD YOU'RE BACK WITH US, SAFE 'N' SOUND!
UH-HUH.

SAFE 'N' SOUND-- EXCEPT FOR THE TARANTULAS DANCING THE POLKA IN MY STOMACH!
DON'T ASK ME HOW --BUT THINGS'RE GONNA GET WORSE BEFORE THIS CRUISE IS OVER!

DESPITE THE DUCK'S PREMONITION...
...THE VOYAGE OF THE DAMNED CONTINUES UNINTERRUPTED PAST SUNDOWN AND INTO THE MOONLIT NIGHT.

MISS SWITZLER, MR. SAME, MISS WESTER-- WELCOME!
THANK YOU, CAPTAIN. NICE OF YOU TO INVITE US.
MM-HMM-- IT'S A WAWITY FOR US TO ATTEND A FORMAL SHINDIG!
YEAH...HOW OFTEN DOES YOUR AVERAGE DUCK GET THE OPPORTUNITY...
...TO DRESS UP THE PENGUIN?

YES, WELL... DO RELAX, ENJOY YOURSELVES...DINNER WILL BE SERVED SHORTLY.
DUM
OKAY, FOLKS-- EVERYBODY DANCE!

SHALL WE TRIP A LITTLE LIGHT FANTASTIC, DUCKY?
SURE-- WHY NOT!
I-I-I-- WANNA ROCK'N' ROLL ALL NIIIGHT--

NOTHIN' MORE EXHILARATING THAN HARD ROCK PLAYED ON PIANO, BASS, AND DRUMS.
REMINDS ME OF MY BEST FRIEND'S BAR MITZVAH.

WHEN THE BAND CONCLUDES ITS STODGY SET...
DINNERTIME, SWEETS.
HOPE THE FOOD'S BET-TER THAN THE MUSIC.
I DON'T CARE IF IT'S RECYCLED SOYBURGERS! I'M STARVED!

LADIES AND GENTLEMEN, YOUR FIRST COURSE.
DON'T PROLONG THE SUSPENSE, PAL. WHAT'VE WE GOT?

DUCK L'ORANGE, SIR. EX-QUISITE, IS IT NOT?

GULP!

MMMPPH
H-HOWARD ...IS THERE ANYTHING I CAN DO?
MM-MMPH

WHICH TRANS-LATES ROUGHLY TO: "YES! CLEAR ME A PATH, AND STRANGLE THE CHEF!"
BEV GETS THE GIST, IF NOT THE SPECIFICS...
BUT THE FOWL IS LONG GONE BEFORE SHE CAN ACT, CLUTCHING HIS BILL, RAC-ING AS IF ON WHEELS...
MMGLURRG

...TO A SECLUDED CORNER OF THE UPPER DECK...
AAAAUGH
...WHERE, AT LAST, HE MAY RETCH IN PEACE.

TH-THAT DID IT... TOTAL ENERVATION! ...I CAN FEEL THE SPIDERS CRAWLING OUTTA MY INTESTINES...
...DOWN MY RUBBERY LEGS...
...AN' INTO THE DECK! CATHARSIS!

I MEAN...HOW MUCH WORSE CAN IT GET, AFTER BEING EX-PECTED TO ENGAGE IN CASUAL CANNIBALISM?!
GOTTA...LIE DOWN... TOO QUEASY TO THINK, LET ALONE STAND...!

YEAH... THIS'S BETTER...
BREATHE IN THAT BRACING SALT AIR... KEEP MY EYES ON THAT INDIGO SKY, DAPPLED WITH SILVER...!
ONCE YA HIT THE PITS IT CAN ONLY IMPROVE, RIGHT?

SUDDENLY--
CRRRAAASSHHHH
AN IMMENSE CHUNK OF GRANITE, DROPPED FROM NOWHERE, IMBEDS ITSELF IN THE DECK.

TH-THIS...IS NOT AN IMPROVEMENT...!
FROM THE PITS...TO THE QUARRY?
WAAAGH

INCHES...THREE, MAYBE FOUR... FIVE, TOPS!
TH-THAT'S ALL THAT STOOD BETWEEN ME AND WAFER-HOOD!
MY GOD... WHAT'S GOING ON HERE?
HOWARD!! WHAT HAPPENED??

WE HEARD A TERRIBLE CRASH, AND...
WELL, YA CAN ALL REST EASY NOW...
THE BOULDER IS UNARMED.

CAPTAIN, WHERE COULD IT HAVE COME FROM?
IS IT A METEOR, DO YOU THINK, OR--?
I DON'T KNOW, MR. SAME. I'VE NEVER SEEN ANYTHING LIKE IT.

MAYBE IT'S AN EGG. MAYBE I LAID IT.
LA-DE-DA
MY INCU-BATORY POSITION ATOP IT IS AWFULLY INCRIMI-NATING.
BUT, NO...IT'S SO BIG!
AN' I'M A MALE!
SO IT MUST'VE FALLEN FROM UP--

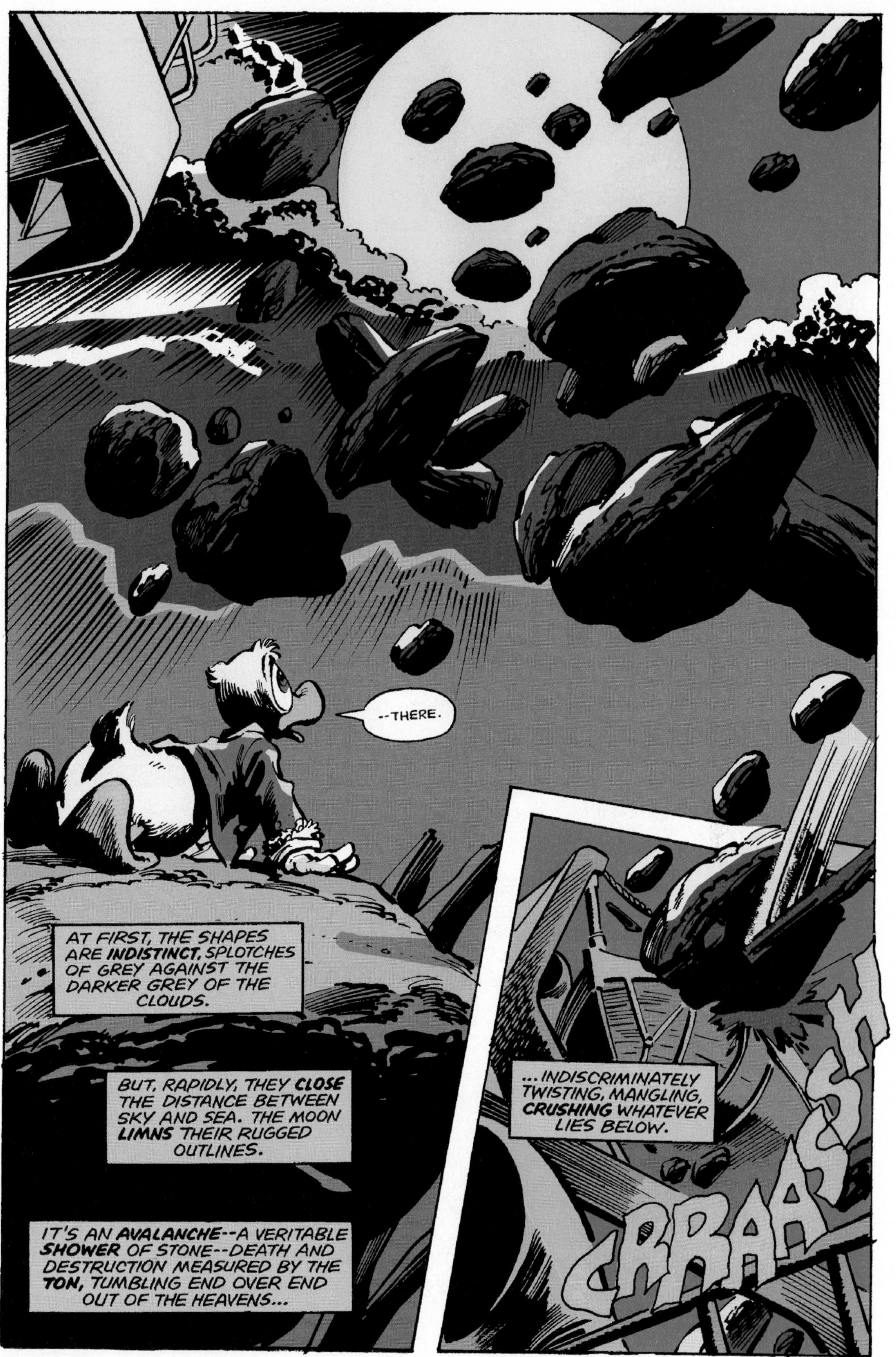
--THERE.
AT FIRST, THE SHAPES ARE INDISTINCT, SPLOTCHES OF GREY AGAINST THE DARKER GREY OF THE CLOUDS.
BUT, RAPIDLY, THEY CLOSE THE DISTANCE BETWEEN SKY AND SEA. THE MOON LIMNS THEIR RUGGED OUTLINES.
IT'S AN AVALANCHE--A VERITABLE SHOWER OF STONE--DEATH AND DESTRUCTION MEASURED BY THE TON, TUMBLING END OVER END OUT OF THE HEAVENS...
...INDISCRIMINATELY TWISTING, MANGLING, CRUSHING WHATEVER LIES BELOW.
CRRAASH

PANIC:
¦GNNAGH¦
THERE IS, OF COURSE, NOWHERE TO RUN...
CLOP
...AND YET, THE ONLY BODIES NOT DARTING ABOUT AIMLESSLY BE-LONG TO HOWARD, AND TO THE DEAD.
SHORTLY, THE STORM ABATES...
S.S. DAMNED
...LEAVING THE SHIP WOBBLING LIKE SOME FREE-FORM SCULP-TURE CAST ADRIFT FROM THE MUSEUM OF MODERN ART.
C-CAPTAIN--THE BRIDGE IS A SHAMBLES --RADIO'S OUT--NAVI-GATIONAL INSTRU-MENTS GONE--
ENGINES SEEM INTACT, SIR--BUT WE'RE SAILING BLIND--
THE MEN ARE AWAIT-ING YOUR ORDERS--SIR?
T-TELL THEM ¦GASP¦ I SAID--TO TRY--ANYTHING AND ¦GASP¦ EVERYTHING!
I MEAN IT!!
SEND UP FLARES--SWEEP THE WATER WITH SEARCHLIGHTS--
YELL FOR SUB-MARINER--WHISTLE FOR FLIPPER--
PUT A MESSAGE IN A BOTTLE--!
I DON'T CARE WHAT IT TAKES--GET US HELP!!

AND THE CREW OBEYS-- EVEN TO THE LETTER.
SPLASH
ZASH
SHOOM
CALLING ALL DOLPHINS!
CALLING PRINCE NAMOR!
FOOSH
AWROOOOGAH
FLARES EXPLODE, BELLS CLANG, SIRENS BLEAT, BULLHORNS BELLOW...!
THE GENTLE WARMTH OF THE MEDITERRANEAN EVENING IS TRANSFORMED INTO A FOURTH OF JULY NIGHTMARE.
ALL I CAN THINK ABOUT IS BOB DYLAN: "EVERYBODY MUST GET STONED."
SOMEHOW, I ALWAYS FIGURED HE MEANT IT THIS WAY.
THAT'S FUNNY-- SO DID I.
POOF
WHO'S BOB DYWAN?
I DUNNO...I JUST HOPE WE'RE QUOTING SURVIVORS, NOT MARTYRS.
HOW TWUE! FWAME OF MIND IS SO IMPOR--
OH!! WOOK!!
WAND HO! WAND HO!!

LAND! A SIGH OF RELIEF RISES LIKE TRAPPED STEAM FROM THE EMBATTLED SHIP.
BONG
BONG
BONG
THERE'S ONLY ONE PROBLEM: THIS BELL-SHAPED ATOLL ISN'T SUPPOSED TO BE HERE!
AND, TOO... THERE'S THE MATTER OF THE BONGING.
BONG
AS THE SHIP DRAWS CLOSER, THE SOUND GROWS LOUDER, SPLITTING NOT ONLY EARS...
...BUT ROCK, AS WELL.
CRRRAACK
AW, NO-- IT IS AN EGG!!
AND FROM IT HATCHES NOTHING LESS BIZARRE THAN --A CONCRETE SWAN...
EEEEYIIII!
...RISING DESPITE ITS WEIGHT, DESPITE ITS UNFLAPPABLE WINGS, INTO THE SKY!
BEV!! LEGGO!!
WAAAGH
BEV-- WHY?
I-- I'M SORRY, DUCKY-- I COULDN'T!
IT HAPPENED TOO QUICKLY-- MY GRIP FROZE--!

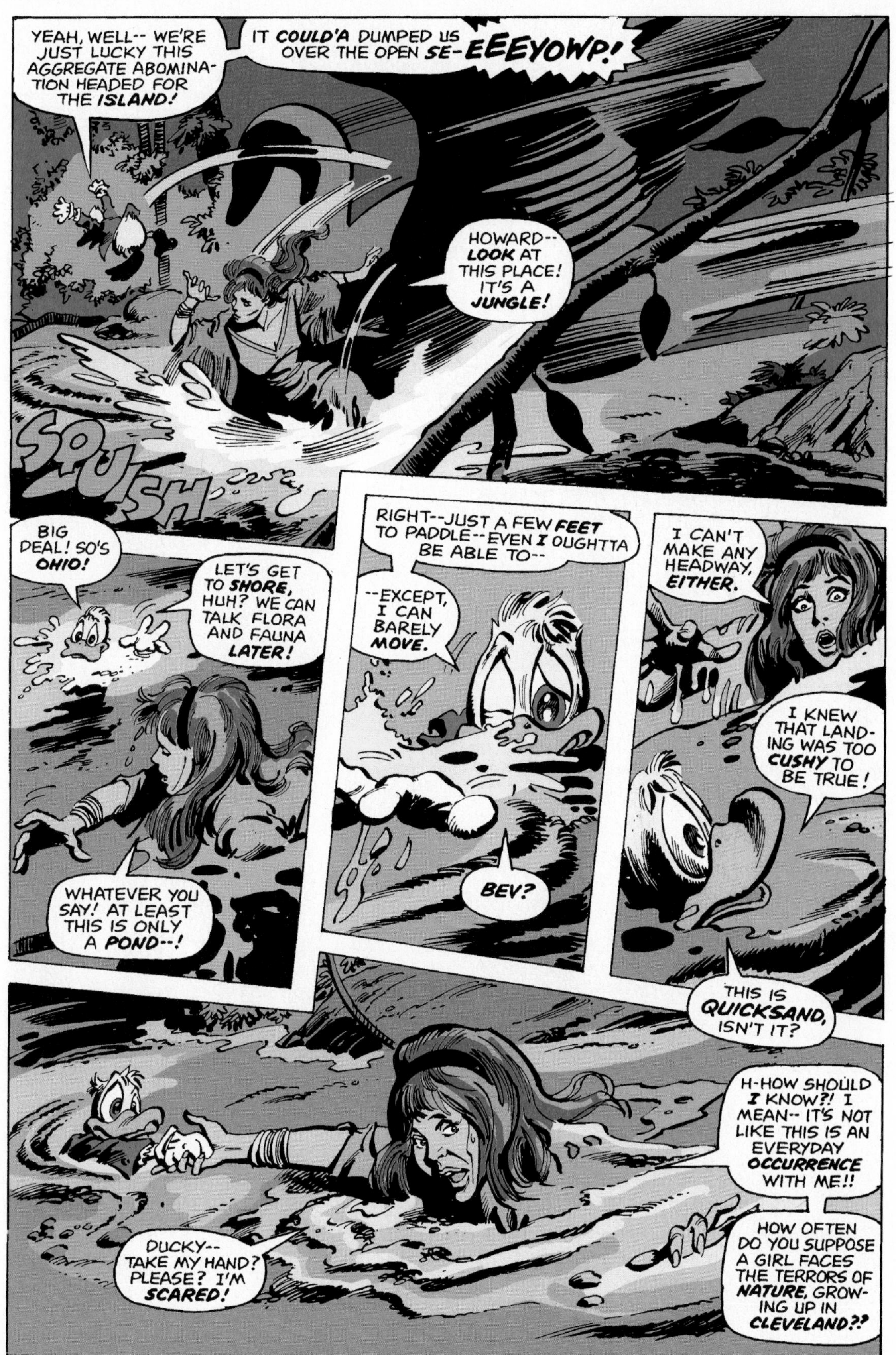
YEAH, WELL-- WE'RE JUST LUCKY THIS AGGREGATE ABOMINATION HEADED FOR THE ISLAND!
IT COULD'A DUMPED US OVER THE OPEN SE-EEEYOWP!
HOWARD-- LOOK AT THIS PLACE! IT'S A JUNGLE!
SPLUSH
BIG DEAL! SO'S OHIO!
LET'S GET TO SHORE, HUH? WE CAN TALK FLORA AND FAUNA LATER!
WHATEVER YOU SAY! AT LEAST THIS IS ONLY A POND--!
RIGHT--JUST A FEW FEET TO PADDLE--EVEN I OUGHTTA BE ABLE TO--
--EXCEPT, I CAN BARELY MOVE.
BEV?
I CAN'T MAKE ANY HEADWAY, EITHER.
I KNEW THAT LANDING WAS TOO CUSHY TO BE TRUE!
THIS IS QUICKSAND, ISN'T IT?
H-HOW SHOULD I KNOW?! I MEAN-- IT'S NOT LIKE THIS IS AN EVERYDAY OCCURRENCE WITH ME!!
HOW OFTEN DO YOU SUPPOSE A GIRL FACES THE TERRORS OF NATURE, GROWING UP IN CLEVELAND??
DUCKY-- TAKE MY HAND? PLEASE? I'M SCARED!

SUDDENLY, IT BEGINS AGAIN: THE DEAFENING PEAL OF THE BELLS:
BONG BONG
BUT THIS TIME, IT'S ACCOMPANIED BY ANOTHER SOUND...
...A RUSTLING IN THE UNDERBRUSH.
AS IF IN ANSWER TO THE BELLS' EERIE SUMMONS, A COTERIE OF BIZARRE BEINGS CREEPS OUT FROM THE TANGLE.
NEEZ!
TH-THEY WANT TO HELP US!!
UHM...NO THANKS. I'LL PASS.
NEEZ?
HONEST-- NO OFFENSE! IT'S JUST...IF YOU GUYS ARE ANY INDICATION OF WHAT'S COMIN'--
--I'D PREFER TO BOW OUT NOW.
DON'T BE FOOLISH, BROTHER. TAKE MY HAND.
WAAUGH
Y-YOU'RE A
DUCK!!

I WAS... UNTIL THE DOCTOR GAVE ME NEEZ.
I KNOW I SHOULD BE REACTING MORE --WHAT? VISIBLY TO THIS MADNESS, BUT--
DON'T APOLOGIZE, TOOTS-- I'VE BEEN THERE.
BONG BONG
AFTER AWHILE, IT'S ALL YA CAN DO TO FAKE THE EXPECTED GASPS AN' MOANS OF--
SURPRISE!
OH JEEZ, NOW WHA--?
OH MY GOSH!!
WHY-- HOW CHARMINGLY INARTICULATE! THANK YOU, MS. SWITZLER.
AND MAY I WELCOME YOU TO THE ISLAND OF--
DR. BONG!
waaaugh
UH... WHAT IF I SAID, "NO, YOU MAY NOT"?

NEXT THE ROCKY ROAD TO ANONYMITY!

HOWARD THE DUCK TM
MARVEL® COMICS GROUP
APPROVED BY THE COMICS CODE AUTHORITY
30¢
16 SEPT 02415
TRAPPED IN A WORLD HE NEVER MADE!
©1977 MARVEL COMICS GROUP
HOWARD THE DUCK TM
SPECIAL ONCE IN A LIFETIME ALBUM ISSUE!
HOWARD AT THE MERCY OF HIS MOST POWERFUL FOE-- THE INCREDIBLE CREATOR!
DEADLINE DOOM!

From the time of his hatching, he was...different. A potentially brilliant scholar who dreaded the structured environment of school, he educated himself in the streets, taking whatever work was available, formulating his philosophy of self from what he learned of the world about him. And then the Cosmic Axis shifted...and that world *changed*. Suddenly, he was stranded in a universe he could not fathom. Without warning, he became a strange fowl in an even stranger land.

Stan Lee Presents: HOWARD THE DUCK!™

I **WAS**...UNTIL THE DOCTOR GAVE ME **NEEZ**.
I KNOW I SHOULD BE REACTING MORE --WHAT?--**VISIBLY** TO THIS MADNESS. BUT--
DON'T APOLOGIZE, TOOTS-- I'VE **BEEN** THERE.
BONG BONG
AFTER AWHILE, IT'S ALL YA CAN DO TO **FAKE** THE EXPECTED GASPS AN' MOANS OF--
SURPRISE!
OH JEEZ, **NOW** WHA--?
OH MY GOSH!!
WHY-- HOW CHARMINGLY **INARTICULATE!** THANK YOU, MS. SWITZLER.
AND MAY I **WELCOME** YOU TO THE ISLAND OF--
DR. BONG!
waaaugh
UH...WHAT IF I SAID, "NO, YOU MAY **NOT**"?
THAT'S WHERE OUR STORY LEFT OFF **LAST ISSUE**. IT'S ALSO WHERE OUR STORY WILL RESUME-- **NEXT ISSUE**. THE ADMITTEDLY OFF THE WALL ADVENTURE INTO ABSURDITY WHICH YOU'RE ABOUT TO READ IN **THIS ISSUE** IS THE RESULT OF. . .TECHNICAL DIFFICULTIES. PLEASE STAND BY.

"Relax," I keep telling myself. "Ease up. Calm down. Cool off. Untense. Hang loose, effendi/pilgrim/true believer. They will understand. Just explain it to them. Candidly, but with dignity. They'll agree—it's better than going reprint."

It is? A comic book without panels, balloons, or even a plot? An essay, for cryin' out loud?!

Uh-uh, Gerbs. This time you've done it for sure. This time you've gone too far. They'll be snickering about your self-indulgent disdain for commerciality from coast to coast. You're through in this business. The only reader who'll remain loyal after this flagrant flouting of comic book convention is Harlan Ellison. Maybe.

"On the other hand, Steve, you could let Duckdom Assembled decide for itself." That inner voice again, gently prodding. "After all, what's the dif? You've already made your decision. The die is cast. No turning back, right?"

Right. But how—?

"The truth, Steve. You tell them the truth, plain and unadorned.

"For the past eight weeks or so (mid-January to mid-April), you've been laboring under tremendous pressure. You've scripted HOWARD #15, the HTD ANNUAL, the first several weeks of continuity for the Duck's newspaper strip, and, almost single-handedly, you've edited, written, and produced the 64-page KISS magazine. This last required your presence in the Bullpen almost daily, for at least a few hours, over that two-month span. Hours which should've been spent at your desk, writing.

"Consequently, you fell severely behind on your deadlines. You caused John Verpoorten, Marvel's production manager, no end of grief. And, incidentally, you shot your nerves completely to hell."

Sob stories are a dime a dozen, inner pal.

"Don't interrupt yourself, Steve. We're just getting to the kicker. While you were busily burning out your mind and body with all this writing and editing and stuff, you were also attempting to clear out your luxurious Hell's Kitchen abode and ship your motley possessions off into the sunset in advance of your impending move to Las Vegas."

Yes. It was heaven, those eight weeks.

"And you cracked under the strain. Come on. Admit it. To yourself first, and then the readers. You fell apart, that's all. For some very good reasons. So you were late sending out the synopsis for HTD #16 to Gene Colan, and it looked like this issue would have to go reprint until—"

—until Colombia, Missouri, midway on my drive to Vegas, when the idea for this special story or essay or true confession, or whatever it is, struck me like a bolt from the smog. Lots of big pictures. Lots of words. All about the relationship between a boy and his Duck. And comics in general. And living at the precipice, playing the Balance Game over the cosmic chasm filled with lime jello.

"Correct. Like an idiot, you voluntarily took on the pressure of producing this instant issue rather than allowing the magazine to go reprint. You did it for the readers."

Uh-huh. And you really think they'll understand?

"I don't know, Stevie-boy. But you've got fourteen pages left in which to convince 'em. If I were you, I'd get on it. Hustle! Go! Go! GO!!"

Swell.

ZEN AND THE ART OF COMIC BOOK WRITING: A COMMUNIQUE FROM COLORADO
STEVE GERBER, WRITER/EDITOR
CAST OF THOUSANDS, ARTISTS
IRV WATANABE, LETTERING
DOC MARTIN, COLORIST
ED HANNIGAN & NELSON YOMTOV, PRODUCTION
ALAN WEISS

I. writers are like people

As mentioned, I am en route to Las Vegas. (To live, not to gamble. Assuming there's a difference.) I've just spent five days on the road, crossing New Jersey, Pennsylvania, Ohio, Indiana, Illinois, Missouri, and Kansas. Five days of refinery fumes, gently rolling boredom, old friends, fast food, Indian burial mounds, family, and flatlands—in that order.

Howard is travelling with me, as he does wherever I roam. He's there in my head. He won't go away. He is as much a highway marker as the green and white signs that weigh heavy on the shoulders of Interstate 70. He is, in a word, real.

We're in Colorado now, in historic Georgetown, a little hamlet about thirty-five minutes west of Denver housing perhaps 700 persons. Moving inexorably from the general to the even more specific, we're seated in a booth in a restaurant called the Happy Cooker, which specializes in Belgian waffles. Like the rest of historic Georgetown, the Cooker is clean, quiet, and quaint. Its large windows look out on the mountains to the south and admit vast quantities of sunshine into the dining area. The plants—in shelves on the windows, on hooks in the ceiling—soak up the rays and turn the precise shade of green to complement the golden brown Belgian waffles. It's a minor miracle of color co-ordination.

Plants are like people. Writers are like plants. Therefore, and this may come as a surprise, writers are like people. Give them light, water, nourishment, a comfortable pot, and an encouraging word, and they'll grow. Really. They'll blossom. They'll create things of beauty.

This principle applies to most varieties of human beings. If other people would accord them as much consideration as they do their plants, they, too, would bloom. Of course, plants don't talk back, which makes them much less annoying to have around the house. This may or may not explain why so many of our institutions seem to devote themselves to the task of turning people into vegetables rather than treating them with the same kindness we lavish upon the already mute. We tend to prefer stumps over trees. You can sit on a stump.

Some writers require more room than others to flourish. Some grow vertically, some laterally or radially, others in vast spaghetti-like tangles. Again, just like plants.

I'm of the spaghetti breed. I'm fascinated by the marinara-splotched pasta of existence, the unrelentingly absurd aspects of human relations and of storytelling. My plots are very thick and zesty.

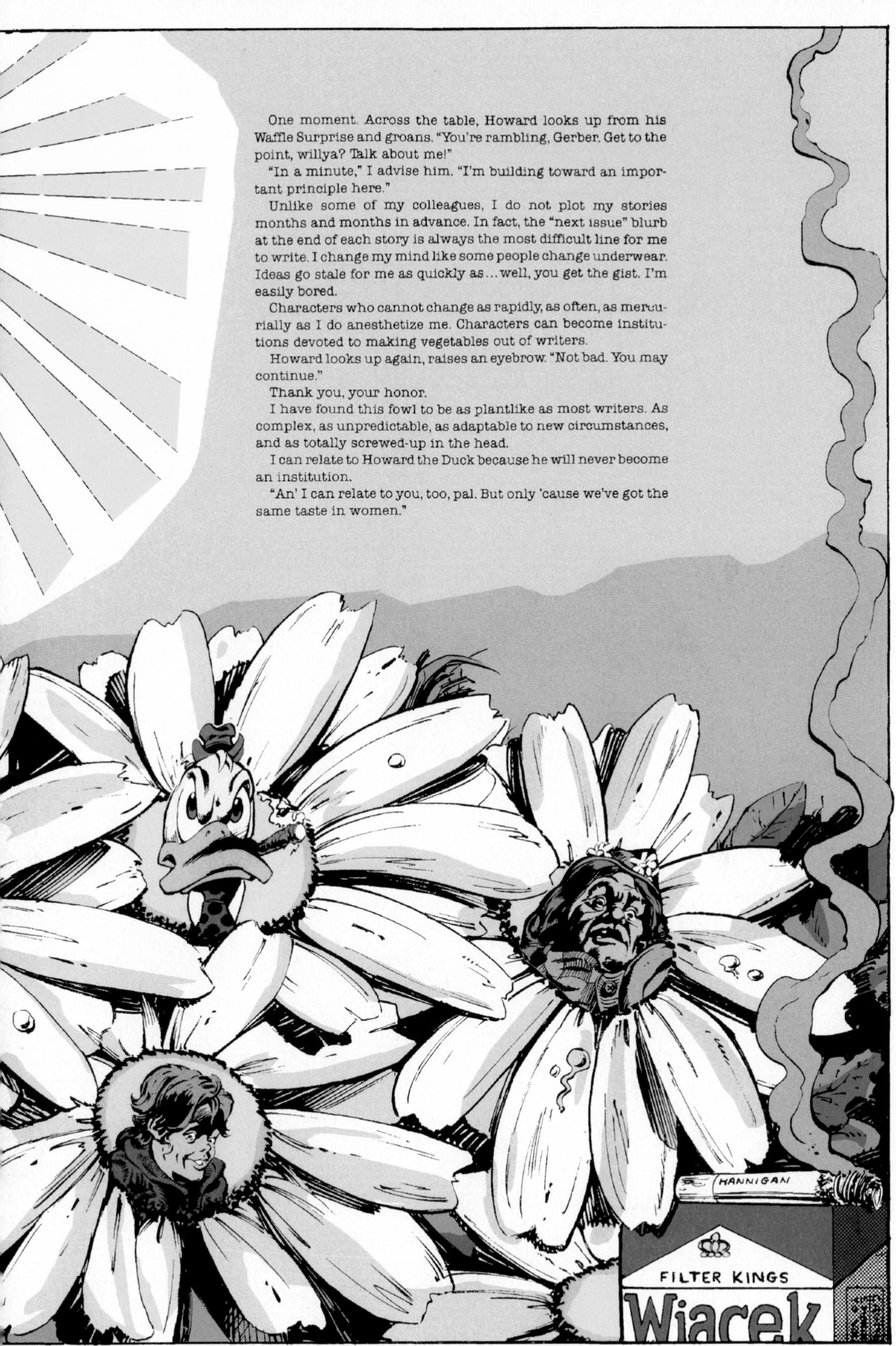

One moment. Across the table, Howard looks up from his Waffle Surprise and groans. "You're rambling, Gerber. Get to the point, willya? Talk about me!"

"In a minute," I advise him. "I'm building toward an important principle here."

Unlike some of my colleagues, I do not plot my stories months and months in advance. In fact, the "next issue" blurb at the end of each story is always the most difficult line for me to write. I change my mind like some people change underwear. Ideas go stale for me as quickly as... well, you get the gist. I'm easily bored.

Characters who cannot change as rapidly, as often, as mercurially as I do anesthetize me. Characters can become institutions devoted to making vegetables out of writers.

Howard looks up again, raises an eyebrow. "Not bad. You may continue."

Thank you, your honor.

I have found this fowl to be as plantlike as most writers. As complex, as unpredictable, as adaptable to new circumstances, and as totally screwed-up in the head.

I can relate to Howard the Duck because he will never become an institution.

"An' I can relate to you, too, pal. But only 'cause we've got the same taste in women."

"Somethin's eatin' at you, Gerber, an' it's not just deadlines or pressures or work, either. I've watched you hairless apes. When you whack out, it's for deeper reasons than that, stuff you can't talk about, or won't."

"Yes, I suppose that's true," I mumble.

"You 'suppose.' That's great. By the way, when did the Human Torch first appear in a solo adventure in the Marvel Age of Comics?"

"Huh? STRANGE TALES #101. Why?"

"And who were the villains in the first fifty issues of FANTASTIC FOUR—in order?"

"Uh... Mole Man, the Skrulls, the Miracle Man, Sub-Mariner, Dr. Doom, Subby and Doom together, Kurrgo, Puppet Master, Sub-Mariner again, Dr. Doom, Impossible Man, Hulk, Red Ghost, Subby again, The Mad Thinker, Dr. Doom, Dr. Doom—"

"Stop!!"

"Whew. Gladly. Thanks. What was the point of—"

"I just wanted ya to see for yourself how much trivia you were carryin' around in yer head! It's gotta be crowdin' out the important stuff, or keepin' it safely suppressed. I bet ya could rattle off a complete list of yer next fifty deadlines, too. But when I ask you about yer psychological posture, you 'suppose'!"

"Now wait just a moment, my web-footed wag! As far as you're concerned, that's not 'trivia', it's history. Where do you figure you'd be today without the first fifty issues of FF? Moreover, that kind of question doesn't require subjective evaluation, just a good memory. When you start asking for opinions about the nature of the mind—!"

"Your mind, Gerber. Not the mind."

"Howard, you're chasing your tail feathers in this conversation. What are you trying to say?"

"I told ya! Somethin's eatin' you, an' ya won't talk about it. You keep retreatin' to the abstract—to suppositions about intangibles like boredom an' institutions an' society. There was a reason you wanted ta write this dumb essay—an' yet you refuse ta let me or the readers in on it!"

"Oh."

"'Oh'?! That's all ya got ta say for yerself?! You, the big humanist, the creative writer, the fragile flower of literature? That's the best ya can do, genius! No wonder my dialogue's been so banal lately!"

"Howard—"

"Y'know what, Gerbs? Deep down, I've always suspected you don't know as much as yer stories would infer. You've learned how ta manipulate words an' pictures ta give a semblance of profundity, but it's all superficial! Cosmetic surgery performed on creaky old ideas an' thoughts! Whaddaya say ta that?!"

"I say that, uhm, on occasion, I've harbored similar suspicions, Howard."

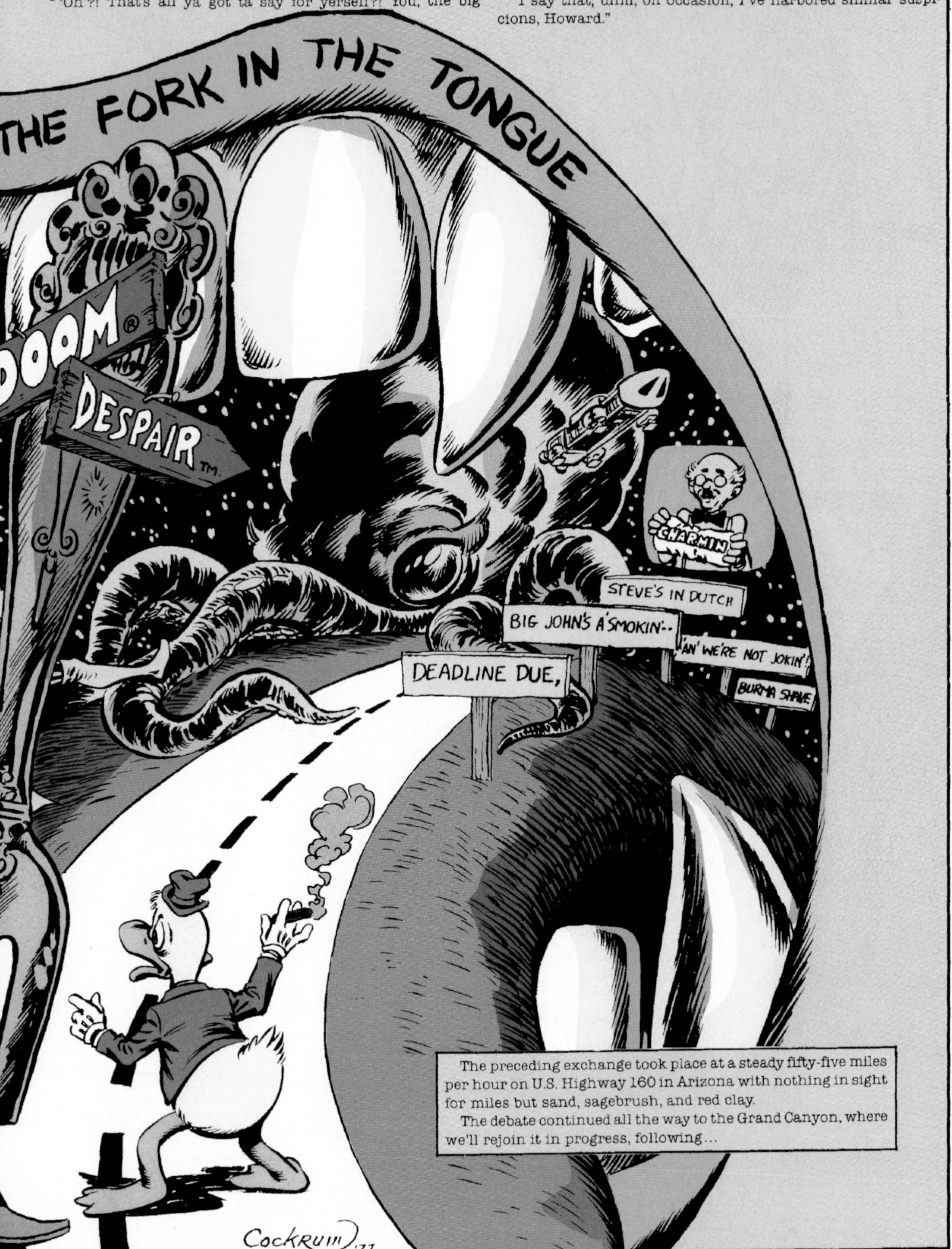

The preceding exchange took place at a steady fifty-five miles per hour on U.S. Highway 160 in Arizona with nothing in sight for miles but sand, sagebrush, and red clay.

The debate continued all the way to the Grand Canyon, where we'll rejoin it in progress, following...

III. obligatory comic book fight scene

There is one rule of comic book writing which simply cannot be violated, even by a writer in search of something as impalpable as his soul or Las Vegas.

Being a visual medium, comics theoretically require at least a modicum of action to engage and sustain reader interest.

Thus, in the interest of sustaining your interest, we reluctantly present this BRAIN-BLASTING BATTLE SCENE, pitting an ostrich and a Las Vegas chorus girl against the MIND-NUMBING MENACE of a KILLER lampshade in a DUEL TO THE DEATH!!

Since we only get one picture for this CLASH OF TITANS, though, we'll have to tell you the outcome. The ostrich sticks its head in a manhole, shrugging off all that's happened and returning to his secret identity as a roadblock. The chorus girl finds herself in the thrill of battle, becomes one with her headdress, and is elevated to goddesshood. The lampshade dies. Basically, it's like most every other comic mag.

57TH ST
MADISON AVE
MARVEL TREASURY EDITION
HOWARD THE DUCK

iv. ...and v

sions of sugar plums

"Majestic, ain't it?" Howard asks, obviously unimpressed.

"Yes," I reply, trying my best to sound contemplative, and failing.

"The Colorado River took eons to carve this steep, sinuous monster objet d'art outta some flat, bland plateau—almost as long as you're takin' gettin' to the point o' this story."

"Howard, it seems vaguely blasphemous to engage in petty banter about human problems in the face of this—this—"

"Hole?"

"I don't believe you said that."

"Look, Gerber, it's not like nature dug this oversized storm drain with the specific intent o' creatin' a tourist attraction! It exists because the river did what it was supposed to do — it flowed. And the rocks did what they were supposed to do—they eroded. Guys like you are just envious 'cause nature didn't haveta put any thought into its work. You wanna be able ta write the same way — only writing isn't a natural process. Nature only hadda make somethin' outta nothin' once in its whole career. You've gotta do it daily. If God had had your temperament, the universe would still be a box o' typewriter paper, waitin' ta be opened!"

I stare dumbly at my friend the Duck, pleading with my eyes for him to continue. He turns away, shaking his head, folding his arms over his chest in disgust. He won't talk to me, and I don't know what to say. After some deliberation, I arrive at the following gem: "Communication ... takes ... a lot of energy, Howard."

He scowls.

I light a cigarette.

We both sit there for a long moment, wordlessly, gazing at the spectacle of the canyon.

"Y'know what that canyon really is, Gerber? It's the world's biggest, most convoluted rut!"

I laugh involuntarily. "I've gotta hand it to you, pal. That's definitely a new interpretation of the phenomenon."

"An' that tight-lipped smile tryin' ta elbow its way onta yer face is the first sign of spontaneity I've seen from you in eleven pages! Loosen up, willya! Save the theorizin' for the speech-communication majors o' the world! You're outta school now, big boy. You're pushin' thirty with a bulldozer. There's no how-to manual on one-to-one interaction between allegedly intelligent beings. The way ta communicate is just—do it!"

"Be myself, you mean. Yeah. Mmm-hmm. That's terrific advice, Howard. Thank you. Wowee. Why didn't I think of that?"

"It ain't that simple, turkey. Ya gotta be yerself without tryin'. Like the river down there."

"Or the eroding rocks, for that matter, huh?"

"Yeah, well, yer not gettin' any younger. But ya got the choice, rocks or river. I figger you've been stonewallin' it too long already." He stands, brushes the dust off his feathers and coat, and turns to walk away. "Listen, I'm gonna grab a bite ta eat. They got a great processed ham sandwich in that restaurant next to the souvenir gift shop with the Taiwan-manufactured Indian beads. Why don't you sit here alone a bit an' meditate on the natural splendor while I gorge myself on preservatives? Free associate. See what ya come up with. Tell the folks at home a story. An' whatever ya do, plan on bein' more interesting next time we meet!"

VI tell the people a story

Ramsludge Hawthorne looked at the assortment of official forms fanned out across the modest expanse of the coffee table. All of the forms began with the same three words: "Please Print Clearly." All of the forms asked for the same information: name, address, city, state, zip, age, married, single, separated, divorced, annual income, father's name, father's address, mother's maiden name, mother's maiden address, health: good, fair, poor, do you certify that you have answered all questions on this form completely and truthfully to the best of your knowledge?, signature, date. The tax forms in the assortment even asked for spare change. Panhandling by mail, Ramsludge thought. Gimme, gimme, gimme. Your money, your word, your life, your every waking moment. And remember, your record will follow you wherever you roam, biting at your heels like a rabid dog. We own you, lock, stock, and zip code.

"You only own me as long as I continue to exist," Ramsludge snarled at the forms, which responded with the same old questions.

Ramsludge's wife the former Remarka Demonstrata, heard

her husband's comment as she entered the living room with her knitting basket. Remarka would almost have been beautiful had she been born a dwarf elm; as a woman, however, she was an aesthetic disaster, short and spindly with a full head of leaves. She plopped herself in the easy chair across the coffee table from the sofa where Ramsludge was still hunched forward, foaming at the forms. "Gonna off yourself, hubby-dubby?" she queried enthusiastically. "Your insurance all paid up, IhopeIhopeIhope?"

"Darling," Ramsludge hissed, "your mind is as barren as your scalp is fecund."

"Yes," Remarka sighed, folding her hands in her lap, turning her gaze heavenward. "That's why we have such a full and happy life together, Rrrrrramsludge!" He hated it when she growled his name.

"Actually," Ramsludge said, "I was thinking of deserting you, going into hiding, adopting a new name and perhaps a puppy from Bide-a-Wee, establishing a new identity for myself, something less... oppressive."

"Aw, g'wan!"

"Okay, I will." And with that, Ramsludge leaped from the sofa, over the coffee table, and bounded into the kitchen. Remarka sighed, smiled stupidly, and undertook to knit a little blue booty. "Tee hee," she giggled at the needles.

It was some hours and one completed booty later that she realized Ramsludge had never returned from the kitchen. "Honey-poo," she called out. "Sweety-charms? Puddin'-pie? Safflower-meat?"

No answer.

"Tch," she tched, and set her knitting on the end table. As she did so, she noted a kind of finality about the act. It disturbed her. She angled her limbs and branches out of the easy chair and her leaves swayed gently into the kitchen.

Omigosh! Omigosh! Omigosh!!

The upper half of the Dutch door leading out to the patio was open, and there were vault marks on the linoleum!

He'd done it!

Ramsludge was gone!

He was free! He'd escaped!

And though Remarka could not know this, in the few hours since his mad dash out of the neighborhood, he'd changed his name to Oralong Haymountain, obtained two oil company credit cards, a Master Charge, and a marriage license and was already over his head in debt again.

Remarka cried, but only for a little while. When she'd exhausted her tear ducts for the evening, she put Helen Reddy on the stereo, and told herself she was strong, she was invincible, she was a woman, not a dwarf elm.

And that's that.

SURPRISE TWIST ENDING: Oralong Haymountain is now known from coast to coast as the man who planted an atomic bomb in the Internal Revenue Service office in Blunderbuss, Vermont, and failed to escape before it detonated. Authorities found his charred molecules tangled in a roll of red tape. Remarka wasn't very happy, either, but her life lasted longer, and she collected Ramsludge's insurance and social security when she turned sixty-two

"Okay, class, now let's analyze the preceding story," says the professor. "I think we can all agree that its literary merit is nil, and thus our approach must be from a psychological viewpoint. Any objections?"

The class shakes its head.

"Good. Then let us proceed. We have here the product of an extremely hostile individual with readily apparent paranoid tendencies. But he is more fearful than angry, more humiliated than vengeful. He can only conceive of escape from a given unpleasant situation. Coping behavior, like communication, requires too great an expenditure of energy. Now, how can we deduce these facts?

"First, ecce icky homo! Behold the icky man! His name perfectly encapsulates his character. 'Ramsludge,' he is called. The strong, masculine—but significantly sheepish—first syllable, coupled with the concept of slime, waste, and unpleasant odors. The writer feels that the male in this society is like a sheep who is allowed to live only so long as he can be shorn. Then he's slaughtered for chops. Obviously, the author also feels both compassion and propinquity with and to his beleaguered protagonist. Do we agree, class?"

The class nods.

"The last name, too, is symbolic, being that of an early American literary figure, now hopelessly outdated, and also that of a tree, which, again surely not coincidentally, is how both author and protagonist view the female. Got that?

"Plodding odiously onward, we find Ramsludge engaged in a conversation with income tax forms, loan forms, insurance forms, etc. We can, I think, infer from this pathetic presentation of the male the author's own attitude toward bureaucracy. There is clearly antipathy extant 'twixt the writer and officialdom. Doo-wah!

"The woman is a stereotypic pre-liberationist caricature, toward whom the author also harbors hostilities. He compares her with a tree, or more accurately a shrub, which takes root and vegetates in one place. Yet she mockingly growls his name, as if to say, 'haha hoho and heehee, I dare you to come and transplant me, tiger.' So, like her analog the tree, her unquestionably superior strength lies in her relatively immovable nature. Obviously, she perceives the hawthorne as crowding out the dwarf elm, eating up all the nutrients in the soil, and she wants the larger, hungrier tree to die. The hawthorne, of course, concedes. The home is her turf. He runs away. Any questions, class?"

The class raises its hand, and the professor nods in its direction.

"Are your suggesting, sir, that the author's theme might be the irreconcilable differences between the sexes?" inquires the class.

"I'm suggesting that this clown doesn't believe two hairless apes can inhabit the same clucking planet if one of 'em happens ta be him!

"See, once he makes his big, dramatic exit, class, he proceeds to embroil himself in the same stupid woes he suffered during his marriage to Remarka. Ultimately, he even blasts himself ta kingdom come! The guy's worse than a born loser—he's a rat who only knows how ta run one maze. He stands in terror of his life pattern, but that's all he does—stands! An' that's where his tree-ness comes inta the picture!"

"Are you saying, Professor Howard, that one can emancipate him or herself from these constricting, stationary positions?"

A shot rings out. The professor lurches backward, hands rising instinctively to his chest. He falls forward onto the classroom floor. The class, horrified, springs from its seat to the professor's side.

The professor looks into the face of his class, winks, and says with a chuckle: "They missed. Does that answer yer question?"

The class, bewildered, shuffles out of the room just as the bell rings.

"By the way, class," says the prof, standing now, brushing the bullet fragments from his gown, "your assignment for tomorrow is ta write a fan letter ta the jerk who wrote that story, an' set 'im straight in time for next issue! Dismissed!"

FLUKE!
MORE OUTRAGED MARVELITES
LEVI
MARKET-PLACE
OUTRAGED MARVELITES
TYPIST
GERBER STRAINED BRAINS
"THIS'LL TEACH YOU TO FEED US PABLUM!"
NASSER / austin
GERBER STRAINED BRAINS

FOR: HOWARD THE DUCK

Dear Steve,

Just finished reading HTD #16, and I'm afraid my reaction to your noble experiment is somewhat ambivalent. I admire your daring, your dedication, and your determination to innovate. But frankly, I don't care much for your writing. If Edison's experiments had worked out as badly as this one, I'd be penning this letter by gaslight.

Still, since I am a HOWARD THE DUCK fan, and since I realize that you'd never be insane enough to attempt this sad sort of charade again, let me enumerate some of the high points of the ish.

Above all, I enjoyed the personal touch in what I assume to be the prologue to the "story." For a change, it's welcome to learn the real circumstances, the particulars behind the euphemism "Dreaded Deadline Doom." We tend to forget that writers like yourself, Marv Wolfman, Len Wein, Doug Moench, Bill Mantlo, Chris Claremont, and the rest of the crew are human beings with finite reserves of stamina. If the other writers push themselves as hard as you do, and I know they do, my admiration for the consistent high quality of Marvel's product is trebled.

I also like Howard's evaluation of the Grand Canyon. It's hard to tell whether he was speaking sarcastically or not (his comment about processed food tends to make think he was), but his estimation of it as the "world's biggest rut" certainly startled me into rethinking my attitudes on the relationship between man and nature.

What I did not like was your self-conscious self-effacement throughout the story. Okay, so maybe you'll never grow up to be another Tom Robbins or Thomas Pynchon. Maybe you are doomed to labor as a "reactionary" writer, in the sense that your material may always consist more of invective than inventiveness. But that's no reason to see yourself as a tree that can't take root! Come on, Gerber! Get with it! How can you wallow in self-pity when HTD is premiering on the nation's newspaper pages this month, and you've finally ejected yourself from the madness of New York and found a warm, dry climate where a professional cactus has just got to grow more prickly than ever?

Back to the high points of the story. I loved the "obligatory fight scene." You've gone a long way toward removing HOWARD from the punch-hit-kill syndrome, but this was the most blatant statement of your position to date. Congratulations. And when is the Las Vegas chorus girl going to get her own book?

Well, I guess that's about it for this time. Wish I could've been more laudatory, but I guess the old maxim holds true: a fill-in issue is a fill-in issue. Too bad. Anyway, I'm still looking forward to the continuation of the Dr. Bong saga next ish. I understand it's dynamite.

So, 'til Howard moults, MAKE MINE MARVEL!

Steve Gerber
Las Vegas, NV 89122

PAR AVION

NEXT ISH: *THE MAN FROM BEVERLY'S PAST! THE POWER OF THE PRESS! THE LADY DUCK WITH THE SILVER TRAY! AND MUCH, MUCH MORE AS WE REJOIN HOWARD AND BEVERLY ON THE MYSTERIOUS ISLAND OF DR. BONG. MEANTIME, JUST PRETEND THIS ISSUE NEVER HAPPENED. YOU HAD A BAD DREAM, THAT'S ALL, AND EVERYTHING'LL BE OKAY IN A SCANT THIRTY DAYS! SEE YOU THEN. Waaaugh!*

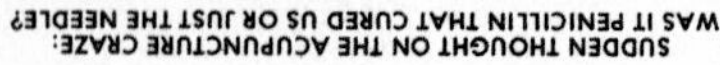

SUDDEN THOUGHT ON THE ACUPUNCTURE CRAZE:
WAS IT PENICILLIN THAT CURED US OR JUST THE NEEDLE?

Ronald Reagan he puts on a great show.
Slapping backs, shaking hands, let's no hate show.
He's brave through thick and thin.
In the end, he does win.
I just saw it last night on "The Late Show!"

Teddy Kennedy, one of the speakers,
Claims that he's not among office-seekers.
By all things 'neath the sun
Swears that he'll never run.
Yet he wears a tuxedo with sneakers!

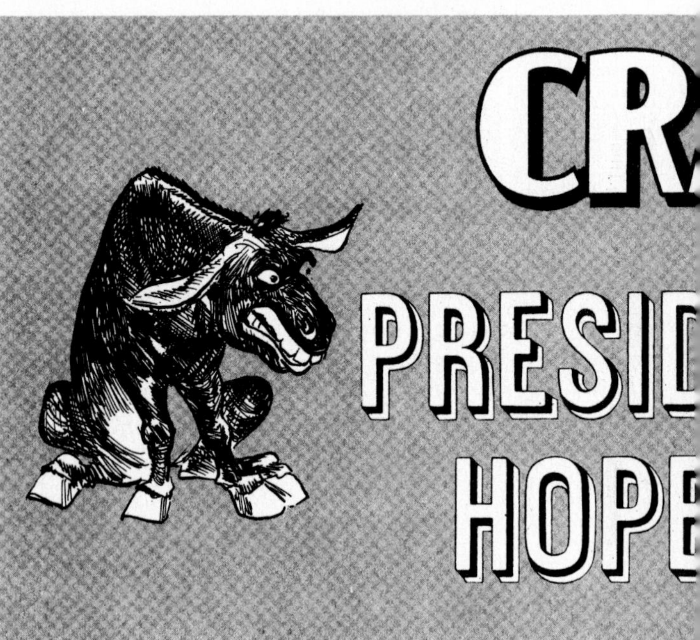

George Wallace, top man in his state,
Says that he'd make a great candidate.
In all kinds of foul weather
Loves when crowds get together.
Get together—but not integrate!

Morris Udall—a candidate classy.
For Environment, he comes on brassy.
Thinks the voters he'll please
By protecting the trees.
He'll get only one vote—and that's Lassie!

From down South came this chap Jimmy Carter.
In New Hampshire, looked like a top-starter.
But in Boston's big race
He fell flat on his face.
Go home and pick cotton—much smarter!

Hubert Humphrey is in a bad panic.
He's so nervous that he's nearly manic.
Wants the President's manse.
What's the odds on that chance?
Like the captain who ran the "Titanic!"

Edmund Muskie is still up in Maine
Gath'ring dust as his chances doth wane.
Queered the top-spot for years
When he burst into tears.
Muskie suffered—but we got the pain!

AZY T 1976 ENTIAL ULS

Writer: Fred Wolfe

Pride of Washington—Henry "Scoop" Jackson
Wins with issues like bussin' and taxin',
Feels the Russians are finks,
And the wheat-deal—it stinks.
And that Kissinger's neck needs an axin'!

The incumbent Republican Ford
Over Reagan he recently scored.
He then offered his prayers.
Came a Voice from "Upstairs"—
"Just like all your talks, Gerald, I'm bored!"

The best candidate? Howard The Duck.
Marvel's hero could win with some luck.
Tho he isn't a human
It would start things a-zoomin'
If the country were run by this cluck!

ATTENTION WORLD: FAY WRAY WAS USING KING KONG TO MAKE BRUCE CABOT JEALOUS!

HOWARD THE DUCK FOR PRESIDENT
GET DOWN, AMERICA!
VOTE HOWARD THE DUCK IN '76
HTD
TE
MARVEL COMICS GROUP
BOX 1827 F.D.R. STATION
NEW YORK, NEW YORK 10022
Forwarding and Return
Postage Guaranteed
Addressed Correction
Requested
BULK RATE
U.S. POSTAGE
PAID
PHILADELPHIA, PA
PERMIT #2190

FOOM
Nº 15
EXTRA-SPECIAL CAMPAIGN ISSUE!
FEATURING: AN IN-DEPTH INTERVIEW WITH STEVE GERBER

This year, the Nation celebrates two hundred years of political quackery by offering its citizens a choice for their leadership from between a Grand Rapids rattletrap and a well-oiled peanut with a roasted-in-the-shell smile.

Well, heck . . . what's another four-year debacle?

We Americans are, after all, a hardy people. We've survived more political and social traumas in the past twenty years than most nations face in a thousand. Korea. McCarthy. The Cold War. The Cuban missiles. Assassinations. Vietnam. Watergate. Campus unrest. Urban unrest. Resthome unrest. And all the rest. We like our sociology spicy.

On the other hand, some of us think we've been living in this bowl of chili too long. Some of us think it's time for a change—not retrogression to some imagined idyllic past, but a brash, bold bump into the future. Some of us who think that way are throwing our support to HOWARD THE DUCK in 1976, because, in the Duck's own words, "I'll throw it right back atcha."

The politics of responsiveness. Ain't it grand?

Well, some of us think it is. And some of us think that you, too, owe it to yourself, your God, your country, and your Great Aunt Jennie to throw your support after our support—good after bad, as it were. Or perhaps pearls after swine. Whatever. It's getting late, and some of us don't think so good in the wee hours of the morning.

Anyway, it's like this. We've got this nifty HTD Presidential Button for sale, see? It's red, white, blue and duck-colored. It measures two inches in every direction except thick. And some of us think you should buy one. If you think so, too, you should send $1.00 plus 25¢ postage & handling for each button you want to HOWARD's campaign headquarters.

And that's not all . . . pilgrim.

If you send another $1.25 to the same address, you've doomed yourself to receive the super-deluxe HTD Campaign Portrait, an 8x10 duck-lover's dream, printed in warm sepia tones on heavy stock, and suitable for framing. It's mailed direct to you in plain brown biodegradable wrapping, suitable for throwing away, after your support.

Use the handy coupon below to order yours. And remember, some of us are watching you!

Okay, Duck-O, shoot the works! Here's the campaign paraphernalia I want:

☐ Official HTD buttons @ $1.25 ea. (incl. pstg).

☐ Official HTD portraits @ $1.25 ea. (incl. pstg).

☐ Mighty bodies with tree-trunk legs and rippling arms @ $229.95 ea. (incl. feet).

Mail to: STEVE GERBER, c/o Mad Genius Associates,
850 Seventh Ave., Room 806, New York, N.Y. 10019

Name ______________________

Address ______________________

City ____________ State ____________ Zip ______

I promise to use my buttons & portrait only in self-defense. Same goes for my body.

The Foom interview:

Steve Gerber

Conducted by
David Anthony Kraft

Articulate, bursting with ideas and opinions, Steve (Baby) Gerber is an absolute wonder to interview – even at 5 o'clock on a muggy Monday morning. He was born 20 September 1947 in St. Louis, Missouri, and graduated from St. Louis University in 1969 with a major in Radio-TV Communications and a minor in Creative Writing. Steve stands six feet tall, has black hair, brown eyes, and is nearsighted ("extremely – which may also account for some of the opinions

expressed in this interview," he admits anxiously.) Despite a pronounced distaste for melodrama in his scripting, he nonetheless persists in living a very melodramatic life. He can't help it; it's an unconscious compulsion. Gerber is also paranoid, and at one point attempted to pass this feature off as an interview with a Life Model Decoy. Gifted with a talent for the weird and offbeat, Steve is the driving force behind that feisty little fowl, Howard the Duck. And now, let's let Steve speak for himself...

FOOM: What kind of childhood did you have?

STEVE: Dull. Well, not *really* dull. I got involved with some pretty strange escapades from time to time. I grew up in a middle-class suburban community, went through the same school system my whole life, lived in the same house from the time I was born until the time I was 22 and married, and then moved into another dwelling. I don't think there was enough instability in the events of my life; any instability was internal. After awhile, with that much sameness in one's existence, if some variety or even some danger doesn't creep in occasionally, and the person is at all a thinking person, I believe he starts to go insane. And, really, that's what happened to me, I think, at some point. I reached a crisis where rebellion became not something fashionable, not something even governed by any particular principles, just something I had to do in order to keep my mind alive. My home had become an anaesthetic, and it was like I was living under that anesthetic, just listening to the voices of my mother and father and brothers and sisters and the television set, which was on constantly, and receiving no new input, so I got involved in the whole hippie culture, but without any deeply-felt commitment. I was a participant/observer, one step back from everything. Close enough to touch, and close enough to get hurt a couple of times, but never fully committed to it. I spent a lot of time in Gaslight Square, which was St. Louis' one-block Greenwich Village, and came in contact with people who were doing drugs and doing the whole flowers and beads thing, and I was involved with the protest against the Viet Nam War. But I was always too academic, too conscientiously critical, to throw myself into it totally. There seemed to be a certain shallowness of philosophy, somehow, and beyond that, even, there was a lot of violence associated with that culture, at least by the time it got to St. Louis in '67 or '68. It was the hippie scene, but it was mixed with the bikers, the Hell's Angels types; also, there was still a decided residue of grease, because St. Louis is kind of a half-breed city. It's sort of Southern, and sort of Midwestern, but it really isn't either. There's a tendency to violence among people in that area of the country, there's no way around that. The easiest way to solve an argument is, y'know, to fight it out, because they don't like to mess with words.

FOOM: Isn't that a correlation to the standard solution in comic book stories?
STEVE: Yeah, it is. It is. I found most of those people, incidentally, to be fascinated with comic books at the time. I loaned my entire *SPIDER-MAN* collection to a houseful of hippies for awhile, and they avidly read through all of them, about a hundred issues.
FOOM: When did you first decide to become a writer — and why?
STEVE: I knew I was going to be a writer, back when I was about five years old, because there didn't really seem to be much else worth doing. That's it. It's the only profession I could think of that looked like it would hold any interest for me.
FOOM: So how did you get into comics?
STEVE: I found out about comic books from watching television. The first contact I ever had with comic books in any form was the *Superman* TV show, and I was utterly fascinated by it. Then, when I found out there were printed stories about this guy, I became interested in those, too, and that led to Batman, and that led to the original Captain Marvel, and that led to about twelve years of reading things, y'know, right up through the first issue of the *FANTASTIC FOUR* and so on. I got into the business as a result of meeting Roy Thomas and corresponding with him for about ten years, off and on, through one of Julius Schwartz's letters pages in an early issue of *Hawkman*.
FOOM: But you're both from St. Louis?
STEVE: Roy's from Jackson, Missouri, which is about 120 miles south of St. Louis, so we saw each other infrequently, and when he moved to Arnold to teach at Fox High School, we saw each other more frequently. Arnold is almost a suburb of St. Louis. And after he went to New York — first to work for National for about a week, and then to Marvel — I came up to visit him for a couple of weeks over vacation the year I graduated from high school. Met Stan for the first time during those two weeks, and then some seven years later I had graduated from college and gone through a couple years of graduate school and was working in an advertising agency — and suffocating — and wrote a letter to Roy that said, "Help! I'm dying. Do something!" It came exactly at the time, luckily, that he was promoted to editor and Stan was appointed publisher, and they were talking about expanding the line greatly. I was taken on as an editorial assistant, and that's how I wound up working in comics.

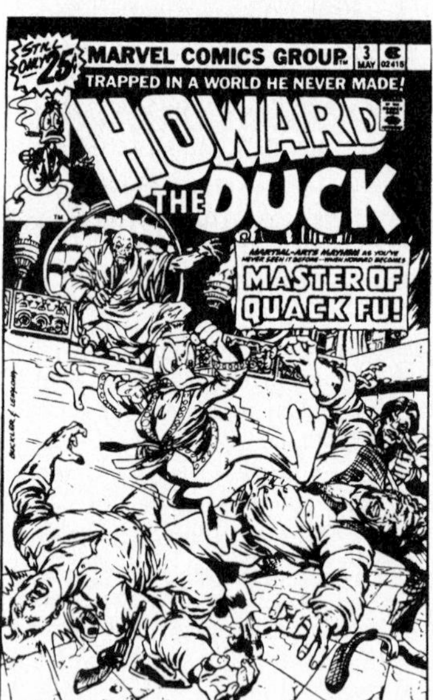

FOOM: Do you have any regrets?
STEVE: Do I have any regrets that I left advertising behind? None. Do I have any regrets that I got into comics? No. Do I have any regrets that I've stayed here this long? Oh, reams and volumes! A lot of things have happened since I've been in the business that I regret, I guess, but it's silly to bother with them. That's passed; I'm more concerned about the future.
FOOM: Who are your influences?
STEVE: Stan. Roy. Gerry Conway was very helpful when I got into the business. In terms of other literary influences, it's very strange, because I didn't read much when I was a kid. I'm reading more now than I ever have at any previous time in my life. So essentially I created my writing style out of my own facility with words. I've been told that it resembles various writers' styles; they seem to be, generally, people who have the same background as myself — Jewish home, middle class, growing up in the 40s and 50s, that sort of thing. I find that interesting, 'cause I have almost really no literary background, despite the fact that one of my studies was English and another was Creative Writing and Communication. I really had very few influences in the past. I'm influenced now by everything I read, and consciously incorporate certain aspects of that input into my work, ex-

perimentally. But there's nobody I can point to, really, as a major influence, except possibly The Beatles. Seriously.
FOOM: Who do you write for — yourself, the fans, or the editor?
STEVE: None of the above. The stories — generally, at their best — seem to tell themselves. I don't ordinarily start with a particular theme or message in mind. I'll begin plotting a story, and it'll take its own direction, and if it's a *good* story, then it'll be written the way it told itself to me, rather than my trying to shape it in any particular direction. Sometimes, of course, there are conscious things you do with structure and with pacing, and that sort of thing, but the actual events of the story and the particular characterizations and things are generally determined by the story or the interplay of the

characters, themselves.
FOOM: Doesn't that mean you please yourself?
STEVE: Well, let's put it this way: When a story presents itself to me that way, it generally pleases me, it sometimes pleases the readers, and it almost never pleases the editors. (Laughter.)
FOOM: Do you feel any sense of moral obligation to the readers of comics?
STEVE: The same obligation I feel to any other human being — not to lie to them. Beyond that — no. Maybe if you defined "moral obligation" more clearly. Do you mean to educate them, or to uplift them, or what?
FOOM: Specifically, then, do you think violence is a necessary part of comics?
STEVE: I think that, yes, actually violence is a necessary part of comics as they're structured today, because, y'know, as I define violence that's the Hulk punching the Abomination in the face or Spider-Man wading into a gang of bank robbers and punching them out and tying them up with webs and leaving them for the police. I mean, we euphemize that and call it "action," because nobody *bleeds* in those sequences. I find the hero/villain aspects the dullest things about any of the books. I've always been much more interested in the interplay of personalities. I do feel — and this gets back to what I said about a moral obligation — that showing somebody being pounded into the ground, and depicting neither combatant suffering pain from it *is* lying, in a sense, and so to that extent, y'know, I think that the same moral obligaion holds.
FOOM: I remember you were having a crisis of sorts, a year ago, about the violence and whether there was anything positive in the comics.
STEVE: I've never completely resolved that crisis. Violence is generally presented as a solution to problems in comics, because, being the illustrated form that they are, they tend to over-simplify, reduce everything to its most basic. Pure

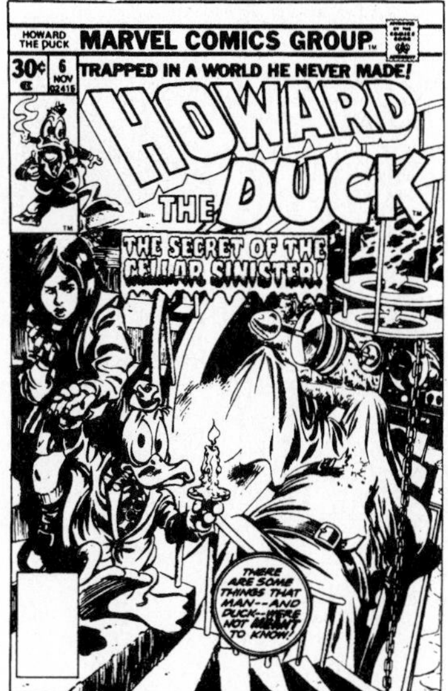

Good vs. Pure Evil, for example, is a conflict which rarely occurs in the real world. It's a set of circumstances that doesn't exist. The way comics are structured now, they teach very positive values and brutal means for achieving them. And readers tend, I think, to take this bizarre lesson seriously, as if it were real. It's why I would prefer, say, to be

doing a strip like *HOWARD THE DUCK* to a strip like ... well ... I could say Spider-Man, but even my own character, *OMEGA*, because with the duck there's a certain amount of unreality presupposed. The creature himself is unreal, and so you can forgive certain other reductivist and retrograde tendencies of the medium. The problem with a strip like *OMEGA*, where the characters are at least pretenses at reality, is that you can never go far enough, you can never show how filthy those streets are in Hell's Kitchen, you can never show the dope dealers in the corridors of the school that James-Michael attends, because the code won't allow it; you can't show what would really happen to somebody if they got beat up as badly as John was beaten up by Nick and his hoods, because even though those kids

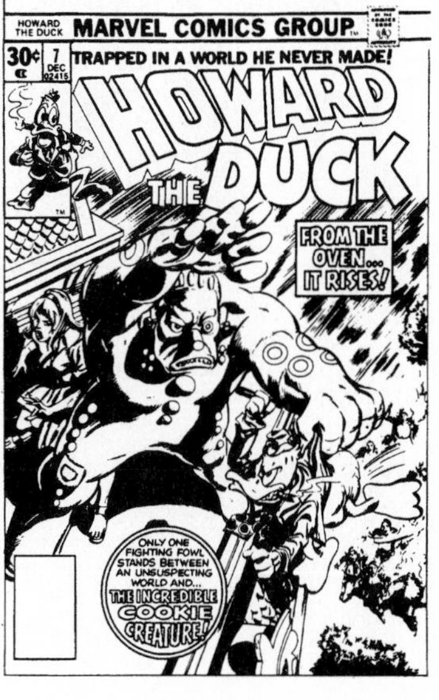

see it every day, it's simply not allowed because it's not "within the bounds of good taste."

FOOM: Are you reaching for anything beyond commercial success with your comic writing?

STEVE: I question your wording there, because I don't think I'm reaching for it; I think I would like to achieve it, but it's not conscious effort most of the time. There are times — like the kung fu story in the Duck book — where I have a particular message I want to get across, and I wanted to do that in a way that would be commercially viable, because I wanted the book to sell and get into people's hands so that they would see the message.

FOOM: Is there anything you think *shouldn't* be depicted in comics?

STEVE: No. Absolutely not. I don't think there's any aspect of life that people shouldn't know about. Ignorance is not bliss. Ignorance is a trap; the less you're aware of, the more easily you can be deceived and seduced. I don't think there's *anything* that shouldn't be presented in comic books, no matter how horrible or, for that matter, how lovely. I wouldn't say comic books should *only* present the negativistic side of things that cannot be depicted presently; there are an awful lot of positive things, too, that we can't show in comic books.

FOOM: Do you find that the production schedules allow for a proper gestation period?

STEVE: Sometimes, yes, and sometimes, no. Sometimes a story will come to you in five minutes, and other times it takes five weeks. In the first case, of course, they allow for it; in the second case, they don't. Sounds like I'm equivocating on every question you ask. (Laughter.)

FOOM: How was Howard the Duck created?

STEVE: As a joke. It was the only sight gag I could think of to top Korrek jumping out of the jar of peanut butter in *FEAR #19*, I told Val to have a duck come waddling out of the bushes. I didn't mention the cigar; the cigar was Val Mayerik's creation. So was Howard's clothing. I just told Val, "Don't make him look too much like Donald, and for God's sake, don't dress him in a sailor suit." Because I included Howard's dialogue for that particular sequence of panels — "Clam up, buddy, you don't know what absurdity is," etc. — I think Val drew the kind of duck who might deliver that line. That's where the cigar came from, and that's where the kind of tacky suit and the rumpled hat came from, and the minute I saw it, without even knowing what the duck's name was (we didn't name him 'til next issue), I knew we had something more on our hands than just, y'know, a four panel gag or something. He was a very real character from the very beginning, and the easiest one of the characters in that whole sequence of bent-out-of-shape-reality stories to write. It was a good indication there was substance there.

FOOM: Did you abandon Howard at that point, or did you think about him in terms of future stories at all?

STEVE: I was asked to abandon him. They were afraid that the appearance of the duck in the Man-Thing storyline was going to spoil the mood of that book, and so I killed him off about halfway into *MAN-THING #1*. My own feeling was that I wished he could be brought back, but I truly felt he was lost, and I figured the readers would probably not respond to this at all. Everytime you try to do something a little outrageous — or, at least, at *that* time — something outside the normal bounds of Marvel reality, you got letters protesting and saying, "Why are you being silly with our funny books?" (Laughter.) "Don't you know funny books are supposed to be serious!" And this time must have been the exception that proves the rule, y'know. People were taken with him immediately. The office was flooded with letters; there was the one wacko who sent a duck carcass from Canada —

FOOM: Yeah, I remember that.

STEVE: — saying, "Murderers, how dare you kill off this duck?" There was the incident at a San Diego Comics Convention where somebody asked Roy, I believe, who was speaking there, whether Howard would ever be coming back, and the entire auditorium stood up and applauded. Stan was being asked about it everyplace he went on the college circuit. It was decided as a result of those incidents to give Howard another shot in the *GIANT-SIZE MAN-THING* book, as a back-up feature, and the response to that led to his getting his own book.

FOOM: How much of Howard is actu-

First the Defenders, and now — ? (Art by Dancin' Dave Wenzel & Fluffy Duffy Vohland.)

Artistic evolution of a duck: the four faces of Howard.

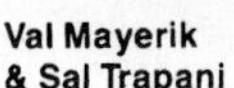

Val Mayerik & Sal Trapani

Frank Brunner & Steve Leialoha

John Buscema & Leialoha

Gene Colan & Leialoha

ally you?

STEVE: Howard is my conscience. It's more like he behaves, generally, the way I would *like* to behave. He's a lot nosier than I am, and a lot more demonstrative, and a lot more sarcastic, usually, than I am. I went through a period like that, I guess, during my college days, but Howard is still like that. A lot more caustic.

FOOM: What's your opinion of the state of comic books today?

STEVE: I think they're atrophying. As things are I think kids are changing, and the books aren't changing nearly fast enough to keep pace with them. We're reaching a very limited segment of people — people who are deeply into a kind of fantasy that bears almost no relation to reality — and I don't think most kids are like that anymore. I think that has a place in their lives, but if you take a look at the changes in children's literature, jesus, they've outdistanced the comics by light years in terms of the subject matter that they're treating. I'm not sure if, according to the provisions of the code, we're even allowed to do a story about a broken home, or about the effects of divorce on a child, or any of the things that really *matter* in a kid's life. If you mention that to many comic book writers now, they look at you as if you're crazy. "That's terrible, that's heavy stuff, the kids don't want to read about that." Well, that's bull, y'know? They're assuming because a story treats a serious subject it can't be entertaining. That assumption indicates to me a too-narrow definition of entertainment, and also (paradoxically, when considered in terms of this medium) a lack of imagination as to how those subjects could be treated. I think there's very little imagination in comics right now.

FOOM: Whose fault do you think that is?

STEVE: I don't think anybody gets off clean on this. The code has a lot to do with it. The fear of the publishers to enact changes in the code or abolish it altogether. The limitations of the writers, most of whom are really not educated in the learning processes of children. And, of course, everybody for that same failure of imagination — for not being able to see how something like that could be accomplished.

FOOM: You keep mentioning children. Do you think the readership consists of children?

STEVE: Primarily, I know it does. Children and adolescents. I mean, of course, there are older readers, but there again, I'm afraid a very specific and limited kind of older reader. We tend to attract the same sort of readers who become Trekkies and Satanists. That's a gross over-generalization, but I sometimes worry that very few of our older readers are what could be called — *normal.* By the same token, I don't want to give anybody the misimpression that *I'm* normal. I think it's okay to be crazy. I think very few people, really, in 20th Century America aren't *slightly* neurotic, in some fashion or another, and I'm not even sure that the most common neuroses are the best, *ie* that what we consider normal is in any way desirable. But what I'm afraid of is that many of the older readers we attract are not just interestingly out of step, or marching to a different drummer, but stumbling around blindly to no beat at all. I'm not *sure* about that — I know it doesn't apply universally — but I think, in large part, it may be true.

FOOM: Don't you think there's a certain amount of the "youth culture" that crosses over from rock music and movies — media freaks, in general?

STEVE: Yeah, and I think those people probably account for the inapplicability of that general statement, but I don't think those people are going to be with us for long, because the innovations are coming too slow. Most of the people in comic books right now were comic book fans, growing up, and I've always had this theory that certain of these people, to a greater or lesser extent, grew up with minds that could be approved by the Comics Code Authority. They could have that seal stamped on their foreheads. They don't understand any of the more complex or sophisticated forms that came into existence in the 60s. Comic books have stayed in the 50s, since the 50s.

FOOM: Exactly what do you *mean* by that?

STEVE: I'm talking about subject matter — *content* — not syle. Stan's method came into effect as a matter of expediency. The whole renaissance in rock

Teen Angel faces off against the fearless fowl in a flight of fantasy by Wenzel & Vohland.

music took place in the 60s, the whole renaissance in film took place in the 60s, there was a whole cultural upheavel. Everything was turned upside down during the decade — except comics, which although they expanded their horizons slightly, mostly because of Stan, pretty much stayed the same in terms of what was acceptable as *subject matter* for comic books. Stan found new ways of treating that old subject matter. He could make an alien race a lot more interesting than the Kryptonians, for example, evolve different kinds of culture and just look at things with a much more cosmic perspective than a lot of the earlier writers could. But there was this incredible change — the whole "psychedelic" thing, for lack of a better word — going on in the 60s that most of the writers of comic books, I'm afraid, because they were so deeply into comic books, as fans, missed entirely.

FOOM: In most other fields, a writer is expected to write from experience, whereas comic book writers...

STEVE: Their primary experience is comics. In fact, that's even true of me to a large extent. What happened was, at about age 15 or 16, I got very fed up with fandom, because I could no longer read the fanzines. They were written in a foreign language, using all sorts of strange abbreviations and truncated forms, and I couldn't tell an LoC from a TBG from an XYZ, after awhile. It was a completely other language, y'know, and when they stopped using English and got into that sort of bastardized argot, I just gave up. I've always had a great loyalty to the English language, even though this interview doesn't show it. Actually, a couple of things *have* changed in comics. For awhile there, until Gerry was instructed to bring Gwen Stacy back into the *SPIDER-MAN* book, we really had people convinced that unexpected things could happen in the books again — that characters *could* die, that the ending of every story was *not* predictable. I think we've since eviscerated that believability again, too; we're right back where we started. In terms of predictability, comic books have reached the stage now where you know, say as on *Star Trek* when Kirk took down Sulu, Spock, and two security guards as part of a landing party, who was going to get "offed." (Laughter.) We're really at that point now, and I think some drastic changes have to be made.

FOOM: Do you think comics are relevant?

STEVE: No, I don't. I use the word relevance in the broadest sense. I don't think they have anything to do with people's lives. I'm not even sure that the comics provide a real and necessary escape anymore.

FOOM: Isn't there a conflict between escapism and relevance?

STEVE: I have never been a big fan of escapist literature, as ridiculous as that sounds. The things I liked about the comics, particularly about Stan's comics in the early '60s, was the fact that by comparison to the Mort Weisinger *Superman* comics of the same era, there

was so much reality. It's what changed the whole shape of the comics industry to begin with — the fact that the heroes began to have personalities, they began to have problems, Spider-Man was enmeshed in an on-going financial crisis. When those elements became commonplace, it seemed like the next step should have been to intensify the reality a little bit. But that never happened.

FOOM: The readers probably expect me to ask your future plans for Howard.

STEVE: I get asked that a lot, particularly at conventions. People really don't understand that I don't have Howard plotted ten issues in advance, and I wouldn't tell anybody what was going to be in those ten issues if I did. I stopped reading *The Comic Reader* when I was a fan, in fact, because I didn't want to know what was happening in the damn books before they came out. Y'know, what's the point of reading them, then? You can just read the synopses, and then put away the books on your shelf, and you don't have to bother with them. Since then, I and several other writers have, I think, wisely refused to give out the endings to any of the stories to TCR. They were upset about that at first, I think, but later came to understand why we were doing it. We wanted to put that element of surprise back in it, even for the fans.

FOOM: What about *OMEGA?* How far in advance do you have that plotted, since it seems to have more of a master structure?

STEVE: It has a definite direction. It does not have incidents plotted out all the way through issue # 100 or anything like that. We know where it's going; we know where James-Michael is going; we know certain things about which characters are going to be introduced into the strip and what part they're going to play. In some ways, it's the most calculated strip I've ever done, and largely that's because of Mary's predisposition toward structure. We know who the teachers are, for instance, that we have introduced into the story. Ruth and Amber were specifically introduced to play off each other in a particular way and create a particular kind of confusion in James-Michael. Richard Rory is going to be coming into the strip — maybe even will be, by the time this interview is published, and he's going to provide the male figure that's been missing from James-Michael's life since his parents were killed. We do know, even though we're probably not going to reveal it for quite awhile, what the relationship between James-Michael and Omega is. So all that stuff actually is "plotted" in that sense. The concepts are all there; exactly how they're going to take shape, I don't know.

FOOM: How do you and Mary Skrenes collaborate?

STEVE: It varies. We plot the books together, generally, just bouncing ideas back and forth off each other. Then, after the panel descriptions have been done, which Mary generally does, either she will sketch in suggestions of dialogue, from which I'll work toward the final

version of the dialogue, or sometimes we just split up the pages and she'll do whole pages and I'll do whole pages. Most of the time I write the captions; Mary is responsible for an awful lot of the dialogue. It's an interesting collaboration. It changes on every issue.
FOOM: How does your present work differ from things you've done in the past?
STEVE: It's a lot better. Have you ever read my Sub-Mariners? (Laughter.) I've gained a certain mastery of the medium since then, y'know. I came into comics, and the first few stories I did—true to the theory of beginner's luck — were not bad, and then by my sixth or seventh story, things really began to get crappy, and stayed that way for about a year while I learned what the hell I was doing. It's been a steady climb ever since then. You can almost date it from the issue Bob Brown took over *DAREDEVIL*. Things have been getting steadily better with occasional, inevitable dips, of course, since then.
FOOM: Do you intend to continue in your present mold, or are you con-

About The Artists:

by Roger Stern

GENIAL GENE COLAN

The only problem with Eugene Colan is that he is just *too* damn good as an artist. Look at a job by Colan — any job — and you will find a degree of professionalism, quality, and style that rivals the biggest guns of the comics industry. The verve and atmosphere of his work shines throughout some eighty issues of DAREDEVIL, over fifty issues of TOMB OF DRACULA, and numerous old IRON MAN, SUB-MARINER, and CAPTAIN AMERICA strips that old-time readers still recall with a wistful smile.

But if Colan is such a great artist, why is it that we so rarely hear his name mentioned when award time rolls around?

Because — like we said — the man is simply *too* good.

A typical letter to a magazine like TOMB OF DRACULA will go on and on about a particular issue's story and subplot developments, and then — almost as an afterthought — will add "Gene and Tom (Palmer) did their usual great job." It's that "usual great job" that has paradoxically stolen some of the limelight which Genial Gene so richly deserves. It's just that readers have gotten so used to getting such a fine quality of art from Gene, that their raves of appreciation have become somewhat tempered with an edge of familiarity. But if his public might be a bit recalcitrant at times about praising his art, Colan's colleagues are far from it.

"I don't believe what that man can do," says long-time DRACULA writer, Marv Wolfman. "Gene's a real miracle worker! No kidding, he can draw anything. I sometimes wish we could shoot the art directly from his pencils, because so few inkers can really do him justice."

"Gene's stuff is really fine," agrees artist Allen Milgrom, "but he's really hard to ink. I mean, I've only done a couple of ink jobs over his pencils — some covers — and I was really only satisfied with one of them. Gene tends to work in tones rather than in lines; he's such a good artist, and he puts so much work into his pencils, that it's really tough to do them justice in the inking. An inker really has to work at it. I personally think that some of Gene's best work is the stuff he's done in wash for the black-and-white magazines."

The quality of Colan's work is something that John David Warner, editor of Marvel's black-and-white magazines, is fully in agreement with. "I've got this BLADE story on file that Gene did himself — and in wash — that's just beautiful, but it sits in the drawer because I don't have a book to put it in. It's really a shame, too, because Gene's stuff *is* so hard to ink, and this wash-job really shows the depth of his work. One of the reasons that TOMB OF DRACULA always looks so great is that Tom Palmer is so successful at translating Gene's pencils to inks with the use of zip-a-tone and a fine pen line."

Just what kind of training goes into the making of such an artist? We contacted Gene at his New Jersey studio for the answer.

"Well, my influences were the usual ones: Alex Raymond, Milt Caniff, and Noel Sickles ... and, of course, Hal Foster. But I got most of my practical training thanks to the late Syd Shores. Syd had a studio, and we turned out work for the old Timely/Atlas line."

It was for that precursor of the present-day Marvel Comics line that much of Gene's early work was produced, although he also turned out work for such companies as Fiction House, Ziff-Davis, Ace, National, and Quality. There was even a story for the late EC comics line. And the work Gene did ran the gamut of everything from science fiction to westerns, from war stories to weird monster stories. Yes, and even to humor and romance comics.

"I always enjoyed the romance stories," says Gene. "They were simple stories — and, sure, there was a lot of formula in most of them — but they were fun to do. For the most part, though, I've always liked the adventure strip. Give me something with a little action to it, maybe even with a little bit of the old mystery or supernatural flavor to it ... like DRACULA."

And certainly, it is his work on TOMB OF DRACULA and on DOCTOR STRANGE for which Gene is most widely known. So, with a background that includes both slam-bang acrobatic super-heroes and the Lord of Vampires — with a reputation for turning out art that has at times been described as moody, brooding, and hauntingly realistic — isn't it just the slightest bit odd for Gene Colan to be delineating the adventures of a cigar-chomping duck?

Perhaps.

"Oh, but I love drawing HOWARD!" exclaims Gene, his normally soft voice becoming insistent. "It's really a kind of off-beat comedy adventure, if you get what I mean. There's all the usual action and excitement of a

templating any big changes?
STEVE: Two answers to that. One, I don't contemplate writing comics forever. Two, I don't want my next strip to be another Howard the Duck. If I do create another comic book series, it's going to be something different, probably totally a 180° polar opposite of Howard. The Howard book and the Omega book debuted at about the same time, and I'm glad that one was a serious series and one was a funny series. (I'm not sure which was which, though.) I don't wanna keep doing the same things over and over again. I don't want people to expect the next Howard the Duck from me. I'm trying, really, to stay one step ahead of the office, and just give them what they don't expect each time. People forget that I live with that duck on a day-to-day basis, y'know, and I almost wish he'd go away and let me alone! (Laughter.) It's like, I love him dearly, but I don't want to spend all my time thinking about it. I'm really more interested in The Next Project now than I am in the duck, in a lot of ways.
FOOM: What is your next project? Do

continued

---

super-hero strip, but with this underlying air of comic relief that's always present."

Or as someone else has said, "I mean, he's a *duck*!"

And as far as Genial Gene Colan is concerned, he's going to keep drawing HTD until they cart him away.

And wouldn't it be something if such a peerless penciler finally got the praise he so richly deserves, thanks to an anthropomorphic fowl?

That would be *too* good to be true.

SURFIN' STEVE LEIALOHA

Night falls in the San Francisco Bay Area, and the fog settles in over the region like a blanket, as a lone figure bends over his drawing board. Carefully, he applies his ink to a series of penciled pages as the clock ticks on. And, while the so-called normal people toss about in their beds, the tall fellow at the board pauses between brush and pen, allows himself to stretch and yawn once or twice, and then — chuckling a bit, perhaps — returns to his work. It is midnight in San Francisco, and Steve Leialoha is inking the Duck.

So how does a tall, bearded young man of some twenty-four summers wind up inking the adventures of America's most fantastic fowl? After all, it's not the most usual form of employment. One might expect him to be occupied by something more prosaic — like, say, playing bass in a rock band. Well, as a matter of fact, although he *does* play bass in a rock band, Steve Leialoha is also possessed by that special sense of wonder that typifies the strange breed of humanity known as comic book people. And, as is the case with many of us folk, Steve's involvement with the medium stems from an old childhood attachment.

As a matter of record, the art of Steve Leialoha first popped into comics-related print back in the mid-sixties in the pages of a couple of New York-based fanzines, *Super-Adventures* and *Stories of Suspense*. (For those of you interested in the "Isn't it a small world?" school of coincidences, both of those fanzines were produced by Marvelous Marv Wolfman.) After several issues of illustrating the escapades of such characters as "Janah the Space Viking," Steve drifted away from the world of fanzines, although he continued to enjoy comics and polish his art. "My influences in those days were mainly Gil Kane and Carmine Infantino," says Steve, "especially when they were inked by Murphy Anderson. Of course, there have been a lot of other influences since then, but those three were the first big ones."

After that early splash in the fanzines, the name of Leialoha was not to be heard of again in connection with comics for nearly a decade — not until the mid-seventies. It was then that the loose grouping of people known as the Marvel Bullpen West came into being. In actuality, Marvel West was just an odd conglomeration of writers, artists, letterers, and other such types who had grown tired of the Big Apple and packed it all off to the somewhat calmer climes of the Bay Area. Of that group, it was Alan Weiss who first encountered Leialoha.

"I had heard about all of these comic book people moving into the area," Steve explains, "and then one day I ran into Al and showed him some of the samples I was working up. He liked 'em, and he told me that I ought to go up and see Jim Starlin."

Starlin, as it happened, was in the market for a good, California-based inker to help in the production of his WARLOCK book. "It's funny! Two strips I'd always wanted to work on were WARLOCK and DOCTOR STRANGE, and there I was, working with Jim on WARLOCK!"

One thing led to another, and when the first issue of HOWARD THE DUCK came out, it was Steve Leialoha who was holding down the honors as embellisher. So what's it like to put the finishing touches on the far-flung adventures of a misplaced duck? "Oh, it has its moments," says Steve. "I really enjoy working with Gene Colan. I've heard other people say that he's a hard artist to ink, but I find his stuff pretty easy, myself. I guess it's all a matter of your point-of-view. His pencils have a lot of gray tones, as opposed to bold line-work, and I like that. As an inker, it gives me a lot of leeway in what I do, and I don't feel so restricted in adding my own touches to it."

As for the future? Well, Steve has some new works planned for Mike Friedrich's STAR*REACH magazine and, of course, there's always music and the band — but what about Leialoha at Marvel?

"Well, it looks like I'll be working with Gene and Marv soon on DOCTOR STRANGE. And ... well, I've always wanted to ink some of Gil Kane's pencils. Now that I'm working for Marvel, I'd like to do that ... even if it's just a cover."

Meanwhile, there's the Duck ... and the fog. And the normal people have no idea just what they're missing!

you plan to diversity in your writing, moving into other fields?

STEVE: I already am, yeah. You know about the book I'm trying to put together on comics. There's a novel I want to write about the comic book business. A collection of short stories I'm working on. I'd like to get back to film, radio and some of the other things. There's the project that Mary, Jim Salicrup and I are working on, *Dione Belmont*. There's another really silly project that I have in mind for anybody who wants it, called *Meatball*. I'm setting up my own production company, although I don't exactly know what Steve Gerber Productions is going to be, yet. We produced the Duck button. I'm thinking about doing an underground.

FOOM: How will your underground work differ from your overground?

STEVE: I was going to say the plots might be more complex, but I'm not really sure about that when I remember that ten-issue *DEFENDERS* "bozos" epic. I don't know if they could get much more complicated than that. The pacing of the stories would probably differ a lot, because I wouldn't have to have a fight scene every three pages. I think there would be a certain freedom of language that you don't have in the code-approved comics, or even in the black-and-whites, and I think that's primarily where it would differ — in the subject matter, the pacing, and the language — because I don't have most of the complaints with the Establishment comics that most of the other underground artists do. It's like, I've found very little of real entertainment value in most of the undergrounds; they tend to be as repetitive in their own way as the overground comics do in theirs. I refuse to say anything about ground level comics. (Laughter.)

FOOM: So, tell me, Steve — what do you do in your spare time?

STEVE: My what? (Laughter.) There's no such thing.

Campaign Bulletin from *Howard the Duck #4*

SPECIAL BULLPEN NOTE:

Marvel Comics has never before endorsed a candidate for office, but now, in this Bicentennial bummer of a year, at this crossroads in the pathway of our nation and civilization, in this impossible era when tumult and social trauma have given way to the mire of mediocrity and monotony...well, it's time to take a stand.

For this reason, we're backing THE candidate with charisma; THE candidate who has no vested interests, owes no favors, and believes all hairless apes were created equal!

WE'RE DRAFTING HOWARD AS A CANDIDATE IN THE 1976 PRESIDENTIAL RACE!

Want to join this burgeoning grassroots movement—and cop yourself a collector's item even Wendell Willkie would be proud to own?

Well, folks, we have a limited quantity of HTD Official Campaign Buttons hot off the presses and ready to unleash upon the public! Each is illustrated in color with the leering face of America's unlikeliest candidate and bears the campaign slogan: "GET DOWN, AMERICA! VOTE HOWARD THE DUCK IN '76!"

To get yours, simply mail $1.00 (plus 25¢ for postage and handling) for each button direct to HTD's campaign manager: STEVE GERBER, % Mad Genius Associates, Room 806, 850 Seventh Avenue, New York, NY 10019. (And make your checks out to Mr. Gerber, okay?)

No, this is not a gag. It's a more-or-less paid political announcement. Order your button now! Today, Cleveland, tomorrow...!

Campaign Bulletin from *Howard the Duck #5*

HTD PRESIDENTIAL CAMPAIGN BULLETIN!

New York, (UDI).——— Though entered in none of the major primaries across the country, the Waddle (ducks don't gallop) Poll shows Howard already several percentage points ahead of President Ford and the entire field of Democratic contenders in a number of key states. The opinion of one Pernell Horowitz, an average Idaho grapefruit grower selected at random from the Boise telephone directory, seems to reflect the mood of the Nation. Mr. Horowitz states, "Shucks, we seen enuff foul play in the White House the past few years. Might as well let a fowl play around with it, an' see what he comes up with, I reckon, woo-woo."

In Washington, a noted radical expressed his approval of the Duck's candidacy, deeming him preferable to the sheep who usually seek the office.

In Honolulu, after meeting in executive session, the usually clandestine Hawaiian Revenge Squad publicly announced its endorsement of Howard. And here in New York, Chinese restaurant entrepreneurs have voted to scratch Mandarin duck from their menues in a gesture of support and respect.

Now, what about you, Mr. John Q. Public, Ms. Average Citizen, you typical American, you?! Isn't it time you joined the crusade for a cleaner, brighter America with no greasy wax build-up? Let's sweep the polls and floors together!

Order your Official HTD For President Button today, by sending $1.00 (plus 25¢ for postage & handling) to Howard's Campaign Manager: STEVE GERBER, c/o Mad Genius Associates, Room 806, 850 Seventh Avenue, New York, N.Y. 10019. (Please make all checks payable to Mr. Gerber. Howard doesn't have a bank account. Sorry: contributions are not tax-deductable.)

GET DOWN, AMERICA!
Vote Howard the Duck in '76!

Campaign Bulletin from *Howard the Duck #6*

HTD CAMPAIGN BULLETIN!!

NEWS FLASH: **To bring you clear, concise coverage of Howard's bid for the presidency, *HOWARD THE DUCK goes monthly as of this issue!* That's right, fowl folk, HTD #7 will be on sale in just thirty days with the first installment of "The Manchurian Duck"—a tale of political intrigue with two desserts.**

* * *

NEWS FLASH: **There's still time to latch onto your Official HOWARD THE DUCK For President button—but believe us, believers, they're going faster than even we ever expected! To get yours, send $1.00 plus 25¢ for postage and handling for *each button* you want to Howard's Campaign Manager:**

STEVE GERBER
c/o Mad Genius Associates
850 Seventh Ave., Rm. 806
New York, NY 10019

For your trouble, you'll receive a genuine brown envelope containing your massive, two-inch-diameter, full-color HTD button and an incredibly sloppy note from Steve on yucchy green paper. (Which reminds us: make your checks and money orders payable to Mr. Gerber.) Give a buck and back the Duck!

* * *

NEWS FLASH: **If you've already received your button and wouldn't mind yet another sloppy note in your mailbox, send a *stamped, self-addressed envelope* to the same New York address for news of HTD Campaign Paraphernalia To Come! (And before you ask: no, we *cannot* return your button in the same envelope! The "handling" part of the postage & handling charge makes it worth some political flunkie's while to *stuff* all those envelopes! Clear?)**

* * *

GOOSE FLESH: **Rumors persist of a Republican/Democratic coalition ticket as a last-ditch measure to halt the Duck's rapid rise to political superstardom. The ticket would offer Gerald Ford as candidate for president, Jimmy Carter as veep, and Ronald Reagan as a new executive branch member, "The Old Ranger."**

* * *

Further bulletins as they break—or in thirty days, whichever comes first! Until then, remember...

GET DOWN, AMERICA!
Vote HOWARD THE DUCK in '76!

Weakly Campaign Update #1, from titles published the 1st week of September 1976

HOWARD THE DUCK Weakly Campaign Update #1

————*Waaaugh,* Mr. & Ms. America and all you folks at sea! Welcome to the first of a series of fragile reports, issued four times a month by mighty Marvel, to keep you informed of the latest developments in our wondrous waterfowl's bid for this nation's highest office. Yes, no longer content to be a big duck in a little pond, Howard is seeking the Presidency of these Untied States! And now from the mountains, the prairies, and the oceans white with toxic foam, here's this week's news roundup!

————According to Mike, Gene, Jon, and Don at *Apache Books* (631 S.E. Morrison, Portland, Ore.), one of our first official HTD local campaign headquarters, the Duck's drive for write-in votes is well underway. Howard received three votes in the Oregon Primary, and at least eleven more politically-weary souls have pledged their ballots for the November election if the two major parties can't come up with anything more inspiring than they've shown us so far.

————Back east, here at Marvel, endorsements are pouring into the office every day, mostly through the ventilator shaft. Perhaps the most surprising pledge of support so far came from Fulvio deBruize, maitre d' at the Brillo Coffee Shop. Fulvio intended for his pledge to pour in, but it was actually *sucked* in—by editor Archie Goodwin, who found it with his straw in the vanilla malt he'd ordered with lunch. Arch was rushed to the nearest hospital on Smilin' Stan's personal dogsled. He's reported recovering rapidly and threatening to vote for Carter if this nonsense doesn't stop at once.

————*The Duck on the Issues!* We asked Howard to take a stand on pollution. Here's his reply: "Stand?! Every time I step outside for a trip to the cigar store, I take a *walk* on pollution! New York isn't an asphalt jungle anymore. Today, even the asphalt is fighting for air from beneath a carpet of broken glass and hamburger wrappers. That wouldn't be so bad, except the air really isn't worth fighting for! If I'm elected, every manufacturer of no-deposit/no-return bottles will take a compulsory course in advanced self-mortification and will be required by law to *eat* every one of those jagged shards in every gutter in America. I'll go a little easier on the hamburger magnates, though—they can get off with just *wearing* their oily wrappers as disposable paper suits. That's what I call recycling!"

————Isn't it time you threw your support to Howard's new species of leadership? You can show the rest of America you care by wearing (a) an oily paper suit or, preferably, (b) the Official HTD Campaign Button! It's yours for just $1.00, plus 25¢ postage and handling for each button, from Howard's campaign manager: STEVE GERBER, c/o Mad Genius Associates, 850 Seventh Ave., Rm.806, New York, N Y 10019. (Make all checks payable to Mr. Gerber. He plans a long vacation in South America after November.) More in seven days!

Weakly Campaign Updates #2-4, from titles published the 1st week of September 1976

HTD WEAKLY CAMPAIGN UPDATE #2:

----Unless you've dwelt in a cave for the past six months and have confined your reading strictly to rare, out-of-print editions of Lin Carter novels, you're probably aware that Marvel's feathered fury, HOWARD THE DUCK, has flung his battered hat into this year's presidential sweepstakes. This lemon-hued rectangle contains the second in our series of feeble reports on our wondrous waterfowl's winding woad to the White House.

---*TRAGEDY STRIKES DUCK CAMPAIGN;* Terre Haute, Ind. (UDI) Danger has become a constant companion to presidential hopefuls, and HTD is no exception. Last week, during the course of a single 30-minute address before the Society of Landlocked Seaweed Enthusiasts here in Terre Haute, *eleven* separate attempts were made to snuff the Duck. Weapons ranged from a letter-bomb skimmed through the air as a paper plane to an exploding cigar with a nuclear triggering device. Ten of these assassination attempts were abortive. The eleventh—involving a bottle of Crazy Glue, a box of Wheat Thins, and an expandable watchband—irreparably scarred one Milos Pitt, a member of the audience. Pitt, already confined to a wheelchair as a result of his participation in the Nixon campaign of '72, found himself directly in the line of fire and unable to dodge. He later commented bitterly, "Sure wish I'd been wearin' one o' them 'Git Down' buttons. Then the watchband would'a bounced right off." Shucks!

---*KRASS KOMMERCIALISM KORNER*: Yes, you can still attach yourself or your clothing to the *Official HTD For President Button* pictured above. The price is $1.00 plus 25¢ postage and handling per button.

----*KRASS KOMMERCIALISM KORNER, Part Two*: If even the button is insufficient to express your fowl ardor, may we recommend our new HTD CAMPAIGN PORTRAIT, produced in association with Magic Mountain Books? Classier than a poster, it's reproduced in subtle sepia on heavy stock, suitable for framing. It, too, is just a buck, plus that inevitable 25¢ for postage and handling. And both the button and portrait are available from Howard's campaign manager:

STEVE GERBER
c/o Mad Genius Associates
850 Seventh Avenue, Rm. 806
New York, NY 10019

(Make all checks payable to Steve; he's still saving up for a copy of HTD #1.) Another report in seven days!

HTD WEAKLY CAMPAIGN UPDATE #3

----With the autumnal equinox now upon us, the campaign trail is beginning to feel the impact of the bombastic bird's web-shodden foot. Reports of growing support arrive daily at HOWARD THE DUCK CAMPAIGN HEADQUARTERS. From DeFuniak Springs, Florida, comes word of a touching personal campaign sacrifice. Mr. and Mrs. R. Walter Sandoz, a local retired couple living on a fixed income, have vowed to live on a diet of grubs, tadpoles, and assorted grains and seeds until election day as a show of support for the Duck. "Heck-fire, a body can't afford to eat like a man with today's prices!" claims Mr. Sandoz. "Might as well eat like a duck! After all, if it's good enough for a presidential candidate, I figure it's good enough for us!"

----*CAMPAIGN MEMORABILIA CLASSICS*: Yes, once election day is past, and the Duck makes his way to that little summer house on the Potomac, you can be proud that you purchased the *Official HTD For President Button.* What?! You haven't yet?! Well, then hurry up and send $1.00 plus 25¢ for postage and handling for your button. You'll be showing your support for the fabulous fowl, *and* you'll be leaving a priceless legacy for your children. (No kidding! Do you know how much McGovern/Eagleton buttons are worth?) And if the button doesn't satisfy your ducky determination enough, then send for our new HTD CAMPAIGN PORTRAIT, produced in association with Magic Mountain Books. Eminently suitable for framing, it also retails for just a buck, plus the usual 25¢ for postage and handling. For your button and/or portrait, make your check payable to Howard's campaign manager:

STEVE GERBER
c/o Mad Genius Associates
850 Seventh Avenue, Rm. 806
New York, NY 10019

And, who knows, maybe Steve will send you a picture postcard from Buenos Aires! More in seven days!

HOWARD THE DUCK CAMPAIGN UPDATE FINAL----Time is short, and so is our space. There's just enough room allotted us for this item:

----*DUCK SUPPORT SWEEPS COUNTRY!* Pie Town, New Mexico (UDI) City Father Harley D. Farnsworth last week declared his full support of the Duck. Speaking before a gathering of the West Central New Mexico Chapter of the Sons of the Sagebrush, Mr. Farnsworth said, "It's about time that this country had a candidate that truly respects the public. There's not a man among us that Howard wouldn't look up to. I say let's put him on a pedestal, and look up to him for a change!"

----For further news on the campaign, on the *Official HTD Button* and related paraphernalia, be sure to catch the next HOWARD THE DUCK letters page. And don't forget to vote!

Campaign Bulletin from *Howard the Duck* #7

WISE QUACKS

c/o MARVEL COMICS GROUP, 575 MADISON AVE. N.Y.C. 10022

HTD CAMPAIGN UPDATE: SPECIAL EXPANDED EDITION

Greetings, Mr. and Ms. America and all you folks at sea. There's good news tonight. But not much. And mostly it concerns the candidacy of Marvel's feathered fury, HOWARD THE DUCK. Now that you've read the story of how he won the All-Night Party's nomination (which actually happened back in August, but comics unfortunately work on a two-month tape delay), here are the latest-breaking developments in Howard's harrowing political career.

——DUCK BREAKS DEVELOPMENT IN NEW YORK; New York (UDI). In a highly unorthodox demonstration of his antipathy toward shoddy, colorless urban redevelopment, All-Night Party candidate Howard the Duck took a vicious swipe at a new high-rise apartment project on the lower east side. The project collapsed. The swipe was taken with a baseball bat and hit a girder on what was to be the ground floor of the structure. Project designer Nils Harbinger was quoted as commenting, "Aw, shucks on ducks!" The city housing administration is investigating the disaster and, according to one unofficial spokesman, hopes to "find room in our tight budget for a bottle of Crazy Glue to help patch things up." To which Howard rejoined, simply: "Waaaugh. What's the use?"

——DUCK OPPOSES CONSTRUCTION OF NUCLEAR POWER PLANT; Fleasville, Ark. (UDI). "We're true ecologists and humanitarians," said engineer Hubert Dunge of his company's proposed plan for energy expansion coupled with population control. "You're sick," replied candidate Duck. And for days the debate raged here in Fleasville over the building a nuclear reactor adjacent to the playground of Our Lady of Unrelenting Sorrows and Vicissitudes Elementary School. "It's perfectly safe," Dunge repeatedly maintained redundantly over and over again. "Why, I'd sleep like a baby at night even if it were built in my backyard." When HTD and a member of the Fleasville City Council offered to sponsor a rezoning measure that would in fact have allowed the reactor's construction on precisely that site, Dunge reneged. "It's perfectly safe, but the noise, on further consideration, *would* keep me awake at night," he admitted. It was later discovered by private detectives that Dunge was expelled from Our Lady... in 1947 for making obscene gestures at his hot lunch. He's craved revenge ever since. Shamefacedly, he acknowledged the truth of the report before a group of outraged parents: "It's true," he said, "but only perfectly safe revenge." The City Council took pity on the long-tortured soul and granted permission for construction of the reactor. To which Howard replied, simply: "Waaaaugh. What's the use?"

——THE DUCK ON THE ISSUES! We asked Howard what he would do, if elected, to solve the problem of unemployment. He replied: "You want the plain, unvarnished truth? The unemployed in this country are just plain lazy — and I *respect* them for it! It takes guts to resist the societal pressure to entrap oneself in a meaningless, boring, socially-unproductive nine-to-five automaton existence. Especially in *this* world, where the first question everybody's conditioned to ask is, 'What do *you* do?' The problem isn't unemployment — it's how to provide you hairless apes with a more convincing rationale for spending half your waking lives battling tedium just to make somebody else rich. Personally, I hope we never succeed in formulating that nifty nugget of persuasion."

——THE DUCK ON THE ISSUES, SHORT TAKES! Fearlessly sticking his beak where other candidates fear to snap, the Duck has made these biting comments. *On the reunion of the Beatles:* "I say fiddle-faddle to the critics who think the four moptops can never live up to their public's expectations. It's an artist's duty to extend his audience's expectations, not merely fulfill them." *On the Middle East:* "I think the U.S. and the Soviet Union should arm both sides with water pistols and let 'em squirt each other to death with oil. As for these hijackings, they've got to stop. Not only are people getting killed, nobody gets to see the end of their in-flight movie anymore." *On Crime in the Streets:* "I'm in favor of licensing muggers, pushers, and all criminals and taxing their profits. Why should the poor middle-class slob be taxed for what's lifted from his pocket?" *On the Ultimate Future of Humanity:* "Waaaaugh. What's the use?"

——CAMPAIGN FUNDING DEPT.: A limited number (roughly equivalent to the annual yield of peanuts in Plains, Ga.) of *Official HTD Campaign Buttons* is still available. Wearing this button will (a) show your support for HTD to the vast majority of Americans who only look at the pictures; (b) get you on half-a-dozen government Enemies Lists; (c) probably improve your love life, but the test results aren't final yet. The button is red, white, blue, and duck-colored, and measures two inches in every direction except thick. You can obtain yours by mailing $1.00, plus 25¢ for postage and handling per button, to the address below.

——CAMPAIGN FUNDING DEPT., *Part Two:* And here's another fine feathered collector's item for you, produced in association with Magic Mountain Books. The *Official HTD Campaign Portrait*, printed in warm, comforting sepia tones on heavy 8″ x 10″ stock, suitable for framing. No patriot's bedroom wall is complete without one. It, too, is just $1.00, plus the inevitable 25¢ per for postage and handling. And you can get it (and/or the button) by writing to Howard's Campaign Manager:

STEVE GERBER
c/o Mad Genius Associates
850 Seventh Ave., Rm. 806
New York, N Y 10019

(Please make all checks payable to Steve. Otherwise, he'll be unable to afford that ambassadorship to Rhode Island when Howard wins.)

——*NEXT ISSUE:* The Nation jumps aboard the HTD Bandwagon, 'cause it's playing our song. Did you know Benjamin Franklin wanted our national bird to be the turkey? See you in thirty days, indigenous ones!

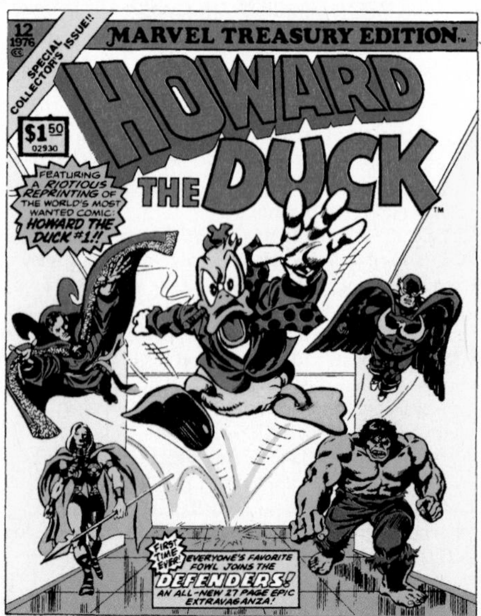

Campaign Bulletin from *Howard the Duck #8*

* * *

HTD PRESIDENTIAL CAMPAIGN UPDATE FINAL

News Flash: DUCK FEVER SWEEPS NATION; MASS IMMUNIZATION PROGRAM PROPOSED. Washington, D.C. (UDI)---Fench Q.T. Hargrove, vice-deputy assistant undersecretary of the Food and Drug Administration, announced today that the FDA would undertake a nationwide innoculation program to halt the epidemic spread of "duck fever." The malady, also known as "Howard's Disease," infests the brains of voters and painfully heightens their sensitivity to absurd political rhetoric. As a result, the spokesman said, "Voters are turning away from Jimmy Carter and President Ford in droves. The disease represents a clear and present danger to the complacent existence of our two-party system." The FDA suspects the disease may be of extraterrestrial origin. Federal microbe hunters are furiously seeking to isolate the virus and destroy it utterly by November 2nd.

News Flash: DUCK PADDLES AHEAD IN STRAW VOTE. New York (UDI)---Although Ford and Carter have made significant gains since the start of the campaign—almost all registered Democrats now favor Carter and three of the four registered Republicans have pledged their support to Ford—HTD has retained his hold on the independent vote. The Waddle Poll therefore expects Howard to carry 49 states; the exception is Wyoming, where there are so few people that chickens are allowed to vote. "Only half the population *eligible* to vote bothers to *register,*" the Waddle report read, "and the established parties comprise barely half of those registered. So we have a situation where 25% of the electorate selects the candidates between which the full 100% are expected compliantly to choose. Voters now seem to comprehend that this is ridiculous and are flocking to Howard as an alternative to a bizarre form of oligarchy."

The Waddle Organization cautions, however, that its poll was conducted before the Bathtub Scandal came to public attention. How will this incident affect the Duck's chances? The report soberly concludes: "Gee whiz, anything could happen now! Golly!!"

Noose Flash: DUCK CAMPAIGN TREASURY AT ALL-TIME LOW; CAMPAIGN MANAGER EMBEZZLING FUNDS, CLAIMS HTD. New York (UDI)---Howard the Duck today accused his campaign manager, Stephen R. Gerber, of embezzling funds from the sale of Official HTD FOR PRESIDENT BUTTONS and CAMPAIGN PORTRAITS of the Duck. Gerber claims that the buttons—resplendent in four-colors, two inches in diameter, and redolent of printer's ink—were his property; as were the 8x10 sepia-tone portraits, produced in association with Magic Mountain Books. When pressed to substantiate this claim, Gerber angrily sputtered, "Besides, that villa on the Riviera was too big a bargain to pass up." Asked if these campaign items were still available to the general public, Gerber seemed to relax somewhat and replied, "You betcha! And they're just $1.00 each, plus 25¢ postage and handling per item from *me*:

STEVE GERBER
c/o Mad Genius Associates
850 Seventh Avenue, Room 806
New York, NY 10019

But hurry if ya want 'em before election day. And supplies are running out fast!."

Speaking of running out, this reporter later learned that Gerber had purchased either a one-way ticket to the south of France or a Greyhound See-America pass from a scalper outside the McCartney and Wings concert at Madison Square Garden last summer. Draw your own inevitable conclusions.

GET DOWN, AMERICA!
Vote HOWARD THE DUCK in '76!

Campaign Bulletin from *Howard the Duck #9*

HTD PRESIDENTIAL CAMPAIGN ROUNDUP: It was a good fight, ma. Unfortunately, they creamed us. But it was a battle to remember...which is why we're hard at work even now preparing a special sort of *souvenir* of the campaign. You'll be hearing more about it in the next month or so. Meanwhile, we still have a few OFFICIAL HTD FOR PRESIDENT BUTTONS left and we figured we'd offer 'em up once more, just as a sentimental gesture, before they become overpriced collector's items. You can still get yours for just $1.00, plus 25¢ per button for postage and handling. Likewise, the HTD CAMPAIGN PORTRAIT is still available. Same price. Same address: *STEVE GERBER, c/o Mad Genius Associates, 850 Seventh Avenue, Room 806, New York, NY 10019.* And that's all the pep talk for this issue. Frankly, we're poor losers and since we can't say anything nice about the other candidates, we'll just clam up. Nuts to you. Grumble, grumble, gnash, gnash, waaaugh.

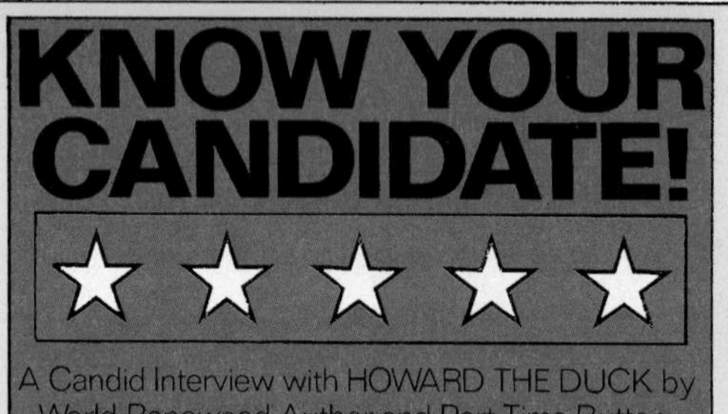

KNOW YOUR CANDIDATE!
A Candid Interview with HOWARD THE DUCK by World-Renowned Author and Part-Time Button Magnate STEVE GERBER

STEVE GERBER: Once they've read this *Marvel Treasury Edition,* Howard, your fans and potential supporters should be fairly conversant with the history of your exploits. But today's voter is interested in more than a candidate's record.

HOWARD THE DUCK: Yeah. I know. They want all the intimate details of their personal lives. Whaddaya think — I've never read *Celebrity* magazine?!

SG: Skip the sarcasm, okay? And let's take this opportunity to let the voters get to know you as a person.

HTD: But I'm *not* a person, you yo-yo! I'm a duck!

SG: Whatever. Let's start with a simple question that should lend some insight into your personal — into the real you, that is. Why do you want to be president?

HTD: All the standard reasons. Your power. Your fame. Your niche in history. But mostly it's the salary. See, I'm currently unemployed, and 200 grand a year would fill the void nicely. Especially with four years' free rent tossed in to sweeten the deal.

SG: Practical, material considerations are your primary motivation, then. Would that same orientation be reflected in a Duck Administraton as well? Would you govern the country pragmatically?

HTD: Shucks, no. Deep down, I'm a cockeyed optimist. I took a course in motel management once. I'd run the country that way — like everybody's name was Smith.

SG: Could you be more specific?

HTD: No.

SG: Oh. Well then, let's talk about your qualifications for office. What's the extent of your political experience?

HTD: I used to work in a loan company branch office.

SG: Apparently that's meant to imply something, but —

HTD: I sold used cars for a while, too.

SG: That's quite an impressive resume, but we seem to be digressing ...

HTD: I distinctly heard you say you wanted to probe the *real me.* Well, that's it. Basically, I'm just as dull as the next nine-to-five automaton. You gotta remember, back where I come from, bein' a duck is nothin' exceptional.

SG: Yes, but even so, I can't picture a fellow with your sardonic bent plodding away at a workaday job.

HTD: How true, how true. I never kept one job more than three an' a half weeks. Which is another advantage of the presidency. They can only fire ya for high crimes an' misdemeanors. That stuff, I don't pull. I just mouth off a lot.

SG: Maybe we'd better steer this discussion toward your positions on the issues.

HTD: Yeah. Let's.

SG: You've expressed dismay at certain trends in popular culture, particularly the glorification of the rogue and the glamorization of violence. Are we to infer from this that you'd advocate some form of media censorship?

HTD: You gotta be kidding! Ya don't eliminate garbage by turnin' it into a black market commodity, an' ya don't elevate tastes by gagging writers an' artists. Look, there's nothin' wrong with makin' heroes outta non-conformists. I'll even admit to a rebellious streak myself. It's just — at the risk o' soundin' pompous — what seems to distinguish *today's* anti-hero from yesteryear's is the former's willingness to callously exploit other people to achieve his own independence from the system. It's the difference between a poet an' a vulture, basically.

SG: That's pretty heavy.

HTD: Yeah. Nearly collapsed under its own weight, didn't it?

SG: I mean, do you think the American public is ready for that degree of subtle reasoning from its president?

HTD: They better be. If you turkeys can't even think *that* deep, this nation's *had* it!

SG: We seem to be gingerly approaching the core of your political philosophy, Howard. You want human beings to *think.*

HTD: Yeah, well, I know it's askin' a *lot* from a hairless ape, but ...!

SG: Realistically, how do you assess your chances for winning the November election?

HTD: Chance, schmance. I'm no gambler. Barring unforeseen factors, it's in the bag.

SG: And should some such factor arise ...?

HTD: I wish ya luck unloadin' those "Get Down America" buttons, pal.

SG: Thank you, Howard the Duck.

HTD: You're welcome, Steve the Teddybear. Now g'wan — beat it!

UNSOLICITED TESTIMONIALS

A glittering gallery of Marvel Super-stars explain in their own words why HOWARD THE DUCK gets their votes in 1976

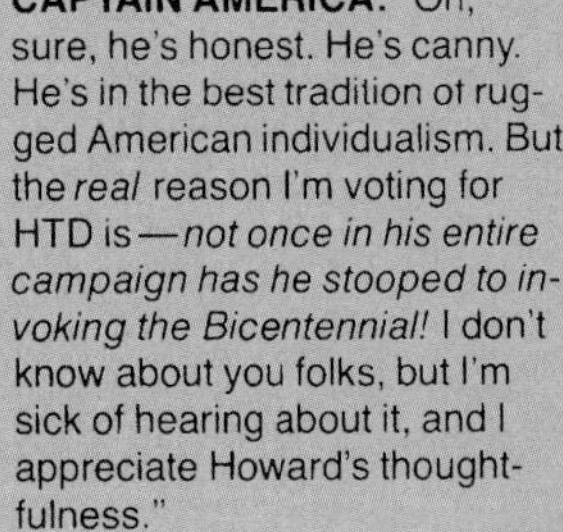

CAPTAIN AMERICA: "Oh, sure, he's honest. He's canny. He's in the best tradition of rugged American individualism. But the *real* reason I'm voting for HTD is—*not once in his entire campaign has he stooped to invoking the Bicentennial!* I don't know about you folks, but I'm sick of hearing about it, and I appreciate Howard's thoughtfulness."

IRON MAN: "He's got a heart of gold and nerves of steel. And he promised Tony Stark that my armor would be tax-deductible as a business expense if he's elected."

BENJAMIN J. GRIMM (a.k.a. The THING): "He smokes a mean stogie. That's good enuff fer me! Go clobber 'em, feather-puss!"

THE MIGHTY THOR: "When thou lookest upon yon slate of candidates, then wilt thou see, with eyes moistened by sorrow, that thou truly hast no choice."

THE INCREDIBLE HULK: "Hulk likes little duck! Duck is Hulk's friend! Vote for duck or Hulk will smash your face!"

DR. STEPHEN STRANGE: "If politics be 'the art of the possible,' then praise the Vishanti we have a candidate who has seen the worlds within worlds and knows for certain—*all things* are possible."

DAREDEVIL: "My super-hearing has been attuned to his heartbeat from the start of the campaign, so I can guarantee—he'll never lie to you."

LUKE CAGE, POWER MAN: "Listen, I work for a livin', see, so I'm runnin' with the candidate who's gonna help feather my nest—Mr. H.T. Duck, not some jive turkey, you dig?"

STAN LEE: "I graciously bowed out of the presidential race this year—so besides Howard, who's left, true believer?"

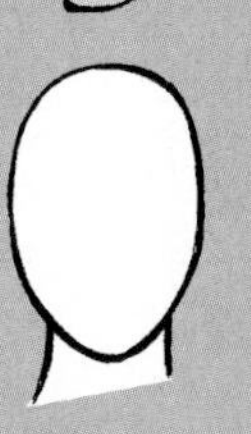

YOU, MARVELITE: It's not enough that Howard has the support of these far-famed fighters for truth and justice, folks. He needs *your* backing, too! That's why we're making this last, unbearably pathetic appeal not only for your vote—but your hard-earned bread as well!

The *OFFICIAL HTD FOR PRESIDENT CAMPAIGN BUTTON,* pictured atop this page is still available. It's printed in full color, measures two (count 'em, two!) inches in diameter, and comes complete with its own pin! What's more, it looks even better decorating your body that it does on this page—that's a campaign promise!

To order yours, rush $1.00, plus 25¢ for postage and handling per button, to Howard's Campaign Manager:

STEVE GERBER
c/o Mad Genius Associates
850 Seventh Ave., Rm. 806
New York, NY 10019

We should also mention that the *OFFICIAL HTD CAMPAIGN PORTRAIT,* an 8 x 10 sepia-tone poster printed on heavy stock and suitable for framing, is available from the same hungry writer at the same address for the same price: $1.00, plus 25¢ postage and handling per portrait. And it's a beauty.

Which leaves but one thing left to be said:

GET DOWN, AMERICA!

Vote HOWARD THE DUCK in 1976!

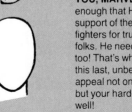

HOWARD THE DUCK COVER CAMPAIGN!
GIANT-SIZE MAN-THING
MARVEL COMICS GROUP
TRAPPED IN A WORLD HE NEVER MADE!
HOWARD THE DUCK
FIRST ISSUE
SPIDER-MAN!
GET DOWN, AMERICA! VOTE HOWARD THE DUCK IN '76
HOWARD
GET DOWN, AMERICA
GIANT-SIZE MAN-THING
THREE FACES OF
YES, WE KNOW HOWARD DOESN'T APPEAR ON THE GIANT-SIZE MAN-THING COVERS. BUT SINCE THOSE ISSUES ARE NOW A DEFINITE PART OF THE DUCK MYTHOS, WE DIDN'T WANT TO DENY ANYONE A GANDER AT THEM. JUST ONE MORE MIGHTY MARVEL PUBLIC SERVICE.

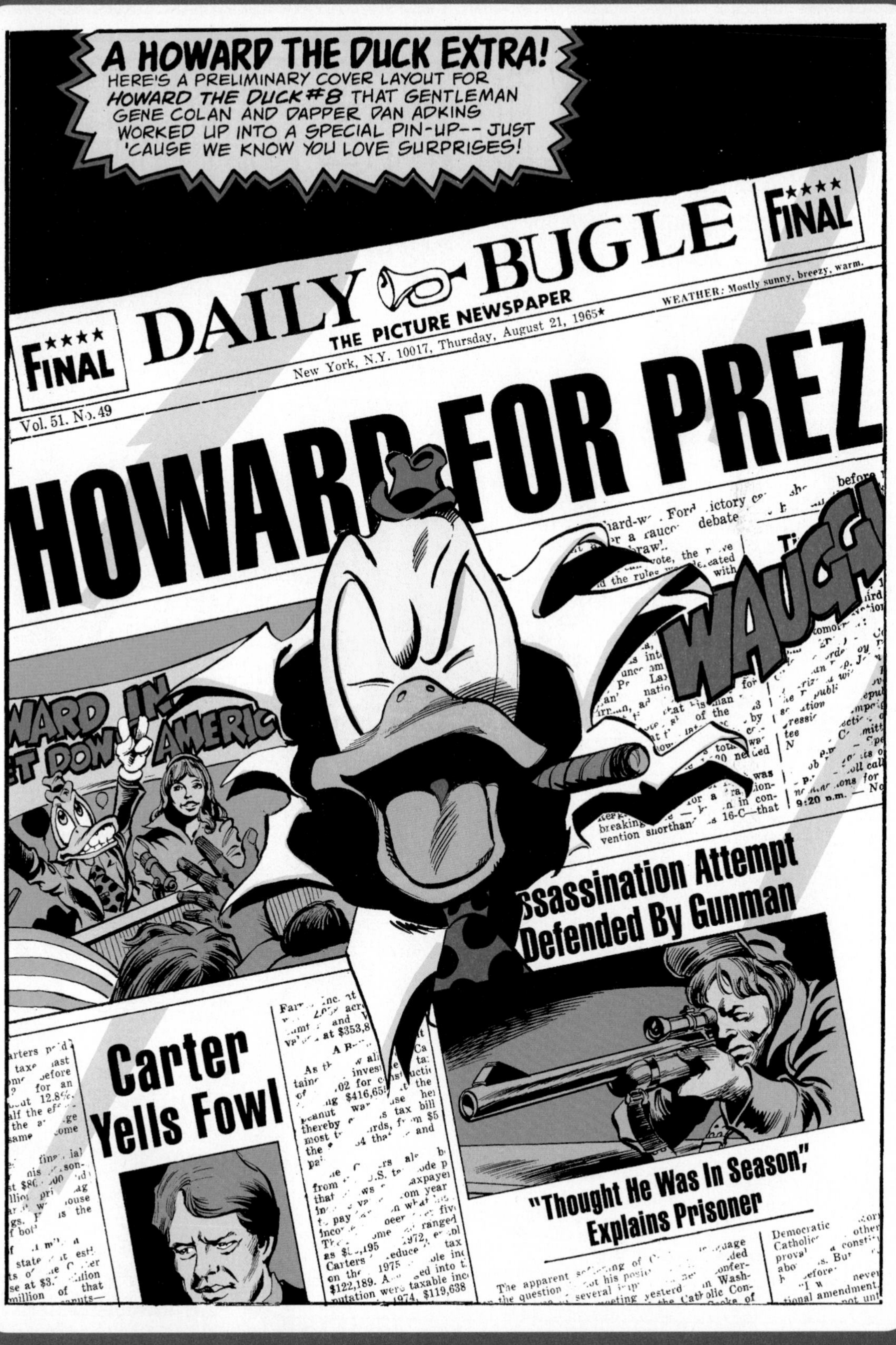
A HOWARD THE DUCK EXTRA!
HERE'S A PRELIMINARY COVER LAYOUT FOR HOWARD THE DUCK #8 THAT GENTLEMAN GENE COLAN AND DAPPER DAN ADKINS WORKED UP INTO A SPECIAL PIN-UP-- JUST 'CAUSE WE KNOW YOU LOVE SURPRISES!
FINAL
DAILY BUGLE
THE PICTURE NEWSPAPER
WEATHER: Mostly sunny, breezy, warm.
New York, N.Y. 10017, Thursday, August 21, 1965★
FINAL
Vol. 51. No. 49
HOWARD FOR PREZ
WAUGH
Assassination Attempt Defended By Gunman
"Thought He Was In Season," Explains Prisoner
Carter Yells Fowl

Marvel Treasury Edition #12 reprinted Howard's first appearance, ***Fear* #19**, with a new 1.5-page opening sequence by Steve Gerber and Val Mayerik.

VOICE FROM ON HIGH: All right, Howard, cut the whining and get on with the synopsis! You have our complete assurance---

HOWARD THE DUCK: Fie on your assurance! You figure I'm gonna settle for a verbal commitment from some disembodied entity I can't even *shake hands* with?! Get off!

VFOH: All right, if that's the way you want it. But it's the *readers* who'll suffer, Howard, not we. We *published* the story. We know it by rote.

HTD: Tryin' ta play on my sympathies, huh? Well, fergit it! I'm no bleedin' heart! Either cough up the cold, hard cash or I keep mum, see?

VFOH: Whatever you say. We can't *force* you to talk. So we'll simply have to narrate the story ourselves. (ahem) As a result of this Duck's flagrant stupidity, the world almost came to an end when---

HTD: Waitaminit! I was a victim, not---

VFOH: Oh? Really? Well, according to *our* records it was all your fault.

HTD: That's a lie! There was this wacko from another dimension who called himself the "Overmaster", see? An' by jiggling the *cosmic axis* around, he caused various planes of reality ---alternate universes--- to meet tangentially. And every time any two o' those worlds *touched,* see, somebody'd blink out of his own reality and into another! That's what happened to *Korrek,* my balmy barbarian buddy--- he blinked outta his home world of Katharta and landed in a jar of peanut butter on earth!

VFOH: Of course! And that's also what befell Jennifer Kale and Dakimh the Enchanter and Man-Thing. Well, that's the story, folks---

HTD: No! No. NO *NO!!* Cripes, Jennifer was an earth-kid who had a sorta natural aptitude for magic. So Dakimh took her to his world as his apprentice--- to help 'im untangle all these jumbled realities. Man-Thing, well--- he lived (if ya can call that livin') in the Everglades, which just happened to be the *nexus point* of all realities! Got that? Yeesh!

VFOH: Mmmm. Then Man-Thing, obviously, was the organizer of the *Congress of Realities* mentioned in the story, so---

HTD: You *sure* you published this story? Listen, pal, the villain of the piece was that "Overmaster" character, who turned out to be *Thog the Nether-Spawn,* ruler of Sominus, which roughly corresponds to Hell ---or maybe New York City--- in this here cosmology. Clear?

VFOH: Clear. So we're joining the story in progress, right? At the moment just before you made your famous entrance.

HTD: Right! For once! Now, any more brilliant questions?

VFOH: Just one. How are you getting home?

HTD: Waaaugh.

Alternate versions of *Marvel Treasury Edition #12*'s front & back covers

STEVE GERBER

How does a man end up writing dialog for a duck?

Steve Gerber claims that Howard was an accident, that the Man-Thing story he first appeared in demanded such a character, a topper as it were to the insanity that preceded it. We know better. We know that Steve Gerber is not accident-prone.

He *is* mad. Totally.

He *is* paranoic. He won't go into a trance unless he's sure nobody's waiting for him there.

And he *is,* undoubtedly, one of the more talented writers ever to hit the Marvel Comics scene.

But how did he get that way?

Let's see. He tells us his worst job ever was as a salesman in a used car lot in St. Louis when he was 22. Seems Steve was too honest. He couldn't lie to any prospective customer and he sure couldn't sell those junkers via the truth. So he was fired by the owner of the lot—his uncle! (And Steve didn't blame him a bit.) He and his family nearly starved to death in the weeks that followed. They were living on food stamps and had no hope at all. For the next couple weeks, they were in a state of passive panic. Passive because they had to conserve their energy. Finally, Steve got a job on a radio station.

Eventually, he got trapped in an ad agency, suffocating as he did commercials for a savings and loan company until, one particularly bad day, he wrote Roy Thomas, a friend of some ten years, and said, "I am an old friend and you must help me. I am dying." Six months later Steve was at Marvel.

There you have it—a typical American success story.

Steve now has 1 wife (Margo, whom he met while teaching Communication—"which I have since forgotten how to do"—at St. Louis U.) 1 daughter (3-year-old Samantha), 2 dogs (Apple and Willy), and 3 cats (Stupid, Stricken, and Kitten). He's currently interested in writing films and has made several films on his own.

The above paragraph sounds like something from *Sixteen.*

And it still doesn't, nor do any of the previous paragraphs, explain how Steve Gerber ended up as:

— a gag-writer for a duck,
— one of America's most prolific writers of morality plays (with a walking pile of muck as the star, for cryin' out loud),
— and one of the wildest humorists we've ever seen.

Except that we don't ask for explanations.

It's enough that he, like the changing of the seasons, is always there at the right time.

(Okay, Steve. We practically deified you. Now will you let Tony's mother go?—

(We told you he was mad.)

Howard the Duck #1 cover art by Frank Brunner

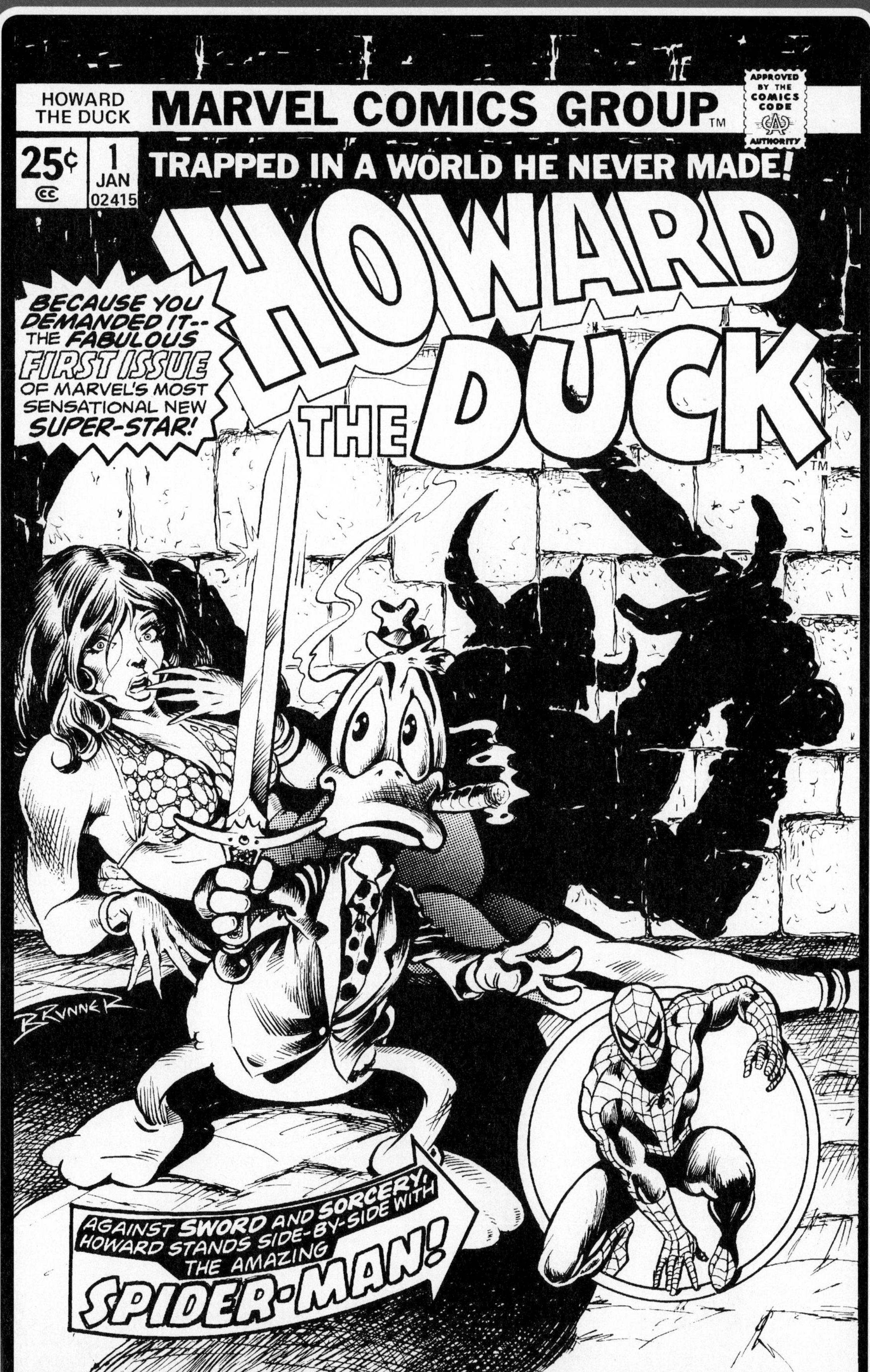

Howard the Duck #1, page 15 art
by Frank Brunner & Steve Leialoha

Howard the Duck #3, page 2
art by John Buscema & Steve Leialoha

Howard the Duck #3, pages 7 & 9 art by Gene Colan & Steve Leialoha

Images courtesy of HeritageAuctions.com

Howard the Duck #15, pages 6 & 17 art by Gene Colan & Steve Leialoha

Howard the Duck #9, pages 4-5 art by Gene Colan & Steve Leialoha

Images courtesy of HeritageAuctions.com

Howard the Duck #1, page 15
color guide by Frank Brunner

Images courtesy of HeritageAuctions.com

1976 campaign button art
by Bernie Wrightson

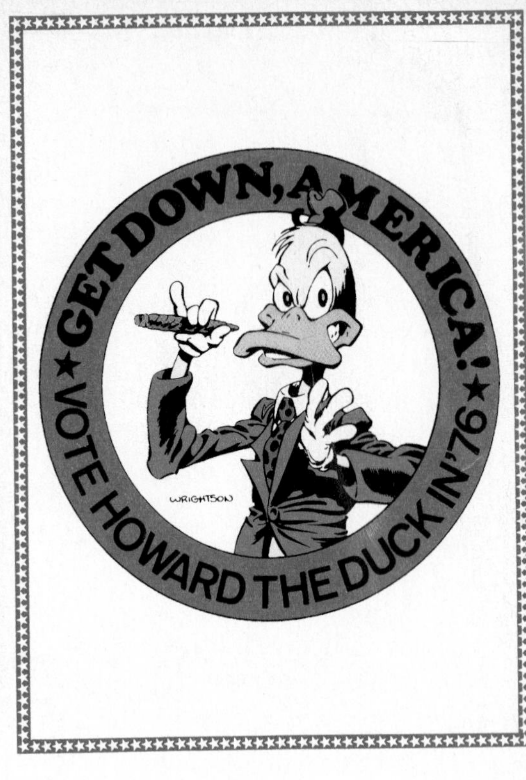

Essential Man-Thing Vol. 1 TPB
cover art by Frank Brunner & Tom Smith

Essential Man-Thing Vol. 2 TPB
back-cover art by Frank Brunner
& Avalon's Matt Milla